REORIENTING THE MIDDLE EAST

REORIENTING *the* MIDDLE EAST

Film and Digital Media Where the Persian Gulf, Arabian Sea, and Indian Ocean Meet

Edited by
DALE HUDSON
and ALIA YUNIS

INDIANA UNIVERSITY PRESS

This book is a publication of

Indiana University Press
Office of Scholarly Publishing
Herman B Wells Library 350
1320 East 10th Street
Bloomington, Indiana 47405 USA

iupress.org

© 2023 by Indiana University Press

All rights reserved

No part of this book may be reproduced or utilized in any form or by any means, electronic or mechanical, including photocopying and recording, or by any information storage and retrieval system, without permission in writing from the publisher. The paper used in this publication meets the minimum requirements of the American National Standard for Information Sciences—Permanence of Paper for Printed Library Materials, ANSI Z39.48–1992.

Manufactured in the United States of America

First printing 2023

Cataloging Information is available from the Library of Congress

ISBN 978-0-253-06756-2 (hardcover)
ISBN 978-0-253-06757-9 (paperback)
ISBN 978-0-253-06758-6 (ebook)

CONTENTS

Introduction: Interconnecting Histories and Migrating Cultures / *Dale Hudson and Alia Yunis*   1

1. Area Studies and Its Afterlives: Perspectives from the Gulf / *Nelida Fuccaro*   55

2. Petrocolonial Genealogies of Cinema in the Gulf / *Firat Oruc*   68

3. Interview with Ammar Al Attar on *Cinemas in the UAE* Exhibition / *Ammar Al Attar and Dale Hudson*   102

4. Audible Love: Letter Songs, Vocal Letters, and the Aurality of Love across the Indian Ocean / *Bindu Menon*   121

5. Ultimate Slaves in the Dead Zone: Blackness in Iranian Sacred Defense Cinema / *Parisa Vaziri*   143

6. *Dreams for Sale* or the Challenges of Representing UAE through the Lens of Malayalam Cinema / *Sebastian Thejus Cherian*   167

7. Transnational Coproductions and Questions of International Festival Films from Saudi Arabia and Oman / *Karolina Ginalska*   185

8. Import-Reexport: Reconsidering the Film Festival as a Port Economy / *Kay Dickinson*   207

9. Peeking behind the Curtain: Gulf Filmmakers
Imagine the Lives of Female Migrant Domestic Workers
in the Arabian Peninsula / *Suzi Mirgani*   229

10. Reorienting the Gaze: Emirati Women behind
the Camera / *Chrysavgi Papagianni*   248

11. Arabia's Ambivalent Auteur: Meshal Al-Jaser's
Cinematic Vision for the New Saudi Arabia / *Sean Foley*   267

12. Covering Critiques: Film and New Media Artwork
in the UAE / *Elizabeth Derderian*   286

13. The Gulf between Students: The First Decade of
the Gulf's Longest-Running Film Festival / *Alia Yunis
and Sascha Ritter*   306

Index   329

REORIENTING THE MIDDLE EAST

INTRODUCTION
Interconnecting Histories and Migrating Cultures

DALE HUDSON and ALIA YUNIS

The first narrative feature film shot and set in the Gulf, the Wonderful World of Disney's *Hamad and the Pirates: The Phantom Dhow* (USA, 1971; prod. Roy Edward Disney), represents the dhow as a maritime vehicle for adventure. Produced in collaboration with Sheikh Isa bin Sulieman al-Khalifah, ruler of Bahrain, the film suggests an early awareness by Gulf states of the power of film. *Hamad and the Pirates* served state narratives that affirm the power of Gulf ruling families yet marginalized the Gulf's transcultural history.[1] Considered the first feature film directed by a Gulf citizen, Khalid Al-Siddiq's *Bas ya Bahar / Cruel Sea* (Kuwait, 1972) framed pre-oil history less romantically but still somewhat nationalistically. Neither film gives much voice to other Arabs, Africans, Indians, Iranians, and other groups who were part of this maritime connection though barely visible as extras in the films. Multicultural communities, including children of Bombay-Kuwait wallahs (Arab men married to Indian women), are conspicuously absent. Selective strategies in depicting the Gulf extend comparable strategies evident in documentaries produced by foreign (European and United States) oil companies to whom the rulers gave concessions. These films depicted the Gulf as a lucrative gig for Westerners and consolidated a repertoire of "empty" or "barren" deserts, nomadic caravans of camels, and Bedouin men with falcons that can still be seen in the catalogues of locations issued by Gulf film commissions today and in films that promote heritage for citizens,

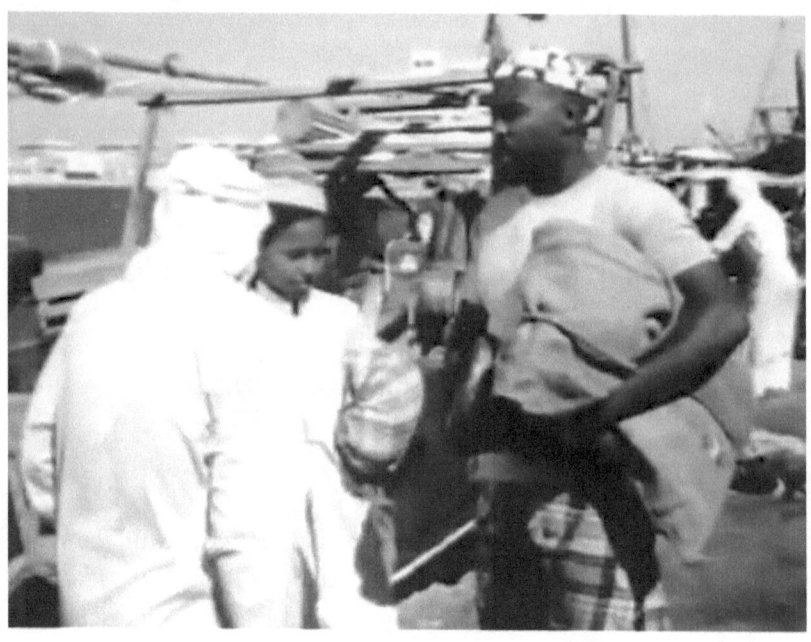

FIGURE 0.1

Boarding the ship in *Hamad and the Pirates: The Phantom Dhow* (USA, 1971; prod. Roy Edward Disney).

expatriates, and tourists—all obscuring the Gulf's long-standing maritime connections.[2]

All of these films convey the effects of the postindependence partitioning of the world into Western-defined states and the post-Cold War partitioning of knowledge into Western-defined regions. Area studies defines regions by land-mass, so the littoral spaces around the Persian Gulf, Arabian Sea, and Red Sea tend to disappear from view through frameworks calibrated to register only what comes into focus through prescriptive areas and regions—"the Middle East," "North Africa," "South Asia"—or individual states, often called "nations." Whether produced by Gulf citizens or by foreigners, such films offer a highly selective image of the Gulf that largely conforms to Western-defined states and regions in area studies and that reproduces itself in Western-defined national, regional, international, and world cinemas in film studies. As a consequence, the Gulf often only comes into focus in relation to autocratic governance, kafala (labor sponsorship laws), "petrodollars," rentier systems, fundamentalism, "veiled" women (who are either oppressed or exceptional), or debates over whether the Gulf is Persian (as Iran and most of the world refer to the body of water) or Arabian (as the Gulf Cooperation Council [GCC] prefers).³

Conventional frameworks can occlude more than they reveal. They can reify essentialist ideas of "the Middle East" and also neo-Orientalist tropes of "Arabia." Cultural and financial interests entwine on the Arabian Peninsula, as is evident in tourism campaigns for "Arabian Nights"–themed hotels that are sometimes difficult to dismiss as entirely Orientalist. More complicated are performances of translocal practices of fijiri (i.e., pearling and sea songs), which are claimed as cultural heritage in ways that can be reductively interpreted in culturalist / nationalist terms as "Khaleeji," especially when Western producers and promoters who lack formal training on the Gulf are hired for their business and technical expertise. Khaleeji literally translates to "from the Gulf," yet, as Attiya Ahmed argues, it "became synonymous with being Arab" (i.e., Gulf Arab and not Arab expatriate) with "national belonging" conceived "in increasingly racialized terms."⁴ Top-down culturalist / nationalist definitions of identity also tend to obscure the presence of marginalized Gulf Arabs without close ties to ruling families. "Gulf states and citizens increasingly treated foreign residents as though they were 'builders of the nation' rather than fellow 'nation builders,'" she observes.⁵ A culture of openness to self-critique remains incipient with many citizens afraid to question state policy openly—and many well-paid expatriates willing to police essentializing definition of culture. While there have been governmental shifts in the United Arab Emirates (UAE) and Qatar in the past five years to reduce cultural exclusivity and acknowledge expatriates, Khaleeji is often used colloquially for a Gulf-Arabized idea of cultural / national identity that is bound within national borders on the Arabian Peninsula rather acknowledging the Persian Gulf's connection to the Arabian Sea and Indian Ocean. In a world increasingly threatened by nationalisms, the Gulf's transcultural interconnections offer another model for conceptualizing knowledge beyond neoliberal cosmopolitanisms and multiculturalisms that obscure inequities and injustices to facilitate financial flows.

Reorienting the Middle East: Film and Digital Media Where the Persian Gulf, Arabian Sea, and Indian Ocean Meet reorients debates on film and digital media in the Middle East by looking to the Gulf for ways to unsettle the field's inheritance of land-based frameworks from post-Cold War Western area studies, which was designed for knowledge and resource extraction and geopolitical control. It aims to focus on film and digital media in the Gulf that has been overlooked within dominant categories such as "Arab," "Middle East," and "MENA (Middle East and North African)" cinemas and to focus attention on how using the lens of the Gulf might serve as a method for noticing details that have been overlooked within films that have conventionally been constituted as distinct from "South Asian" or "African." It does so by recognizing the Gulf as a *fluid and transcultural space*, whose interconnecting histories and migrating cultures can help scholarship reconfigure critical frameworks that focus strategically on territorial states and their official histories and cultures within Western-defined regions. Rather than accept the Persian Gulf as a *border* between distinct Arab and Iranian cultures, the collection focuses on the Persian Gulf as a *conduit* between multiple overlapping cultures whose complex identity exceeds the limiting imagination of nations and regions in area and film studies. The same holds for the Arabian Sea and the Indian Ocean. They are conduits, not borders. Moreover, this interconnected history predates what Amitav Ghosh calls the "interruption" of Western imperialism. He describes the disappearance of physical traces of the "small, indistinguishable, intertwined histories [of] Indian and Egyptian, Muslim and Jewish, Hindu and Muslim, [that were] partitioned long ago," thereby erasing entire categories of knowledge.[6]

Located between the Western-defined regions of Africa (i.e., sub-Saharan Africa), the Middle East (i.e., Southwest Asia and North Africa), and South Asia, the Gulf is often addressed in film and digital media scholarship as the Arabian Peninsula and ignores the huge expatriate populations that today amount to as much as 90 percent of the residents of Qatar and UAE, many from places connected to the Gulf for centuries.[7] Culture across the Arabian Peninsula and littoral parts of East Africa, South Asia, and Southwest Asia reflect maritime links that predate the arrival of Ottoman, Portuguese, and British imperialists. The Persian Gulf has long connected the Arabian Peninsula to southern Iraq and Iran, which itself has been connected to the eastern Mediterranean through the land routes pioneered by Nabatean Arab traders some one thousand years ago. The Gulf flows into the Arabian Sea, which connects Southwest Asia to South Asia. These connections are evident in shared cultural practices—in clothing, food, music, and words across different languages and dialects. However, the imperial "interruption" of these transcultural connections laid the groundwork for carving the Gulf into a self-contained region of independent states.[8] As such, scholars often approach the Gulf with national and regional frameworks developed without sufficient attention to the assumptions of nations and regions. This collection inverts the focus of most maps from land to water.

We use the term "the Middle East" in this collection's title, rather than Southwest Asia, with trepidation. The power of the term is institutionalized in academic publishing, journalism, and keyword searches. Encompassing Iran, Israel, and Turkey, the term has been deployed to undermine pan-Arabism. Criticisms of the term are hardly new. In the late 1960s, C. G. Smith described the Middle East as "the best known yet geographically least justifiable of the various regional names" adopted after the second World War, attributing its longevity to its vagueness as a "borderland between Europe, Monsoon Asia, and Africa south of the Sahara" and "bridge land between their continents."[9] Karen Culcasi traces the term to British imperialism, which was oriented toward South Asia, making it "the middle of the journey east to India, hence the term 'Middle East.'"[10] She finds "the reason it is difficult to define the region culturally, historically, economically, politically, or physically is the absence of uniform characteristics that world regions ostensibly maintain."[11] We highlight the term in our title prefaced by the gerund *reorienting* to underscore how the book might help correct misassumptions based on Western geopolitics by adopting an orientation to open seas rather than partitioned lands.

Gulf Cooperation Council (GCC) rulers favored a Bedouin Arab identity over other identities, notably Hawala and Ajam (Arabized Persians or Persianized Arabs) and African. Ahmed Kanna finds that "Arab identity in the post-oil period has been constructed largely in opposition to other identities increasingly categorized, officially, as non-Arab."[12] GCC states are not alone in this regard. Iranian identity is often defined as exclusively Persian, erasing littoral communities of Arabs and Afro-Iranians plus minoritized ethnic groups, particularly after the Iran-Iraq War (1980–1988). On both sides of the Persian Gulf, a transcultural history is reduced to the Western-defined structure of nation-states—wherein cultural or national identity allegedly align perfectly with territorial borders—that extends a divide-and-conquer logic from Western interventions since the Sykes-Picot Agreement of 1916, when Britain and France divided Southwest Asia between themselves after the defeat of the Ottomans. Excluding expatriates from academic scholarship on the Arabian Peninsula is a misleading practice, as Neha Vora and Nathalie Koch argue.[13]

In Western media, the Gulf is still equated with the caricature of "the oil sheik" (a perversion of the cultural figure of the sheikh as a wise leader), whose corrupting "petrodollars" are imagined capable of tarnishing even Western consumerist capitalism.[14] Such stereotypes reinforce Gulf exceptionalism, as Yasser Elsheshtawy notes, as a *negative* exceptionalism, rather than the positive exceptionalism associated with the United States.[15] However, positive elements of Gulf exceptionalism—business-friendly free zones, political stability, state feminism, religious tolerance, Western-aligned military and surveillance interests—also demand examination for what they conceal. Transnational capitalism impels Gulf states to engage in cultural policy strategies that mobilize a kind of *strategic essentialism* with very different politics than those proposed (and later disavowed) by Gayatri Spivak as *resistance* to colonialism and imperialism in both its domestic and foreign forms; instead, strategic essentialism becomes *participation* with dominating forces through deliberately "altering and transforming local and national cultures for global consumption."[16] In opposition to these state-defined discourses, the Gulf's heterogeneity is reflected in its citizen and expatriate populations—and in the films and digital media produced and consumed by its residents. Such strategic practices are evident in some of the first filmed images of the Gulf in home movies shot in the 1930s by the wives of British colonial officials. They document events commemorating agreements between colonizers and ruling families, yet they sometimes also capture traces of maritime interconnections to Africa, Iran, and South Asia. British colonial officers and US oil companies encouraged sheikhs throughout the Gulf to model themselves after the British monarchy.

FIGURE 0.2

African music celebrations to mark the accession of Shaikh Hamad bin Isa, the Shaikh of Bahrain, at Manama, Bahrain in Dalyell Collection Reel 10, Christmas Party, Bahrain, 1933–1934 (Colonial Film: Moving Images of the British Empire).

This collection takes a broad historical look at film and digital media and attempts to open new pathways for critical inquiry. Objects of study in this book's chapters range from professionally produced media to amateur audio, visual, and audiovisual media; from open-air cinemas run by oil companies to film festivals; from the first freestanding cinemas to paper flyers that selectively advertise digitally mediated performance art; from the compromises of accepting transnational coproduction funding to compromises demanded by independent filmmaking; from films and digital media that confront issues of gender, ethnoracial, and religious inequality to those that ignore them. The collection is not encyclopedic. It theorizes the Gulf as a means of deconstructing dominant categories in area studies and film studies to contribute to future research and by linking previously parallel conversations within and across these disciplines. The Gulf shares much in common with other spaces with heterogeneous populations and media cultures. We hope that this reorienting of the Middle East *with the Gulf as a concept and method* will contribute to critical frameworks for film research to make visible multiple narratives elsewhere.¹⁷

THE GULF AS CONCEPT AND METHOD

Rather the conventional terms of areas and regions or national, regional, international, and world cinemas, this collection argues that film and digital media in the Gulf is better understood with terms like *arenas, contact zones, encounters, presences, relations,* and *scapes* that foreground historical, colonial/imperial, and transnational forces that shape transcultural stories and identities. We define the Gulf as a *concept* that is most evident in the littoral parts of Southwest Asia that physically touch the Persian Gulf. These spaces are connected both by *land* to the other parts of Southwest Asia, North Africa, and Central Asia, and by *water* to East Africa, South Asia, and Southeast Asia. In some cases, state capitals are located on the Persian Gulf, as with Abu Dhabi, Doha, and Kuwait City; in other cases, they are located inland, as with Baghdad, Riyadh, and Tehran. The Gulf is where the Persian Gulf, Arabian Sea, and Indian Ocean meet. Thus, the Gulf is a *contact zone* in Mary Louise Pratt's sense of "social spaces where disparate cultures meet, clash, and grapple with each other, often in highly asymmetrical relations of domination and subordination—such as colonialism and slavery, or their aftermaths as they are lived out across the globe today."¹⁸

The Gulf evokes other fluid spaces that have been theorized, such as the Caribbean. Édouard Glissant proposes a way of understanding identities premised on *relations*. He conceived "a poetics of relations" as a rhizome that "maintains [. . .] the idea of rootedness but challenges that of a totalitarian root."¹⁹ This conception allows for indigeneity and rooted connections among people who might not have migrated voluntarily to coexist, something often lost under national and regional categories. Glissant challenges Gilles Deleuze and Félix Guattari's idea of nomadism as emancipatory to consider whether it might be "a form of obedience to contingencies that are restrictive."[20] Errancy begins by moving "beyond" a limiting definition of identity, which is defined "from the beginning" as "opposed to" Western states (especially when masquerading as nations); that is, errancy prompts "knowledge that identity is no longer completely within the root but also within the Relation," which "is spoken multilingually."[21] The multilingual articulation of the Caribbean offers a conceptual framework to bring to the Gulf, with its multiple Arabic dialects and other languages, into focus, particularly for film studies derived from early Middle East Studies and from Orientalist Studies before it. Much like Glissant's poetics of relation, Tarik Sabry proposes that Arab culture might be better defined by *encounters*—both maritime and territorial—between Arabs and others, thus showing that Arab cultures are multifaceted.[22]

Contact, relations, and encounters all allow for noncontiguous interconnections, which is why we hesitate to reduce the Gulf to a quadrant of an Indian Ocean World. The Gulf evokes Nile Green's preference for the concept of *arenas*, rather than "areas" or "worlds."[23] He argues that arenas emphasize interactions and contacts that are dynamic, evolving, and multilayered, thus challenging the Orientalist notions of fixed and timeless places.[24] He cautions against adding the word *world*, as in "Indian Ocean World," since it carries "suggestions of holistic entirety and self-sufficiency" that "run the risk of replicating the problems of the area model on a larger (often maritime) scale."[25] He proposes three intersecting arenas—Mediterranean, Inter Asian, and Indian Ocean—for what area studies defines as a single Middle Eastern region. Green recommends geographical frameworks based on "maritime conceptions of space" after the "oceanic turn" in history that produced "new research questions."[26] Similarly, Fahad Bishara advocates for dismantling "stale narratives and stagnant historiographies," so we notice the significance of places like Muscat, Basra, and the Gulf common whose histories engage India and East Africa.[27] Such reconfigurations within area studies confront long-standing limitations. Oceanic concepts reorient without erasing later connections to Britain and the United States.

The Gulf is also very much shaped by the present moment of global capitalism. Arjun Appadurai defines five *scapes*—ethnoscapes, mediascapes, technoscapes, financescapes, and ideoscapes—that suggest its peripheral horizons as a process that is visible, though never in totality.[28] Given investments in infrastructure to facilitate trade, finance, and media, the Gulf is a hub within an ever-increasingly complex network of connections to the world. Its investments can be located across the planet. Scapes prompt us to rethink how power operates in capitalism. Many Gulf cities share more in common with the statist cosmopolitanism of Singapore than with Cairo, more with Delhi than with Beirut, and more with London than Casablanca, suggesting ways that transnational capital affects the kinds of media produced and consumed and the social production of spaces within the Gulf.

The Gulf serves as a *method* for decolonizing and deimperializing the Arabian Peninsula and littoral parts of Southwest Asia, much like Kuan-Hsing Chen's "Asia as method" serves as one for decolonizing and deimperializing East Asia cultures from Cold War ideologies.[29] This work extends critiques of Eurocentrism by Samir Amin and by Ella Shohat and Robert Stam, who pointed to how Eurocentrism is largely unconscious within Western fields.[30] It can contribute to what Saër Maty Bâ and Will Higbee consider "an alternative 'un-centered' version of knowledge that gives credit to multiple viewpoints in order to arrive at original and innovative ways of studying film history, theory, and practice" as part of a broader project of de-Westernizing the field.[31] The Gulf is one of many places of convergence within a more complex film history that collectively unsettles dominant historiographic concepts of national, regional, international, and world cinemas.

UNPARTITIONING FILM STUDIES

Within the frameworks of national, regional, international, and world cinemas, the Gulf may seem to offer little. Indeed, the Gulf does not widely register in books on Arab or Middle Eastern film. With the exception of articles on Kerala, scholarship on South Asian cinema also does not include the Gulf substantively, even as an important market for Bollywood films. Books on African and African diasporic film also ignore the African presence in the Gulf. The absence of the Gulf in much African, Arab,

Middle Eastern, and South Asian film scholarship reflects exclusionary practices that are structured into rigid critical frameworks.

When scholarship focuses on details that conventional film studies overlooks, it notices limitations in extant critical frameworks. Film studies has partitioned knowledge through its dominant frameworks of national, regional, international, and world cinemas, as well as its focus on art house films to the minimization of other media forms, especially nonprofessional and amateur forms. Dominant practices in Western (i.e., "international") film festivals, distribution, journalism, and scholarship obscure transcultural dimensions, often by claiming to focus on the "national" and "regional" within universalizing frameworks of a depoliticized and dehistoricized "international" or "world." Essentialism often extends assumptions from Cold War–era area studies, when fields of inquiry partitioned cultures, including film culture, according to economic, geopolitical, and military logic. Although national cinema might seem a way to resist the cultural imperialism of Hollywood, the concept can also naturalize "internal cultural colonialism," as Andrew Higson explains.[32] Although area studies partly contributes to statist and regionalist frameworks within film studies, it has also brought attention to detail into the field. A new generation of scholars from the Gulf understand culture and heritage as "living" and bring locally-situated, place-based knowledge to their work on Gulf film and digital media, as happened in art history back in the 1970s.[33] We cite many of these scholars in our introduction.

Film festivals like those in Berlin, Cannes, Amsterdam (International Documentary Festival Amsterdam [IDFA]), and Venice select films as though motivated by an imperialist logic that distorts via universalizing tropes of humanism or under exoticizing lenses that focus only on the primitive and poor. Distributors largely follow these festival selections, which predetermine films that film scholars examine, as scholars rarely have access to work that is not commercially distributed. Western festivals favor filmmakers brought to their attention by their European mentors and funders, such as Fonds Sud (1984–2011, rebranded and continued as "aide aux Cinémas du monde" or "world cinema aid"), Hubert Bals Fund (est. 1988), Jan Vrijman Fund (est. 1998, now IDFA Bertha Fund), and Berlinale Talent Campus (est. 2007). This limited selection of films is consumed by limited audiences as though they offer a semitransparent window into "foreign" cultures.

Selective programming of such films reinforces stereotypes—not only in content and theme but also in form and style—that exclude people and platforms that complicate national, regional, international, and world cinemas.[34] Western commercial cinema presents its historical prejudices in negative stereotypes that Jack Shaheen calls "reel bad Arabs."[35] Comparably, Ramachandra Guha finds four categories of Indians in the Orientalist and imperialist imagination that range from the fabulous and mystical to the benighted and pathetic.[36] Stereotypes of Africa and Africans are remarkably consistent in a selective focus on "unspoiled nature" and "nightmare of danger and chaos."[37] Okaka Opio Dokotum examines the Dark Continent myth in 112 years of films of white saviors, who allegedly battle savagery, cannibalism, and virology (i.e., Africa is the source of deadly viruses), and white colonizers, who allegedly bring civilization (i.e., Africa as Edenic utopia or tabula rasa).[38]

While such stereotypes in Western commercial cinema seem obvious today, adding non-Western art films does not completely solve the problem. Lúcia Nagib describes the four requirements for support of non-Western filmmaking by European Union television funding and the Sundance Institute: "local color," "realism," "private hero," and "improbable but convincing event."[39] In other words, stories must be told in a Western format to be distributable. These unmarked selection criteria are carried into film studies, most evident when Hollywood industry awards (i.e., Academy Awards, Golden Globes) and festivals (i.e., Sundance, SXSW, Toronto, Tribeca) are accepted as arbiters of merit for all films everywhere.[40] Until scholars intervened, most introductory film studies textbooks erased Arab film entirely. Youssef Chahine's *Bab el-Hadid / Cairo Station* (Egypt, 1958) was perhaps the first Arab film to enter the Western canon. Its use of cinematic devices from film noir allowed Western audiences to see Egypt beyond the Orientalism in Western films on ancient and biblical Egypt. *Cairo Station* offered a social analysis that spans ability, class, and gender, along with rural and urban cultures, yet it leaves the ethnoracial identity among Egyptians untouched. The film thus conforms to Western definitions of a nation-state while pointing to its shortcomings.

Egyptian popular cinema was screened throughout North Africa and Southwest Asia, but it is excluded from Western film studies—or belittled with epithets, such as "Hollywood on the Nile." By ignoring Egyptian popular cinema, film studies effectively repartitioned Arab culture into so-called national cinemas. The field looks narrowly to art house films that reinforce the concept of national identity, thus largely accepting the Western-defined state as a natural and inevitable form of polity, society, and even culture, as postcolonial feminist scholarship has argued.[41] When Arab films are selected by Western festivals, these festivals tend to categorize them by state of production, according to an international framework for understanding the world as political states that represent so-called nations. As such, Arab films are forced to conform to certain definitions of national cinemas that amplify national narratives—and consequently marginalize or erase minoritized perspectives. When Arab films from the Gulf are selected, multiple cultures that exists alongside Arab cultures tend to be dismissed as ambience or background. Film critics, scholars, filmmakers, and audiences perpetuate such national frameworks as though they were unproblematic—and unharmful. Such simplifications manifest in Gulf filmmaking. Iraqi filmmaking seldom features the Gulf despite having sizable populations in the Persian Gulf.[42] Comparably, Iranian cinema tends to obscure its stories from littoral areas, where there continues to be much mixing with the Arab side of the Gulf, to conform to a national cinema that constructs Iranian identity as fully Persian. Film studies obscures historical perspectives that are important parts of film history.

Western fantasies that the world aspires to imitate Hollywood are just as unfounded. The first Iranian talkie, *Dokhtar-e Lor, ya Iran-e Diruz va Iran-e Emruz / The Lor Girl, or Yesterday's Iran and Today's Iran* (Iran, 1933; dir. Abdolhosain Sepanta), was actually produced in India with the assistance of Ardeshir Irani, a Parsee from Bombay.[43] Irani also directed India's first Urdu- and English-language films.[44] *The Lor Girl* suggests the connections across the Gulf that do not register under conventional frameworks as significant to film history. "The exchange relations between Indian cinema and Iranian cinema thus went beyond exporting Indian films to Iran, for they involved genre transfers as well," argues Hamid

Naficy; the film's use of four musical numbers became a "formula, which Sepanta borrowed from Indian cinema, [and which] became the engine of future popular melodramas and stewpot movies."[45]

At the same time, *The Lor Girl* conveys "the Pahlavi ideology of syncretic Westernization: anti-Arabism," which is evident in the story of a Lor tribal chief, who robs caravans, murders, and kidnaps.[46] The hero Jafar (played by Sepanta) saves the young Lor girl Golnar (Ruhangiz Saminezhad) from "a bullish Arab sheikh," who has paid the tribal chief for her time and feels entitled to rape her. Jafar and Golnar escape to Bombay and only return to Iran after Reza Shah has come to power and modernized the country, thus weaving Pahlavi nationalism in with the sixth-century Muslim conquest of Iran.[47] Set "before the jubilant Pahlavi era" when "regions in the south and west of Iran were under the influence of various tribes and nomads," according to the intertitles, the state commissioned further films to consolidate Persian identity as civilized in contrast to Arab identity.[48]

Critical examination of potentially limiting frameworks within Middle East Studies can be brought to film studies. Timothy Mitchell finds categories of Western social sciences, such as demography and geography, are not always useful for understanding history, culture, and politics.[49] He and others advocate for critical paradigms within area studies that interrogate naturalized categories used by researchers.[50] Ella Shohat focuses attention on "some of the dangers of studying women and gender in isolation, within ghettoized and geographically defined discursive spaces such as area studies," noting that "Eurocentric versions of global feminism (not unlike the paradigms that inform the sociology of modernization, the economics of development studies, and the aesthetics of postmodernism) assume a telos of evolution toward a reductive identity practice" that is generally "performed within the discursive framework of development and modernization."[51] Film scholarship can unwittingly reinforce neo-imperialist or globalist interests.

Since Middle East Studies has historically claimed the Gulf, South Asian Studies largely ignored it until the oil era, when skilled and managerial labor was recruited from Bangladesh, India, Nepal, Pakistan, and Sri Lanka. Sometimes called the Indian subcontinent, Jambudvipa, or

Bharatvarsh, the term South Asia gained currency in US geopolitics only after Bangladesh gained independence in 1971—and Afghanistan was added after 9/11.[52] South Asian film studies must continually critique the overemphasis on contemporary Bollywood as representative of Indian film, especially after *Devdas* (India, 2002; dir. Sanjay Leela Bhansali) premiered at Cannes, but Bollywood's antecedents in Bombay cinema were overlooked because the spectacle of alternative modernities did not conform to Western expectations of realism. Western attention to films about South Asia produced by *white* filmmakers, from *Gandhi* (UK/India/USA, 1982; dir. Richard Attenborough) and *A Passage to India* (UK/USA, 1984; dir. David Lean) to *Born into Brothels* (USA, 2004; dir. Ross Kauffman and Zana Briski) and *Slumdog Millionaire* (UK/USA, 2008; dir. Danny Boyle), underscores how festivals and venues, notably Sundance and the Academy Awards, not only reinforce but also reward the colonial gaze. UAE and Qatar have contributed and complicated such assumptions.[53]

Nicholas Dirks traces the development of South Asian Studies from Orientalist obsessions, which produced "dominant tropes for the representation of South Asia" as either "ancient India" or contemporary India's "most remote hinterlands."[54] Film studies adopted such early lenses. Festivals favored Satyajit Ray's *Pather Panchali* (India, 1955) over the alternative modernity of Bombay cinema, the more experimental work by Mrinal Sen and Ritwik Ghatak, or even Ray's films set in cities. Despite the use of Western realist conventions in *Pather Panchali*, Western institutions overlooked the film's artistry in favor of an imaged transparent window into rural India, which Ray knew mostly through novels.[55] The film was awarded Best Human Documentary at Cannes in 1956, but his films about middle-class urban families found a less enthusiastic reception in the Western canon. Bombay "mythologicals," characterized by complex mixing of various aesthetics, narratives, and visual strategies, were dismissed as naïve by European / North American writers, whose criteria for evaluation, as Rosie Thomas points out, were "at best, irrelevant and also often racist."[56] Consequently, many English-language introductory textbooks omitted Bombay cinema—along with postliberalization Bollywood—until fairly recently. They also rarely acknowledge filmmaking in Afghanistan, Bangladesh, and Pakistan, unless related to abuse of women. Even when other South Asian states are included, festival programming and international distribution favors stories that are contained within individual states, rather than those whose plots or characters move across states. More recently, Vebhuti Duggal, Bindu Menon, and Spandan Bhattacharya published an India-center introductory textbook in English to decolonize the field for students in Indian universities.[57]

African Studies has also minimized the Gulf, from its historical ties to the Swahili coast through pilgrimage, slavery, and trade across the western Indian Ocean. "From the perspective of the area studies establishment," argues Pearl Robinson, "Africa's place at the bottom of those hierarchies was never in question" with "Social Darwinism buttressed by the principles of *réal politique*."[58] She describes historical obstacles, such as recognizing North Africa as part of Africa: area studies severed North Africa from the rest of Africa, undercutting Egypt's iconic Cold War pan-Arabist leader Jamal Abdul Nasser's idea of Egypt as *both* Arab *and* African. Scholarship on African filmmaking historically prioritized South African filmmaking and Francophone filmmaking in West Africa, notably Ousmane Sembène's *La Noire de... / Black Girl* (France/Sénégal, 1965) about the dangers of identifying too closely with Western former colonizers. Sembène later made films in Wolof, countering the French habits of coopting work from its former colonies into the postimperial category of Francophone cinema.

By reframing these films, we model ways that film studies can adopt elements of the deep knowledge that area studies affords when disengaged with the limiting Cold War–era categories. Film scholarship has nonetheless begun to recognize connections between Africa, South Asia, and Southwest Asia with a particular focus on *popular cinema* that was consumed by audiences yet ignored by Western festivals. Scholars note the popularity of Bombay and Hong Kong films in Africa among audiences who understood neither Hindi nor Cantonese, as well as the appeal of Bombay and Bollywood films in Pakistan (despite their frequent Islamophobia), since the films offer an alternative to Western modernity.[59] Other scholarship has considered commercial filmmaking in Bombay and Cairo during both the colonial and postindependence eras—films that sometimes appropriated Western stories, styles, and infrastructures—but more frequently ignored them, or appropriated elements from each other.⁶⁰ A focus on these connections reveals the limiting focus of a conventional approach to film studies.

Shohat and Stam nudged the field to "unthink" its Eurocentrism, which was largely unconscious in the "unthinking" habits of Westerners and their allies.⁶¹ Teshome Gabriel devised a working framework to understand filmmaking on its own terms, rejecting the "proper technique" that Western industries attempt to naturalize as a goal for everyone without any awareness of how styles and structures invariably carry cultural biases.⁶² Similarly, the long-standing methods of the Gulf's network of storytelling are illegible under Western lenses. One is Nabati oral poetry, born in what is now Saudi Arabia's Nejd Plateau and memorized and performed across the Gulf for at least seven hundred years, and the other is the pearl-diving music, born of the mingling of African slaves and traders and divers from South Asia and the Arab and Iranian sides of the Gulf. Storytelling is often considered to have come about only through exposure to Western arts, and film studies mirrors this assertion. Not coincidentally, when such filmmaking practices developed, Western film studies consolidated its Eurocentric approaches to film history and film theory, as Stam demonstrates, often disregarding non-Western theory as merely "identity politics" devoid of intellectual complexity.⁶³

Subsequent scholars explored ways non-Western exilic and diasporic films navigate different ideas of filmmaking, as well as "cinema of small nations" and "cinema at the periphery."⁶⁴ Transnational models interrogate the inequities and injustices embedded into the political economies of film financing, film festivals, and film journalism.⁶⁵ The transcultural approaches that this collection describes can de-emphasize the homogenizing effects of the national within the transnational as a concept. Rather than segregation by culture, nation, or region, transcultural comparison needs to be part of the ongoing work of deprovincializing the field. Transcultural approaches also refute narratives portraying the Gulf as a desolate desert bursting into modernity upon its "discovery" by Western adventurers and oil companies.

COLONIAL AND CONCESSION ORIGINS OF FILMMAKING AND FILM SCREENING

Although most states in the Arabian Peninsula did not engage in anticolonial struggles, imperial power asymmetries are nonetheless apparent. Gulf filmmaking celebrates its origins in the work of early Kuwaiti and Bahraini filmmakers, who produced documentaries for the newly independent states, such as Siddiq's twenty-five-minute documentary *Al-Saqr / The Falcon* (Kuwait, 1965) and Bahraini Khalifa Shaheen's feature documentary *Marah fi Robo'a Lebnan / Fun throughout Lebanon* (Bahrain, 1971).[66] Shaheen trained himself while working in the Bapco (Bahrain Petroleum Company) Film Department and went on to teach other aspiring documentary filmmakers. In 1967, Bahrain established the Bahrain Cinema Company to help "several film-makers including Ali Abbas and Majid Shams succeeded in producing short dramas and documentaries in Bahrain in the 1970s," notes Anne Ciecko.[67]

Although these films resemble those by oil companies, they also depart from their conventions. Oil company films were as self-interested as they were self-assured of their narratives. Todd Reisz finds that World Wide Pictures' *These Are the Trucial States* (UK, 1958) navigates British desires to access oil while also addressing criticisms of the "Gulf problem," that is, Britain's inability to continue financing its empire.[68] Mona Damluji argues that the Anglo-Iranian Oil Company's *Persian Story* (UK, 1952; dir. Ralph Keene) established an exchange of oil concessions from Iran for "the promise of modernity" from Britain.[69] They produced a narrative of benevolent tutelage and cooperation. When Westerners defer to Gulf rulers, however, familiar tropes of capricious, almost irrational, Arabs return, as in the case of the UAE's Sheikh Zayed dismissing a plan for a new souq after months of hard work by Western architects in British Petroleum's *Abu Dhabi* (UK, 1969; dir. Julian Spiro). The film includes the silent presence of Palestinian teachers who, along with other expatriate Arabs, contributed to the early infrastructure of the UAE, but it does not recognize their contributions. Only Westerners are acknowledged as helping the ruling families. The films largely minimize Africans and South Asians from this history.

FIGURE 0.3

Photograph of film projector at Company House,
Msheireb Museums, Doha, June 12, 2019.

Ethnoracial hierarchies on screen did not always correspond with who had access to the first cinemas in the Gulf. British colonial officers and Western oil companies attempted "civilize" with British and Hollywood films, but Gulf residents generally preferred Egyptian and Indian films. Screenings segregated audiences by nationality. Cinema arrived in Saudi Arabia in 1937, when the first families of Aramco (Arabian American Oil Company)'s senior managers arrived, as Robert Vitalis argues. "Arabs were forbidden to attend," he explains, "but they were about five deep all about the house peeking in the windows" to see images of Ann Harding in *Gallant Lady* (USA, 1933; dir. Gregory La Cava).[70] Saudi workers later challenged the company system of racial segregation, which operated from 1945 to 1956, based on US Jim Crow laws, when denied admission to a screening of Charlie Chaplin's *Limelight* (USA, 1952).[71] The "company movie theater" became a "symbol of privileges that foreigners, in this instance Pakistanis and Palestinians, enjoyed but were denied Saudi workers."[72] Gulf residents soon began to define exhibition and production often within the space created by the oil companies.

GULF FESTIVALS AND FILMMAKING AS POST-OIL ECONOMIC DIVERSIFICATION

In his research on film financing, production, distribution, and exhibition, Abdulrahman Alghanem complicates assumptions about so-called national and regional cinemas by pointing to the GCC Customs Union's role in distribution and exhibition.[73] He finds each state's print and publication laws to be mostly a "call to protect national security, economy and moral values" by adhering to "local norms" and providing Arabic subtitles on foreign films rather than the ever-allusive censorship document that many Westerners imagine.[74] His research also highlights ways that investment in production infrastructure in Qatar and UAE seldom benefits independent filmmaking by Qataris, Emiratis, and other Gulf nationals—and sometimes even hinders it by escalating production costs. Furthermore, he challenges assumptions that only foreign (Hollywood) film marketing strategies can be profitable through a comparative analysis of Rakan's *Edhay in Abu Dhabi / Dhhayy fi Abu Dhabi* (UAE, 2016), which played well in cinemas in neighborhoods with predominantly nationals as residents and deployed the strategy of Khaleeji celebrities, unlike the box-office indifference to Ali F. Mostafa's *From A to B / Min Alif ila Ba'* (UAE, 2014) with its web campaign and roadshow marketing cost.[75] Image Nation's importation of Hollywood industry practices and practitioners to "mentor local talent" seem to have reversed Mostafa's popularity after his self-produced *City of Life / Dar al-Haya* (UAE, 2008), whose attention to nuances in UAE is largely absent in *From A to B*, which attempts to appeal to non-Gulf Arabs.[76] The composition of Gulf residents in his first feature offers a challenge to most frameworks devised for national, regional, and transnational filmmaking.

Multiplex cinemas in shopping malls today reflect diverse resident populations, which largely self-segregate.[77] Commercial cinema offers hits from Egypt and Hollywood, alongside films from India and the

Philippines—not to mention a few locally produced ones, especially in Kuwait, Saudi Arabia and the UAE. Despite the heterogeneity of theatrical exhibition, as well as the availability of films on satellite television and streaming platforms, attention to film culture in the Gulf has focused mostly on extravagant festivals.[78] Before they were canceled, Dubai International Film Festival (DIFF, 2004–2017), Abu Dhabi Film Festival (ADFF, 2007–2014, originally Middle East International Film Festival), and Doha Tribeca Film Festival (DTFF, 2009–2012) elicited skepticism, among citizens, residents, and press over their big budgets and short histories. They approached film differently than festivals founded during the era of decolonization, such as Les Journées Cinématographiques de Carthage (JCC or Carthage Film Festival, est. 1966) and Festival panafricain du cinéma et de la télévision de Ouagadougou (Fespaco, or Panafrican Film and Television Festival of Ouagadougou, est. 1969), which considered film as integral to decolonize media from centuries of Western colonialism and served as sites for contentious debates on national consciousness and transnational solidarities. The Damascus International Film Festival (est. 1979) later joined.

DIFF and ADFF seemed to extend the work of JCC or Fespaco for a few years with their funding and prizes for emerging filmmakers, free or inexpensive tickets for audiences, relaxed censorship, and venues for serious conversations about filmmaking. They later shifted focus to promote production infrastructure, free zones, and tourism.[79] Nonetheless, they did offer competitions with generous cash prizes and financial support for Gulf and other Arab filmmakers, which have largely vanished. Only the Doha Film Institute (DFI), which sponsored DTFF, continues to assist Arabic-language filmmaking with grants and also hosts two smaller festivals Ajyal and Qumra, which emphasize culture over finance. DIFF and ADFF promoted the UAE as an alternative to location shooting in Israel, Jordan, Morocco, or Tunisia and to offshore production in Australia, Canada, Europe, and elsewhere. The festivals "synergized" with the burgeoning tourism industries, as important components of post-oil economic planning. Saudi Arabia is now pursuing comparable policies. In 2018, Saudi cinemas reopened after having been closed since 1980.[80] Today, film is part of Saudi Arabia's post-oil strategy to attract foreign direct investment (FDI), including the new Red Sea International Film Festival, which launched with much international fanfare and huge crowds in 2022 after being postponed due to the COVID-19 pandemic.[81]

Tensions between financial and cultural objectives are evident in the ways these states have inaugurated film production by serving as financiers on several high-profile Hollywood and independent films. More problematic, however, is the commissioning of Western filmmakers to produce romanticized narratives about the past. *Black Gold / Day of the Falcon* (France/Italy/Qatar/Tunisia, 2011; dir. Jean-Jacques Annaud), *Born a King* (Spain/UK, 2019; dir. Agustí Villaronga), and *Khorfakkan* (UAE, 2020; dir. Ben Mole and Maurice Sweeney) were a mix of nationalist and Orientalist discourses.[82] They represent the Gulf only through interaction between Gulf Arabs and Westerners. They resemble Western nostalgia or heritage cinema of the 1980s and 1990s, evident in their high production values, stars, and nationalist histories.[83] With the release of *Al Kameen / The Ambush* (UAE, 2021; dir. Pierre Morel), a film about Emirati soldiers who went to rescue their compatriot soldiers in Yemen, nationalism is also fostered. The film garnered the largest number of ticket sales for an Arabic-language film in UAE.[84] It was directed, produced, and written by Westerners with almost no knowledge about UAE.

These feature films share government support with other high-budget visual productions, namely for museums and tourism, also part of the post-oil economic focus. Commissioned for the National Museum of Qatar in Doha, Mira Nair's film *Nafas / Breath* (Qatar, 2019) offers a fragmented impression of pearl diving across its gallery walls of Jean Nouvel's "desert rose" design.[85] "The images are displayed on site through 114 4K projectors with 308 speakers spread throughout 11 galleries," according to one report, emphasizing technical achievement over historical accuracy.[86] Audiences are denied the privileged position of a disinterested voyeur and instead become immersed in a series of subjective impressions in a lavish audiovisual experience.[87] Unlike other films at the museum, *Nafas* conveys a history that is not exclusively Gulf Arab, yet cultural differences fade behind a heterosexual romance between two Gulf Arabs. In an oil exploration film, only Westerners appear alongside Gulf Arabs.

FIGURE 0.4

Installation view of Mira Nair's multiscreen film *Nafas / Breath* in the National Museum of Qatar in Doha, June 11, 2019.

Film culture also folds into tourism marketing and promotions. Dubai Tourism's multiplatform series *#BeMyGuest* (UAE, 2017–2019) with Bollywood superstar Shah Rukh Khan combines neoliberal leisure activities with Orientalist fantasies. Ada Petiwala situates the campaign in relation to Indian prime minister Narendra Modi's Brand India campaigns to rebrand India as a "key diplomatic and cultural-infrastructural partner."[88] She argues that "the sore topic of migrant exploitation is only paid mere lip service in Modi's branding strategy (when addressed) to launch a new and seamless relationship with the Emirates and other Gulf countries," such that *#BeMyGuest* and its "fair-skinned and upper-class tourists" become "a form of image rehabilitation" for Indian in the Arab World.[89] The hiring of foreign celebrities thus intersects with politics that transcend individual states. Dubai Tourism also commissioned *A Story Takes Flight* (UAE, 2019; dir. Reed Morano) in which Hollywood stars Kate Hudson, Gwyneth Paltrow, and Zoe Saldana project Orientalist fantasies on "colorful" locals at a working-class souq.[90] The official music video for Expo 2020 brands Dubai as a place where only Emiratis live but also where everyone is welcome to come and be wowed by an extravagant future.

In tandem with Dubai Expo 2020, Hollywood stars Jessica Alba and Zac Efron perform beside Dubai landmarks in *Dubai Presents: A Five-Star Mission* (UAE, 2021; dir. Craig Gillespie), which exploits city pride when *Mission: Impossible—Ghost Protocol* (USA/UAE, 2011; dir. Brad Bird) became publicity for Studio City Dubai.

Television has a much longer and active history in the Gulf. Most countries had government-operated local channels by 1970, relying on censored programming from abroad alongside local news broadcasts and game shows. Kuwaiti TV was an exception. During the 1970s and 1980s—locally called Kuwait's Golden Age of Television—its musalsalat (limited television series) comedically tackled social issues of modernity.[91] With the launch of satellite television in the 1990s, pan-Arab news channels, most notably Qatar's Al Jazeera, boomed in the Gulf, as have television series. Production incentives, economic power, and the war in Syria have shifted musalsalat production from Damascus and Cairo to the Gulf, especially Abu Dhabi and Dubai. Arabic-language television in the Gulf is increasingly consumed through platforms like Netflix and Saudi Arabia's MBC (Middle East Broadcasting Center) with its Shahid.net. It continues to overshadow film consumption and production. In this way, the Gulf with its government-owned production facilities now controls the pan-Arab visual media landscape financially and culturally.

In 2002, aspiring Gulf filmmakers, citizens, and residents formed the Emirates Film Competition (EFC). They hosted an annual film festival, which was merged into ADFF in 2010. EFC exhibited films that conveyed compelling stories about conflicted identities within controversial topics such as school bullying and dating, which are absent in film produced by state-sponsored initiatives, such as Image Nation Abu Dhabi's Arab Film Studio in the twofour54 free zone. EFC's institutional support for independent filmmaking no longer exists.[92] The Gulf Film Festival (2007–2013) was also abruptly canceled, leaving no space for independent film screenings until Cinema Akil (Dubai) opened in 2014, Sharjah Film Platform opened in 2018, and Cinema El-Housh in Jeddah in 2019. Offering free screenings to the public, Cinema Space (Abu Dhabi) has operated since 2014. Mohammed Alobthani's documentary *Branding Global Image: Filmmaking and Complicating National Identity in the UAE* (UK/UAE,

2021) investigates how UAE citizens and residents understand cultural space in the cities of Abu Dhabi and Dubai, which differs from how state agencies construct such spaces for foreign investment and tourism, particularly through institutions designed to support filmmaking. He contrasts top-down branding initiatives that "plug into" neoliberal capitalism with daily lives of Emirati and expatriate filmmakers.[93]

REORIENTING THE GULF IN AFRICAN, MIDDLE EASTERN, AND SOUTH ASIAN FILMS

More than other Gulf cities, Dubai has become an iconic of a so-called region and a mythical place for global dreams of consumerism, evident in Chinese, Hollywood, Indian, and Nigerian commercial films set against its iconic cityscape.[94] Although Bollywood represents Dubai today as a holiday destination for middle-class Indians, it previously stereotyped the city as a location for hawala ("transfer" in the sense of recruitment and remittances), associated with trafficking of gold, drugs, and terrorism in the late 1990s and early 2000s. The Gulf is imagined as corrupting good Indians and attracting bad ones, even in comedies such as the box-office hit *Happy New Year* (India, 2014; dir. Farah Khan), in which a street fighter (Shah Rukh Khan) wants to steal the same emeralds his rival does and frames him in the process. However, this view of the Gulf is only a small part of its larger presence in South Asian filmmaking. Ada Petiwala describes the ways that Bollywood is changing in response to increased interconnections with UAE, evident in "a small but diverse cohort of globally-loved 'Arabized' Bollywood songs" that "reflect new transnational priorities and realities, pursuing less the strict translation of lyrics into Arabic than something more flexible and ambiguous: an overall 'Arabic mood,'" as well as the emergence of correct Arabic-language signage in Bollywood films shot in Abu Dhabi like *Tiger Zinda Hai* (India, 2017; dir. Ali Abbas Zafar), which contrast with Hollywood's frequent bot-translated texts that are printed with backwards and unconnected letters.[95]

The first films set in the Gulf are considered to be *Dubai Chalo / Let's Go to Dubai* (Pakistan, 1979; dir. Haider Chaudhry) and *Vilkanundu Swapnangal / Dreams for Sale* (India, 1980; dir. Azad).[96] Significantly, the dialogues in these films are in Punjabi and Malayalam, respectively, not in the hegemonic languages of what might be assumed to be national cinema: Urdu (Pakistan) and Hindi (India). They tell stories that might not be prioritized in typical scholarship on South Asian film, and they tell stories from perspectives that are seldom heard in Southwest Asia or South Asia. Dubai appears in titles to films in multiple languages, including Punjabi-language *Dubai* (India, 2001; dir. Joshi), Telugu-language *Dubai Seenu* (India, 2007; dir. Sreenu Vaitla), and Hindi-language *Hungama in Dubai* (India, 2007; dir. Masood). For South Asian expatriates in the Gulf, these films often intentionally include practical information about navigating separation from family and possible exploitation by sponsors and agents.

Ratheesh Radhakrishnan finds that Malayalam cinema has been influenced by a three-decades-long relationship with the Gulf, as in 1970s films that were called "art house," thus distinct from commercial films due to their narratives, notably Adoor Gopalakrishnan's *Swayamvaram / Marriage by Choice* (India, 1972) and *Elippathayam / The Rat Trap* (India, 1981), in which "objects and the opulence of the Gulf returnee" and a "smuggler" character badly affect the films' Nair (Hindu Kshatriya caste) protagonists.[97] In the 1980s, other films were released simultaneously in Kerala and throughout the Gulf on VHS tapes with Arabic subtitles; more recently, the term "Gulfukaran" has been destigmatized from meaning an undesirable Gulf migrant to a desirable NRK (Nonresident Keralite).[98] Shot in Qatar on a micro-budget, Salam Kodiyathur's *Parethan Thirichu Varunnu / The Deceased Returns* (India, 2004) initiated Malayalam Home Cinema (or Islamic Home Cinema), which bypasses commercial distribution by circulating privately on VCD or DVD between Kerala and the Peninsula, and now on YouTube, with more than two hundred films produced in the last decade, as Bindu Menon and T. T. Sreekumar explain.[99] The films often convey unhappy stories of sacrifice that are absent in commercial films.

Films made for South Asian expatriates in the Gulf and their families at home constitute another audience. The "Gulfiwood" film, dubbed so for its low-budget production affinities with early Nollywood films, addresses issues relevant to the Mappila Muslim community, including attitudes toward women and wealth as well as remittances from migrants, 94 percent of whom are male, working in the Gulf. Films set in the all-male world of the Malayali Gulf include *Aliyanu Oru Free Visa / Free Visa for Brother-in-Law* in Kuwait, *Paathiyaathrakkoru Ticket / Half-way Ticket* in Qatar, and *Oru Dirham Koodi / One More Dirham* in the UAE.[100] The migrant community has also been a market for Malayalam soft porn films, and the Gulf is a transit point for hardcore porn into India. In the context of the India's Malayalam soft porn industry before its decline in 2005, Darshana Mini describes how the Gulf often functions as "an imagination of 'elsewhere,'" used by producers to account for the production of "cut pieces," "extra reels," or "the bits" (e.g., "shots of cleavage and thighs, massage and bath scenes, and dubbed-over moaning to signify sexual pleasure and climax") that would not pass Indian film censorship.[101] Moreover, financing for the films often included "remittances from Gulf-returned Malayalis who thought of soft porn as a shortcut to easy money."[102] Marketed to a much wider audiences, *Aadujeevitham* (India/USA/Haïti, 2023; dir. Blessy) is adapted from Benyamin's 2008 novel, which was translated as *Goat Days* in 2012. It was shot in Algeria and Jordan as well as Kerala, since it tells the story of an Indian man coerced into working as an enslaved goatherd in Saudi Arabia.

The Gulf also appears in films from the Philippines. Filipina/os became a desirable class of expatriates beginning in the mid-1980s for white-collar and service jobs, especially nurses and hospitality staff, since they are highly educated and speak English. The Gulf enters into Philippine cinema with both stories of horror, as in *The Sarah Balabagan Story* (Philippines, 1997; dir. Joel Lamangan) about a Filipina woman who was returned to the Philippines from "Saudi" (euphemism for Al Ain, UAE) after being sentenced to death for murdering her employer as he attempted to rape her, a story based on news reports in the region, to *Dubai* (Philippines, 2005; dir. Rory B. Quintos), about two Filipino brothers who find opportunity in the UAE unavailable in the Philippines. Like Malayalam films, these tend to address specific audiences in the Gulf and families at home.

Dubai's allure and its dangers have entered into Nollywood films. During their "Dubai runs" to purchase the latest fashions for their boutiques back in Nigeria, young Nigerian women engage in prostitution, thus conveying a sense that bling comes at a price that they are willing to pay in

FIGURE 0.5

Raffy (Aga Muhlach) shows his brother Andrew (John Lloyd Cruz) the Dubai of "kababayan" (fellow countryperson in Tagalog), the Overseas Filipino Worker (OSW) community, in *Dubai* (Philippines, 2005; dir. Rory B. Quintos).

Dubai Runs 1 and *Dubai Runs 2* (Nigeria, 2007; dir. Mac-Collins Chidebe). Dubai also features as a wedding destination in *The Wedding Party 2: Destination Dubai* (Nigeria, 2017; dir. Niyi Akinmolayan), which was actually shot partly on location in Dubai. Ali F. Mostafa is "keen to connect to Nollywood" on a sequel to *City of Life* that examines Chinese, Nigerian, and Saudi stories.[103] Film and digital media in the Gulf continue to develop as an interpretation and manifestation of how the Gulf intersects with those living in the Gulf.

REORIENTING THE MIDDLE EAST WITH GULF FILMS

As a fluid and transcultural space of interconnected histories and migrating cultures due to encounters, presences, and relations with arenas, contact zones, and scapes, the Gulf brings new insights into feature films—not only productions by foreign filmmakers but also by those from the Gulf. Most recognized are Khaled Al-Siddiq's *Bas ya Bahar / Cruel Sea* (Kuwait, 1972) and Haifaa Al-Mansour's *Wadjda* (Germany/Saudi Arabia, 2012) both of which garnered praise at Western film festivals. Our analysis of these films and others focuses less on the main narratives of the hazards of pearl diving in pre-oil Kuwait (*Bas ya Bahar*) or the obstacles to bicycle riding for women in the Saudi capital (*Wajda*) to notice details that convey a sense of the Gulf's transcultural realities, which include encounters and relations with Africa and South Asia evident in Arab characters. Comparably, Marzieh Meshkini's *Roozi khe zan shodam / The Day I Became a Woman* (Iran, 2000) captured attention at Western film festivals, though often only for its focus on hijab. As an Iranian film directed by a woman about obligatory postrevolutionary hijab, Western audiences praised the bold behavior of three Iranian women, one of whom rides a bicycle much like the girl in Mansour's film. But critics often overlooked the third part of the film, set along the Gulf, far from the capital of Tehran, and where the presence of Africans and Arabs is evident. Like *Wadjda*, Meshkini's film offers insights into Iranian politics that are more complicated than gender alone. The third story in Meshkini's film also evokes Bahram Beizai's controversial *Bashu, Gharibeye Koochak / Bashu, the Little Stranger* (Iran, 1989), which is set during the Iran-Iraq War (or first Gulf War), when Arab groups in Iran where suspected of allegiance to Iraq and persecuted. Comparably, Bassam Al Thawadi's *Hekaya Bahrainiya / A Bahraini Tale* (Bahrain, 2006) examines the historical era of the end of pan-Arabism with the fall of Gamal Abdel Nasser. Like *Bashu*, it focuses on the effects of US proxy wars and reflects how they disrupted the transcultural and multicultural communities that have lived alongside one another for centuries. In addition to their stories, their style departs from Western expectations.

Although Siddiq cast actors from Kuwaiti television for his film, he directed them to act in a more naturalist style. By contrast, Thawadi's actors act in the stylized performance modes of musalsalat (television serials). Despite the film's acknowledgment of rising tensions, its overly melodramatic style makes the film largely illegible to the gatekeepers of Western film festivals. Not only are the emotions more overt in Thawadi's film than in ones by Siddiq, Mansour, and Meshkini but so too are the social tensions with the multicultural society of Gulf cities that were gradually being purified into one that conforms to state narratives of national identity.

By contrast, Siddiq's *Bas ya Bahar* screened at festivals in Damascus, Tehran, and Tunis, as well as Chicago and Venice. "The film world was astounded," writes one critic since "Kuwait was a country with practically no cinematic tradition" yet the film "demonstrated great artistry."[104] The film conveys the precarity of pearl diving after the British siege on Gulf trade routes but before the collapse of pearling with the manufacturing of cheaper cultured pearls from Japan in the 1930s. Whereas scholars have typically focused on the film's representation of pearling, Najat Alsheridah examines its representation of women. Inside gender-segregated space, they dance and ululate in yalwa (cleansing and cleaning) wedding rituals; outside, they sing and dance in public to mark Alqufal (local dialect for the closing of diving season) and ensure the safe return of their husbands and sons.[105] "Significantly, in Kuwait, directors tend to hire women from African ancestry to perform ritual dance as this allows them to get through censorship restrictions more easily," Alsheridah explains; "In the eyes of the censors this preserves the 'purity' of the Kuwaiti woman's image."[106] Kuwaiti actors without visible African ancestry are contained to scenes inside the domestic space.

Bas ya Bahar claimed a space for Gulf Arabs in debates on New Arab Cinema, which had appeared only tangentially in New Arab Cinema—and often unfavorably.[107] Screened in the same year, *Al-Makhdu'un / The Dupes* (Syria, 1972; dir. Tewfik Saleh) depicts Palestinian refugees who encounter self-interested Iraqis unwilling to reduce their fees for transport from Basra to Kuwait City and a calculating Palestinian refugee who smuggles them inside an empty water tank in midsummer. The men suffocate as the driver haggles with Kuwaiti customs officials, who punctuate their fascination with lascivious stories about female dancers with the sound of prayer beads (*misbaha*), implying hypocrisy within conservative Gulf morals. In the film, the Gulf becomes a site for betrayal of a Palestinian cause, a principle of Arab nationalism.

Bas ya Bahar was understood through the lenses of Arab or Middle Eastern cinema—rather than as transcultural cinema. Siddiq defines

FIGURE 0.6

Corrupt Gulf Arab "oil sheikh" stereotype in *Al-makhdu'un / The Dupes* (Syria, 1972; dir. Tewfik Saleh).

Kuwait as primarily Gulf Arab, though pearling required slave labor from Africa, which was estimated to constitute 17 percent of the population in 1900, a proportion equivalent to that in Oman, whose connections to Africa are well established.[108] It also included South Asian traders, whose connections to the Arabian Peninsula date back to the sixteenth century. British colonialism institutionalized bureaucratic ties to India by governing its protectorates from Bombay and issuing a Gulf rupee from 1959 to 1966. *Bas ya Bahar* is remarkable for recognition of sexualized violence within marriage in a terrifying rape scene that Kuwaiti censors cut, but considering the film's erasure of Africans, South Asians, and other Arabs requires a critical framework that deconstructs purified ideas of nations and regions.

Forty years after Siddiq's film, Mansour's *Wadjda* became a favorite at Western festivals for acknowledging the limited mobility of Saudi women at the time.[109] The film's story was often universalized by Westerners to reinforce Western constructions of "saving Muslim women," which also erased questions about working-class society in Riyadh that cannot be reduced to gender alone.[110] The story rewards white feminist desire for "girl power" from "a girl on a bike" without much regard for the more complicated intersections of class, gender, ethnicity/race, and citizenship. Western celebrations of Mansour's determination, reportedly directing her cinematographer from inside a parked van, reproduces state discourses of "exceptional Saudi women," who rise despite legal barriers. The character of Wadjda embodies this figure.

In the film, a young girl, Wadjda (Waad Mohammed), wants a bicycle of her own to move freely through the city with her male friend Abdullah (Abdullrahman Al Gohani). Meanwhile, Wadjda's mother (Reem Abdullah) is contained, both by laws that prevent her from driving and by customs that encourage her husband to obey his mother and marry another woman, who might bear him a son. Direct critiques of guardianship laws and religious police are difficult to make, but they do appear. Tariq Al Haydar, however, notes that when Wadjda finally rides her bicycle, the camera pauses and focuses on a public bus, adorned with the state flag and rulers that includes the state slogan: "May the Glory of the Nation Endure." For him, the scene undercuts the film's critique of state policy.[111] Audiences, however, might also notice that Wadjda rides past the bus with utter indifference to its symbolic power. *Wadjda* underscores how acts of resistance are necessarily provisional. Wadjda's mother returns a red dress with which she had hoped to secure her husband's affections, so that she can purchase a green bicycle for her daughter. She creates a space within limitations. The film asks us to consider such acts as revolutionary.

Wadjda's story also includes social problems that are not determined by gender, religion, or ruling family, occluding economic conditions for the Saudi working class as another form of immobility. Wadjda's father sees her infrequently due to work. Even more vulnerable, the family's South Asian driver, Iqbal (Mohammed Zahir), sees Wadjda's mother each day when he drives her to work, but he has not returned to see his own family for several years. Both he and Wadjda's mother have access to certain kinds of mobility yet are denied other kinds. Their relationship is fraught, as both vie for power over the other in a system that limits power for both. Iqbal's insubordination to Wadjda's mother often shocks audiences, accustomed to seeing absolute obedience by South Asians to Gulf Arabs, especially women. Mansour represents abuses of citizenship when Abdullah defends Wadjda by Iqbal with deportation. Abdullah's uncle works in the government, and his mustachioed face appears on posters throughout the neighborhood. Also, when Wadjda is told she should donate her money to help the Palestinians, her annoyance reflects the trivialization of the Palestinian story in certain parts of Gulf society.

The film's story, then, is more nuanced and about more than the gendered oppression with which Westerners obsess; it is also about how class, ethnicity/race, family/tribe, gender, and generation intersect to make visible the precarious state of women's rights within Riyadh's lower middle class and those with the legal status of "migrant workers" or "bachelors," two colloquial expressions for working-class expatriates—neither of which can sponsor their families. *Wadjda*'s Western reception paid no attention to how Wadjda benefits from the reproduction of racism that Abdullah mobilizes by belittling Iqbal. Wadjda might be an exceptional young Saudi girl for Western audiences, but she shows no signs of discomfort—or even recognition—of the racism and abuses of power that her Saudi male friend mobilizes to impress her. Riyadh becomes a contact zone in which the legacies of British colonialism and US imperialism intersect with states constructed around ruling families within the scapes of a globalized media culture.

Wadjda is not unique for including inequitable relations between citizens and noncitizens, often through relegating the latter to the background or making them comedic foils or villains. The complexity of multicultural Gulf societies is the subject of *A Bahraini Tale*, which defines preindependence Bahrain as a space where sectarian tensions are beginning to develop between Muslim and Jewish Arabs and between Shia and Sunni Muslims.[112] It also recovers characteristics of the Gulf that Nelida Fuccaro defines as a social heterogeneity—one that would disappear in neighboring Manama by the 1970s.[113] The film conveys Bahraini modernity as a site where ethics developed not only from reading the Qur'an but also

FIGURE 0.7

Wadjda confronts her mother's South Asian driver in *Wadjda* (Germany/Saudi Arabia, 2012; dir. Haifaa Al-Mansour).

from reading Karl Marx. The Gulf devised its own configurations of "cultural encounters" that Tarik Sabry describes elsewhere in Arab-majority states.[114] Another aspect of the film's depiction of Bahrain in the late 1960s is a love of Hindi cinema. In the film, a mixed-gender crowd flocks to a screening of Raj Kapoor's *Sangam* (India, 1964). Not only do Hindi films claim visual prominence, but the film's dialogues remind us that Bahraini Arabs understood Hindi. The presence of Indian films evokes the presence of Indian merchants, some of whom settled on the Peninsula, as did former African slaves, as part of Indian Ocean encounters. For Western film festival programmers, however, *A Bahraini Tale*'s production values and acting styles are too "televisual" to be "cinematic" and thus it did not have international play nor has it been the subject of much academic scholarship. The film's marginalization by Western film festivals suggests the power of these festivals as gatekeepers to the stories about the Gulf, but the film points to how the Gulf's history can unsettle assumptions within area and film studies in productive ways.

Reorienting with the Gulf also allows for a reconsideration not only of Arab cinema but also Iranian cinema. Representations of Africans, Arabs, and

INTRODUCTION 35

FIGURE 0.8

Posters for Hindi films outside a 1960s Bahraini cinema in *Hekaya Bahrainiya/A Bahraini Tale* (Bahrain, 2006; dir. Bassam Al Thawadi).

other "ethnic minorities" are political in Iranian art cinema. Beizai's *Bashu, the Little Stranger* was censored, as Hamid Naficy argues, for its representation of Arab blackness and its use of Arabic language in an Iranian film, made all the more controversial since it coincided with the Iran-Iraq War.[115] Arabness and blackness become "foreign" and are equated with national betrayal within the shifting relations of power. Naii (Susan Taslimi) is ostracized for caring for the traumatized orphan black Arab Bashu (Adnan Afravian). The film received some attention in Western festivals but very little in comparison with director Abbas Kiarostami's on much safer topics and a style that is often more French than Iranian (even in films set in Iran).

A multiple award winner at Western festivals, Meshkini's *The Day I Became a Woman* sets one of its three interwoven stories on the Persian Gulf island of Kish. It tells a story of three women on a day when their physical mobility is determined by their sex. The nine-year-old Hava (Fatemeh Cherag Akhar) is no longer free to play with her male friend Hassan (Hassan Nebhan) on the beach. The married Ahoo (Shabnam Toloui) is divorced by her husband (Sirous Kahvarinegad) and berated by her male family for bicycle racing with other women. The widowed Hoora (Azizeh Sedighi), by contrast, celebrates her husband's death by retiring to Kish, where she purchases everything denied to her in life except a son. The film is considered a celebration of strength, dignity, and defiance. Less frequently discussed by critics, it is one of the few Iranian films to acknowledge racism against Afro-Iranians as part of a critique of patriarchy. Hoora disparages the blackness of a young boy, who helps her travel with her caravan of consumer goods from a shopping mall to the beach. Afro-Iranian and Afro-Arab identities introduce a history that predates purified notions of Persian-Iranian identity.

The fluidity of the Gulf as a space defined by encounters, presences, and relations through a maritime arena—one that is overlaid by colonial / imperial contact and globalizing scapes—allows for exploration and allows for a closer examination of content, not just distribution. Such fluidity can be extended beyond the Gulf, allowing for interconnections between nations and regions to become more apparent. For example, Merzak Allouache's *Omar Gatlato / Umar Qatlatu Al-Rudjla* (Algeria, 1976) depicts its protagonist secretly recording Hindi "filmi" music in an Algerian cinema. The film deconstructs failures of pan-Arab masculinity in Algeria's war for independence as tied to the heroic FLN (National Liberation Front). Although Omar (Boualem Benani) is intimidated by modern woman Selma (Farida Guenaneche) and unable to project the masculine bravado of his father's generation, he is able to express his feelings through the lyrics and rhythms of Hindi music, offering an alternative model through Bombay superstars like Dev Anand, Dharmendra, Rishi Kapoor, and—above all—Amitabh Bachchan, whose "angry young man" characters resonated with disenfranchised male audiences in Egypt yet still suggested ways to adapt to modern working women. Bachchan enters into Egyptian New Realist Cinema as part of Egyptian film culture in the 1980s, argues Claire Cooley, so that "a globally circulating Hindi cinema addresses concerns and fills absences within an Egyptian society that is adjusting to changes associated with economic liberalization."[116] Egyptians were attracted to Bachchan's "angry young man" character, which emerged during India's Emergency (1975–1977), when citizen trust in an increasingly authoritarian state had waned. Indian films were always banned in Egypt to protect the local theatrical market, but videocassettes, whether legal or pirated, circulated. At the same time, through the politics

FIGURE 0.9

On the island of Kish, Hoora and her young helpers in *Roozi khe zan shodam / The Day I Became a Woman* (Iran, 2000; dir. Marzieh Meshkini).

of relations, we can consider why Bombay cinema produced numerous "Arabian Nights" fantasies, along with colorist "junglee" (savage) characters at the same time as Egyptian cinema's "wuhush" (savage) characters.[117] These connections put film cultures in conversation without the direct imposition of Western paradigms.

Even the Gulf does not escape caricature in both Indian and Egyptian films. In *Don* (India, 1978; dir. Chandra Barot), Bachchan navigates an Indian underworld of illicit cabarets, filled with Gulf Arabs and Christian Indians. Negative stereotypes of Gulf Arabs are also evident in Egyptian art films just before the (second) Gulf War (1990–1991), such as Chahine's *Iskanderija, Kaman oue Kaman / Alexandria Again and Forever* (France/Egypt, 1989), which satirizes the Gulf as controlling in a scene with a Gulf Arab in national dress demanding that a scene with alcohol be removed from a film. Saudi Arabia was one of the largest importers of popular Egyptian film for private screenings, but Chahine makes a joke about Egyptian film being corrupted by "petrodollars" when film distribution shifted from

Lebanon to Kuwait in the 1980s. Echoing the concerns of committed Egyptian filmmakers, Viola Shafik notes how this change led Egyptian cinema "to be hijacked and adapted for the needs of neighboring countries with stronger economies" and sanitized into "clean cinema" (*sinema nazifa*) according to a "so-called new morality and religiosity, strongly inspired by the Saudi Arabian fundamentalist Wahhabism."[118] Egyptian popular cinema had declined in the 1970s, evident in *Zi'ab la Ta'kol al-Lahm / Wolves that Don't Eat Meat / Kuwait Connection* (Egypt, 1973; dir. Samir A. Khouri) with its gratuitous female nudity, associated again with the Gulf. At the same time, Egyptian commercial filmmaking's dependency on the Saudi market affected the ability for independent Egyptian filmmakers to critique social problems in Egypt. The development of a commercial Saudi film industry under Mohammed bin Salman, along with other liberalization, promises to change the relationship further. Indeed, Egypt, Saudi Arabia, and UAE have discussed coordination before 2019.

The Gulf as a concept, however, is more substantive than merely calling attention to perceptions of conservative Gulf pressures to impose themselves on Egyptian films or hypocritical Gulf sheikhs enjoying forbidden sex and alcohol amid Western hippies and Christian Indians in Bombay cabarets. It can focus attention on the absences of transcultural interconnections in the films that have been selected as canonical examples of Arab, Middle Eastern, and South Asian cinemas. Although invisible in Chahine's *Cairo Station*, as a social analysis of ways that the transportation center of modern Egypt excludes rural migrants, portrayals of other groups are excluded from modern nations and national cinemas. Nubians, for example, are featured in Egyptian popular cinema, often as "naïve, honest, kind-hearted, and humorous" nannies, servants, doorkeepers, waiters, who spoke with rustic accents or broken Arabic, if at all.[119] By conceiving spaces as fluid and transcultural, rather than fixed and territorial, such characters come into focus. Film studies has never focused much on ways that such forms of circulation inform the kinds of films produced.

FILM AND DIGITAL MEDIA ON SOCIAL MEDIA

In addition to limiting visions of feature narratives, dominant categories in film studies also tend to exclude nonprofessional media, which is the majority of Gulf media—and increasingly more so with affordable film and distribution options that bypass censorship (although self-censorship continues).[120] By focusing on types of media that film studies typically overlooks, the Gulf encourages us to examine official and unofficial archives. The Gulf's media consumption is driven by the youth market, with 60 percent of the population being under age thirty in almost all states—most of whom have come of age online. Social media platforms have taken the place of television. Television focuses primarily on reality shows and dramas based on Hollywood formats, like MBC's *Arabs Got Talent* (Lebanon, 2011–2019; cr. Simon Cowell) and Image Nation Abu Dhabi / Netflix's *Qalb al-Adala / Justice* (UAE, 2017; cr. William Finklestein and Walter Parkes), both produced in the UAE.[121] Television also includes large numbers of Indian serials and programs. Sreya Mitra examines how Emirati audiences are increasingly watching Bollywood films on cable and satellite television, dubbed into Arabic on channels such as Zee Aflam, Zee Alwan, and MBC Bollywood.[122] Comparably, Darshana Mini describes different uses of Malayalam-language satellite channels that range from entrepreneurship to looking for missing persons, that is, what the states used to do for their citizens.[123]

Social media has fewer limitations than television. YouTube does not require official approval by censors and has become a platform for young Gulf media producers and creators of all ethnoracial and socioeconomic backgrounds. This demographic publishes short comedy sketches and web series that range from the sophisticated comedy and high production values of Telfaz11 and the web series *Takki* (Saudi Arabia, 2012–2015; dir. Mohammad Makki), which was eventually Netflixized for a third season in 2021, to video diaries and vlogs from the perspectives of middle-class expatriates, including second- and third-generation expatriates, on navigating laws, customs, and expectations.[124] These videos also critique the ethnoracial biases within the Gulf. Jordindian, the duo of Naser Al Azzeh and Vineeth "Beep" Kumar, poke fun at the convergence of multiple cultures as Arab and South Asian youth navigate adulthood, making them popular across the Gulf. The use of social media and messaging services is the highest in the world and has contributed to tribal survival across different nation-states, to forming "digital majlis," and to the maintenance of oral poetry.[125] Indeed, much of the youths' output on social media platforms reflects a nostalgia for a time not even their parents remember. Uploaded to YouTube, these old Kuwait musalsalat find new generations of audiences and become part of an informal cultural heritage of negotiating modernity. Heritage thrives through music videos as well, most notably "Amatiyah" by the group Bin Abady. The video, directed by two of the band's members, swept through the Arab World after its Eid Adha release in 2022. The video juxtaposes images of traditional Omani dress, like the burqa and thobe with contemporary activities like rollerblading. The dialogue in the video opted for the local dialect of the Omani province Batiyeh; this caused discussions on social media throughout the Arabic-speaking world about dialects and heritage.

Social media also allows performance artists to use digital mediation as a mode of engaging with socially sensitive subjects without the risk of on-site performances.[126] For example, Meshal Al-Jaser's *Ṭaz bi al-Kuffar / Screw the Infidels* (Saudi Arabia, 2015) went viral on YouTube, parodying and critiquing Islamophobia in Hollywood, Daesh (Islamic State) recruitment videos, and Arab hip-hop. While the media that Telfaz11 and others create is not activist, it is political, breaking with foreign stereotypes of the Arabian Peninsula that portray Gulf Arabs as superficial, whether consumerist or fundamentalist, and utterly lacking in self-reflection or self-criticism. Colorism is another topic that has been addressed only tangentially in much scholarship on African, South Asian, and Southwest Asian media and the Gulf with its many intersecting cultures and identities. Although stories about the use of blackface in Egyptian cinema from AJE circulate on social media, occasional social influencers or other celebrities in dark makeup that have been critiqued as perpetuating such practices.[127] It reproduces racial and ethnic hierarchies from the colonial era, yet it also accumulates meaning from Hollywood and other US media that circulate widely in cinemas, on television, and via streaming platforms today, including media that confronts racism.[128] Fluid and non-territorial critical concepts like gulfs, seas, and oceans allow more nuanced understandings of the racism/colorism/shadeism that allows for discrimination against working-class African, South Asian, and Southeast Asian expatriates in many Gulf states, along with prejudices against "half Emiratis" with darker or lighter features as they pertain to passport

FIGURE 0.10

Scene from *Ana mafi khof min Kafeel/I'm Not Scared of Kafeel* (Saudi Arabia, 2015; dir. Saleh Haddad).

privileges of noncitizen parents. Colorism in UAE filmmaking is seldom thematized. Although it can appear in stereotypes, public discussion has not developed.[129] Discussions of colorism, of course, can also obscure discussions of prejudice based on caste, ethnicity, race, and tribe.

Whether online or onscreen, Gulf media production and consumption reveal a cultural space shared by many, debated and interpreted by filmmakers and media producers living within and well beyond its political borders (but connected to it through labor migration and trade), and an intersection where visual stories emerge through professional and amateur filmmaking. It is not a place of exceptionality but of multiple interconnections, many of which are evident in film and digital media. Film and digital media in the Gulf thus required multiple disciplines and multiple critical lenses to analyze its complexities. This collection brings together scholars in different fields and expertise to cross-pollinate conversations and facilitate dialogues between area studies and film studies, as well as between African, Arab, Middle Eastern, and South Asian film and digital media. The study addresses the marginalization of the Gulf within film studies and the marginalization of film and digital media within area studies by redefining conceptual frameworks to render images and stories from the Gulf more legible. However, it is not intended to be comprehensive and contains noteworthy gaps, such as analyses of the power of influencers on social media. The collection provides useful frameworks and examples for future scholarship.

The essays frame how the Gulf can serve as an opportunity to reorient assumptions and expectations. Nelida Fuccaro examines area studies in relation to the Gulf, particularly its afterlives, alongside the genealogies of Gulf studies. She notes the significance of Gulf cities as potential correctives to Gulf isolationism and exceptionalism. Firat Oruc examines oil company documentaries in Bahrain and the development of some of the first semipublic cinemas, both of which were partly shaped when Bahrain was a British protectorate, and governed the Bombay Office. Dale Hudson's interview with Emirati artist Ammar Al Attar on his photographs of some of the first freestanding cinemas in the UAE shows the complex formal and informal networks by which films from Egypt, Hollywood, India, Palestine, and Pakistan, and elsewhere came to audiences. Attar exhibits the photos as part of installations that include objects salvaged from the cinemas. Bindu Menon examines the migration of audio cassettes as precursors to amateur videos, between Kerala and the Peninsula, focusing on themes of love and longing among the Mappilas, who exchange *kathupattu* (letter songs). Examining two of the most celebrated sacred defense genre films, Mohsen Makhmalbaf's *Arūsī-yi Khūbān / Marriage of the Blessed* (1989) and Ebrahim Hatami-Kia's *Azhans-i Shīshah-yī / The Glass Agency* (1998), Parisa Vaziri focuses on blackness in Iranian cinema, which does not conform to conventional frameworks of black diaspora. Sebastian Thejus Cherian looks at the Malayalam film *Vilkanundu Swapnangal* (1980), which narrates the difficulties of migrant life and whose production embodies the challenges faced by filmmakers in their attempt to shoot the first Indian film in the Gulf.

Karolina Ginalska analyzes the limitations of transnational cooperation on narrative feature films produced in the Gulf, comparing festival hit *Wadjda*, which received much international funding, and lesser known *Alboom* (Oman, 2006; dir. Khalid AbdulRahim Al-Zadjali), which was made solely with the funding of individual Omanis.[130] Kay Dickinson examines the DIFF and Dubai Studio City in relation to free zones, calibrated to maximize profit from the circulation of capital, workers, visitors, and goods. Suzi Mirgani considers how short films and videos can articulate overt or covert political statements about female domestic workers in Kuwait, Qatar, Saudi Arabia, and UAE, thus offering a space for civic discourse despite an absence of rights to protest. Chrysavgi Papagianni reexamines the Western preoccupation of gendered oppression by examining the film practiced by two Emirati filmmakers, who mobilize their social privilege to convey complicated and often controversial stories on film. Sean Foley describes the emergence of a new generation of Saudi artists by focusing on Meshal Al-Jaser, whose viral videos articulate perspectives that resonate with youth throughout the Gulf and include non-Gulf Arabs. Beth Derderian looks at the possibility of political arts practice from the perspective of Gulf-born noncitizen artists, focusing on Walid Al Wawi's use of digital platforms for performance art. Finally, Alia Yunis and Sasha Ritter discuss the Zayed University Middle East Film Festival (ZUMEFF) as a grassroots institution that has weathered shifting investments in film education and culture to be the longest-running film festival in the Gulf.

NOTE ON LANGUAGES AND TRANSLITERATIONS

Although we would have liked to have retained each contributor's own English, we agreed to translate from British English and Indian English into US English, including the MDY date format (rather than DMY or YMD), for ease in indexing and copyediting. We have left transliterations from Arabic and Persian alphabets in the form (with or without diacritics) used by each contributor.

ACKNOWLEDGMENTS

Most chapters develop from presentations at the conference Film and Visual Media in the Gulf: Images, Infrastructures, and Institutions: Connecting Africa, the Middle East, South Asia, and the World, which was convened at New York University Abu Dhabi (NYUAD) Institute in October 2018. We are grateful to the NYUAD Institute for hosting the conference that made this volume possible, especially Gila Besserat-Waels, who encouraged us to submit a proposal, and Robert J. C. Young, who endorsed it as NYUAD's Dean of Arts and Humanities. We also thank Sharon Bergman, Tarek Chehab, Manal Demaghlatrous, Antoine El Khayat, Reindert Falkenburg, Philip Kennedy, Ralph Raymond, and Nora Yousif at the NYUAD Institute, all of whom helped realize the conference. At Nirvana Travel, we thank Subi Jayadevan, Adnan Mukadam, and Farahnaaz Waels, who helped nonresidents get to Abu Dhabi. Other papers from this conference appear as a special double issue of the *Middle Eastern Journal of Culture and Communication*, which is particularly rich in media related to Kerala in southwestern India and to Bollywood but also includes chapters on Kuwait's first official photographs and tribal uses of social media across state borders.

We thank Nahed Ahmed at the NYUAD Institute for making it possible for us to host a screening *Bas ya Bahar* with filmmaker Khalid Al-Siddiq to discuss the film. The public screening is likely the last that he attended. At the NYUAD Art Gallery, we thank Maya Allison and Kris Mortensen for making Ammar Al Attar's *Cinemas in the UAE* exhibition possible. We thank Maysoon Mubarak in Public Affairs for helping the exhibition receive excellent reception by both Arabic- and English-language press. We are also grateful to colleagues who lent their expertise to the conference by chairing panels and offering responses, including Brad Bauer, Alejandra Val Cubero, Owen Bennett Jones, Terri Ginsberg, Lena Jayussi, Arvind Rajagopal, and Nadia Yaqub, as well as Gianluca Chakra, Alaa Karkouti, Butheina Kazim, Lina Matta, and Gregory Unrau, who participated on an insightful and candid panel discussion of the film industry, which was moderated by Jay Weissberg. The collection also benefits from discussions with colleagues outside the conference, including Fawzia Afzal-Khan, Awam Amkpa, Laure Assaf, Sheetal Majithia, Salwa Mikdadi, Robert Parthesius, Gaelle Picherit-Duthler, Ella Shohat, Robert Stam, and Woodman Taylor. We are also incredibly fortunate to be part of the Middle East Moving Image Collective (MEMIC), where we receive generous feedback on an early draft of this introduction from Hend Alawadhi, Samirah Alkassim, Greg Burris,

Donatella della Ratta, Terri Ginsberg, Iman Hammad, Bindu Menon, Wissam Mouawad, Zeina Tarraf, and Negar Taymoorzadeh. We are indebted to the anonymous reviewers of this book's manuscript for their incredibly generous feedback and suggestions. Finally, we are grateful to Allison Chaplin at Indiana University Press for her support of our work and this book.

> DALE HUDSON is Associate Professor of Film and New Media at New York University Abu Dhabi. He is author of *Vampires, Race, and Transnational Hollywoods* and, with Patricia R. Zimmermann, of *Thinking Through Digital Media: Transnational Environments and Locative Places.*
>
> ALIA YUNIS is a scholar, writer, and filmmaker. She is currently a research fellow at the Arab Gulf States Institute in Washington, DC.

NOTES

1. Lawrence G. Potter, "Introduction," in *The Persian Gulf in Modern Times: People, Ports, and History*, ed. Lawrence G. Potter (New York: Palgrave Macmillan, 2014), 8–10; and Ahmed al-Dailami, "'Purity and Confusion': The Hawala between Persians and Arabs in the Contemporary Gulf," in *The Persian Gulf in Modern Times*, 299–325; Abdulrahman al Salimi, "The Banians of Muscat: A South Asian Merchant Community in Oman and the Gulf, c. 1500–1700," in *The Gulf in World History: Arabia at the Global Crossroads*, ed. Allen James Fromherz (Edinburgh: Edinburgh University Press, 2018), 105–119; Johan Mathew, "Khaliji Hindustan: Towards a Diasporic History of Khalijis in South Asia from the 1780s to the 1960s," in *The Gulf in World History*, 120–138; Matthew S. Hopper, "Africans and the Gulf: Between Diaspora and Cosmopolitanism," in *The Gulf in World History*, 139–159. Also see work in history and anthropology, such as: R. Said Zhalan, *The Origins of the United Arab Emirates: A Political and Social History of the Trucial States* (London: Macmillan, 1978); Jill Crystal, *Oil and Politics in the Gulf: Rulers and Merchants in Kuwait and Qatar*, updated version (Cambridge: Cambridge University Press, 1995); Anh Nga Longva, *Walls Built on Sand: Migration, Exclusion, And Society In Kuwait* (London: Routledge, 1997); Christopher M. Davidson, *Abu Dhabi: Oil and Beyond* (New York: Columbia University Press, 2009); Nelida Fuccaro, *Histories of City and State in the Persian Gulf: Manama since 1800* (Cambridge: Cambridge University Press, 2009); Lawrence G. Potter, ed., *The Persian Gulf in History* (New York: Palgrave Macmillan, 2009); Rebecca L. Torstrick and Elizabeth Faie, *Culture and Customs of the Arab Gulf States* (Westport, CT: Greenwood Press, 2009); Yasser Elsheshtawy, *Dubai: Behind an Urban Spectacle* (New York: Routledge, 2010); Nabil A. Sultan, David Weir, and Zeinab Karake-Shalhoub, eds., *The New Post-Oil Arab Gulf: Managing People*

and Wealth (London: Saqi, 2011); David Commins, *The Gulf States: A Modern History* (London: I. B. Tauris, 2012); Allen. J. Fromherz, *Qatar: A Modern History* (Washington, DC: Georgetown University Press, 2012); David Held and Kristian Ulrichsen Coates, eds., *The Transformation of the Gulf: Politics, Economics, and the Global Order* (London: Routledge, 2012); Mehran Kamrava, *Qatar: Small State, Big Politics* (Ithaca, NY: Cornell University Press, 2013); Neha Vora, *Impossible Citizens: Dubai's Indian Diaspora* (Durham, NC: Duke University Press, 2013); Lawrence G. Potter, ed., *The Persian Gulf in Modern Times: People, Ports, and History* (New York: Palgrave Macmillan, 2014); Miriam Cooke, *Tribal Modern: Branding New Nations in the Arab Gulf* (Berkeley: University of California Press, 2015); Matthew S. Hopper, *Slaves of One Master: Globalization and Slavery in Arabia in the Age of Empire* (New Haven, CT: Yale University Press, 2015); Andrew Ross, ed., *The Gulf: High Culture/Hard Labor* (New York: OR Books, 2015); Farah Al-Nakib, *Kuwait Transformed: A History of Oil and Urban Life* (Stanford, CA: Stanford University Press, 2016); Kristian Coates Ulrichsen, *The United Arab Emirates: Power, Politics, and the Policy Making* (London: Routledge, 2017); Alia Yunis, "Coming Soon: Encounters on the Road to Heritage and Film in the UAE" (PhD diss., University of Amsterdam, 2020).

2. James Onley, "Transnational Merchants in the Nineteenth-century Gulf: The Case of the Safar Family," in *Transnational Connections and the Arab Gulf*, ed. Madawi Al-Rasheed (London: Routledge, 2005), 59–110. Nidhi Mahajan, "Dhow Itineraries: The Making of a Shadow Economy in the Western Indian Ocean," *Comparative Studies of South Asia, Africa and the Middle East* 39, no. 3 (2019): 407–418; Nisha Mathew, "At the Crossroads of Empire and Nation-State: Partition, Gold Smuggling, and Port Cities in the Western Indian Ocean," *Modern Asian Studies* 54, no. 3 (2020): 898–929.

3. With the start of the Iran-Iraq War, the Arab Gulf rulers formed an economic and political alliance in 1981 that deletes Iran and Iraq from their definition of Gulf. The Gulf Cooperation Council (GCC) includes Bahrain, Kuwait, Oman, Qatar, Saudi Arabia, and the United Arab Emirates (UAE).

4. Attiya Ahmad, "Beyond Labor: Foreign Residents in the Persian Gulf States," in *Migrant Labor in the Persian Gulf*, ed. Mehran Kamrava and Zahra Babar (New York: Columbia University Press, 2012), 25.

5. Ahmad, "Beyond Labor," 25.

6. Amitav Ghosh, *In an Antique Land: History in the Guise of a Traveler's Tale* (New York: Vintage, 1992), 339.

7. CIA World Factbook provides annual population data for all the Gulf countries broken down by citizenship.

8. Amitav Ghosh describes an Indian Ocean interrupted by Western imperialism in the novels *Sea of Poppies* (2008), *River of Smoke* (2011), *Flood of Fire* (2015), and *Gun Island* (2019).

9. C. G. Smith, "The Emergence of the Middle East," *Journal of Contemporary History* 3, no. 3 (1968): 3, 9.

10. Karen Culcasi, "Constructing and Naturalizing the Middle East," *Geographical Review* 100, no. 4 (2010): 585.

11. Culcasi, "Constructing and Naturalizing the Middle East," 593.

12. Ahmed Kanna, *Dubai: The City as Corporation* (Minnesota: University of Minnesota Press, 2011), 11.

13. Neha Vora and Natalie Koch, "Everyday Inclusions: Rethinking Ethnocracy, *Kafala*, and Belonging in the Arabian Peninsula," *Studies in Ethnicity and Nationalism* 15, no. 3 (2015): 542.

14. Jack Shaheen, *Reel Bad Arabs* (2001), 3rd ed. (Northampton: Olive Branch Press, 2012); Alia Yunis and Gaelle Picherit-Duthler, "Tramps vs. Sweethearts: Changing Images of Arab and American Women in Hollywood Films," *Middle East Journal of Culture and Communication* 4, no. 2 (2011): 225–243.

15. Yasser Elsheshtawy, *Temporary Cities: Resisting Transience in Arabia* (London: Routledge, 2019), 252. See also Ahmed Kanna, Amélie Le Renard, and Neha Vora, *Beyond Exceptionalism: New Interpretations of the Arabian Peninsula* (Ithaca, NY: Cornell University Press, 2020).

16. Gayatri Chakravorty Spivak, *Other Asias* (Malden: Blackwell, 2008). Diana Crane, "Culture and Globalization: Theoretical Models and Emerging Trends," in *Global Culture: Media, Arts, Policy, and Globalization*, ed. Diana Crane, Nobuko Kawashima, and Ken-ichi Kawasaki (London: Routledge, 2002), 4.

17. See articles in Kaveh Askari and Samhita Sunya's special issue of *Film History*, "South by Southwest" 32, no. 3 (2020); Frédérique Lagrange and Clio Ceveneau's special issue of *Arabian Humanities*, "Pop Culture in the Arabian Peninsula" 14 (2020); and our special double issue of the *Middle East Journal of Culture and Communication*, "Film and Visual Media in the Gulf: Historical and Contemporary Perspectives" 14, nos. 1–2 (2021).

18. Mary Louise Pratt, *Imperial Eyes: Travel Writing and Transculturation*, 2nd ed. (New York: Routledge, 2008), 7.

19. Édourd Glissant, *Poetics of Relations*, trans. Betsy Wing (Ann Arbor: University of Michigan Press, 1997), 11.

20. Glissant, *Poetics of Relations*, 12.

21. Glissant, *Poetics of Relations*, 17–19. He juxtaposes "errancy" against "a totalitarian drive for a single, unique root" (14), which is a legacy of contact with colonizers and imperialists, impose limits as "monolingual" (15) or "settled way of life of Western nations" (16) whereby movement is reduced to discovery, conquest, or voyage.

22. Tarik Sabry, *Cultural Encounters in the Arab World: On Media, the Modern and the Everyday* (London: I. B. Tauris, 2010).

23. Nile Green, "Rethinking the 'Middle East' after the Oceanic Turn," *Comparative Studies of South Asia, Africa, and the Middle East* 34, no. 3 (2014): 558.

24. Green, "Rethinking the 'Middle East,'" 558.

25. Green, "Rethinking the 'Middle East,'" 558.

26. Green, "Rethinking the 'Middle East,'" 556.

27. Fahad Ahmed Bishara, "Ships Passing in the Night? Reflections on the Middle East in the Indian Ocean," *International Journal of Middle East Studies* 48, no. 4 (2016): 759.

28. Arjun Appadurai, *Modernity at Large: Cultural Dimensions of Globalization* (Minneapolis: University of Minnesota Press, 1995).

29. Kuan-Hsing Chen, *Asia as Method: Toward Deimperialization* (Durham, NC: Duke University Press, 2010).

30. Samir Amin, *L'eurocentrisme: Critique d'une ideologie* (Paris: Anthropos-Economica, 1988); Ella Shohat and Robert T. Stam, *Unthinking Eurocentrism: Multiculturalism and the Media* (1994), updated edition (New York: Routledge, 2014).

31. Saër Maty Bâ and Will Higbee, "Introduction De-Westernizing Film Studies," in *De-Westernizing Film Studies*, ed. Saër Maty Bâ and Will Higbee (New York: Routledge, 2012), 13.

32. Andrew Higson, "The Concept of National Cinema," *Screen* 30, no. 4 (1989): 44.

33. Nasser Rabbat, "What is Islamic Architecture Anyway?," *Journal of Art Historiography* 6 (2012): 1–15.

34. For a discussion of the ethnoracial hierarchies in the production of "international cinema" in the United States, see, for example, "International Hollywood Vampires: Cosmopolitanisms of 'Foreign Movies,'" in Dale Hudson, *Vampires, Race, and Transnational Hollywoods* (Edinburgh: Edinburgh University Press, 2017), 100–133.

35. He identifies five types. Three were historically unmoored as "timeless" and "unchanging" essences: irrationally evil villains, buffoonish and avaricious sheiks (sheikh or شيخ becomes "sheik," severing associations with wisdom and community leadership), and hapless and sexualized maidens. The other two were situated within selective histories: ancient Egyptians, removing Egypt from modernity, and bloodthirsty terrorist Palestinians, enacting violence divorced from anticolonial struggle. Shaheen, *Reel Bad Arabs: How Hollywood Vilifies a People* (2001); updated edition (Northampton: Olive Branch Press, 2009).

36. He explains: "(1) the fabulous Indians, the maharajas and magicians coupled with equally exotic animals such as tigers and elephants; (2) the mystical Indians, a people who were 'deep, contemplative, tranquil, profound'; (3) the benighted Indians, who worshipped animals and many-headed gods, living in a country that was even more heathen than China; and (4) the pathetic Indians, plagued by poverty and crippled by disease—children with fly-encircled eyes, with swollen stomachs, children dying in the streets, rivers choked with bodies." Ramachandra Guha, *India after Gandhi: The History of the World's Largest Democracy* (London: Macmillan, 2007).

37. Wairimũ Ngarũiya Njambi and William E. O'Brien, "Hollywood's Africa: Lessons in Race, Gender, and Stereotype," *Review of Education, Pedagogy, and Cultural Studies* 40 (2018): 361–362.

38. Okaka Opio Dokotum, *Hollywood and Africa: Recycling the "Dark Continent" Myth from 1908–2020* (Makhanda: African Humanities Program), 1.

39. Lúcia Nagib, "Going Global: The Brazilian Scripted Film," in *Trading Culture: Global Traffic and Local Cultures in Film and Television*, ed. Sylvia Harvey (Eastleigh: John Libbey, 2007), 96–98.

40. Dale Hudson, "#OscarMustFall: On Refusing to Give Power to Unjust Definitions of 'Merit,'" *Jump Cut* 61 (2022), https://www.ejumpcut.org/currentissue/DaleHudson/index.html, republished with new postscript by African Film Festival New York (19 September 2022), https://africanfilmny.org/articles/oscarmustfall-on-refusing-to-give-power-to-unjust-definitions-of-merit/.

41. See, for example, Ella Shohat, "The Cinema of Displacement: Gender, Nation, and Diaspora," in *Dreams of a Nation: On Palestinian Cinema*, ed. Hamid Dabashi (London: Verso, 2006), 70–89.

42. See Alia Yunis, "Iraqi Cinema, Then and Now," in *Cinema: Made in the Middle East*, ed. James Neil (Volendam: LM Publishers, in press).

43. Hamid Reza Sadr, *Iranian Cinema: A Political History* (London: I. B. Tauris, 2006), 27.

44. Hamid Naficy, *A Social History of Iranian Cinema, Vol. 1: The Artisanal Era, 1897–1941* (Durham, NC: Duke University Press, 2011), 232.

45. Naficy, *A Social History of Iranian Cinema*, 1:235.

46. The Pahlavi dynasty (1925–1975) was backed by Britain and the United States, most directly in the 1953 coup of democratically elected Mohammad Mosaddegh, who sought to nationalize the Anglo-Iranian Oil Company, which was a private British corporation.

47. Naficy, *Social History of Iranian Cinema*, 1: 233–236.

48. Golbarg Rekabtalaei, *Iranian Cosmopolitanism: A Cinematic History* (New York: Cambridge University Press, 2019), 309.

49. Timothy Mitchell, "The Middle East in the Past and Future of Social Science," in *The Politics of Knowledge: Area Studies and the Disciplines*, ed. David L. Szanton (Berkeley: University of California Press, 2004), 74–118.

50. See chapters in Szanton, *The Politics of Knowledge*, and Michael E. Bonine, Abbas Amanat, and Michael Ezekiel Gasper, eds., *Is There a Middle East?: The Evolution of a Geopolitical Concept* (Stanford, CA: Stanford University Press, 2010).

51. Ella Shohat, "Area Studies, Transnationalism, and the Feminist Production of Knowledge," *Signs* 26, no. 4 (2001): 1269.

52. Michaela Stone Cross, "The Murky History of 'South Asia,'" *Juggernaut*, May 5, 2020, https://www.thejuggernaut.com/south-asia-term.

53. Image Nation Abu Dhabi supported John Madden's Orientalist fantasies *The Best Exotic Marigold Hotel* (UK/USA/UAE, 2011) and *The Second Best Exotic Marigold Hotel* (UK/USA 2015). By contrast, the Doha Film Institute supported Mira Nair's *The Reluctant Fundamentalist* (USA/UK/Qatar, 2013), which deconstructs both racism and internalized racism.

54. Nicholas B. Dirks, "South Asian Studies," in Szanton, *The Politics of Knowledge*, 351.

55. Chandak Sengoopta, "'The Universal Film for All of Us, Everywhere in the World': Satyajit Ray's *Pather Panchali* (1955) and the Shadow of Robert Flaherty," *Historical Journal of Film, Radio and Television* 29, no. 3 (2009): 277–293.

56. Rosie Thomas, "Indian Cinema: Pleasure and Popularity: An Introduction," *Screen* 26, nos. 3–4 (1985): 117.

57. Vebhuti Duggal, Bindu Menon, and Spandan Bhattacharya, eds., *Film Studies: An Introduction* (Delhi: Worldview, 2022).

58. Pearl T. Robinson, "Area Studies in Search of Africa," in *The Politics of Knowledge*, 119, 137.

59. Brian Larkin, "Indian Films and Nigerian Lovers: Media and the Creation of Parallel Modernities," *Africa* 67, no. 3 (1997): 406–440; Shahnaz Khan, "Consumer Citizens and Troubling Desires: Reading Hindi Cinema in Pakistan," *Studies in South Asian Film and Media* 3, no. 2 (2012): 65–85.

60. Sumita S. Chakravarty, *National Identity in Indian Popular Cinema, 1947–1987* (Austin: University of Texas Press, 1993); M. Madhava Prasad, *Ideology of the Hindi Film: A Historical Construction* (New Delhi: Oxford University Press, 2000); Ravi S. Vasudevan, *Making Meaning in Indian Cinema* (New Delhi: Oxford University Press, 2000); Viola Shafik, *Popular Egyptian Cinema: Gender, Class, and Nation* (Cairo: American University of Cairo, 2006); Walter Armbrust, "The Ubiquitous Nonpresence of India: Peripheral Visions from Egyptian Popular Culture," in *Global Bollywood: Travels of Hindi Song and*

Dance, ed. Sangita Gopal and Sujata Moorti (Minneapolis: University of Minnesota Press, 2008), 200–220.

61. Shohat and Stam, *Unthinking Eurocentrism*.

62. Teshome H. Gabriel, *Third Cinema in the Third World: The Aesthetics of Liberation* (Ann Arbor: UMI Research, 1982). Also see Roy Armes, *Third World Film Making and the West* (Berkeley: University of California Press, 1987); Jim Pines and Paul Willemen, eds., *Questions of Third Cinema* (London: British Film Institute, 1990).

63. Robert Stam, *Film Theory: An Introduction* (Malden: Blackwell, 2000), 286.

64. Laura U. Marks, *The Skin of the Film: Intercultural Cinema, Embodiment, and the Senses* (Durham, NC: Duke University Press, 2000); Hamid Naficy, *An Accented Cinema: Exilic and Diasporic Filmmaking* (Princeton, NJ: Princeton University Press, 2001); Mette Hjort and Scott Mackenzie, eds., *The Cinema of Small Nations* (Bloomington: Indiana University Press, 2007); Dina Iordanova, David Martin-Jones, and Belén Vidal, eds., *Cinema at the Periphery* (Detroit, MI: Wayne State University Press, 2010).

65. Elizabeth Ezra and Terry Rowden, eds., *Transnational Cinema: The Film Reader* (New York: Routledge, 2006); Nataša Ďurovičová and Kathleen Newman, eds., *World Cinema, Transnational Perspectives* (New York: Routledge, 2010); Dale Hudson and Patricia R. Zimmermann, *Thinking through Digital Media: Transnational Environments and Locative Places* (New York: Palgrave Macmillan, 2015); Katarzyna Marciniak and Bruce Bennett, eds., *Teaching Transnational Cinema: Politics and Pedagogy* (New York: Routledge, 2016).

66. "Three Film Professionals to Receive GFF Honours," *Emirates 27/7*, March 29, 2009, https://www.emirates247.com/eb247/companies-markets/media/three-film-professionals-to-receive-gff-honours-2009-03-29-1.95461.

67. Anne Ciecko, "What the Sea Brings: Cinema at the Shoreline in Bahrain's First Feature Production and Film Culture," *Continuum: Journal of Media and Cultural Studies* 27, no. 5 (2013): 705.

68. Todd Reisz, "Landscapes of Production: Filming Dubai and the Trucial States," *Journal of Urban History* 44, no. 2 (2018): 301.

69. Mona Damluji, "The Oil City in Focus: The Cinematic Spaces of Abadan in the Anglo-Iranian Oil Company's *Persian Story*," *Comparative Studies of South Asia, Africa and the Middle East* 33, no.1 (2013): 82.

70. Robert Vitalis, *America's Kingdom: Mythmaking on the Saudi Oil Frontier* (London: Verso, 2009), 60.

71. Vitalis, *America's Kingdom*, 153.

72. Vitalis, *America's Kingdom*, 159.

73. Abdulrahman Alghanem, "Pushing the Boundaries: The Development of Film Industries in the Gulf Countries from 2004 to 2017" (PhD diss., University of St. Andrews, 2021).

74. Alghanem, "Pushing the Boundaries," 86.

75. Alghanem, "Pushing the Boundaries," 168–174.

76. *City of Life* explores Dubai through neoliberalism's segmented spaces, where Emiratis from different social and economic classes occasionally interact with Arab and Western expatriates but none of these groups interact with Indian expatriates of any social or economic class to any significant degree. Despite the large number of professionals from the Philippines, Filipinas appear only as arm-candy for an Indian mujra (dance bar) owner and Filipinos only through the character of Old Filipino who collects corrugated

cardboard. Dale Hudson, "Toward a Cinema of Contact Zones: Intersecting Globalizations, Dubai, and *City of Life*," *Afterimage* 47, no. 4 (2020): 26–49.

77. Klaus Schoenbach, Robb Wood, and Mariam Saeed, *Media Industries in the Middle East, 2016* (Doha: Northwestern University in Qatar, 2016), https://www.qatar.northwestern.edu/docs/publications/research/2016-middle-east-media-industries-report.pdf.

78. Exceptions are the media use studies conducted by Northwestern University in Qatar: Everette E. Dennis, Robb Wood, and Justin D. Martin, *Entertainment Media Use in the Middle East a Six-Nation Survey* (Doha: Northwestern University in Qatar, 2014), http://www.mideastmedia.org/survey/2014/files/2014_NUQ_Media_Use_Full_Report.pdf; Schoenbach et al., *Media Industries in the Middle East, 2016*. For an analysis of assumptions in these studies, see Dale Hudson, "UAE Filmmaking beyond Arabization, Cosmopolitanism, and Exceptionalism," in "La culture pop dans la péninsule Arabique," ed. Frédéric Lagrange and Clio Chaveneau, special issue, *Arabian Humanities* 14 (2020), 1–27.

79. Jeffrey Ruoff, "Ten Nights in Tunisia: Les Journées Cinématographiques de Carthage," *Film International* 6, no. 4 (2008): 46; Kay Dickinson, *Arab Cinema Travels: Transnational Syria, Palestine, Dubai and Beyond* (London: British Film Institute, 2016), 119–162.

80. Saudis nonetheless continued to go to cinemas with an estimated 230,000 engaging in "film tourism" in Dubai between 1980 and 2018 as reported by Alex Ritman, "Escape to the Movies: How Saudi Cinema Ban Benefits UAE Tourism," *The National*, March 22, 2012, http://www.thenational.ae/arts-culture/film/escape-to-the-movies-how-saudi-cinema-ban-benefits-uae-tourism#full.

81. Cinemas are owned and managed by foreign companies, including AMC Entertainment of the United States, Cinepolis of México, and VOX Cinemas of the UAE. Next Generation and Muvi Cinemas are the only Saudi companies licensed to open cinemas.

82. Hollywood producers have allegedly been at work on a biopic about UAE founder Sheikh Zayed, under the direction of Shekhar Kapur. Khaoula Ghanem, "There's a Sheikh Zayed Hollywood Biopic in the Works," *Vogue Arabia*, June 3, 2018, https://en.vogue.me/culture/theres-a-sheikh-zayed-hollywood-biopic-in-the-works/.

83. On nostalgia or heritage cinema see *Film/Literature/Heritage a Sight and Sound Reader*, ed. Ginette Vincendeau (London: British Film Institute, 2001).

84. Janice Rodrigues, "Emirati Film *Al Kameen* Breaks Records in the UAE," *The National*, December 4, 2021, https://www.thenationalnews.com/arts-culture/film/2021/12/04/emirati-film-al-kameen-breaks-records-in-the-uae/.

85. The museum presents a seven-thousand-year history that culminates with twentieth-century Qatar as "the world's biggest video installation." The site-specific films are the work of international filmmakers and video artists, including Doug Aitken, Jananne Al-Ani, Christophe Cheysson, Mira Nair, Jacques Perrin, John Sanborn Abderrahmane Sissako, and Peter Webber. None are Qatari.

86. Bryant Frazer, "National Museum of Qatar: Behind the Scenes," *Studio Daily*, May 8, 2019, https://www.studiodaily.com/2019/05/national-museum-qatar-behind-scenes/.

87. Dale Hudson, "Songs from India and Zanzibar: Documenting the Gulf in Migration," *Studies in South Asian Film and Media* 10, no. 2 (2019): 91–112.

88. Ada Petiwala, "A 'New India' for the Arab World: Brands Bollywood and Modi in the U.A.E.," *Middle East Journal of Culture and Communication* 16 (2023): 1–20.

89. Petiwala, "A 'New India' for the Arab World," 6, 13.

90. Kate Hudson's appearance, however, did revive a debate on human rights. International Campaign for Freedom in the United Arab Emirates, "Kate Hudson's Dubai Tourism Video Met with Human Rights Backlash," ICFUAE, January 16, 2020, https://icfuae.org.uk/news/kate-hudsons-dubai-tourism-video-met-human-rights-backlash. Perhaps due to associations with her Goop products, Paltrow's appearance was unremarkable.

91. The most celebrated writer of the Kuwait musalsalat was Tareq Othman, a Palestinian, and the people behind the camera still remain primarily from the Levant, particularly Lebanon and Syria, where they come with training not available in the Gulf. Arabic-language series also compete with locally popular Korean and Turkish series.

92. All of the EFC films are stored at the UAE National Film Library and Archive at Zayed University in Abu Dhabi, but the collection is in its infancy and no one has worked on it in almost ten years. Moreover, the university cannot actually archive the films. Initiated before this aspirational archive, the NYUAD Library's special collections also contain many of the EFC films, as well as Films from The Gulf, sponsored by the Association of Gulf and Arabian Peninsula Studies (AGAPS) at the MESA (Middle East Studies Association) Film Festival, and individual Gulf filmmakers.

93. Mohammed Omar A Alobthani, "Branding Global Image: Filmmaking and Complicating National Identity in the UAE" (PhD diss., University of Birmingham, 2021).

94. Hudson, "Toward a Cinema of Contact Zones."

95. Ada Petiwala, "Of Echoes and Utterances: A Brief Sketch of Arabic Hauntings in Hindi Cinema and Song," *International Journal of Middle East Studies* (2023), 1–6.

96. See Sebastian Thejus Cherian's chapter in this volume.

97. Ratheesh Radhakrishnan, "The Gulf in the Imagination: Migration, Malayalam Cinema and Regional Identity," *Contributions to Indian Sociology* 43, no. 2 (2009): 225.

98. Radhakrishnan, "The Gulf in the Imagination," 234, 239.

99. Bindu Menon and T. T. Sreekumar, "'One More Dirham': Migration, Emotional Politics and Religion in the Home Films of Kerala," *Migration, Mobility, & Displacement* 2, no. 2 (2016): 4–23; Sudarshan Purohit, "Gulfiwood Culture and Society in South Asian Arabia," *Bidoun*, 2012, https://bidoun.org/articles/gulfiwood.

100. Menon and Sreekumar, "'One More Dirham'"; Purohit, "Gulfiwood"; Mohamed Shafeeq Karinkurayil, "'It Was Not a Planned Move': Salam Kodiyathur on Home Cinema," *MCH Film Club Journal* 1, no. 3 (2018), http://mcphfilmclub.org/not-planned-move-salam-kodiyathur-home-cinema/.

101. Darshana Sreedhar Mini, "The Rise of Soft Porn in Malayalam Cinema and the Precarious Stardom of Shakeela," *Feminist Media Histories* 5, no. 2 (2019): 58, 56.

102. Mini, "The Rise of Soft Porn," 70.

103. Melanie Goodfellow, "Ali F. Mostafa Reveals Next Film Will Be A Standalone Sequel To 2009 Breakout, Dubai-Set Debut 'City Of Life,'" *Deadline*, December 8, 2022, https://deadline.com/2022/12/ali-f-mostafa-new-film-sequel-city-of-life-1235191564/.

104. Kiki Kennedy-Day, "Cinema in Lebanon, Syria, Iraq, and Kuwait," in *Companion Encyclopedia of Middle Eastern and North African Film*, ed. Oliver Leaman (New York: Routledge, 2001), 404.

105. Najat Alsheridah, "Woman and Dance in Kuwaiti Cinema" (PhD diss., University of East London, 2019), 63–77.

106. Alsheridah, "Woman and Dance in Kuwaiti Cinema," 76.

107. See Viola Shafik, "Cultural Identity and Genre," in *Arab Cinema: History and Cultural Identity* (1999), updated with a new postscript (Cairo: American University of Cairo Press, 2016), 121–207, for an overview of the various self-critical approaches by Arab filmmakers (or "auteurs," as she calls them), including New Egyptian Realism (*al-waq'iya al-djadida*), Algerian New Cinema (*sinima djidad*), Young Cinema in Egypt (*sinima al'shabab*), and Alternative Cinema in Syria (*al-sinima al-badila*). Also see *Caméra arabe / Camera Arab: The Young Arab Cinema* (Tunisia, 1987; dir. Férid Boughedir), which include interviews by many of the Arab filmmakers who debated the various approaches to a new Arab filmmaking at JCC.

108. Potter, "Introduction," 8.

109. Much like subsequent changes in law that will allow Saudi women to drive in particular circumstances in 2018, the film was superficially celebrated without consideration for its subtle complexities. For examples of such reviews, see Isabel Stevens, "Kid on a Bike" (review of *Wadjda*), *Sight and Sound* 23, no. 8 (August 2013): 28–31.

110. Lila Abu-Lughod, "Do Muslim Women Need Saving? Anthropological Reflections on Cultural Relativism and Its Others," *American Anthropologist* 104, no. 3 (2002): 783–790; Charles Hirschkind and Saba Mahmood, "Feminism, the Taliban, and the Politics of Counter-Insurgency," *Anthropological Quarterly* 75, no. 2 (2002): 107–122.

111. Tariq Al Haydar, "Haifaa Al Mansour's *Wadjda*: Revolutionary Art or Pro-State Propaganda?," *Jadaliyya*, January 13, 2014, http://www.jadaliyya.com/pages/index/15996/haifaa-al-mansours-wadjda_revolutionary-art-or-pro.

112. The film examines the emotional effects of Egyptian president Gamal Abdel Nasser's resignation after the humiliating defeat of Arab states by Israel in 1967, four years before Bahrain became a state.

113. Fuccaro, *Histories of City and State in the Persian Gulf*.

114. Sabry, *Cultural Encounters in the Arab World*.

115. Hamid Naficy, *A Social History of Iranian Cinema, Volume 4: The Globalizing Era, 1984–2010* (Durham, NC: Duke University Press, 2011), 34–38.

116. Claire Cooley, "Bachchan Superman: Hindi Cinema in Egypt, 1985–1991," *Jump Cut* 59 (2019), https://www.ejumpcut.org/archive/jc59.2019/Cooley-Bachchan/.

117. See Rosie Thomas, "Thieves of the Orient: The Arabian Nights in Early Indian Cinema," in *Bombay before Bollywood: Film City Fantasies* (Albany: State University of New York Press, 2013), 31–65; Ifdal Elsaket, "Jungle Films in Egypt: Race, Anti-Blackness, and Empire," *Arab Studies Journal* 25, no. 2 (2017): 8–33.

118. Shafik, *Arab Cinema*, 214–215. Comparable shifts appear in television dramas with the advent of satellite television and Gulf financing of series for pan-Arab channels in the 1990s. Christa Salamandra, "Arab Television Drama Production in the Satellite Era," in *Soap Operas and Telenovelas in the Digital Age: Global Industries and New Audiences*, ed. Diana Isabel Arredondo Ríos and Mari Castañeda (New York: Peter Lang, 2011), 279.

119. Shafik, *Arab Cinema*, 66–68, 72–73, 85. Subjected to slavery due to their black skin, Nubians were sometimes called "barbari," a colloquial expression for an "incomprehensible black coming from somewhere south of Aswan" (67).

120. Self-censorship is discussed in Alia Yunis and Sasha Ritter's chapter in this volume.

121. One exception is *Shayer al Million* (Million's Poet) in which young poets compete with each other in what, since 2009, has been the highest-rated television show in the Gulf, an indication of the desire of Gulf Arabs to construct "heritage."

122. Sreya Mitra, "Beyond the Nation and the Diaspora: Examining Bollywood's Transnational Appeal in the United Arab Emirates," *Middle East Journal of Culture and Communication* 14, nos. 1–2 (2021): 135–157.

123. Darshana Sreedhar Mini, "Satellites of Belonging: Televisual Infrastructures and the Gulf-Malayali," *Middle East Journal of Culture and Communication* 14, nos. 1–2 (2021): 81–111.

124. On Saudi videos, see Sean Foley's chapter in this volume. On expatriate media, see Nele Lenze, "Representations of Non-Resident Indians from the Gulf in Online Comedy Videos," *Middle East Journal of Culture and Communication* 14, nos. 1–2 (2021): 158–176; Bindu Menon, "Migrant Images: Lateral Agency and Affective Citizenship in Dubai," *Middle East Journal of Culture and Communication* 14, nos. 1–2 (2021): 225–249.

125. For data on media usage, see Northwestern Qatar's biannual report *Media Use in the Middle East*.

126. On mediated performance, see Elizabeth Derderian's chapter in this volume. On tribal use of social media, see Hassan Hussain, "Cyber Tribes: Social Media and the Representation and Revitalization of Arab Tribal Identities in the Internet Age," *Middle East Journal of Culture and Communication* 14, nos. 1–2 (2021): 112–134.

127. AJE, "Kuwaiti Makeup Artist Slammed for Posting Blackface Photo," *Al Jazeera English*, January 2, 2020, https://www.aljazeera.com/news/2020/01/kuwaiti-makeup-artist-slammed-posting-blackface-photo-200102170213776.html; Mustafa Marie, "Kuwaiti Actress Hayat al-Fahd Sparks Controversy over COVID-19 Crisis," *Egypt Today*, April 2, 2020, https://www.egypttoday.com/Article/4/83281/Kuwaiti-actress-Hayat-al-Fahd-sparks-controversy-over-COVID-19.

128. The murder of George Floyd by US police in 2020 globalized the Black Lives Matter (BLM) movement, so that people everywhere are more aware of the biases and prejudices based on ethnoracial categories that have for so long gone unaddressed in terms of racism.

129. For example, *Dhil al Bahr / Sea Shadow* (UAE, 2011; dir. Nawaf Al Janahi), *Mazraat Yado 2 / Grandmother's Farm, Part 2* (UAE, 2015; dir. Ahmed Zain), *Ḥajwala / Hajwala: The Missing Engine* (UAE, 2016; dir. Ali Bin Matar and Ibrahim Bin Mohammad), *Hajwala 2: The Mysterious Mission* (UAE, 2018; dir. Ibrahim Bin Mohamed and Hasan Aljaberi), *Shaghghalatua Arjantiniyya / Our Argentinian Maid* (UAE, 2018; dir. Hamed Saleh), *Ali wa Alia / Ali and Alia* (UAE, 2019; dir. Hussein Alansari), *Al-'amm Naji i l-Iarat / Uncle Naji in UAE* (UAE, 2019; dir. Ahmed Zain), and most egregiously *Rashed & Rajab* (UAE, 2019; dir. Mohammed Saeed Harib). An exception is *Khallik Shanab / Sport a Moustache* (UAE, 2019; dir. Hani Al Shaibani). See Hudson, "UAE Filmmaking beyond Arabization, Cosmopolitanism, and Exceptionalism."

130. In some ways, *Alboom* recalls Siddiq's *Bas ya Bahar*, as well as other Gulf films, like the Emirati *Jumaa wa al-Bahr / Jumaa and the Sea* (UAE, 2007; dir. Hani Al Shaibani). They focus on everyday hardships rather than the "hot topics" of civil wars, religious fundamentalism, gendered oppression, and terrorism that are "showcased" at foreign festivals according to Western expectation of "typical concerns" for Arabs in the Middle East.

1

AREA STUDIES AND ITS AFTERLIVES
Perspectives from the Gulf

NELIDA FUCCARO

Commenting on the afterlife of area studies, H. D. Harootunian and Masao Miyoshi eloquently refer to a post–area studies era and to revisionist moments of strategy and reflection that seek to deconstruct and reconstruct knowledge by pushing it further away from the historical Euro-American axis:

> The afterlife [of area studies] thus refers to the moment that has decentered the truths, practices, and even institutions that belonged to a time that could still believe in the identity of some conception of humanity and universality with a Eurocentric endowment and to the acknowledgment that its "provinciality" must now be succeeded by what Said called "a contrapuntal orientation in history."[1]

Born as an enterprise in the translation of regions and cultures outside Europe and North America, area studies is often still considered a byword for the arbitrary and political nature of knowledge production and of the epistemological and geographical borders that have underpinned and defined this knowledge. As a process of place learning actualized through fieldwork, area studies has also been equated to isomorphic practices of colonial extraction in which local knowledge is collected and then processed through the lens of Euro-American universalism.[2]

Given the above, it is no surprise that for some time academics and public intellectuals from different persuasions and backgrounds engaged with Asia, Africa, and the Middle East have been asking several key questions: Are we entering (or should we enter) the post–area studies era (i.e., its afterlife)? And is the notion of critical area studies marking this transition? Does this mean that in questioning area studies, we ultimately want to abandon them? Crucially, what are the implications for the Gulf region, whose status on the area studies map has long been uncertain? And by extension, what are the implications for the Arab World and Middle East, which the Gulf has been until recently identified and closely associated with?

BOUNDING AND UNBOUNDING REGIONS

At this early point in the troubled twenty-first century, many of us find area studies intellectually and ethically problematic. The reasons for this are both synchronic and diachronic. On the one hand, established geographical, political, and cultural boundaries are increasingly prone to dissolving under our eyes, undermining traditional regions as units of scholarly investigation. This widespread phenomenon of deterritorialization seems to have also affected the disciplines, whose epistemic boundaries have been increasingly transgressed. On the other hand, the conundrum posed by area studies is a question of historical legacy, closely linked to the construction of a world order neatly arranged in regions (and ultimately defined by power relations) that underpinned the development of area studies in Anglo-Saxon academia after the Second World War. To a large extent, the collusion between academia, governments, and corporations shaped area studies as we know it today. The involvement of the CIA in sponsoring research in the second half of the twentieth century is a case in point; so is the fact that after the 1950s, oil-bearing regions like Saudi Arabia became a target of US government funding. The identification of area studies with the Cold War is reinforced by the fact that it entered a period of crisis (at least in the United States) in the 1990s after the fall of the Soviet Union. Yet, as Timothy Mitchell warns us, it was not only the Cold War that propagated area studies but also the new political project attached to the social sciences that reflected a drive to spread a new globalized American modernity.[3]

In the 1970s, a new wave of critical scholarship triggered by the consolidation of dependency theory (which supplanted modernization theory) and the publication of Edward Said's *Orientalism* had far-reaching implications for area studies. By pushing the terms of the scholarly debate closer to historical peripheries, these two new paradigms impacted area studies in general and scholarship on the Middle East and South Asia in particular. Said's *Orientalism* sent shockwaves through the field of Middle Eastern Studies, which was still closely identified with Orientalism, without radically transforming it. By contrast, Said's work (alongside that of the anthropologist Bernard Cohn) partially reshaped South Asian Studies as a field of postcolonial theory, driven by disciplines such as literature, anthropology, history, and cultural studies.[4] Some have argued that postcolonial studies are area studies by other means. Yet postcolonial studies' confinement to particular disciplinary fields is perhaps evidence of its inability to radically transform the production of knowledge on the postcolony as a whole.[5]

Regardless of its history of often ambivalent and uneven relationships, the discipline of area studies has created politically driven epistemic borderlines through a process of "scaling of localities, ethnicities, languages, religions and cultures."[6] Recently, the idea of scaling has served as an analytical platform to debunk the spatially constructed framework of fixed boundaries of nation-states on the one hand and unbounded scenarios of globalization on the other. Drawing attention to states' practices of "verticality" and "encompassment," James Ferguson and Akhil Gupta, for instance, have critiqued the notion of national space as contained and as a given, and highlighted instead how states generate the local, the regional, and the global as central features of their reproductive systems.[7] A number of *trans* paradigms have also successfully challenged traditional and state-bound horizons of area studies, core / periphery binaries, and fixed geographies more generally. The *trans* paradigms in question are rooted in the so-called mobility turn, a busy and heterogenous area of critical engagement that is closely associated with Arjun Appadurai's seminal notion of global cultural flows.[8] These paradigms are often interdisciplinary and multidisciplinary, from transnationalism and translocality to transculturalism and transindividuality, the latter pair being particularly relevant to media and new media studies with their focus on the relationship between the individual, technology, and society.[9] In the name of new connectivities, these approaches have forced us academics to rethink strategies of "doing" area studies to secure its afterlife. And this fluidity has had transformative effects on the Gulf and Arabian Peninsula as regions sandwiched between established regional blocs.

Research on media has often accepted the geographical and epistemic boundaries of area studies at face value, particularly in the case of conventional media such as cinema and television. Yet at both the regional and national levels, literature on the Gulf is overall still underdeveloped. It tends to undervalue (and often exclude) important historical and contemporary visual media such as oil company documentaries, photographs, YouTube web series, and Instagram feeds. It also ignores nonprofessional media, such as blogs produced by marginalized expatriate communities. Further, while there is some work on media zones and the business side of television, there is little analysis of media content.[10] The media landscape of Asia is undoubtedly much richer and more inclusive than that of the Gulf. In movies produced in Asia, Gulf cities feature prominently as places of migration and livelihood for large numbers of Indian, Pakistani, and Filipino workers. Media scholarship on Asia is also developing new platforms of critical thinking, drawing on the idea of mediated experience to refute the geographical materiality of area studies, as well as normative attitudes toward the West and the nation form. With its representational practices of local content and transnational readability, cinema is an excellent testing ground to revisit spatial and temporal hierarchies, as well as binaries such as tradition versus modernity, East versus West, and development versus underdevelopment. In short, cinema presents complex chronotopes that cut across material, political, and epistemic boundaries, challenging both conventional geographies and official histories.[11]

GULF STUDIES AND ITS GENEALOGIES

Today, a considerable number of policymaking, teaching, and research outfits across the globe bear the name of "Gulf Studies." Of late, this field seems to have also reached a degree of self-reflection. Take for instance the programmatic agenda of the Gulf conference held at Exeter University in 2018, one of the first academic institutions to engage with the region back in the early 1980s. The call for papers summarized the conference objectives as aiming "to plot new trajectories in Gulf Studies" to "explore the identity and viability of this very notion."[12] The agenda also shows an appreciation of the ethics and responsibility of knowledge production and an acute awareness of thorny issues of fieldwork, access, and censorship.

In the past, some area studies specialists, particularly those working on the Middle East and the Arab World, have contested the validity of Gulf Studies as an independent area of teaching and research and even questioned its right to exist. The history of the field is jagged and relatively recent. Yet like area studies, it is unmistakably wedded to neocolonial, postcolonial, and regional power politics, all of which have contributed to constitute the Gulf as a region. The arrival of US oil companies after 1945 marked the entry of US imperialism and the beginning of the progressive consolidation of US economic, political, and cultural hegemony in the Gulf. But the advent of petroleum capitalism also became enmeshed with the broader globalized political / academic project linked to the American social sciences discussed by Timothy Mitchell. The oil industry in general, and Aramco in particular, entered a partnership with US academics who started to collect and systematize knowledge on local economy, societies, and culture. Arguably, in the 1950s and in the 1960s, this partnership kick-started the first wave of studies on modern and contemporary Saudi Arabia.[13]

On the other side of the Atlantic, in Great Britain, the leftist and anti-colonial discourse of the 1970s catapulted the study of the Gulf and Arabian Peninsula beyond classical archaeology and Orientalist scholarship. This was not so much part of the revisionist wave that swept area studies in the 1970s as a result of the consolidation of the dependency paradigm and the publication of Said's *Orientalism* but of political developments on the ground—namely anti-colonial and anti-reactionary uprisings in Aden and Bahrain and the Dhofar liberation movement in Oman. These events spearheaded the establishment of the Gulf Committee in London in 1975 by a handful of academics and public intellectuals that included prominent scholars such as Fred Halliday. The Gulf Committee mirrored the recently established Middle East Research and Information Project (MERIP) in the United States as a left-wing collective that through research and publications sought a new and politically engaged relationship with the region and its peoples. Although the Gulf Committee was short-lived, scholars like Halliday continued their academic and political mission for some years, inspired as they were by Marxist and internationalist ideologies.[14]

Regional politics and their entanglements with British and European academia were also important factors that shaped Gulf Studies in the image of the Arab World. By the early 1990s, the Gulf's Arab credentials had become well established, with a concomitant separation of the region from Iran and South Asia, the latter an important imperial foreland for centuries. Inside the region, connections to the Arab World gained political momentum as a result of the anti-colonial (mostly anti-British) radical Arabism popularized by the Egyptian president Jamal ʿAbd al-Nasir (Nasser) in the 1950s and continued into the 1960s and 1970s under the shadow of Baʾathist propaganda coming from Iraq. In the 1980s, as the Iran-Iraq War raged, the newly established Gulf Cooperation Council took matters into its own hands as the regional organization that supported postindependence state building. Arguably, it was the creation of Arab states in conjunction with oil wealth that deepened the obfuscation of the hybrid and cosmopolitan past of the Gulf coast and Oman that had been initiated in the 1950s under the aegis of al-Nasir's Arabism.[15]

The first known efforts to shape and showcase an academic agenda driven by Arabism in both the humanities and social sciences came from Baʾathist Iraq on the eve of the outbreak of the war with Iran. In 1979, a conference organized by the Center of Arab Gulf Studies of the University of Basra delineated the contours of the Gulf's modern and contemporary Arab civilization that fit with the regional ambitions of the Baʿath leadership. The participation of British and European academics was most notable, offering an early example of cooperation (many would say collusion) between European academia and the Iraqi regime at a time when it was still enjoying the support of Western governments. Under the title of "Man and Society in the Arab Gulf" (*Al-Insan wa al-Mujtamaʿ fi al-Khalij al-ʿArabi*) the event offered a granular yet reified portrayal of the individual inhabiting the region as a *Homo Arabicus*. As Arab identity was placed at the center of Gulf societies, conference delegates scrutinized its past, present, and future from the perspective of identity politics, mobility, economic development, urbanization, and heritage, among other factors.[16] Despite the impressive thematic range and heterogenous participation in the conference, the political aims of the organizers were clear. As explained in the introduction to the conference proceedings:

> At present the Arab individual and Arab society as a whole is exposed to the results of the awful plot that aims at destroying the personality of the Arab man and the Arab nation and to transform our Arab peoples into small weak nations that can be blackmailed by the Zionists and the Imperialists. Therefore, this meeting should not ignore this issue but raise to the occasion and address it.[17]

Propped up by the Ba'ath regime, the profile of the *Homo Arabicus* carried with it a set of "civilizational" assumptions that are reminiscent of a classical Orientalist / Islamic Studies / Indological tradition that is closely connected to the historical formation of the Middle East and South Asian Studies. Much like the *Homo Islamicus* discussed by Zachary Lockman, the *Homo Arabicus* emerging from the Basra conference suggested the construction of an organic and totalizing knowledge that did not leave enough room for geographical specificities or marginalities.[18]

The center that hosted the conference (established in 1974 in Basra's modern al-Ashar district) left a powerful imprint on the nascent Gulf Studies discipline, which was amplified by the published journal *al-Khalij al-'Arabi* (The Arab gulf).[19] In the West, Gulf Studies started to gain traction in the 1980s as a term for scholarship on the region primarily thanks to the activities of the Centre for Arab Gulf Studies based at the University of Exeter in the United Kingdom. Established in 1978 by former Foreign Office officials who had served in different capacities in the Gulf region and in the Middle East, the center maintained close connections with its homonymous center in Basra at least until the early 1980s and trained generations of academics specializing in the region.[20] Tim Niblock, one of the center's first academic staff members, who became a prolific writer on the politics of Saudi Arabia and the Gulf, wrote the following in 1979:

> The rationale for taking the Arab Gulf as an area for separate study is that this area is evidently of crucial international importance; that the social, economic and political problems facing the peoples of the area are

complex—and distinct from the problems facing peoples in most other Middle Eastern states; and that a disturbingly small amount of research effort is currently being directed towards the area. Even in centres devoted to Middle Eastern studies, the Arab Gulf area seems to have attracted only limited attention.[21]

Since 1979, the center (now part of the Institute of Arab and Islamic Studies) has organized Gulf conferences that over the years have not only showcased research and regional expertise but also helped to define research agendas. Until the late 1990s, conferences tended to focus on national units or—if conceived at the regional scale—to be inspired by international relations, dependency, or developmental approaches. The research presented at the Exeter Gulf conferences, which was also published in influential edited volumes, was pioneering—based on fieldwork and rich data analysis. Yet it can be taken as representative of a general field of study that until the late 1990s remained largely uncritical and in some cases served to validate empirically and policy-driven objectives. A case in point is the widespread popularity enjoyed by the rentier state theory, first introduced by the Iranian economist Hossein Mahdavy in 1970 and then developed by Hazem Beblawi in the Arab context. The brainchild of modernization and dependency paradigms, this theory has served to essentialize key analytical categories such as state, society, and the economy, besides replicating a statist-driven and structurally self-determined approach to the region.[22] Ironically, and in spite of the Arabist streak of earlier Gulf Studies, the abundant literature on the rentier state, modernization, and development has contributed to fuel the myth of Gulf exceptionalism by placing emphasis on the unique oil and state-formation experience of Gulf countries, often in relation to the rest of the Middle East.

NEW GEOGRAPHIES OF THE AFTERLIFE

In the last twenty years or so, literature on the Gulf has displayed a particularly expansive geographical imagination. In many respects, this literature has contributed to shape the afterlife of Middle Eastern area studies by drawing on the *trans* approaches that have galvanized research on world regions. The Gulf's location along the fault lines of established area studies regions and the rising awareness of the possibilities offered by the methodological and epistemological openness of the field have undoubtedly contributed to de- and recentering geographies. The wave of historical and anthropological research on Gulf transnational flows initiated by a project sponsored by the British Economic and Social Research Council (ESRC) between 2000 and 2003 is a case in point. This project brought together a new generation of academics whose work started to challenge the isolationist nature of earlier scholarship on the region in the modern and contemporary periods, which had been dominated by topics such as tribe, state, British imperialism, and security studies.[23]

Since then, Gulf literature has been increasingly relational and comparative and has brought to the fore geographical, epistemological, and theoretical connections with a multitude of regions beyond the Arab World and Middle East, South Asia, and Africa to name the most evident. In this respect, prolific strands of research such as those focusing on diaspora communities and migratory waves to the Gulf both before and after the 1970s have added considerably to the portfolio of both Asian and African studies, having had a particularly far-reaching and long-lasting impact on the study of South Asia and the Indian Ocean Worlds.[24] Scholarship on port cities and on non-Arab Indigenous communities has overcome the theoretical historical barrier between the Arab Gulf and Iran, long considered one of the enduring bastions of academic conservatism.[25] This type of scholarship has also benefited immensely from the seaborne upheaval brought to the Gulf by the new thalassology of Indian Ocean studies, which has turned the scholarly gaze away from the land masses and the fixity of national boundaries.[26]

It can be argued that just the sheer volume of research published on the Gulf in the last ten years or so has helped to challenge regional centrisms by shifting the focus of scholarly attention toward a geographical area that, until recently, humanists, cultural studies scholars, and many social scientists considered a periphery. The implications for the Arab and Middle East area studies concentration are quite intriguing. In an important respect—albeit in a different economy of scale—the impact of Gulf Studies on its parent field resonates with the earlier evolution of area studies in the United States as a platform for the decentralization of the social sciences. The recent surge in scholarship on the Gulf has undoubtedly helped to bring diverse datasets, theoretical paradigms, and concepts to bear on the study of the modern and contemporary Arab World and the Middle East. In this respect, it has helped to democratize and de-parochialize Arab and Middle Eastern studies by helping to make the field more flexible, polycentric, farsighted, theoretically engaged, and comparative.

Cities are an example of this democratization, as the study of cities in the Gulf region has helped shape depictions of Middle Eastern, Arab, and global urbanism. In some cases, this has also signposted the importance of studying smaller cities in areas that do not display the classical types of Arab / Islamic cities, helping debunk an enduring Orientalist urban myth. The study of Gulf urbanism before and after oil, with its corollary of mobility, transnationalism, and cultural hybridity, has provided primary examples of Richard Sennett's hinge city; this helps us to concentrate on relational aspects of city formation and living and of cities as crossroads rather than central places.[27] In recent years, urban environments have also functioned as hinges interlocking the Gulf and South Asia as a result of their prominent role in cinematic narrations of migration and diasporic communities. Gulf cities feature more often in Indian and Pakistani filmography than in movies produced elsewhere, as exemplified by the Malayalam film scene.[28] By reading urban space not merely as a backdrop but as the visual and experiential site of geographically connected stories and representations of self and other, cinema studies has contributed substantially to the *trans* agenda of Gulf scholarship, effectively integrating Gulf cities into South Asian human and cultural landscapes on the one hand and diasporic communities into the multicultural sociopolitical orders of the Gulf's urban worlds on the other.

This partnership between the Gulf city, the South Asian diaspora, and cinema studies is just an example of the regenerative power of the new geographies created by the afterlife of Gulf Studies. The very existence of these geographies (and the enduring territorial and epistemological logic that underpins them), however, does not necessarily mean that area studies has transitioned into a completely new conceptual space. It is difficult to imagine the study of the Gulf without the sense of *placeness* that area studies has afforded to several generations of scholars in both the humanities and social sciences. Hence, the emancipation of the region from its precarious position in the hierarchy of the geopolitics of knowledge production inevitably entails challenging this production from within through a critical reformulation and strategic redeployment of area studies tools and methodologies of place learning. This means that in the case of the Gulf, questioning area studies (at least for the moment) does not necessarily mean abandonment of the field; it means continuing to offer correctives to portrayals of the region's past isolationism, exceptionalism, and its essentialist portrayals as the exclusive appendix of the Arab World. These are key tropes that, more than others, have been the signifiers of the asymmetrical power balances that have defined the study of the region and its peoples.

> NELIDA FUCCARO is Professor of Middle Eastern history at New York University Abu Dhabi specializing in the Persian Gulf and Arabian Peninsula. She is author of *Histories of City and State in the Persian Gulf: Manama since 1800* and of *The Other Kurds: Yazidis in Colonial Iraq*. She is editor of *Violence and the City in the Modern Middle East* and (with Ulrike Freitag, Claudia Ghrawi, and Nora Lafi) of *Urban Violence in the Middle East: Changing Cityscapes in the Transition from Empire to Nation State*.

NOTES

1. H. D. Harootunian and Masao Miyoshi, "Introduction: The 'Afterlife' of Area Studies," in *Learning Places: The Afterlives of Area Studies*, ed. Masao Miyoshi and H. D. Harootunian (Durham, NC: Duke University Press, 2002), 14.

2. Harootunian and Myoshi, "Introduction," 7.

3. See Timothy Mitchell, "Middle East," 74–118, particularly 76, 89–92, and 93–94. For an earlier critique of US funding of the study of the Arabian Peninsula see Gwenn Okruklik, "From Imagined Scholarship to Gendered Discourse: Bringing the Peninsula in from the Periphery," *Middle East Report* 204 (July–September 1997): 36–37.

4. Mitchell, "Middle East," 92–98; Dirks, "South Asian Studies," 362–375.

5. Harry D. Harootunian, "Postcoloniality's Unconscious/Area Studies' Desire," in Miyoshi and Harootunian, *Learning Places*, 151–152.

6. Claudia Derichs, "Shifting Epistemologies in Area Studies: From Space to Scale," *Middle East Topics and Arguments* 4 (2015): 30.

7. James Ferguson and Akhil Gupta, "Spatializing States: Toward an Ethnography of Neo-Liberal Governmentality," *American Ethnologist* 29, no. 4 (2002): 981–1002.

8. Arjun Appadurai, *Modernity at Large: Cultural Dimensions of Globalization* (Minneapolis: University of Minnesota Press, 1995).

9. Harootunian and Miyoshi, "Introduction," 14; Adrian Smith, "Trans-Locals, Critical Area Studies and Geography's Others, or Why 'Development' Should Not Be Geography's Organizing Framework: A Response to Potter," *Area* 34, no. 2 (June 2002): 210–213; Katja Mielke and Anna-Katharina Hornidge, "Introduction: Knowledge Production, Area Studies and the Mobility Turn," in *Area Studies at the Crossroads*, ed. Katja Mielke and Anna-Katharina Hornidge (London: Palgrave Macmillan, 2017), 3–15; Thomas Lamarre, "Platformativity: Media Studies, Area Studies," *Asiascape: Digital Asia* 4 (2017): 285–305; Ines Braune and Achim Rohde, "Critical Area Studies," *Middle East Topics and Arguments* 4 (2015): 5–11.

10. See the editor's introduction in this volume.

11. Arnika Fuhrmann, "This Area Is [NOT] under Quarantine: Rethinking Southeast /Asia through Studies of the Cinema," in Mielke and Hornidge, *Area Studies at the Crossroads*, 251–257.

12. 30th Exeter Gulf Conference, "Beyond Oil, Sheikhs and Security: Plotting New Trajectories in Gulf Studies," July 2–3, 2018. Personal communication of the author, April 12, 2018.

13. See for instance *The ARAMCO Reports on Al-Hasa and Oman 1950–1955* by F. S Vidal, William E Mulligan and Arabian American Oil Company (Archive Editions, 1990), 4 vols.

14. The first two issues of the review *Gulf Studies* published by the committee dealt with the anti-colonial struggle in Aden, insurgency in Oman, and class struggle in Bahrain. "Armed Struggle in Arabia," *Gulf Studies* 1 (1976); "Bahrain: Service Boom and Armed Struggle," *Gulf Studies* 2 (1977). Before the publication of this review, the committee commissioned independent studies on political prisoners in the Gulf States and arms buildup in the Indian Ocean and the Gulf. See also "Gulf Committee: British Troops in Oman," *New Left Review* I/92 (July/August 1975), https://newleftreview.org/issues/I92/articles /gulf-committee-british-troops-in-oman; F. Halliday, *Arabia without Sultans: A Political Survey of Instability in the Arab World* (New York: Vintage, 1975).

15. On the adoption of the term Arab Gulf as opposed to the Persian Gulf, see Martin H. Levinson, "Mapping the Persian Gulf Name Dispute," *ETC: A Review of General Semantics* 68, no. 3 (July 2011): 279–287.

16. *al-Insan wa al-Mujtama' fi al-Khaliij al-'Arabi: Buhuth al-Nadwah—Man and Society in the Arab Gulf*, The Third International Symposium of the Centre for Arab Gulf Studies held at the University of Basrah, March 29–31, 1979 (Baghdād: Matba'a al-Irshad, 1979), 3 vols.

17. *al-Insan wa al-Mujtama'*, 1, 27.

18. Mitchell, "Middle East," 80–81; Zachary Lockman, *Contending Visions of the Middle East: The History and Politics of Orientalism* (Cambridge: Cambridge University Press, 2004), 7–83. In contemporary parlance *Homo Islamicus* is primarily used as a counterpoint to *Homo Economicus* in the context of discussions on self-interest versus communitarian behavior in Islamic economics.

19. David Brady, "The Centre for Arab Gulf Studies of the University of Basrah," *British Journal of Middle Eastern Studies* 6, no. 1 (1979): 58–59.

20. Including the author of this article who held the position of postdoctoral researcher and lecturer at the center from 1997 to 2003. Mohamed A. Shaaban, "Centre for Arab Gulf Studies—University of Exeter," *Middle East Studies Association Bulletin* 14, no. 2 (December 1980): 91–92.

21. Timothy C. Niblock, "The Centre for Arab Gulf Studies University of Exeter," *Bulletin (British Society for Middle Eastern Studies)* 6, no. 2 (1979): 116–118.

22. Harootunian, "Postcoloniality's Unconscious / Area Studies' Desire," 159; Steffen Hertog, "Shaping the Saudi State: Human Agency's Shifting Role in Rentier State Formation," *International Journal of Middle East Studies* 39, no. 4 (2007): 539–563.

23. The project was led by Madawi al-Rasheed, James Piscatori, and Paul Dresch. It resulted in two edited volumes: M. al-Rasheed, ed., *Transnational Connections and the Arab Gulf* (New York: Routledge, 2005) and Paul Dresch and James P. Piscatori, *Monarchies and Nations: Globalization and Identity and the Arab States of the Gulf* (New York: Bloomsbury Academic, 2005). For a critique of Gulf exceptionalism and history writing see Nelida Fuccaro, *Histories of City and State in the Persian Gulf: Manama since 1800* (Cambridge: Cambridge University Press, 2009), 1–2.

24. For earlier work on migrants see Sharon Nagy, "Making Room for Migrants, Making Sense of Difference: Spatial and Ideological Expressions of Social Diversity in Urban Qatar," *Urban Studies* 43, no. 1 (2006): 119–137; Andrew Gardiner, *City of Strangers: Gulf Migration and the Indian Community in Bahrain* (Ithaca, NY: Cornell University Press, 2010).

25. See Potter, *Persian Gulf in History*; Potter, *Persian Gulf in Modern Times*. For a critique of the ethno- and empire-centric historiography of the Gulf, see Nelida Fuccaro, "Rethinking the History of Port Cities in the Gulf," in Potter, *Persian Gulf in Modern Times*, 24–25.

26. For an excellent example of Indian Ocean–oriented historiography, see Fahad A. Bishara, *A Sea of Debt: Law and Economic Life in the Western Indian Ocean, 1780–1950* (Cambridge: Cambridge University Press, 2017).

27. Nelida Fuccaro, "Preface: Urban Studies in the Arabian Peninsula: Six Thoughts on the Field," *Arabian Humanities* 2 (2013), http://cy.revues.org/2530.

28. See Cherian in this volume.

2

Petrocolonial Genealogies of Cinema in the Gulf

FIRAT ORUC

> *I hear a rumour that an "Arab" is arranging to establish a cinema here. . . . If the rumour is true, I think that prohibiting the establishment of a cinema should be carefully considered, and in any case that censorship should be provided for. I cannot but think that His Excellency Shaikh Hamad would regard with distaste the type of film which experience elsewhere tells me is likely to be shown.*

Thus begins the first correspondence in the "Bahrain Cinemas" file of the India Office Records, a confidential letter dated April 7, 1934, from Lieutenant Colonel Percy Gordon Loch, the political agent in Bahrain, to Charles Dalrymple Belgrave, the British adviser (*al-mustashar*) to the government of Bahrain.[1] The "Arab" whom Loch mentioned in the circulating "rumour" was Hussein Yateem, a local merchant who had approached the government of Bahrain to obtain a license for establishing a public cinema.[2] Hussein Yateem belonged to a well-established merchant family that was particularly interested in importing new media technologies of that time, such as gramophones and cameras.[3]

But what was Political Agent Loch referring to by "experience elsewhere"? His point of reference was none other than India. As a circulating imperial officer, Loch had held numerous posts in India between 1919 and 1932 in the Multan, Gilgit, Rewa, Kathiawar, and Mysore regions prior to his appointment to Bahrain (1932–1937).[4] Loch was in India during

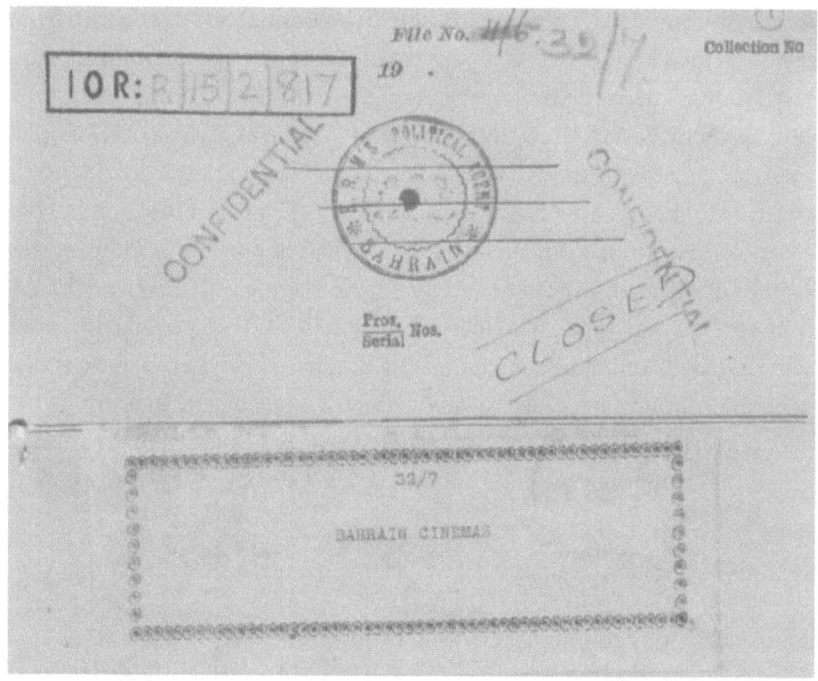

FIGURE 2.1

Bahrain Cinemas cover page.

precisely the period when there was a panic over the moral and political effects of film in the British Empire. Strikingly enough, Belgrave's diary notes during a recruitment trip to India in late 1927, approximately a year after his arrival in Bahrain, show that Adviser Belgrave saw several silent-era films, including Henry Otto's *Dante's Inferno* (Fox Film, 1924) and Alexander Korda's *The Private Life of Helen of Troy* (First International, 1927) in Karachi's cinemas.[5] Critiquing those adaptations of two major European classics to the screen as "decadent," "depressing," and "dreary," Belgrave ended this diary entry as follows: "I can't imagine what an Indian audience made of it."[6] Belgrave did not elaborate on his remark, but we can safely infer that he was convinced that those films were not fit for a "native" audience.[7]

Loch and Belgrave's initial reactions to the rumors about the opening of a public cinema in Bahrain reflected a set of anxieties that were circulating in the late imperial period among British colonial administrators who were alarmed by the increasing appeal of cinema as a popular form of entertainment among colonial subjects. The "Bahrain Cinemas" files of the India Office Records show the extent to which the experiences of colonial India shaped the formative years of cinema culture in the Gulf.[8] Administrators looked to how cinema was handled in India for ideas on how to create similar policies in Bahrain. The arrival of cinema in Bahrain was closely monitored and regulated by the British colonial network of administrative personnel, who meticulously followed the general film policies that were implemented across the empire.[9] The bureaucratic traffic over the submissions of early public cinema petitions in Bahrain shows how regulatory practices and norms of governance over cinematic spheres circulated from one colonial context (South Asia) to another (the Gulf).

CINEMA AS A CIRCULATING QUESTION

As cultural anthropologist Brian Larkin points out, to the extent that empire functioned as a network of repeating and multiplying circulations afforded by "a ceaseless movement of persons, laws, administrative practices, commodities, texts, [and] images," the panic over the new medium was characterized by "the diversity of situations in which cinema found itself, and the regularity of the stories narrated about those films."[10] It was, therefore, no coincidence that Loch and Belgrave shared the same discomfort about how colonial subjects viewed and interpreted films with, for instance, Governor Sir Henry Hesketh Bell in Northern Nigeria, expatriate journalist George Bilainkin in Malaya, or writer Aldous Huxley in Java.

But the cinema question did not remain limited to a mere epistemological curiosity concerning what the colonial audiences were thinking about the onscreen images they saw. As popular cinema, particularly Hollywood cinema, made its way to the colonies, it was accompanied by metropolitan concerns about governance and mass culture. The British Empire strove to control, survey, and supervise the emergent circulation of films in the colonies, responding to the question of how moving images affected "the mind and morals" of individuals and destabilized proper citizen conduct.[11] As Larkin argues, controversy over the effects of film in the empire was part of a wider moment in which cinema was constituted as a public sphere of regulation, with intense efforts made by governmental and private bodies to control and limit its exhibition. By 1914, domestic debates in England about the demoralizing effects of film on "immature minds" (most especially children) were being transferred into concerns about the influence of films in colonial territories. The concern for the influence of film in Empire was in part an outgrowth of debates about the moral effects of film within Britain itself.[12]

But in the colonial context, the cinema question was not merely a sociological issue; rather, it was a politically charged question that challenged "white prestige."

In 1927, while Loch was still posted to India, the government of India formed the Indian Cinematograph Committee (ICC) to report on the influence of films on the native subjects and their ability to properly decode them. Cinema presented a paradox for the colonial order: on the one hand, it provided "an unprecedentedly efficacious means for conveying the blandishments of civilization," but on the other hand, it embodied an overwhelmingly powerful "visceral appeal to the senses."[13] As a sensuous experience, cinema stimulated feelings of excitement and passion that challenged Victorian notions of a civilizing mission and an imperial pedagogy in the colonies. The concerns over the effects of the cinema were predicated on the notion that native spectators (at least the uneducated, non-Europeanized lower classes) were not ready to process the sensory stimuli of the cinema. The interviews of the ICC centered on rhetorical questions that implied that the new visual medium could not be properly understood and decoded by colonial subjects: "Do you consider that the differences in social customs and outlook between the West and the East necessitate special consideration of films in this country?" "Have any of the films exhibited in India a tendency to misrepresent Western civilization or to lower it in the eyes of Indians? Is it a fact that films representing Western life are generally unintelligible to an uneducated Indian or are largely misunderstood by him?"[14] The expected answer to each of these questions was "yes."

As scholars of late colonial cinema have consistently shown, although framed in cultural and moral terms, the cinema question was a symptom of deeper concerns triggered by the challenges the new medium posed to colonial governmentality and state control.[15] More than the images themselves, what was at stake was "how this symbolic flow was reconstituted within colonial power relations."[16] Cinema, after all, brought into contact populations that had been distant to each other, particularly due to its affordances of "spatial intimacy ... across national, racial, and gender boundaries."[17] As such, the social topography of cinema undermined established colonial divisions and hierarchies. Films, specifically Hollywood productions, undermined the white European image that had been established in the colonies over centuries and exposed private metropolitan life to native viewers. Just imagine the scandalous gaze of the brown man on the white woman on the screen, or the unsettling experience of sharing the same space with people from lower social classes in the cinema house.[18] One of the British interviewees for the ICC would express this sense of losing the representation of superiority: "It is useless to expect the coloured people to respect the white races when they see these false representations of so-called 'civilised life.'"[19] In response to these colonial anxieties, and in line with the late imperial attitude of British self-insulation,[20] the ICC called for a spatial separation of Western(ized) versus local cinemas based on audiences, tastes, exhibition patterns, and literacies.[21]

CINEMA AND PETROCOLONIALITY

The Gulf, it must also be noted, differed in one significant aspect from India: the discovery of oil in the 1930s. This discovery came at precisely the time when the natural pearling economy the coastal towns depended on had begun to decline irrecoverably due to the global dominance of cultured pearls in the aftermath of the Great Depression. The transition from one extractive mode of production to another resulted in an epochal shift.[22] Oil signified the seemingly marvelous arrival of a hydrocarbon modernity, which, in addition to a whole set of technological, infrastructural, urban, and economic developments, generated a new cultural dynamic that contemporary scholars of energy humanities have termed "petroculture" to designate oil's influence on the (trans)formation of modern everyday life in material and immaterial ways.[23] The primary cultural form that came with oil capitalism in the Gulf was film.[24] Cinema was embraced as a key site of leisure for the oil settlements precisely at a time when British administrators' suspicious attitude toward Hollywood's impact in the colonies was at its height.

Yet, as I demonstrate below, despite hydrocarbon modernity's promise of what Mark Simpson calls "lubricity"—oil's enabling of exceptionally smooth flows of people, material resources, lifestyles, and cultural forms—the circulatory energies made possible by fossil fuels (in both a literal and metaphorical sense) were managed through a new logic of governance that I call "petrocolonial" in so far as the term captures the very intersectionality of bureaucratic imperial power and capitalist energy extraction in the Gulf.[25] If, as Timothy Mitchell argues, carbon-based energy—coal in the nineteenth century and oil in the twentieth—played a fundamental role in shaping modern governance, in the Gulf context, it led to the constitution of the petrocolonial state as a result of the coming together of British imperialism and US venture capitalism.[26]

The embeddedness of cinema in the formation of hydrocarbon modernity allowed the Gulf to generate a set of characteristics that were resonant with, but also different from, other cinematic formations in the Middle East and South Asia. The petrocolonial configurations of cinema in the Gulf were refracted through three spheres of moving-image culture: private, corporate-sponsored, and commercial public cinemas. Although these moving-image practices are often examined separately, I show that in the Gulf context they were intricately connected. What was common to these three spheres was a certain logic of exclusion and restricted access norms. The private cinema sphere was exclusive to the colonial and Indigenous elite; the corporate cinema was confined to the Euro-American staff of the oil companies; and the commercial public cinema was reserved for the local and labor migrant audience. The triumvirate of the political agent, the government adviser, and the oil company in Bahrain regulated each cinema sphere. The processes of socialization, interaction, and acculturation they facilitated used legal codes and restricted access norms, adopting, in particular, patterns of colonial paternalism already well established in India.

The story of the opening of the first public cinema in the Gulf constitutes a significant yet mostly overlooked episode in the transregional history of the circuits of cinema across South Asia and the Middle East. Bahrain Cinema opened its doors to its local audience, under rules of censorship and conduct adopted from the government of India, to screen, as its first film, the iconic Egyptian singer Umm Kulthum's first musical *Wedad* (Studio Misr, 1936). Prior to film industry exchanges in the 1960s and 1970s, circulation from South Asia to the Middle East started in the Gulf under regulations by censorship manuals and segregation systems and with anxieties over the influence of cinema on native populations. The films that were screened across the exclusive Euro-American clubhouse theaters of the oil company settlements in the Gulf were obtained from distributors in India. Indian entrepreneurs, moreover, were the first foreign investors to petition for a license to operate a commercial cinema open for the local Arab population as well as South Asian migrant communities in the Gulf. This was the natural result of the increased labor flow from South Asia to the Gulf fostered by the rise of the oil economy and the strong historical connections between South Asian and Gulf merchants. Soon Bombay and Karachi began to emerge as central hubs of film industry in the early twentieth century.[27] Belgrave's diaries suggest that prominent pearl merchants of the Gulf would have their first cinema experience during their travel to Bombay.[28] The following sections offer a historical account of the three aforementioned moving-image cultures by focusing primarily on Bahrain, which, in the wake of its ascendancy as the regional nodal point in the British colonial network in the early decades of the twentieth century, became the first country in the Gulf where the distribution of cinema unfolded in all the circulatory forms outlined above.

ENCLAVES OF PRIVATE CINEMA

Following the discovery of oil in 1932, Bahrain entered a new phase in its history. As hydrocarbon modernity gave rise to new spaces of urban culture, the interest in establishing a public cinema in Bahrain was invigorated and further stimulated by the growing popularity of sound film as a global entertainment phenomenon.[29] Reporting on the progress of evangelical activities of the Arabian Mission of the Reformed Church in Bahrain, Rev. Gerrit Van Peursem would observe with astonishment the growing interest in new media technologies and visual culture as follows:

> There are still a few of the older men who object to phonographs, radios and musical instruments of any sort. But they are few. The radio is getting very general, and the phonograph is used in the public coffee shop except during the fast month of Ramadhan.... The same thing can be said of pictures in Islam. Time was when coolies and boys took to their heels at the sight of the camera. Some said pictures were images and thus smacked of idolatry. Others thought there was Jinn [sic] inside the box of the camera. Behold, what a change! It is difficult to exclude the crowd from the photo. The more the merrier. The more poses the better. Kodaks and films are sold in the bazaar to Arabs as well as to Europeans. The Shaikhs are especially pleased to have their pictures taken and the subjects aspire to be near their rulers.... There is not yet a public cinema in Bahrain, however, the lantern slides given in our hospital every week and in the men's mejlis are thoroughly appreciated in spite of the fact that the pictures illustrate the Bible story.[30]

Although Rev. Gerrit Van Peursem's account comes with a strong Orientalist as well as evangelical rhetoric in its description of the "miraculous" attraction of "the locals" to media technologies (taken as a sign of progress), it also demonstrates that even prior to the licensing of public cinemas, private nontheatrical spaces (the political agent's residence, the oil company clubhouse, the ruler's palace, the mission hospital, and so on) played a significant role in the formation of cinematic experiences in the Gulf.[31]

In its early years, film exhibition in the Gulf remained restricted to a highly select group: the British colonial administrative staff, members of the local ruling elite and their entourages, oil company employees, military personnel, and foreign visitors. According to the archival records of British offices in the Arabian Peninsula, "private cinema shows" were the most common form of spectatorship during the interwar period. In the January 1934 report of the British Legation in Jeddah, we read: "Picnics, wireless auditions, private cinema shows, and all the apparatus of occidental civilisation, now compete with the rigours of life among the

Wahhabis."[32] The Annual Report of the same year also mentioned private cinema performances as a new addition to "the resources of Europeans" for enjoyment and leisure, while also stressing that local restrictions on entertainment activities were "as a whole weighed very lightly" on the British subjects.[33] The private cinema form also enabled the Indigenous ruling elite to enjoy films in the comfort of their own exclusive courtly spaces, without having to worry about any religious or cultural criticism of the moving image.

The leading figure in both producing and screening private cinema in Bahrain was none other than Eleanor Isabel Wilkie-Dalyell, Political Agent Gordon Loch's wife. Following formal receptions, Dalyell would share her amateur films—short fragments of real footage about local events and public gatherings in Bahrain—with invited guests in the "cinema parties" at the agency residence.[34] Adviser Belgrave was among the regular attendees and recorded notes about these cinema shows in his diary entries between 1933 and 1936.[35] Dalyell's cinema parties are extensively detailed in the etiquette records of the political agency in Bahrain as well.[36]

Dalyell was a practitioner of what historian of imperial visual culture Annamaria Motrescu-Mayes calls late colonial home moviemaking. Although amateur moviemaking may not at first glance look relevant to the exclusionary practices in the physical cinematic space itself, Dalyell's films in fact reproduced the segregationist logic not only in terms of where and to whom they were exhibited but also through their formal elements and thematic material. During Lieutenant Colonel Loch's post in Bahrain between 1932 and 1937, Dalyell shot numerous intertitled 16 mm films using the Kodacolor lenticular system—a relatively rare and expensive experimental color process.[37] Following its standardization in 1923, the portable cine-camera had become a sought-after commodity for nonprofessionals who wanted to make films. The cine-camera was popular particularly among upper-class colonial expatriates who not only could afford to purchase one but also enjoyed relatively greater mobility than their compatriots.

Amateur filmmaking was notably embraced by women in the colonial outposts for whom it provided a lens for "taking an intelligent interest in the country, in the natives, and in [their] own immediate surroundings."[38] Filmmaking encouraged them to come out of the private sphere, participate in public life, and record scenes of "life away from home": administrative, entrepreneurial, and military activities and spectacles of the empire; touristic outings in "exotic" landscapes; and ethnographic encounters with native populations and customs.[39] By the same token, Dalyell's short films in Bahrain fell into two categories.[40] The first category included official visits by high-ranking British bureaucrats, Imperial Airways planes, and Royal Navy warships; official parades, police marches, and soldier drills; and expatriate leisure activities. The second category reflected the typical ethnographic style of filmmaking in the colonies in the 1930s, with extensive footage of dhow sailing, camel riding, pearl diving, horse racing, hunting, wedding ceremonies, religious celebrations, and royal parades. The anthropological subjects of Dalyell's films included local women drawing water, dancing, singing, and carrying shrines; villagers and vendors in the market; and "emancipated slaves" playing drums and dancing outside the agency residence. In these films, Dalyell followed the major generic visual strategies of colonial amateur filmmaking: (1) panoramic shots to emphasize the gap between filmmaker and subject; (2) surreptitious shots of natives to produce the effect of neutrality and authenticity; (3) smooth cinematographic organization of landscapes to limit the traces of dislocation and disorientation; and (4) shots that would invoke exotic contrasts to life at home.[41]

According to Annamaria Motrescu-Mayes, the amateur film work of Dalyell and other British women offers us uncensored and unedited visual texts about life in the colonies beyond the limited view of the official imperial representations. "Such fortuitous records," she writes, "were usually filmed by chance, eluded the filmmaker's initial thematic choice, and were never edited. . . . Some of these films now reveal unexpected details of British imperial identities and cultures."[42] Similarly, in his work on amateur filmmaking in the Dutch East Indies, Nico De Klerk maintains that colonial private films—"being the closest visual records of the 'grassroots' level of interaction in the colony"—demonstrate that daily life did not always coincide with colonial ideologies.[43] But it would be too far-fetched to say that Dalyell and other late colonial amateur filmmakers intentionally subverted the colonial governmental framework: except for a few fleeting moments in which the colonial native was "accidentally" recorded, they remained the ethnographic object, not subject, of the film. As Patricia R. Zimmermann writes: "Although the argument that these films present resistance to the aesthetic prerogatives predominating this period could be made, their shaky camerawork, inability to change composition, and absence of conscious narrative may more simply demonstrate that amateur camera usage was not situated within the discourse of filmmaking, but operated more within the discourse of hunting—to bag a prize, to get a trophy, to capture the experience, and project it on a screen."[44]

Late colonial home movies ultimately reasserted the imperial gaze. Their ability to cross private and public spheres and transgress feminine and masculine settings was guaranteed by their privileged status in the exclusive colonial structures.

THE CORPORATE SCREEN OF THE OIL COMPANY

In tandem with the private cinema—an exclusive domain of the governing elite—the oil company cinema emerged as a second film sphere in the Gulf. In 1935, the Bahrain Petroleum Company (BAPCO)—a subsidiary of Standard Oil of California—applied for permission to equip its clubhouse in Awali with "a modern Talking Cinema for the entertainment of their employees and their friends among the British residents of Manama."[45] Awali was the first oil settlement (*madinah al-naft*) in the Gulf.[46] The company management demanded exemption from censorship on the grounds that BAPCO's cinema would be a noncommercial space "confined to British and American audiences."[47] BAPCO's request was based on the assumption that only films screened for locals needed to be subject to censorship. Loch and Belgrave honored BAPCO's request with slight modifications. While the company management was given freedom over the selection of films, the government reserved a nominal right of censorship.[48] By reserving the right of censorship, Belgrave would be able to prevent the screening of films at the BAPCO theater that could pose problems to either the British administration or the government of Bahrain.

In addition to the issue of censorship, Political Agent Loch's private notes on his conversations with BAPCO's representatives reveal that he was still acting on the assumption that "the lower ranks or local inhabitants" would misconstrue films: "About the 10th January 1935 I spoke to the Chief Local Representatives Mr. Russell and Mr. Davies on the subject of the proposed B. A. P. C. O. cinema.... I told Mr. Davies at some length of the unfortunate results which follow the exhibition of films which are perfectly suitable in their own countries in places like Bahrain, where people get entirely wrong impressions from what may be to *us* [emphasis added] a perfectly ordinary film."[49]

Loch, in other words, reiterated the colonial claim that films that were otherwise appropriate for, and properly processed by, Western audiences would be interpreted by native spectators in problematic ways. In Saudi Arabia, where the first movies arrived in 1937 with the so-called early ARAMCO pioneers who settled in Dhahran, exclusionary measures were also in place. Tom Barger, one of the iconic figures of the early years after the discovery of oil, would write in one of his letters to his family that "Arabs were forbidden to attend" the film screenings.[50]

Notwithstanding restricted access, during the interwar years, cinema became the primary means of entertainment in the oil company camps.[51] BAPCO's agents in Bombay (together with their Saudi counterparts from the Arabian American Oil Company, ARAMCO) rented films (usually two per week) from Indian distributors for studios such as Metro-Goldwyn-Mayer, Warner Bros., RKO, and Paramount.[52] The films were shown first in Awali, and later in Saudi Arabia's oil towns such as Dhahran, Ras Tanura, Dammam, and Abqaiq in the Eastern Province. By 1945, BAPCO had to request priority air freight from the British Overseas Airways Corporation to transport 120 kilograms of film a week to India.[53] Although as a government official Belgrave was painstakingly particular about rules and regulations, he himself was a regular moviegoer. His diary entries between 1935 and 1947 refer to more than eighty titles of Hollywood (and some British) films he saw in Bahrain. The oil company cinemas received a wide variety of films in the popular genres of the period such as biopics, musicals, dramas, cartoons, and (in steadily increasing numbers) war films.

FIGURE 2.2

Aramco company cinema in Dhahran, circa 1951.

BAPCO and other oil companies in the Gulf nevertheless kept their strict measures to ban laborers (local and foreign alike) from the cinema well into the late 1950s. As social historians of oil in the Middle East have pointed out, despite the material welfare and prosperity that hydrocarbon modernity promised, the oil conurbations in the Gulf were structurally influenced by "colonialist, racist ideas about managing a multi-ethnic, overcrowded society."[54] All early oil settlements were built on the same model of segregation, "of dual character, partly planned by [the oil company] and partly wild-grown formations that were shaped by a steady influx of job seekers ... and their families."[55] The degree of segregation in the oil settlements strongly echoed Frantz Fanon's portrayal of the colonial city as strictly compartmentalized in its ordering and geographical layout, enforced by "the principle of exclusivity."[56] This was particularly the case for ARAMCO, which followed a strictly enforced regime of segregation between "the American camp" and "the Saudi Camp": "Americans and

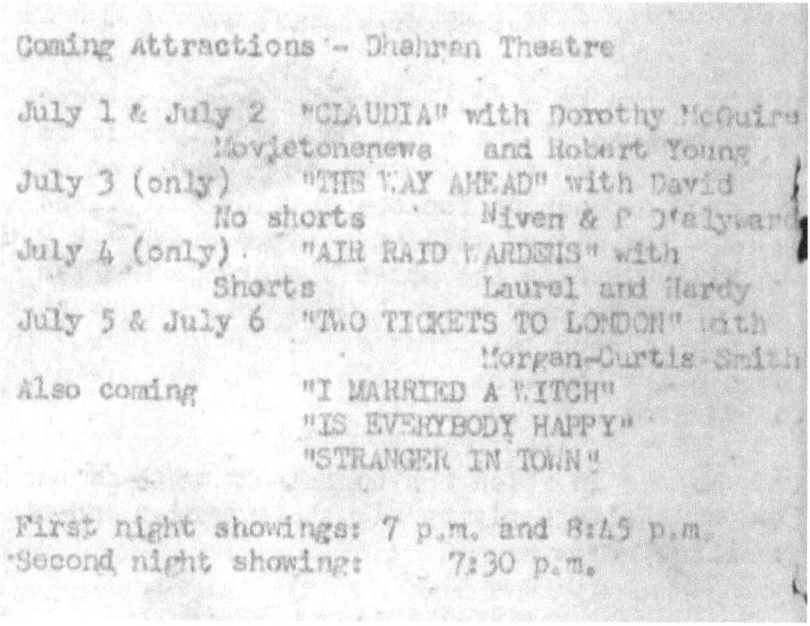

```
Coming Attractions - Dhahran Theatre

July 1 & July 2    "CLAUDIA" with Dorothy McGuire
                   Movietonenews    and Robert Young
July 3 (only)      "THE WAY AHEAD" with David
                   No shorts        Niven & P D'elyvar
July 4 (only)      "AIR RAID WARDENS" with
                   Shorts           Laurel and Hardy
July 5 & July 6    "TWO TICKETS TO LONDON" with
                                    Morgan-Curtis-Smith
Also coming        "I MARRIED A WITCH"
                   "IS EVERYBODY HAPPY"
                   "STRANGER IN TOWN"

First night showings: 7 p.m. and 8:45 p.m.
Second night showing:    7:30 p.m.
```

FIGURE 2.3

Film notices in Aramco's weekly community newspaper *The Dust Rag*, July 1, 1945.

Saudis lived in two worlds apart. The fenced American camps provided a living standard similar to that of middle class suburbs in the United States, including lush greenery and ample recreational areas. Saudi workers were housed in tents or concrete dormitories in separate areas that were bare of vegetation and thus directly exposed to heat and dust. Company services such as transportation, hospitals, cafeterias and water fountains were provided separately for Americans and Saudis and differed considerably in quality."[57]

Formal classification of the employees into professional ranks—senior, intermediate, and general—overlapped almost entirely with divisions across national, ethnic, and racial lines. American expatriates occupied the top of the hierarchy, various "semi-skilled" migrant laborers (primarily Indians, Pakistanis, and Italians from Eritrea) the intermediate level, and local Saudi workers the lowest ranking.[58] The three staff levels, marked by colored badges, lived in separate camps with different standards of amenities. By 1953, in the oil towns of the Eastern Province, Saudi workers numbered more than 13,500, whereas the Saudi employees at the senior staff level numbered less than a dozen.[59]

In ARAMCO's recreated Jim Crow world (to use Robert Vitalis's apt description), not only was work life organized according to "norms of separate and unequal rights and privileges," there was also a structural resistance to cross-cultural interaction and socialization.[60] In so far as it was a privilege granted exclusively to the American senior staff, cinema appeared as one of the strongest markers of the segregation regime of the oil camps. ARAMCO's local employees were excluded from the movie theater even as the job-nationality hierarchy began to change slightly and a limited number of non-American staff members rose to senior levels. Abdullah al-Tariki, who was among the first of the few Saudi nationals to reside in the American camp and who would later become Saudi Arabia's first oil minister and cofounder of OPEC (Organization of Petroleum Exporting Countries), would recall that ARAMCO's movie theater displayed an explicit "for Americans only" sign, and that he was questioned each time he wanted to enter the theater.[61]

It was no wonder that during the labor strikes of the 1950s against ARAMCO, access to the cinema became a key issue when contesting the types of privileges that only Western staff members could enjoy.[62] As discontent over work and living conditions grew, in 1953, a Saudi staff member, Abd al-Aziz Abu Sunayd (director of the Permits and Contracts Division of ARAMCO's Labor Department in Dammam), wrote a letter of protest to ARAMCO's president.[63] In his letter, Abu Sunayd objected to having been denied entry to the senior staff movie theater in Dhahran to see Charlie Chaplin's *Limelight* (1952). He censured ARAMCO for implementing a Jim Crow system in his native country, recalling how he had also been banned from entering a movie theater when he was training in the United States, due to the color line then in place.[64] Three years later, in 1956, as ARAMCO workers held another general strike for better working and living conditions and union rights, they stormed the cinema in ARAMCO's Intermediate Camp—which housed middle level foreign employees—in Ras Tanura.[65] The movie theater, open to white attendees only, epitomized the deep-rooted segregation of the oil town. As tensions rose, the workers occupied the movie theater as a symbolic claim to a range of amenities that they demanded from the company. Storming the cinema transgressed the system of segregation and racial color lines that had circulated globally, reproducing itself at each new site of extraction in the United States, Mexico, Iran, the Dutch Indies, and the Gulf.[66] The oil company responded harshly to the strike, fearing in particular that it could spread to other oil conurbations. The workers were severely beaten, leaders were jailed, and unions were banned.[67]

THE PUBLIC CINEMA IN THE COLONIAL CIRCUIT

Rewinding back to 1935, in his final letter to the BAPCO Club Manager, Belgrave stressed that the company had been granted an exclusive privilege denied to "various persons asking permission to open cinema."[68] He was not exaggerating. Until 1937, he and the British political agent did reject all requests to establish a commercial public cinema for local citizens and foreign immigrant workers. During this time period, the British officials received four petitions from South Asian entrepreneurs outside Bahrain: from Abadan, Bangalore, Bombay, and Karachi. All the petitioners were essentially trying to convince the British officials to lift the effective ban on public cinemas. Taking an almost excessively reverential tone, the petitioners argued for a more positive and inclusive discourse on cinema, modernity, and mass culture, dwelling on three main points: (1) public cinemas would enhance the rising image of Bahrain as a modern country in the Gulf; (2) public cinemas would meet the popular demand for leisure created by the increasing urbanization, prosperity, and mobility that was taking place in Bahrain; and (3) public cinemas would enable laborers to break away from the alienating monotony of industrial work.

On June 3, 1935, just two months after BAPCO's cinema was approved, two entrepreneurs named Mohammed Faqir and Daulatram Rochiran applied for a license to establish a public cinema in Manama. In their letter, they made their case in the idioms of laissez-faire liberalism. But despite their experience and commercial success as owners of the Koh-i Nur Cinemas in Iran's oil cities (Khorramshahr—then Muhemmarah—Ahwaz, and Abadan), they wrote, trade restrictions on foreign merchants in Iran were becoming unbearable: "We hardly feel safe to invest large sums of money in Business in Iran nowadays."[69] A public cinema in Manama, they claimed, would not only enhance the rising image of Bahrain as "the most progressive" country in the Gulf but would also provide a leisure outlet for the increasing "influx of large numbers of foreigners who are migrating to Manamah day in and day out."[70] Cinema, in other words, would demonstrate Bahrain's modernity as well as its openness to foreign labor. Two days after submitting the petition, Rochiran traveled from Abadan to Bahrain to make their case in person. But Political Agent Loch told him firmly in a brief interview that "there was not a hope" and directed him to Adviser Belgrave. Belgrave noted in his diary on June 6, 1935, that the application was categorically rejected: "A M[erchant?] from Abadan came & asked if he could open a cinema here—I said no."[71]

Roughly one year later, an Indian named M. A. Sam, who worked as a sound mechanic in "The Paramount Talkies" in Bangalore, wrote a letter to the political resident in Bushehr for a license to establish a public cinema in Bahrain. Sam's rationale was quite similar to Faqir and Rochiran's.[72] "With large influx of foreigners and the general improvement on the Bahrain island," he wrote, "the presence of such amenities of life as a Talkie Theater would, I have no doubt, be very welcome."[73] Sam also similarly emphasized the labor-leisure nexus: "After a day's hard work," he argued, "one requires some sort of amusement and diversion from the humdrum routine of life, in common with the rest of the world."[74] Hence, the general public as well as immigrant workers deserved access to films. He also referred to BAPCO's successful petition "to have a Talkie for their European and American personnel only." Based on this precedent, M. A. Sam asked the British political resident in Bushehr "to extend the same privilege to the general public on the Island [to] fill a crying need."[75] Concluding his letter on a more pragmatic note, he indicated that he would be content with limiting admissions to foreign residents only.

The political resident in Bushehr forwarded the request to the political agent in Bahrain, who in turn passed it to Belgrave. Sam was told that the question of establishing a public cinema was under consideration, but no decision was made.[76] Meanwhile, Lieutenant Colonel Loch contacted the political resident in Mysore to inquire about Sam, the financial situation of the firm he worked for, and "whether the firm in question [was] reputable, in particular as regards the type of films that they show[ed]."[77] Four months later, the residency in Mysore sent a report on Sam, which had been prepared by "the Chief Secretary to the Government of His Highness the Maharaja of Mysore."[78] The report confirmed that Sam belonged to a respectable family in Bangalore, that he owned two houses, and that he intended to "make his fortune by running a Talkie House of [h]is own investing the cash he has at present and supplementing the same by raising a loan."[79] More importantly, it included a signed statement by Sam himself that if he were to be granted a license to operate a cinema in Bahrain, he would "exhibit only English films [approved] by Bombay and Bengal Censor Boards."[80] But in the end, despite this clear background check, Sam failed to acquire a permit.

Meanwhile, the local "Arab" whose petition was discussed in the opening of this chapter, Hussein Yateem, along with several business partners, came up with a new strategy for acquiring a license to establish a commercial public cinema. They solicited the patronage of two nephews of the Shaikh of Bahrain—Ali bin Mohamed al-Khalifa and Ali bin Abdullah al-Khalifa. As members of the ruling family, these two had a natural advantage to pressure the British on Yateem's behalf. The petition once again began to circulate in the British administrative circuit when Shaikh Hamad forwarded his nephews' request to Charles Belgrave. Although Belgrave was still adamant that Bahrain was not "sufficiently advanced for a cinema," he also began to accept that it was getting increasingly difficult to delay its arrival.[81] He sent a memo to the political agency for input. The officiating agent, Tom Hickinbotham, who was supervising the office in Loch's absence, passed it to the Persian Gulf Residency in Bushehr.[82] Like Belgrave, Hickinbotham submitted that it would not be possible to officially prevent the establishment of a public cinema in Bahrain. But the government of Bahrain would have to agree to a Board of Censors that would be authorized to revoke the operation license and/or fine the cinema management "in case a really undesirable film was shown."[83] Despite these conditions, Hickinbotham reassured his supervisors that his experience "in other parts of Arabia" had shown him that movies never caused trouble or elicited complaints from a moral and religious point of view.⁸⁴ Accordingly, he embraced public cinema as a sign of opening the Gulf to the outside world: "I . . . do not think that we can live out of the world for ever here."⁸⁵

In turn, Trenchard Craven William Fowle, the political resident in Bushehr, contacted O. K. Caroe, the deputy secretary to the government of India in Shimla, for guidance on the idea of starting a cinema in Bahrain, exclaiming half-sarcastically: "Such is progress in the Gulf!"⁸⁶ Although in principle Fowle was against the idea, he also acknowledged that as it was increasingly difficult to "prevent a cinema being started," the only alternative was "to try and censor the films."⁸⁷ Once again, for the colonial administrators, the introduction of cinema must be contingent on maintaining control over the film experience of local spectatorship. Due to the absence of any established cinema guidelines in the Gulf, the resident asked the government of India's advice on censorship rules and movie house regulations. In response, in September 1936, the Foreign and Political Department sent two copies of the Manual of the Bengal Board of Censors to Bushehr.⁸⁸ The manual included the 1918 Cinematograph Act and, more strikingly, a copy of the Report of the Indian Cinematograph Committee, 1927–1928. The ICC report gave detailed instructions for film inspectors in charge of making censorship decisions in India.

The most striking feature of the ICC report was the extent to which it was based on what we might call a reception theory of colonial difference. The report reminded inspectors that movies would have a different impact on "an average audience in India, which includes a not inconsiderable proportion of illiterate people or those of immature judgment."⁸⁹ Crime films, for instance, could "normalize" certain illegal conduct as reoccurring incidents of everyday life and thus "undermine the teachings of morality" among the native populations by "casting a halo . . . round heads of the vicious."⁹⁰ Moralistic concerns aside, censorship in the colonial context reflected deeper political anxieties. As Babli Sinha notes, "Although it was felt that licentious films were undermining British rule, the censorship board did not ban them. Most of the films that were banned outright . . . had overtly political content that was thought to promote revolution."⁹¹ Films that represented British or Indian officers "in an odious light, and otherwise attempt[ed] to suggest the disloyalty of Native States or bringing into disrepute British prestige in the Empire," that were "calculated ... to foment social unrest and discontent," that depicted "the violence that results in an actual conflict between capital and labour," and that "promote[d] disaffection or resistance to Government" were all subject to forms of censorship.[92] In such cases, the inspectors were authorized to remove subtitles, modify the narrative, or cut out portions of the film.

The two copies of the manual reached the political resident's office in Bahrain on October 14, 1936. In January 1937, the Shaikh's nephews approached Belgrave again for a cinema permit. Reluctantly accepting the inevitable, Belgrave obtained one of the copies and began drafting the contract for Bahrain's first public cinema. On April 12, 1937, he sent the contract to the political agent in Bahrain and then the political resident in Bushehr.[93] The contract granted a nontransferable five-year exclusive license and mandated that the cinema begin operations within eleven months of the date of the letter, according to the regulations in India and any other regulations required by the government of Bahrain. Again providing direction, the government of Bombay dispatched copies of license forms and electrical installation guidelines outlined in a booklet titled "Rules for Places of Public Amusement in the City of Bombay 1914."[94] Finally, on August 2, 1938, the British Commandant of the State Police of Bahrain (who was authorized with suspending or closing the cinema) met with the owners to inspect the films scheduled to be shown the following week.[95] After more than a decade of deliberations, the first commercial public cinema in the Gulf, "Bahrain Cinema," opened in Manama with Umm Kulthum's debut film *Wedad* (1936).[96] A musical based on a story from *The One Thousand and One Nights*, *Wedad* was Studio Misr's first international success and helped it on its path to becoming the leading force in the Egyptian film industry under the directorship of German expatriate Fritz Kramp.[97]

Bahrain Cinema remained the only public commercial cinema in the country throughout the interwar period. After the Second World War, another entrepreneur from India, S. M. G. Badshah (apparently encouraged by the physical dilapidation and permit expiration of Bahrain Cinema)

FIGURE 2.4

Bahrain Cinema, the first commercial public cinema in the Gulf.

applied for a permit to open a new cinema. His letter was the same in tone, content, and rationale as the earlier petitions of foreign entrepreneurs:

> The fact that Bahrein [sic] Islands are lacking in Public entertainments of any kind is keenly felt by the ever increasing local population and foreigners, like Indians etc., and this is a great hindrance for the social uplift if no recreational facilities are forthcoming in a country.... After a hard days work, if a man never gets any sort of entertainments, thereby enabling him to refresh himself, his life will be nothing but a morose and melancholy one. The present only one Cinema Theatre of an antique type now running in Manama, instead of giving some entertainments to the public, has become a source of nuisance, for want of modern machinery equipments and sanitary conditions.... In view of the above mentioned circumstances, I would like to state that I am prepared for the construction of an up to date Cinema Theatre, with well furnished furniture, and equipped with the most modern up to date machinery.... My aim is to exhibit Indian and Arabic Films and also some English Pictures at intervals, so that the public

may derive the best benefits for the money they spend.... I need not mention that exhibition of pictures has got its own education value also.⁹⁸

What is striking in Badshah's text is the *strategic repurposing* of the discourses of cinema as a functional, harmless, and hygienic space of leisure fit for working-class spectatorship. In the new post–Second World War cultural climate, as a certain understanding of "useful cinema" was being steadily embraced by the colonial administrators and the oil companies, Badshah's application was quickly approved.⁹⁹

Even in the post–Second World War years, however, Belgrave and the British administration remained reluctant to approve local cinemas.¹⁰⁰ But at this time, they were not as much concerned with Hollywood films as they were with Indian and Arab ones. The following passage from the memoirs of British journalist H. V. Mapp, who arrived in Bahrain in 1950 to work as an editor for BAPCO's magazine *Bahrain Islander*, illustrates strikingly that even after three decades, the early alarmist discourse on the bad influence of film was still in circulation (this time projected onto Hindi films):

> Belgrave had no qualms about attending Awali's open air free cinema [at the BAPCO Club], making occasional visits to see Hollywood epics as a sophisticate without fear of corruption, but was distressed by films shown in Manama—probably Hindi productions with their emphasis on dramatic events such as suttee, where a widow perishes on her husband's funeral pyre. Films had a bad effect on a comparatively primitive people, in Bahrain causing deterioration in manners and morals, even to committing suicide pouring petrol over their clothes and setting them alight, he said.¹⁰¹

Although I could not locate any record that confirms Belgrave's claim, his invocation of petroleum, film, and sati in the same breath is telling. Hindi films, in his view, encouraged bad customs such as sati and the use of oil for self-inflected violence. For those who work on the history of colonial discourse in South Asia, the reference to sati cannot be missed here. When the practice was abolished in 1829, the British colonial rulers in India had celebrated the act as a landmark moment in their moral civilizing mission and reform. But as postcolonial critics such as Gayatri Spivak have argued, the prohibition of the rite of sati was based on the imperialist superiority discourse of "white men saving brown women from brown men."¹⁰²

FIGURE 2.5

Charles Belgrave, circa 1945.

In effect, Belgrave's dismissal of the films shown in Bahrain's cinemas was repurposing the same idea as "saving brown audiences from brown cinemas." For him, film could not be allowed to deviate from the hydrocarbon modernization project toward supposedly regressive native practices.

Moreover, although film scholars such as Brian Larkin and Babli Sinha rightfully argue that in the colonies Hollywood subverted the British Empire's media and communication orders and generated an alternative infrastructure, the above anecdote shows that during the formative decades of cinema in the Gulf, the British colonial personnel would still prefer Hollywood to the emergent regional Indian and Egyptian film industries.[103] Thus, the lasting British reliance on Hollywood presents an important and overlooked dimension of the phenomenon of competing for imperial infrastructures. In fact, during wartime and its aftermath, as the British administration in the Gulf (reflecting a pattern in other colonies and protectorates across the empire) became more concerned about maintaining the support of the local population, the Public Relations Office in Bahrain began to screen the Hollywood films that BAPCO rented from distributors in India in various local clubs, administrative buildings, schools, and private residences in Manama as part of its publicity efforts.[104]

CONCLUSION

Decades of negative discourse and regulatory practices could not prevent the steady increase in the number of public cinemas across the Gulf. Cinema eventually became a permanent component of "the repository of new patterns of leisure" in a hydrocarbon modernized urban life.[105] Both local and South Asian entrepreneurs established new cinemas, which screened a variety of Hollywood, Egyptian, and Indian films in a range of popular genres. The only specific mention of the Egyptian and Indian films that were screened in the public cinemas appears in the 1948 Bahrain Intelligence Summary: "The staple fare of the Bahraini cinema goer is the Egyptian film, but many Indian films are shown and there are large audiences for them. 'Kismet' and 'Mun Ki Jeet' were very popular, and at the moment 'The Flying Prince' which features a pugilistic heroine is providing a rival attraction to the Egyptian Cinema stars, Abdul Wahab, in 'Yom Said,' and Omme Kalsoum, in 'Sallamah.'"[106]

By the 1950s, Bahrain would have a total of five cinemas: Al-Lu'lu, Al Hamra, Al-Nasr, Al-Ahali, and Al Jazeera. In Kuwait, the Kuwait Cinema Company opened Al-Sharqiah in 1954, followed by Al Hamra and Al Firdous cinemas. As urban historian Farah Al-Nakib points out, the cinemas functioned as key public "spaces of diversity" not only for the screening of Arabic, English, and Hindi films but also for holding large meetings organized by the emergent nationalist middle classes.[107] In the 1960s and early 1970s, cinema as an affordable popular medium of entertainment spread to other Gulf cities, including Dubai (Al-Nasr, Plaza, and Deria), Muscat (Al Hamra and Rivoli), and Doha (Gulf and Doha). Meanwhile, as the rising nationalist movement in Bahrain demanded more say in the ruling of the country, Belgrave (once hailed as "Chief of the Gulf") became

FIGURE 2.6

Al Firdous Cinema in Kuwait, circa 1965.

increasingly unpopular. In 1957, after thirty years of running the government of Bahrain single-handedly, it was time for him to depart.

Film scholars such as Lee Grieveson have shown that in the formative decades of North American and European cinema, the discourses and regulatory practices of cultural and political elites focused on constraining the film medium to "harmless and culturally affirmative entertainment," that catered to "the common interest."[108] The colonial history of the regulation of cinema shows how these early structures were carried over to other contexts of governance. In the oil colonies of the Gulf, the primary concern across the different kinds of moving-image practices and spheres that were covered in this article centered on *who* was entitled to cinema. The core political issue of the emergence of a cinema culture in the Gulf was the restriction of cinematic medium and space to certain populations. As such, "policing cinema" was linked to the question of managing the social forces of hydrocarbon modernity that the discovery of oil unleashed. In short, the arrival of cinema in the Gulf took place in an exclusionary and uneven world, entangled with circulations of colonial practices, regimes of segregation, expansionist oil capital, international labor, and of course, film cans.

The predominant reliance on documents from the colonial archive raises an important limitation in my historical account of the formative years of cinema in the Gulf. Whether in the form of official circulars or personal writings, the objects of the archive are riddled with prejudices, silences, and elisions that their authors usually did not bother to hide. Therefore, rather than treating these records as authoritative and objective sources for constructing the history of the emergence of cinema in the Gulf, I approach the internal and often confidential exchanges in these documents as an "ethnography of the archive" that Ann Laura Stoler and Nicholas Dirks, among other historical anthropologists, have proposed for the study of colonial administrative apparatuses. "To engage in an ethnography of the archive," writes Dirks, "entails going well beyond seeing it as an assemblage of texts, a depository of and for history. The archive is a discursive formation in the totalizing sense that it reflects the categories and operations of the state itself."[109] The primacy of official records in the study of the colonial histories of cinema, including that of the Gulf, is in itself a symptom of the extent to which colonial administrations regulated its arrival and lays bare the logic of control. My extensive citation of the colonial archive, therefore, does not mean an endorsement of the problematic rhetoric that it is built on. Equally important, the archive (often against the will of the administrative power) is inherently polyphonic and heteroglossic. In the case of the records that I study in this article, the voices of various "other" actors appear through the correspondences they have with the British political agents as well as the US oil companies. An alternative oral history project of the formative years of cinema in the Gulf could potentially make up for the paucity of records outside the colonial archives.

> FIRAT ORUC is Associate Professor at Georgetown University School of Foreign Service in Qatar, where he directs the Program in Media and Politics. He specializes in contemporary global literatures, cultural studies of the Middle East, energy humanities, and world cinema. He is editor of *Sites of Pluralism: Community Politics in the Middle East* and (with Françoise Lionnet) of "Indian Ocean Literary

Circularities," a special issue of *Comparative Literature*. His current book project explores the cultural and political history of film in the Arabian Peninsula.

NOTES

1. "File 32/7 (4/6) Bahrain Cinemas," IOR/R/15/2/817, India Office Records and Private Papers, British Library. Hereafter IOR/R/15/2/817. The India Office Records also comprises the archives of the British Agencies that operated in the Gulf.

2. Belgrave to Loch, April 9, 1934, IOR/R/15/2/817. It is not clear why Loch put the word Arab in quotation marks. But in any case, it signifies the multiethnic and multireligious demographic composition of Bahrain, as noted also in other correspondence among British officials. In his report to the foreign secretary to the government of India, for instance, H. V. Briscoe, the British political resident in the Persian Gulf, would describe the population in Bahrain as "heterogeneous and divided by racial and religious difference—Nejdis, Wahhabis, Persians, Sunnis, Shias and large colonies of Muhammedan and Hindu Indians." As quoted in Nelida Fuccaro, *Histories of City and State in the Persian Gulf: Manama Since 1800* (Cambridge: Cambridge University Press, 2009), 55.

3. "Kingdom Mourns Death of Builder of Modern Bahrain," DT News, December 20, 2015, http://www.newsofbahrain.com/viewNews.php?ppId=11032&TYPE=Posts&pid=21&MNU=2&SUB.

4. Paul John Rich, *Creating the Arabian Gulf: The British Raj and the Invasions of the Gulf* (Plymouth: Lexington Books, 2009), 223.

5. A modernized allegory of pre-Depression American capitalism, *Dante's Inferno* was about a villainous slumlord "tormented" by scenes of Hell as a warning about the consequences of abusing his poor tenant. *The Private Life of Helen of Troy* was based on John Erskine's best-selling novel adaptation and satirized husband-wife relationships through ancient mythology.

6. Charles Dalrymple Belgrave, *Papers of Charles Dalrymple Belgrave 1926–1957*, http://www.scribd.com/collections/2285562/Charles-Belgrave-Diaries, 118, 123.

7. Throughout the article, the term *native* should be read as if it were in scare quotes. Here it takes on the colonial administrative usage of the term to describe the "local" peoples administered by the empire.

8. Throughout the article, "the Gulf" will be used as a geographical designation to refer to the Arabic-speaking coastal areas (*al-khalij*) of the Persian Gulf. Today, what is called the Arab(ian) Gulf comprises the Gulf Cooperation Countries (GCC) of Kuwait, Saudi Arabia, Bahrain, Qatar, United Arab Emirates, and Oman. In the British colonial records of the time period that this article covers, the term Gulf is also used in reference to a region that included Iran and Iraq.

9. In addition to cinema permits, the sales and exhibition rights of foreign films were also subject to the British special treaty relationships. Film licenses obtained in neighboring Iran and Iraq, for instance, could not be extended into the shaikhdoms of Bahrain and Kuwait. India Office to Radio Pictures Ltd., November 15, 1935, IOR/R/15/2/817.

10. Brian Larkin, "Circulating Empires: Colonial Authority and the Immoral, Subversive Power of American Film," in *Globalizing American Studies*, ed. Brian Edwards and Dilip Gaonkar (Chicago: University of Chicago Press, 2010), 174, 155.

11. Lee Grieveson, "Cinema Studies and the Conduct of Conduct," in *Inventing Film Studies*, ed. Lee Grieveson and Haidee Wasson (Durham, NC: Duke University Press, 2008), 5.

12. Larkin, "Circulating Empires," 164.

13. William Mazzarella, "Making Sense of the Cinema in Late Colonial India," in *Censorship in South Asia: Cultural Regulation from Sedition to Seduction*, ed. Raminder Kaur and William Mazzarella (Bloomington: Indiana University Press, 2009), 66.

14. Quoted in Babli Sinha, "'Lowering Our Prestige': American Cinema, Mass Consumerism, and Racial Anxiety in Colonial India," *Comparative Studies of South Asia, Africa and the Middle East* 29, no. 2 (2009): 291–292.

15. Priya Jaikumar, "More than Morality: The Indian Cinematograph Committee Interviews (1927)," *Moving Image* 3 (2003): 82–109. In her *Cinema at the End of Empire: A Politics of Transition in Britain and India* (Durham, NC: Duke University Press, 2006), Jaikumar also shows that the ICC emerged out of Britain's commercial concerns over Hollywood's increasing global dominance in the film markets.

16. Larkin, "Circulating Empires," 173.

17. Sinha, "'Lowering Our Prestige,'" 292–293.

18. Poonam Arora, "'Imperiling the Prestige of the White Woman': Colonial Anxiety and Film Censorship in British India," *Visual Anthropology Review* 11, no. 2 (1995): 38.

19. Quoted in Prem Chowdhry, *Colonial India and the Making of Empire Cinema: Image, Ideology and Identity* (Manchester: Manchester University Press, 2000), 20–21. These anxieties about film spectatorship were not exclusive to India and the Gulf. For a discussion of the situation in colonial Africa, see James Burns, "Watching Africans Watch Movies: Theories of Spectatorship in British Colonial Africa," *Historical Journal of Film, Radio, and Television* 20, no. 2 (2000): 197–211.

20. Mazzarella, "Making Sense of the Cinema in Late Colonial India," 65.

21. Manishita Dass, "The Crowd Outside the Lettered City: Imagining the Mass Audience in 1920s," *Cinema Journal* 48, no. 4 (2009), 85; Sinha, "'Lowering Our Prestige,'" 293.

22. For detailed historical accounts of the transition from pearl trade to oil industry, see Lawrence G. Potter, "Society in the Persian Gulf: Before and after Oil," *CIRS Occasional Papers*, vol. 18 (Doha: Georgetown University School of Foreign Service, 2017); Andrew M. Gardner, "Pearls, Oil, and the British Empire: A Short History of Bahrain," in *City of Strangers: Gulf Migration and the Indian Community in Bahrain* (Ithaca, NY: Cornell University Press, 2010), 24–48; Nelida Fuccaro, "Pearl Towns and Early Oil Cities: Migration and Integration in the Arab Coast of the Persian Gulf," in *The City in the Ottoman Empire: Migration and the Making of Urban Modernity*, ed. Ulrike Freitag et al. (London: Routledge, 2011), 99–116.

23. For a global critical examination of the cultural affordances of oil, see Sheena Wilson, Adam Carlson, and Imre Szeman, eds., *Petrocultures: Oil, Energy, Culture* (Montreal: McGill Queens University Press, 2017); Ross Barrett and Daniel Worden, eds., *Oil Culture* (Minneapolis: University of Minnesota Press, 2014).

24. For further scholarship on the role of the oil company in the formation of cinema culture in oil-producing countries of the Middle East, see Hamid Naficy, *A Social History of Iranian Cinema, Volume 1: The Artisanal Era, 1897–1941* (Durham, NC: Duke University Press, 2011), 183–186; Mona Damluji, "Petrofilms and the Image World of Middle Eastern Oil," in *Subterranean Estates: Life Worlds of Oil and Gas*, ed. Hannah Appel, Arthur Mason, and Michael Watts (Ithaca, NY: Cornell University Press, 2015), 147–164; Rasmus

Christian Elling, "Abadan: Unfulfilled Promises of Oil Modernity and Revolution in Iran," Ajam Media Collective, February 26, 2015, https://ajammc.com/2015/02/16/abadan-oil-city-dreams.

25. Mark Simpson, "Lubricity: Smooth Oil's Political Frictions," in *Petrocultures: Oil, Energy, Culture*, ed. Sheena Wilson, Adam Carlson, and Imre Szeman (Montreal: McGill Queen's University Press, 2017), 287–318.

26. Timothy Mitchell, *Carbon Democracy: Political Power in the Age of Oil* (London: Verso, 2011).

27. In her *Histories of City and State in the Persian Gulf*, Nelida Fuccaro writes: "The merchants looked at Bombay as the commercial, cultural and religious capital of the region with its import-export offices, Arabic printing presses, and thriving religious and intellectual life. They invested in urban properties and maintained family residences in the Indian port. The primary and secondary schools of Bombay, which offered both scientific and commercial education, further fashioned the Arab urban elites of the turn of the century" (64). Also see James Onley, "Transnational Merchant Families in the Nineteenth- and Twentieth-Century Gulf," in *The Gulf Family: Kinship Policies and Modernity*, ed. Alanoud Alsharekh (London: Saqi in association with London Middle East Institute, SOAS, 2007), 37–57.

28. Belgrave, *Papers*, 364.

29. See Douglas Gomery, *The Coming of Sound: A History* (New York: Routledge, 2005).

30. Rev. G[errit] Van Peursem, "Can We Report Progress?," *Neglected Arabia*, no. 172 (July–August–September 1935): 9–10. But the American Mission's correlation of pictures and music with progress was predicated on their moral function. In contrast to Van Peursem, John Coert Rylaarsdam deplored how the young white-collar class (the "Effendi") in Basrah would waste their time in "an evil smelling cinema," since there were "no public centers for recreation or study." Coert Rylaarsdam, "My Friend—The 'Efendi,'" *Neglected Arabia*, no. 169 (July–December 1934): 6.

31. On the history of utilizing of film in various nontheatrical institutional settings, see Dan Streible, Martina Roepke, and Anke Mebold, "Introduction: Nontheatrical Film," *Film History* 19, no. 4, Special Issue: Nontheatrical Film (2007): 339–343.

32. Sir Andrew Ryan to Sir John Simon, February 3, 1934, Enclosure Jedda Report for January 1934, *The Jedda Diaries, 1919–1940. Volume 3. 1928–1934*, ed. Robert L. Jarman (London: Archive Editions, 1990), 475.

33. Sir Andrew Ryan to Sir John Simon, May 18, 1935, Enclosure Annual Report 1934, *Political Diaries of the Arab World: Saudi Arabia. Volume 5. Annual reports, 1930–1940*, ed. Robert L. Jarman (London: Archive Editions, 1998), 229.

34. Private screenings of amateur films were seen in other British administrative functions in the Arabian Peninsula, too. The May 1935 monthly report of the British Legation in Jeddah recorded that the consulate himself, Mr. Oppenheim, held a screening session to show his film about a journey from Liverpool to Jeddah. Mr. Oppenheim to Sir Samuel Hoare, June 24, 1935, Enclosure Jedda Report for May 1935. *The Jedda Diaries, 1919–1940. Volume 4. 1935–1940*, ed. Robert L. Jarman (London: Archive Editions, 1990), 33.

35. Belgrave, *Papers*, 826, 843, 861, 869, 1144, 1152, 1154. From Belgrave's diaries, we also learn that Shaikh Hamad himself attended the screenings. In his May 27, 1933 entry, Belgrave wrote: "I found the Shaikh sitting on the long mud bench in front of the mosque with about thirty Arabs sitting in a long line in front of him, he was talking to them about

"movies" and saying how wonderful they are, he saw Mrs Loch's one at the Agency, he then told them about "talkies." Some of his servants had seen the film which Mrs L[och] took at the Coronation time, they complained that they moved too fast." Belgrave, *Papers*, 782.

36. "27/2 I Etiquette," IOR/R/15/2/646, India Office Records and Private Papers, British Library.

37. Annamaria Motrescu-Mayes, "Women, Personal Films and Colonial Intimacies," *Close Up: Film and Media Studies* 1, no. 2 (2013): 48. On the history of Kodacolor film and its role in home moviemaking, see Marsha Gordon, "Lenticular Spectacles: Kodacolor's Fit in the Amateur Arsenal," *Film History* 25, no. 4 (2013): 36–61.

38. Mary A. Procida, *Married to the Empire: Gender, Politics and Imperialism in India, 1883–1947* (Manchester: Manchester University Press), 105. The etiquette records indicate that Eleanor Dalyell not only learned Arabic but also regularly connected with upper-class Bahraini women. Dalyell's cinema appears as a regular conversation topic during these social occasions.

39. Prior to her Bahrain films, Dalyell accompanied Loch during his expeditions to the North West Frontier Province in India and filmed his meetings with the tribal chieftains. For a reference to Dalyell's films on infantry troops in the North West Frontier Province, see Gajendra Singh, *The Testimonies of Indian Soldiers and the Two World Wars: Between Self and Sepoy* (London: Bloomsbury, 2014), xii.

40. Now housed in the British Empire and Commonwealth Museum, the Dalyell collection is approximately 230 minutes long and includes 37 short films shot in India (1926–1931) and Bahrain (1932–1937). For a sample film, see "The Dalyell collection (Reel 10): Christmas Party, Bahrain 1933–1934," Colonial Film: Moving Images of the British Empire, 2010, http://www.colonialfilm.org.uk/node/2109.

41. Patricia R. Zimmermann, "Geographies of Desire: Cartographies of Gender, Race, Nation and Empire in Amateur Film," *Film History* 8 (1996): 89–90.

42. Annamaria Motrescu-Mayes, "Uncensored British Imperial Politics in Late Colonial Home Movies: Memsahibs, Indian Bearers and Chinese Communist Insurgents," in *The Home Movie, the Archive, the Web*, ed. Laura Rascaroli, Gwenda Young, and Barry Monahan (London: Bloomsbury Academic, 2014), 95.

43. Nico De Klerk, "Home Away from Home: Private Films from The Dutch East Indies," in *Mining the Home Movie: Excavations in Histories and Memories*, ed. Karen Ishizuka and Patricia Zimmermann (Berkeley: University of California Press, 2008), 152. Also see Christine Grandy, "Empire, Repetition, and Reluctant Subjects: British Home Movies of Kenya, 1928–1972," *Journal of Imperial and Commonwealth History* 46, no.1 (2018): 121–143.

44. Zimmermann, "Geographies of Desire," 90.

45. J.M. Russell, BAPCO Chief Local Representative to Political Agent, March 22, 1935, IOR/R/15/2/817.

46. On the formation of oil cities in the Gulf littoral, see Nelida Fuccaro, ed., "Special Issue: Histories of Oil and Urban Modernity in the Middle East," *Comparative Studies of South Asia, Africa and the Middle East* 33, no.1 (2013): 1–88.

47. J.M. Russell, BAPCO Chief Local Representative to Political Agent, March 22, 1935, IOR/R/15/2/817.

48. Belgrave to Political Agent, April 4, 1935, IOR/R/15/2/817.

49. Loch, Private Paper no. 8, January 24, 1935, IOR/R/15/2/817.

50. Quoted in Robert Vitalis, *America's Kingdom: Mythmaking on the Saudi Oil Frontier* (Stanford, CA: Stanford University Press, 2007), 60. The film that Barger mentioned in his letter was Gregory La Cava's precode melodrama *Gallant Lady* (1933).

51. The Anglo-Persian Oil Company (AIOC) in Iran was the first company to establish a cinema for its employees in 1926. Before the movie theater, in 1912, AIOC brought the first portable projector to Abadan for the exclusive entertainment of British employees. In the 1940s, the company would lead the establishment of fully equipped cinema complexes such as Taj (Crown) and Naft (Oil) Cinemas in Abadan. Elling, "Abadan."

52. W. P. Anderson, BAPCO Chief Local Representative to Political Agent Captain R.E.R. Bird, 20 November 1945. "File 16/32 VII Correspondence with the Bushire Residency," IOR/R/15/2/1535, India Office Records and Private Papers, British Library.

53. "Priority Air Freight for BAPCO Cinema Films," IOR/R/15/2/445, India Office Records and Private Papers, British Library. In his petition to the Political Agent, BAPCO's chief local representative wrote: "The distributors are seriously disturbed by the loss of revenue sustained by them through the frequent late arrival of films in Karachi and we fear that a continuation of these delays might easily result in the cancellation of the contracts. This would mean a serious loss of entertainment to the detriment of morale."

54. Elling, "Abadan."

55. Claudia Ghrawi, "Structural and Physical Violence in Saudi Arabian Oil Towns, 1953–1956," in *Urban Violence in the Middle East: Changing Cityscapes in the Transition from Empire to Nation State*, ed. Ulrike Freitag et al. (New York: Berghahn Books, 2015), 243.

56. Frantz Fanon, *The Wretched of the Earth*, trans. Constance Farrington (New York: Grove Press, 1968), 37.

57. Claudia Ghrawi, "Political and Civic Life at the Dawn of the Saudi Petro Age," *Middle East in London* 10, no. 4 (2014): 19–20.

58. The category of "local" workers also included those from Bahrain and other Arabic-speaking Gulf countries. Ian Seccombe and Richard Lawless, *Work Camps and Company Towns: Settlement Patterns and the Gulf Oil Industry* (Durham: University of Durham, 1987), 37–39.

59. Ghrawi, "Structural and Physical Violence in Saudi Arabian Oil Towns," 245.

60. Robert Vitalis, "Aramco World: Business and Culture on the Arabian Oil Frontier," in *Counter-Narratives: History, Contemporary Society, and Politics in Saudi Arabia and Yemen*, ed. Madawi Al-Rasheed and Robert Vitalis (New York: Palgrave Macmillan, 2004), 154, 163.

61. Loring M. Danforth, *Crossing the Kingdom: Portraits of Saudi Arabia* (Berkeley: University of California Press, 2016), 44, 49.

62. Fueled also by the nationalization of oil in Iran, anti-colonial sentiment, and the pan-Arab nationalism of the Egyptian revolution, labor strikes hit Dhahran, Ras Tanura, and Abqaiq (Saudi Arabia) in 1953 and 1956, Dukhan and Umm Said (Qatar) in 1955, Manama and Awali (Bahrain) in 1954 and Ahmadi (Kuwait) in 1956.

63. Influenced by the nascent leftist movements in the Arab world, Abu Sunayd promoted the Egyptian communist magazine *Al-Fajr Al-Jadid* (The new dawn) among the oil workers but also presided over the Workers Committee that would lead the first labor strikes in the Eastern Province of Saudi Arabia. Claudia Ghrawi, "In the Service of the

Whole Community? Civic Engagement in Saudi Arabia (1950s–1960s)," Jadaliyya, May 6, 2014.

64. Vitalis, *America's Kingdom*, 153.

65. Vitalis, *America's Kingdom*, 159.

66. In her *Living Oil: Petroleum Culture in the American Century* (New York: Oxford University Press, 2014), Stephanie LeMenager explains this segregationist circularity as follows: "The growth of U.S. oil interests into Bahrain and Saudi Arabia followed closely on Mexican oil development of the 1920s, and racial lessons learned in Mexico carried into the Middle East" (94).

67. Toby Matthiesen, "Migration, Minorities and Radical Networks: Labour Movements and Opposition Groups in Saudi Arabia, 1950–1975," *International Review of Social History* 59, no. 3 (2014): 473–504.

68. Belgrave to Political Agent, April 4, 1935, IOR/R/15/2/817. The only exception was HMS Jufair, the British Royal Navy Base in Bahrain. Two years after BAPCO, it acquired permission to operate a cinema for the crews of British ships (and, if space available, for the staff of the British offices located in Bahrain), "provided that the exhibition of films [was] not open to the general public." Political Agent in Bahrain to The Senior Naval Officer, Persian Gulf Division, April 3, 1937, IOR/R/15/2/817. The military cinemas would serve as a major nontheatrical space well into the 1950s.

69. Proprietors, Koh-i-Nur Cinema to Political Agent in Bahrain, June 3, 1935, IOR/R/15/2/817. Mohammed was referring to the highly centralized economic nationalization program launched by Reza Shah Pahlavi, who, after taking power in 1925, sought to abolish capitulations to foreigners.

70. Proprietors, Koh-i-Nur Cinema to Political Agent in Bahrain, June 3, 1935, IOR/R/15/2/817.

71. Belgrave, *Papers*, 1099.

72. Built in 1905, Paramount was one of the first cinema halls in the Bangalore Cantonment. Lakshmi Srinivas, *House Full: Indian Cinema and the Active Audience* (Chicago: University of Chicago Press, 2016), 69.

73. M.A. Sam to Political Resident in Bushire, November 2, 1936, IOR/R/15/2/817.

74. M.A. Sam to Political Resident in Bushire, November 2, 1936, IOR/R/15/2/817.

75. M.A. Sam to Political Resident in Bushire, November 2, 1936, IOR/R/15/2/817.

76. Loch to M.A. Sam, December 9, 1936; Loch to Belgrave, December 9, 1936, IOR/R/15/2/817.

77. Loch to Political Resident in Mysore, December 9, 1936, IOR/R/15/2/817.

78. Political Resident in Mysore to Political Agent Loch, March 10, 1937, IOR/R/15/2/817.

79. Political Resident in Mysore to Political Agent Loch, March 10, 1937, IOR/R/15/2/817.

80. Political Resident in Mysore to Political Agent Loch, March 10, 1937, IOR/R/15/2/817.

81. Belgrave to Political Agent, May 31, 1936, IOR/R/15/2/817.

82. Officiating Political Agent to Belgrave, June 4, 1936, IOR/R/15/2/817.

83. Officiating Political Agent to Political Resident in Bushehr, June 3, 1936, IOR/R/15/2/817.

84. Hickinbotham had previously served as a colonial officer in Kuwait and Yemen (Aden).

85. Officiating Political Agent to Political Resident in Bushehr, June 3, 1936, IOR/R/15/2/817.

86. Political Resident in Bushehr to O.K. Caroe, Deputy Secretary to the Government of India in Shimla, July 4, 1936, IOR/R/15/2/817.

87. Political Resident in Bushehr to O.K. Caroe, Deputy Secretary to the Government of India in Shimla, July 4, 1936, IOR/R/15/2/817.

88. Following the Cinematograph Act of 1918, censor boards were set up in major provinces of India—Bombay, Calcutta, Madras, Rangoon, and (later) Lahore. Each board was headed by the British commissioner of police and was composed of representatives from each local community. Chowdhry, *Colonial India*, 19.

89. Suggestions to Inspectors of Film. Bombay Board of Film Censors General Principles. IOR/R/15/2/817.

90. Suggestions to Inspectors of Film. Bombay Board of Film Censors General Principles. IOR/R/15/2/817.

91. Sinha, "'Lowering Our Prestige,'" 296–297.

92. Suggestions to Inspectors of Film. Bombay Board of Film Censors General Principles, IOR/R/15/2/817.

93. Belgrave to Political Agent, April 12, 1937, IOR/R/15/2/817.

94. H. Weightman, Political Agent in Bahrain to the Electrical Inspector, Government of Bombay, April 28, 1938; The Electrical Inspector, Government of Bombay to the Political Agent in Bahrain, May 10, 1938, IOR/R/15/2/817.

95. Commandant State Police to Political Agent in Bahrain, August 2, 1938, IOR/R/15/2/817. Film inspection would be conducted every week.

96. Mansoor Mohammed Sarhan, *Tarikh al-sinima fi al-Bahrain* [The History of Cinema in Bahrain] (Manama: AlAyam Publishing, 2005), 15. The establishment of Bahrain Cinema is recorded in the 1938–1939 Annual Report of the Political Agent as follows: "Bahrain Theatre Company. The cinema owned by the company was opened in the summer. A different picture is shown every week, Indian, Egyptian, and American films are exhibited in rotation. Films are subject to Government censorship but so far only one has been prohibited as being likely to offend local taste. It is understood that the venture is proving a financial success." "Government of Bahrain Annual Report for Year 1357 (March 1938–February 1939)," IOR/R/15/1/750/3 India Office Records and Private Papers, British Library.

97. Incidentally, *Wedad* also invokes an early example of film song circulation between Egyptian and Indian cinemas. One of the songs that Umm Kulthum performs in *Wedad*, "'Ala balad al-maḥbub" ("Take me to the country of the beloved"), would appear in Hindi form in Raj Kapoor's great classic *Awaara* (1951) as "Ghar aaya mera pardesi" ("Here, my stranger returns home").

98. S.M.G. Badshah to The Political Agent in Bahrain, September 29, 1946, IOR/R/15/2/817.

99. I borrow the term from Haidee Wasson and Charles Ackland, eds., *Useful Cinema* (Durham, NC: Duke University Press, 2011).

100. The 1948 Bahrain Intelligence Summary reiterates the same distance as follows: "The European community goes either to the Bapco cinema at Awali or the R.A.F. [Royal Air Force] cinema at Muharraq." "File 8/16 Bahrain Intelligence Summary," IOR/R/15/2/319, India Office Records and Private Papers, British Library.

101. H. V. Mapp, *Leave Well Alone! Where Oil Shapes Dynasties and Destinies* (Essex: Prittle Brook Publishers, 1994), 86.

102. Gayatri C. Spivak, "Can the Subaltern Speak?," in *Colonial Discourse and Post-Colonial Theory: A Reader*, ed. Patrick Williams and Laura Chrisman (New York: Columbia University Press, 1994), 93.

103. Babli Sinha, *Cinema, Transnationalism, and Colonial India: Entertaining the Raj* (New York: Routledge, 2013).

104. "File 16/63 Cinema Programmes," IOR/R/15/2/1575, India Office Records and Private Papers, British Library. I examine the British propaganda and public relation efforts through film in the Gulf in a separate article. See Firat Oruc, "'Cinema Programmes' of the British Public Relations Office in the Persian Gulf, 1944–1948," *Film History: An International Journal* 32, no. 3 (2020): 197-209.

105. Nelida Fuccaro, "Shaping the Urban Life of Oil in Bahrain: Consumerism, Leisure, and Public Communication in Manama and in the Oil Camps, 1932–1960s," *Comparative Studies of South Asia, Africa and the Middle East* 33, no. 1 (2013): 62.

106. "File 8/16 Bahrain Intelligence Summary," IOR/R/15/2/319. The films that this record refers to are Gyan Mukherjee's blockbuster drama *Kismet* (Bombay Talkies, 1943), Wahid-ud-din Zia-ud-din Ahmed Man's *Man Ki Jeet*—an adaptation of Thomas Hardy's *Tess of the D' Urbervilles*—(Shalimar Pictures, 1944), Homi Wadia's fantasy action film *Flying Prince* (Basant Pictures, 1946), Mohammed Karim adventure drama *Yawm sa'id / Un Jour Heureux* ("A Happy Day," 1940), and Togo Mizrahi's musical melodrama *Salamah* (1945), respectively.

107. Farah Al-Nakib, *Kuwait Transformed: A History of Oil and Urban Life* (Stanford, CA: Stanford University Press, 2016), 48, 165.

108. Lee Grieveson, *Policing Cinema: Movies and Censorship in Early Twentieth-Century America* (Berkeley: University of California Press, 2004).

109. Nicholas Dirks, "Annals of the Archive: Ethnographic Notes on the Sources of History," in *From the Margins: Historical Anthropology and Its Future*, ed. Brian Keith Axel (Durham, NC: Duke University Press, 2002), 59. Also see Ann Laura Stoler, "Colonial Archives and the Arts of Governance" *Archival Science* 2, no.1–2 (2002): 87–109.

3

Interview with Ammar Al Attar on *Cinemas in the UAE* Exhibition

AMMAR AL ATTAR and DALE HUDSON

In *Cinemas in the UAE* (2018), Ammar Al Attar investigates cultural practices of cinema in the United Arab Emirates in an installation of artifacts that he salvaged from some of the first freestanding and purpose-built cinemas and his own original photographs of these cinemas before they closed for business and the buildings were either repurposed or demolished. The exhibition invites audiences to investigate a history of cinemas that predates not only the emergence of multiplexes in shopping malls in the 1990s but also the UAE's formation in 1971.

Public screenings of films in the UAE (United Arab Emirates) began in 1948 with the opening of the Royal Air Force Cinema in Al Mahatta, Sharjah, which first exhibited mostly British and Hollywood films and then began to include Indian ones. Weekly screenings were open to the community. After the UAE's independence from Britain, private cinemas opened across the emirates, catering to the tastes of local audiences, which included expatriates who had come to help build the UAE. As a result, Emirati audiences had access to a wide variety of films.

One wall of Al Attar's exhibition contains his photographs of the closing and demolition of the cinemas. These photos not only recall a rapidly disappearing moment in film history but also preserve a sense of its heterogeneity, revealing the multiplicity of ways that cinema-going as a social practice was adapted to the UAE by theater managers, film distributors, and audiences. Rather than standardized multiplexes, with their

FIGURE 3.1

Ammar Al Attar in his Sharjah studio.

FIGURE 3.2

Demolition of the Golden Cinema in Dubai. Photo: Ammar Al Attar.

dark-colored and mass-produced patterned carpets and wall coverings guiding the eyes to brightly illuminated products on offer (like sugary and salty snack foods) or ones for later consumption (such as product tie-ins as part of a Bollywood or Hollywood marketing strategy), these cinemas varied in style and content.

What distinguishes cinemas in the UAE from ones elsewhere is rapidly disappearing like the video shops that once populated the storefronts in every city and town. At the time of the exhibition, UAE audiences got to see Bollywood films before the rest of the world since films opened on Thursdays in UAE, rather than on Fridays like other places. New films thus opened in UAE one day before their global release, so producers could see how films fared here as an indication of how they would fare elsewhere. With the shift to the Saturday-and-Sunday weekend in 2022, UAE cinemas no longer see Bollywood films in advance of the rest of the world. Currently, mall cineplexes offer a standardized fare of Indian and Hollywood hits available almost anywhere in the world, plus Egyptian commercial films available throughout the Arab World, but previously cinemas conveyed a place-based sense of how different cultures and classes of people navigate a shared space of the UAE. At the same time, these cinemas marked an important moment of transition from outdoor cinemas to indoor ones, complete with air conditioning and comfortable rows of seats.

Neon signs in Arabic and English signaled that these early indoor cinemas were spaces of enchanting stories and technological innovation, such as Dolby Stereo and Digital DTS (Digital Theater Sound). Removable plastic letters appeared on marquees to advertise films and showtimes, revealing traces of physical labor and occasional improvisation when a particular letter or number was in short supply. These signs of handwork are lost today with computer-programmed LED (light-emitting diode) screens. Some cinemas even displayed handwritten schedules. Films were projected on 35 mm reels. Al Attar's photographs of cinemas convey tactile properties of analogue film culture that are increasingly disappearing as film is replaced by digital content files that are projected onto screens from remote locations. As these cinemas close, there are fewer and fewer opportunities to learn about the UAE through from perspectives that are different from globalized mall cinema experiences. These buildings form one contour of a shared public space for weekly family moviegoing rituals,

FIGURE 3.3

Cinemas in the UAE exhibition, New York University Abu Dhabi Art Gallery, October 21, 2018.

offering glimpses into the history of film culture and theatrical film exhibition that is being forgotten and replaced with the emergence of the more segregating spaces of mall cinemas. These newer venues are less accessible to many in the UAE, yet they are promoted as cosmopolitan since they understand film more as a financial opportunity than a cultural practice.

The rest of Al Attar's exhibition consists of objects that he has collected from the cinemas. On a pedestal in the center of the gallery is a dented 75 mm film reel from *Sholay* (India, 1975; dir. Ramesh Sippy). Documents reveal formal and informal business practices by local cinema operators, including official correspondence with film distributors and censorship officials and locally produced posters and tickets. These objects also carry with them associations of earlier moments in UAE film culture, when audiences congregated in cinemas both for the films and for the social interaction. Cinemas were part of the social production of spaces throughout the UAE. They offered a sense of participating in an increasingly globalized film culture by screening the latest Hollywood blockbusters decades before the arrival of satellite television.

Cinemas also offered a sense of connection to more culturally familiar and geographically proximate places, including Egypt, India, Lebanon, and Pakistan, evident in the posters that Al Attar includes on one wall of the exhibit. Brightly colored posters from foreign distributors are localized with cinema names, run times, and the occasional stamp of approval for exhibition in UAE. Inside display cases, Al Attar arranges booklets of paper tickets that document a range of prices, paper flyers that would have been posted on walls around the city, and paper receipts from distributors for print rentals. There are also letters that reveal a complex system of handwritten requests in Arabic and English for complimentary tickets to VIPs or hand-typed approvals—and occasional disapprovals—on official letterhead for the right to exhibit certain films. The fragile materiality of these paper artifacts conveys the fragility of the history of cinema itself, endangered by physical disintegration of celluloid, much like memories of participants in this film culture fade with the passing of years. These ephemera would have been lost had Al Attar not salvaged them before the cinemas were closed.

Other objects seem more solid but are no less susceptible to deterioration. Glass slides are arranged on a light box, so audiences can see advertisements for coming attractions, tailoring shops, televisions, automobiles, and maintenance deals. In between these advertisements are messages from the management about audience etiquette—"no smoking," "use of mobile phone is strictly prohibited," or "using of laser light is forbidden"—and holiday greetings, such as "Happy New Year" and "Eid Mubarak." One of the slides pointedly notes that "photography or videography focused on the screen is strictly forbidden," suggesting practices of video piracy that inevitably brought the films to other audiences unable to come to the cinema. Still other slides mark the "interval" conventional in most South Asian films—an important part of the experience of cinema where audiences would break to socialize and discuss the film.

Another wall of the exhibit displays color movie posters in Arabic and English. Hindi-language films range from the iconic *Mother India* (India, 1957; dir. Mehboob), staring Nargis, to the vendetta tale *Jeene Ki Arzoo* (India, 1981; dir. Rajashekhar). *Suraj* (India, 1966; dir. T. Prakash Rao)

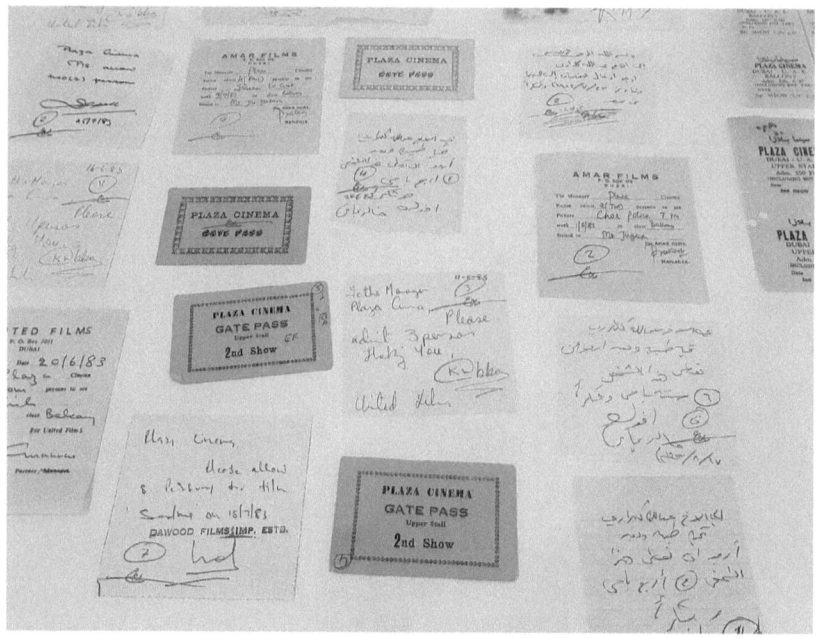

FIGURE 3.4

Display of tickets and passes in *Cinemas in the UAE* exhibition, New York University Abu Dhabi Art Gallery, October 17, 2018.

is promoted in Arabic as "سوراج." There is also a wall displaying wooden seatbacks from the fifteen-hundred-seat Plaza Cinema in Bur Dubai, each numbered by spray paint and stencil. Later renamed Golden Cinema, the Plaza opened in 1972 and became a gathering point for the expatriates who arrived just after the UAE's founding to contribute to the construction of the new state. The Plaza was located within walking distance of bus stations, taxi stands, and abra stands, making it more accessible to a wider array of patrons than mall cinemas of today. As he arranged the wooden seat backs on the wall, Al Attar included seats whose condition ranged from almost pristine to splintered.

Rows of the seats from the Plaza / Golden Cinema were also rescued by Cinema Akil, the Gulf's first art house cinema, where they now serve new audiences. Founded by Butheina Kazim as a nomadic pop-up cinema in 2014, in 2018 Cinema Akil moved to a permanent space in Dubai's AlSerkal Avenue, located in a warehouse district that has been refashioned

FIGURE 3.5

Display of posters in *Cinemas in the UAE* exhibition, NYUAD Art Gallery Project Space, October 17, 2018.

as an art hub. Al Attar's first installation, *Plaza Cinema* (2017), which focused on the Plaza / Golden Cinema, was exhibited at AlSerkal. As Al Attar's photographs in the exhibition documented, the last film screened at Golden Cinema before it closed was the world premiere of the Tamil-language *Uttama Villain* (India 2015; dir. Ramesh Aravind) about a film superstar, played by Kamal Hassan, who searches for a successor to complete a film project due to his imminent death—an appropriate film to mourn the cinema's own death.

Al Attar's present installation, *Cinema of UAE*, extended beyond the gallery space into the ground level of the New York University Abu Dhabi (NYUAD) campus, where students, faculty, staff, families, and guests of the university encountered reproductions of posters promoting *The Brides of Fu Manchu* (UK, 1966; dir. Don Sharp), *On Her Majesty's Secret Service* (UK/Switzerland, 1969; dir. Peter Hunt), *Fuzz* (USA, 1972; dir.

FIGURE 3.6

Seat back from Plaza Cinema in *Cinemas in the UAE* exhibition,
NYUAD Art Gallery Project Space, October 17, 2018.

Richard A. Colla), *I Escaped from Devil's Island* (USA, 1973; dir. William Witney), *Pratiggya* (India, 1975; dir. Dulal Guha), and *Kifah hatta al-Tahrir / Struggle until Liberation* (Jordan, 1969; dir. Abd al-Wahab al-Hindi). The posters and wooden frames were hung outside the gallery windows to suggest how film posters were often displayed outside cinemas. Their presence reasserts the heterogeneity of early film cultures into the space of a university that was itself once integrated into Abu Dhabi's downtown neighborhoods, not far from the iconic Eldorado Cinema on Airport Road, but now stands in sanitized isolation on Saadiyat Island, populated by hotels, villas, museums, and a golf course, all of which are inaccessible or unwelcoming to most of the city's residents.

The *Cinemas in the UAE* installation thus provides a starting point for ongoing investigations into a history that survives primarily in salvaged fragments and fading personal memories. It provides a provisional context for the richness of cinema culture in the UAE by recalling a wide range of stories that are often either not acknowledged or unknown. It asks us to think about micro-histories, based in the granularity of interpersonal relations that helped shape cinema culture in the UAE, which in turn offers opportunities to gain insights into the lives of people who helped create the UAE as we now know it. The stories that have been told around the objects and photographs in Al Attar's work might have been forgotten. They would likely have been overlooked by historians, who typically write history based on international treaties and state policies, not on handwritten notes by theater owners to ticket collectors permitting someone to see a new film free of charge.

The exhibition extends the university's contribution to public film culture that began with screening films from Southwest Asia (the Middle East), North Africa, and South Asia in a collaboration between the NYUAD Institute and the Abu Dhabi Film Festival (ADFF). When the university was located in downtown Abu Dhabi, the NYUAD Institute also hosted the film series *Muslim Cultures of Bombay Cinema* (2009), organized by Richard Allen and Ira Bhaskar in collaboration with Abu Dhabi Culture and Heritage, which highlighted Muslim South Asia, and the *Mahfouz Film Series* (2011) organized by Peter Scarlett and Philip Kennedy in collaboration with ADFF, which celebrated the contribution of novelist Naguib Mahfouz to the Egyptian film industry. Even these very recent contributions have largely been erased from the university's institutional history, further illustrating the precarity of history. The interview with Ammar Al Attar presented here thus contributes to collaborative ongoing efforts to document and reevaluate film cultures in UAE.

* * *

Cinemas in the UAE *was on view October 21–November 5, 2018, in the NYUAD Art Gallery's Project Space on the New York University Abu Dhabi campus. The exhibition was made possible by the generous support of the NYUAD Art Gallery in conjunction with the Film and Visual Media in the Gulf conference at the NYUAD Institute. Cinemas in the UAE would not have been possible without the invaluable support of Maya Allison and Kris Mortensen at the NYUAD Art Gallery. For more information on Ammar Al Attar's photography, exhibitions, and workshops, visit:* www.ammaralattar.com.

INTERVIEW

Dale Hudson: Congratulations on this exhibition. Alia Yunis and I were so happy to have it on view during the conference, and we have both heard that many participants found it to be one of the highlights of the visit to Abu Dhabi. We were also thrilled by the media coverage, which spanned the Arabic- and English-language newspapers. It was really important for us that the conference, exhibition, and screening of *Bas ya Bahar / Cruel Sea* (Kuwait, 1972) with director Khalid Al-Siddiq reach a wider audience than the conference participants. I also want to thank Tairone Bastien at Alserkal Avenue for introducing us in 2016.

When did you first think about photographing cinemas? Which photographs have resonated most with audiences who have attended your exhibitions of them?

Ammar Al Attar: Regarding the cinema project, my interest started in documenting them. In 2015, when I first heard about the Golden Cinema in Dubai, which would be demolished, one of my friends who lives nearby said to me: "Let's go by and document it before they demolish it." So, we went and documented the last show and the last party that they had. Over the next two years, we documented the demolition process. At the time, I wanted to discover more cinemas in the UAE, so I went to different emirates, asking people where cinemas used to be, whether they knew about others, where they were located, and what happened to the buildings. Some cinema buildings still exist, but their function has changed now, which was another interesting aspect of my project.

I continued documenting until 2017, when I first exhibited the work at AlSerkal Avenue, which commissioned the *Plaza Cinema* exhibit for one of their warehouses. It was interesting to see the reaction of people and hear what they thought of the demolition. I showed the entire process in 630 images. I shot more, of course, but the exhibit focused on a timeline from the last show to the end of demolition process. The one photo that makes everybody feel sad is one of Golden Cinema, which I shot as the board with the cinema's name was being demolished. I was lucky to be there on that day and at that time. As the wrecking ball was breaking down the front of the Golden Cinema, I was taking photographs. Demolishing these cinemas is like demolishing cultural icons, so that photo resonates in my mind.

DH: Your collection of documents and objects from cinemas that are no longer open is incredibly rich for the stories and history that they tell. How did you first conceive the idea of salvaging artifacts from the cinemas?

AA: When I went to Golden Cinema, which used to be Plaza Cinema, I started to collect anything that seemed to hold memories of the cinema. I even went into small rooms. Some of them hadn't been opened since the previous owner. Golden Cinema was owned by the Galadari family, and they kept all the business's files and documents in storage rooms. There were even some reels behind the building. In 2006, they sold it to another company—I think, Gulf Cinema House or something like this—so I found all of these artifacts. I wanted to save it since much of it was in really bad condition. Some had dust on it. Some had deteriorated due to bad storage. I found very interesting papers that showed the history of cinema, and I found papers from other cinemas as well.

My project was not only documenting and photographing the cinemas but also trying to save whatever documents that I could keep, so that one day I could use them in my work or somebody else could benefit from them. I found a lot of documents and lots of correspondence with the government during the 1960s and 1970s. There were many small old posters and leaflets depicting the movies that were shown at that time. I also found documents from the Ministry of Information to allow the showing of these movies, documents from the people who used to come around to monitor and censor these films. All this information is here, so I knew that it is important to keep it and to go through it.

DH: What are some of the most interesting documents or objects that you've recovered from cinemas before the building was either repurposed or demolished?

AA: Dispatch documents and posters showed that the cinemas were screening different kinds of movies, which were approved at the time by the Ministry of Information, rather than the Ministry of Culture, which today would likely not approve such films. Some documents show that certain movies were banned, such as one Malayalam movie. I tried to ask why, but nobody remembers. The information in these documents tells us a lot about the past and how businesses used to operate. One of the objects that I found most interesting is a projector for slide advertisements, which they used in the days before digital when they showed analog. It's still in my studio, and I have set some of the slides up during the exhibitions. I also tried to save some reels, though most of the film canisters are demolished, and the film prints are not usable anymore.

DH: Who were some of the key distributors of films in the UAE? What stories have they shared with you?

AA: One of the most important I met is Ahmad Golchin. He is the owner of Phars Films, which has been here in the UAE since 1964. He came from Iran in 1964 and started distributing movies here. He is still here and remains one of the main distributors for Indian, especially Malayalam, movies and also some of the Hollywood movies. He was not only the distributor but he also managed some of the cinemas like Eldorado Cinema in Abu Dhabi and, I think, Jumeirah Cinema in Dubai—and also Ajman Cinema in Ajman. He told me some of the stories about the first owners of some of the cinemas like Dubai Cinema and Deira Cinema in Dubai. These cinemas were not owned by him, but he was managing them for the owners. He is one of the first people to distribute movies in UAE.

One of the interesting stories was that most of the cinemas were without roofs. They were open-air cinemas. Sometimes it rains in the winter, so they would have to stop the movies and return all of the money to everyone who bought tickets. Another story is that when they started putting roofs on the cinemas, they used to put on temporary roofs, not concrete ones. One day, there were very strong winds, which blew the roof off, and rain came inside; so they had to stop the movie and reimburse all the viewers who came to the cinema. He told me that he started to distribute

FIGURE 3.7

Display of glass slides recovered from demolished cinemas. Photo: Ammar Al Attar.

movies, not only in UAE but also in the Gulf—in Bahrain, Qatar, Kuwait, and Oman. He started in Dubai and then distributed in different places in the Gulf and maybe the Middle East.

DH: I'm fascinated by some of the stories of the informal distribution of films between various cinemas that you shared with me as we were planning and mounting the exhibition at NYUAD; they reveal alternative histories to the ones that might be reconstructed from official records. Could you share some of them?

AA: The story of distributing movies is something that I noticed from posters. I saw one of the posters that I had obtained from Golden Cinema, formerly Plaza Cinema. There are two theaters nearby. On one side of Dubai Creek was Plaza Cinema; on other side, Dubai Cinema. I asked one of the managers, who I met and used to manage Plaza Cinema in the

1970s, about two cinema names on the poster. He told me that they used to start the film at Plaza Cinema, say, at 3:00 p.m., then after half an hour, we start that movie at Dubai Cinema on the other side of Bur Dubai. The Plaza Cinema was located in Bur Dubai, and the Dubai Cinema was in Deira. What they would do is start one reel, and when the reel finished, they put the second reel on. Each movie was about ten reels with each reel about fifteen to twenty minutes. When the reel was finished, they gave it to the guy for delivery. Sometimes they delivered by car since there was not much traffic in the 1970s, and sometimes the delivery was by abra. They take it in the abra to the other side of the creek and give it to the next cinema. The film started at one cinema at 3:00 p.m. and at the other cinema at 3:30. They would keep doing it for each of the reels. That was one of the interesting stories that I heard from the people who worked in the cinema.

DH: Another fascinating part of the documents that you have collected are the tickets and the letters from the censorship board. What are some of the more interesting stories that you have pieced together from these documents?

AA: The tickets show the different kinds of seats and the pricing. At the time, the prices were very cheap, not like today. Some of the prices were one dirham, two dirhams, or three dirhams. Now, the price for a similar seat would be forty-five dirhams, which shows you the different economics of the cinema business. Some of the censorship documents show that they were banned in the 1970s. They banned the Malayalam movie. I don't know why. These are some of the interesting stories from that time. If someone researches, there will be more stories connected to this one. Another interesting thing that I found was that sometimes they used small pieces of paper, and they are written from the municipality to the manager of the Plaza Cinema, for example, to allow a person to enter the cinema for free. I found letters from different people to the manager of the cinema requesting free tickets for people. It was like a free coupon.

DH: What were some of the more surprising films that you learned were exhibited? I remember being surprised by the variety, which ranged from the popular genre films that one would expect to occasional Palestinian documentaries and even exploitation films.

AA: I heard from my family that they used to show mostly Indian and Egyptian movies, maybe some Arabic movies and some Iranian movies. I learned that they used to show more diverse types of films. They used to show documentaries. They used to show English movies. And they used to show movies that have sexual—maybe soft porn scenes in them. I found one poster that promoted the film as like *Kaam Shastra* [India, 1975; dir. Prem Kapoor], which I am sure they are not showing these days in the cinemas. I heard from one of my uncles that they used to show a lot of porn scenes—well, not porn, but soft porn and nudity. There was not a lot of censorship of it. Later on, they started to do more censorship in the late 1980s. But in the beginning, there was not much monitoring or censorship. I was surprised that some posters were approved by the Ministry. There was a stamp on it so that it was of interest.

DH: You include reproductions of posters that were made by the local cinemas to promote the films, which you display in wooded frames protected by wire. For the exhibition, they were hung outside the gallery space, so that the exhibition entered the university campus. Could you discuss the significance of this way of exhibiting them?

AA: The idea came to my mind when I saw a couple of wooden boxes promoting some movies. I asked some of my old friends and older generations in my family how they used to promote movies. They told me that they used to use these wooden boxes with chicken mesh in front of it, and they used to lock it, so people wouldn't take the posters. I wanted to re-create that, so I went and gathered wood, not new wood but used, to assemble the boxes. I wanted to use them for the exhibition to show that there is an exhibition about cinema and history, so that was the idea behind those posters.

DH: How do you think your photographs and the exhibitions of them with the documents and objects might contribute to preserving social

FIGURE 3.8

Poster for *Kaam Shastram* (India, 1975) at Plaza Cinema, Dubai. Photo: Ammar Al Attar.

history in the UAE? I'm thinking in particular of the different ways that people used to go to cinemas and the different films that were on offer. This is in stark contrast with today's film culture when all mall cinemas and streaming platforms offer a fairly similar selection of films, mostly from the major commercial industries in India, Egypt, the United States, and the Philippines.

AA: I think it's a very important issue, not only socially and culturally but also economically. We can see the differences in prices to understand what was considered important. We can see who the owners were both then and now. All of the cinemas used to be in a separate building. Going to the cinema used to be a very important outing for people. Some of the cinemas used to be places for people to gather—unlike today. Now it's in a mall, so some people stick to the idea of going to the cinema as a fun thing to do and entertainment. Sometimes I will go to the mall just for cinema.

With all the new technologies that are available today on-demand—TV like Netflix—has, of course, affected the cinema business. Still, there is some charm to going to the cinema. The big screen has an effect unlike anything else. Documenting the era is important since there is not much written on that period, especially after the first cinemas in Sharjah at the Royal Air Force (RAF) camp. After that, there is very little documentation. Maybe they were documented as a building, but that's it. No detail on who would go to it, what was showing, how they censored or allowed it—and all this information. I hope one day that there will be a book to document this history.

DH: It is interesting that this history survives largely in artifacts that you have collected and also in memoires of people who participated in this film culture. What are your earliest memories of going to a cinema?

AA: I remember the first movie that I saw in Nasr Cinema in Dubai, but actually, it wasn't a movie. It was a theater play but screened on a movie cinema screen, so it was like showing a video of a stage play. That was my first. But my first movie was *Titanic* [USA/Mexico/Australia/Canada, 1997; dir. James Cameron]. I saw it at the Metropolitan Hotel, which was on Sheikh Zayed Road. They had a Metropolitan Cinema, and I saw the movie there, the first movie that I saw.

DH: What are some of your most memorable moments of going to the cinema? Do you remember particular films, or was it the collective experience that you most remember?

AA: The most memorable moments were going with my friends. I remember that we used to go every Thursday night. We used to go to the cinema, and, of course, buy nachos or popcorn. There are some interesting movies that I saw like *The Lord of the Rings* [New Zealand/USA, 2001; dir. Peter Jackson], which I can't imagine watching on a small TV screen. Some movies you have to watch in a movie theater.

DH: Do you continue to attend film screenings at cinemas today?

AA: Yes, of course, of course. I haven't gone to the cinema since the pandemic, but I am trying to go. I still go, of course, because even if you have these options at home, watching a movie in a theater has a different charm for me.

DH: Were you able to see films at any of the freestanding cinemas? Or had they stopped being places where families would go by that time, so that you only hear stories from family about the experience of going to these cinemas?

AA: As I remember, I think I went once to the car cinema [drive-in theater], called the Rex Cinema in Mirdef in Dubai. I was very young and not sure which movie I saw, but I remember that they gave two speakers for your car, so you can hear to the movie and a fan in summer.

DH: Who were some of the influential people, and what were some of the supportive institutions that have enabled you to become an artist?

AA: My family used to take photographs of us when we were kids. Photography is in our DNA. When I started taking photos, I never thought that I would become an artist one day and that my photos would become an exhibit until 2006 when I joined the Emirates Photography Society. My mother-in-law, who is an artist, said to me: you have a good eye for photography, so why don't you join the Emirates Photography Society and take some actual courses and go to workshops—and maybe you can exhibit the work there. And from there it started. The first time that people knew about me as a photographer was in 2009 when I had a photo exhibition at Tashkeel. Afterward, I continued to learn more. I attended courses in UAE and abroad, so my story of becoming an artist started there. Now I have a studio in the Sharjah Art Foundation, which supports by giving space and a studio for artists to work.

DH: Could you say a little more about how the Sharjah Art Foundation supports you and other artists with studio space? Would your work on the cinemas have been possible without it, not only logistically in terms of a physical studio but intellectually and artistically in the sense of helping to create a vibrant art culture in UAE?

AA: Before Sharjah Art Foundation (SAF) studio, I had a shared space in Tashkeel, where I started my studio practice. As the project grew with more and more found objects from the different cinemas that I visited, I approached Sharjah Art Foundation in late 2015 to inquire about a private studio and larger space. They have studio spaces in some of their buildings, and they kindly gave me an excellent one, which helped me in managing my storage and also going through the archive. It is closer to my home, so I don't have to commute far to reach the studio. SAF has created a great vibe in that part of Sharjah, which makes my studio visits very rewarding—and also offers opportunities to meet people easily.

> AMMAR AL ATTAR is a photographer and mixed media artist living in Ajman, United Arab Emirates. Completely self-taught, Al Attar's practice seeks to not only document and translate but also methodically research and examine aspects of Emirati ritual, material culture, and geographic orientation that are increasingly elusive in this rapidly globalizing society.
>
> DALE HUDSON is Associate Professor of Film and New Media at New York University Abu Dhabi. He is author of *Vampires, Race, and Transnational Hollywoods* and, with Patricia R. Zimmermann, of *Thinking Through Digital Media: Transnational Environments and Locative Places*.

4

Audible Love

Letter Songs, Vocal Letters, and the Aurality of Love across the Indian Ocean

BINDU MENON

The recent turn toward connections across the Indian Ocean within the larger field of humanities, migration studies, and South Asian history resurrects obsolete media forms, such as audiocassettes, as an archive of migrant life. As archives of migration, visual media have received much scholarly attention recently, but the same cannot be said about the sonic worldmaking of migration.[1] In this chapter, I excavate the traces of aural registers of migrant memory and locate them in the broader history of media infrastructure and senses that enabled exchanges between the present-day nation-states of the Gulf Cooperation Council (GCC) and the Indian state of Kerala, at the southwestern coast of India. By closely reading a specific music genre of audiocassettes and the recording practices for audiocassettes, I link histories of infrastructures and media technologies and metaphysics of format, genres, and auditory practices to bring new insights into the operations of power and pleasure across the Persian Gulf and the Arabian Sea.

To explore such aural registers of migration, I consider the specific audiocassette genre of *Dubaikathu* and the practice of recording private vocal letters. Because my project queries sonic memories, I consider sound texts, in this case recorded music texts, lyrical structures, and other sonic elements. My research also parallels and is colocated with interviews of members of migrant households and migrants from Kerala to the GCC. Taking forward the insights of existing scholarship on media as archives of migration, I attempt a sonically tuned exploration of audio media archives to reveal that the documentation of local expressive aural practices is entangled in processes of migration and in emergent media technologies. This chapter examines audile techniques of letter writing, dwelling on the aural sensory registers and voice. Furthermore, by exploring the place of voice in migrant exchanges, the chapter attempts to theorize the relationship between aurality and migration. This essay pays attention to listening across spaces and sensory perception of mediated voice. In my inquiry then, practices of music making, listening, and aural perceptions appear dispersed across several sites of inscription, such as song genres, vocal letters, and music videos as well as multiple textualities that involve cassette songs, video texts, and television texts.

AUDIOCASSETTES: MIGRATION AND THE SONIC

The audiocassette genre kathupattu (letter songs) became the iconic song genre of migrants from the Malabar coast to the GCC in the 1970s. Drawing from the century-long literary genre in Arabi-Malayalam, the lingua sacra of the Mappilakuslims, the genre of *kathupattu* grew into a transmedia phenomenon through audiocassettes, live recordings, music albums, and television shows that span four decades of migration to the Arabian Peninsula.[2] This transmedia corpus of *kathupattu* calls attention to media textuality's increasingly contingent nature, while situating itself within the specific practices of the converging television and music industries and mobile phone technologies.

This century-old poetic performance tradition—and its recalibration as a predominant genre of affective migrant life—signals its relationship to migration through a specific intersection of media technologies, memory, and cultural practices. Even though the early interest in audiocassettes and stereophony in India was uneven on their introduction in the 1970s, the popularity and use of audiocassettes grew rapidly across Indian vernaculars by the early years of the 1980s. With minimal regulation, cassette culture grew and spread geographically to address a fractured, "local" set of audiences. Heterogenous in their content, audiocassettes presented a rich and variegated soundscape of devotional music, lyrical songs, classical music, folk music, religious sermons, jazz, film music, and voco-centric mimicry, that is, the practice of vocal mimicking of famous personalities, birds, animals, and other natural and mechanical sounds to stage a sonic narrative. This growth in the market for audiocassettes was in part due to the opening of Indian markets for consumer goods. A culture of consumption of media products attended the economic measures implemented after the end of an internal emergency act in 1975, and the associated easing of market regulations led to a greater inflow of media goods into the Indian market.[3] The open markets in the Gulf and East Asia, along with this increased movement of goods into India, made possible the circulation of media goods across the Indian Ocean littoral.

Earlier scholarship on audiocassette culture in the Indian context has been largely limited to the geographic region of northern India, where audiocassettes were analyzed as a novel and syncretic popular technology that challenged and taunted the boundaries of urban / rural, public / private, high culture / low culture that emerged during the 1970s.[4]

Following Peter Manuel's seminal work, much of musicology has focused on folk music and cassette culture in the northern Indian states as well.[5] Given the twin developments of the medial properties of storage and portability of cassettes along with the large-scale mobility of Indian labor outside the nation, it is surprising that audiocassette's widespread aesthetic and social implications have been largely ignored in music, sound, and media studies. Echoing Bruno Latour's words, the audiocassette seems to have been "made invisible by its own success" and masked by its familiarity like many other pervasive technologies.[6] Researchers may also have overlooked the circulation of audiocassettes because of the absence of a framework of diasporic and migration music studies in the humanities until the early 2000s. An exception to this is Tejaswini Niranjana's work on Trinidadian Indian music and its overlapping histories with indentured labor migration, Indian nationalism, and music imaginaries.[7] Identifying gaps in both histories of audio technologies and migration studies will steer us toward a set of relations between audio technologies, acoustic spaces (physical and virtual), listening techniques, scientific and commercial discourses, economic conditions, and reception contexts for migration. Conceived within these sets of relations, this chapter's inquiry centers on audiocassette practices that include speech and music exchanges between Malayalee migrants in the Arabian Gulf and their homes on the Kerala coast, marking a specific interlude between paper-based exchanges of the 1960s and the digital turn in the 1990s toward transoceanic communication through satellite television, internet, and mobile communication systems.

In considering the term *senses*, I draw on two understandings of the meaning: the first is focused on the ear and practices of hearing or listening and the second on machinic senses, thus treating the audiocassette as an apparatus that can both sense and store sound. When conceiving of the audiocassette, the acts of recording and listening—that is, the audiocassette-as-technological object and audiocassette-as-media infrastructure—are brought together. In other words, the audiocassette variously functions as metaphor, object, and practice over the course of this essay. This is a worthwhile exercise in thinking about the audiocassette and its sensorium in the form of a totality that accounts for the material technology, circulation patterns, and medial properties This totality allows us to think through an ecology of listening with respect to audio cassettes, particularly in the context of migration and how it constituted audile techniques.

The term *affect* is mobilized in this essay to hold the two understandings of the senses together and to consequently think of the audiocassette in terms of affect. Affect, here, becomes the set of relations between the human and the machine / technology (audiocassette). The bodies become participants—as both producers and bodies receiving affect. Affect thus spills across these domains, becoming sonic, material processes.[8] The emphasis on the affective becomes crucial for positioning the listener and the migrant as well as the migrant-listener together as a sensuous and affective being.

ELEMENTARY AFFECTS: AUDIO CASSETTES AND THE MACHINE-SENSORY

The audio cassettes in the constellations mapped above are more than media objects and emerge as sensory technological objects. Firstly, given the audio cassette's acts of producing sensory experiences, through the storage, transmission, and amplification of varying sounds (e.g., music, sound effects, static, speech), they mark themselves as participants in the production of sonic sensory experiences and sonic affects. In fact, as I will explain later in the essay, the marking of mood on the audio cassette was precisely an understanding of the audio cassette as sensuous. Secondly, I would like to consider the manner in which most people experience the audio cassettes. The sense-memory of switching on/recording on tape recorders/stereos would often become a physical shorthand when interlocutors remembered the sounds of the audio cassettes. In those gestures, the audio cassettes became not only an object to hear, but also one to touch.

However, the audiocassette was also a sensing body transmitting the flow of the sounds of distant homes or the speech that so many would describe as a "friend" across the ocean. The words *audiocassette* and *friend* were often woven in with each other in media stories about audiocassettes that were manufactured and circulated to bring in geographic location and distant conditions in one swoop. Digging deeper into geography and media technologies, we could trace a long history of thinking about oceanic distances, maritime sea voyages, and connectivity. Despite the development of undersea networks in the early twentieth century, sound and visual bytes were not readily transmissible across the ocean until the 1990s. While early undersea networks and channels were described as "symbol[s] of maritime voyage" by Sterne and Rodgers, which rendered sound through "a masculinist and colonial rhetoric that promotes the bold traversal and technological mastery of turbulent waves and maritime frontiers," in practice their use was limited to sonar research and has only recently been linked to broadcast and communication purposes.[9] The desire for a "liquid media," where the liquid properties of the ocean meet the aerial properties of sound, remained elusive. Into this void, the portable tape recorder stepped, and the analog sound inscribed in audiocassettes engendered new affordances and listening practices in the 1970s. The oil economy of the Gulf region increasingly enabled and disabled the movement of goods, people, and ideas and continues to function as a pivotal node for the circulation of goods. A brief look at the history of audio infrastructure helps locate these relations more specifically.

The circulation of media goods was not channeled merely through the legal routes of migration but mobilized expansively through the speculative economy of smuggling through the sea routes between the port cities of Gulf (Dubai, in particular) and the western Indian Ocean ports. The significance of piracy for Indian media and modernity has been sufficiently theorized from the very early days of audiocassette piracy.[10] Relying on the relatively laissez-faire economy of the United Arab Emirates (UAE) ports, especially Dubai, and the merchant-state nexus in India, the already existing commercial synergies between these port cities grew into smuggling networks in the 1970s. Much like the pirate media ecology that furthered a recycled modernity, the speculative economy of smuggled audio goods enabled a media modernity of novel objects in the 1970s.[11] If we collocate and populate this speculative economy with a history of migrants who inaugurated music shops in the Gulf cities and in their homelands, an infrastructure of labor, goods, and capital emerges across the Indian Ocean.[12] In these ways, the spread of audiocassette culture in the Malabar coast is intrinsically connected to the Gulf. Thus, the movement of the audio goods between the Gulf coast and the Malabar coast help identify the contexts of sensuous, affective relationships between the tape recorder machine, oceanic containments, and media storage.

The broader cultural and social context of audiocassette circulation must be mapped in relation to three elements of the format of audio—temporality, definition, and mobility—which are key in understanding the inscriptions and metaphysics of what constitutes this audio mobility. The notion of time as a continuous linear flow, coupled with the idea that all analog media share this continuity with natural time, suggests a legitimate claim for sonic experience of audiocassettes as contemporaneous with real time. In what follows, I focus on two specific practices in audiocassette culture—one musical and the other speech-oriented—emerging between the Gulf and the Malabar coast.

DUBAI KATHU: VOCAL MASQUERADES AND SONIC AFFECTS

The trade links between the port cities of today's Gulf states and southwestern India can be traced back to the first century CE, evident in cultural and material effects in agricultural practices, food, architecture, clothing, marital relations with Arab merchants, and the spread of the Arab diaspora in the Malabar coast.[13] In the 1960s, the oil-fueled migration to the Gulf states followed the sea trade routes in dhows, motorized sailing vessels, and cargo ships. In the 1970s, following visa regulations instituted to meet the need for labor in the Gulf states, migration traversed more legal channels. Many Mappila Muslims, including technicians, professionals, and both white-collar and blue-collar workers, formed part of this phenomenal labor migration to the post-oil economies of the Gulf. Through migrant mobility, an increased circulation of consumer goods, technologies, novel practices, and tastes merged with a long-standing cosmopolitanism in both the Kerala coast and the Peninsular Gulf region. Following Anna Tsing's call to resist tendencies to theorize all interactions between places as globalization, anthropologists Filippo Osella and Caroline Osella read these novel practices in the Mappila Muslim zones of interaction as *circulation*, that is, a series of highly situated, historically specific collaborations that could create specific cultural forms of capitalism.[14] I read the increased flow of media and other consumer goods along these routes of migration as circulation in this specific sense.

One of the few registers in which the migrant Mappila community expressed social and moral anxieties is the corpus of songs that came to be referred to as *Dubaikathu* or Dubai letters, a poetic subgenre that emerged in the late 1970s. *Dubaikathu* is a derivative of the precolonial Mappila genre of *kathupattu* or letter songs. The song that established the genre was "Dubai Kathu," written and sung by male singer S. A. Jameel, who expressed the plight of Muslim women left behind at home. A marital counselor and a popular writer, Jameel assumed the longing voice of an imagined Muslim woman whose husband is away laboring in Dubai. He was moved by the love and longing of the women he counseled, a group of women eventually known as Gulf wives, a category much explored in literature, popular culture, and migration scholarship.[15] The loneliness and trauma of separation emerges as the single largest issue among Gulf wives.[16] According to demographers, one out of two households in the Malabar region had an emigrant in the Gulf by 1998.[17] Written and performed in 1977, "Dubai Kathu" brings out the intimate fears, loneliness, and social tensions that began to shape their lives. Jameel's visit to Abu

Dhabi in 1978 gave him a closer picture of the migrant husbands' lives in labor camps, and he wrote "Marupadi Kathu" (a response song) that dwells on the reality of being absentee husbands and fathers.

Jameel's poetic assemblage is a direct derivative of the Arabi-Malayalam *kathupattu* or letter-song tradition that has been traced back to the late nineteenth century. In its address, voice, and register, the *Dubaikathu* is closest to the late nineteenth-century letter song "Mariyakuttipattu," in which the imagined protagonist Mariyakutty, the wronged wife of Hassan Kutty, speaks to her husband, now imprisoned by the British for his actions in events related to the Malabar Rebellion. Widely speculated by popular historians to be written by Pulikkottil Hyder, a renowned nineteenth-century Arabi-Malayalam poet, the song addressed the husband and expressed the ordeal of a woman left behind, her life plagued by rumors and ostracization.[18] The epistolary genre, a form of writing present from the early Christian texts onward, appears in diverse cultures and languages. Letter songs primarily served to bridge spatial distance separating communicants and found a place in community imaginaries around distance. The resulting multifunctional nature of letters started absorbing various musical and lyric poetry practices beginning in the nineteenth century. The very flexibility of the epistolary genre allowed for the possibility of such inflections.

As Arafath identifies in his rich cultural history of the letter song tradition, the emergence of *kathupattu* as an audiocassette genre was concomitant with the increasing popularity of Panasonic sound recorders, which dominated the media market in the 1970s.[19] Tape recorders and cassettes acquired a new place in the emotional geography of Mappila migration, sonically connecting husband to wife and father to children across long distances and overriding earlier forms of communication through written letters. Mappila literati composed new songs in the genre of *kathupattukal* that found their way into Mappila homes through performance cultures, orchestra music, and audiocassettes. These songs emerged as the major emotional register through which the *pravasi* (nonresident Malayalee) and their wives negotiated the grim isolation of everyday life.

The question that arises in the context of Jameel's attempts to understand the Gulf wife from the narratives that he encountered is, Who do these songs address? "Dubai Kathu" and "Marupadi Kathu" sketch contrasting political economies of gendered difference where men and women are positioned differently, yet they unify these differences by interpreting them as temporary states that are necessary and in suspension. Through technical mediation and affective musical registers, "Dubai Kathu" and "Marupadi Kathu" sought to resolve marital discord and crisis. And yet, as we see, the songs were unable to resolve tensions by consolidating social structures.

Through its expressions of female desires, the staging of which happened through asking which of the two contracts—the marriage contract or the labor contract—should take priority, "Dubai Kathu" scandalized the public, both in Kerala and among the nonresident Malayalee in the GCC. The dominant narrative of strong marital contracts and harmonious conjugality even at a distance seemed to have suddenly started raising new issues for the community. The anxiety that the songs created among many sections of the Mappila community led to instances where community members were dissuaded from singing them.[20] However, letters and cassettes containing *kathupattu* as referential objects populated the discourse of the figure of the Gulf wife and opened new questions about marital integrity, conjugality, and status within the community. "Dubai Kathu" became an integral part of male social gatherings in the Gulf cities, as reminisced by several Gulf returnees, repeatedly played on public stereo players and listened to collectively.[21] These former migrants express the pain of everyday emotions of longing and separation in the pravasi households and among the labor quarters in the Gulf. Although addressed to the absentee husbands in the Gulf, Arafath suggests "Dubai Kathu" had gathered a larger audience for migrant Malayalee workers and traders in other metropolises of India and elsewhere.[22]

The first rendition of "Dubai Kathu" by Jameel, at a huge gathering of migrant Malayalees in Abu Dhabi in 1978, is reported to have received phenomenal appreciation and led to cathartic expressions of emotion among the audience members.[23] As they listened, it was described that many migrant men behaved as if they were possessed by the protagonist. The song assumes a woman's voice and narrates how her son misses his father and how she would like her husband to perform his fatherly duties—how she feels lost as if in the ocean. She swears her loyalty to her husband but ends on a cautionary note that she is a woman with desires and not an angel. The song ends on a note asking what worth money is if one cannot relish it. In the repartee song, the husband seems shattered, pained, and broken beyond repair, but he accepts that she has needs and her sexual transgression is brought about by his failure to meet them.

The song articulates a restless, fevered passion, with simultaneous expressions of despair, betrayal, and burning anger—an intense and nonconformist feminine anger. The figure of the deviant woman is present in different literary genres—where she is often met with containment, domestication, or in some cases even death. What is remarkable about the figurations of *Dubaikathu* is that the narrative resolutions of the songs do not uphold acceptable social structures. The intense, melodramatic articulation of feminine desire and anger questions the gender norms regarding these very structures. The *marupadikathu*, the song in response, addresses the affective and emotional surplus with the recognition that it can never be accommodated, accepting it in humbled defeat.

The gendered infrastructures of *Dubaikathu and marupadikathu* evade full comprehension within sociological or thematic analysis. Both the songs are sung by male singers and present novel techniques of deploying voice. The genre is for men and by a man; as a conceptual enterprise, women and femininity are conceived as knowable epistemic objects. Jameel's attempt at assuming a woman's voice marks both absence and presence. The vocal masquerade is seen more ubiquitously in Sufi performance traditions and Urdu poetry. In Sufi performance traditions, the search for a wholeness and oneness between the devotee and the saint/ prophet are mediated through devotion. The male devotee rarely assumes the grammatical and lyrical voice of a female in this play of voice.[24] Rather, in search of a nonexistent original wholeness, the male singer presents a woman as the representation of that search, forever excluded from language and subjectivity while always present as its mark.

I envision vocal masquerade as a broad analytical category to help us understand and distinguish the vocal guise that Jameel performed from practices and impersonations in South Asia such as transvestism and crossdressing. The question then arises: Does the concealing of indexical references amount to concealing the illusory bodies? If we were to approach the question of voice through perceptual frames of masquerade and guise, it would be necessary to attune our analysis towards the boundaries between the embodied origins of voices and the illusory, surrogate bodies that voices conjure into existence. If we circle back to where we began, to the beginnings of the *kathupattu* genre in the nineteenth century, we can safely assume a specific kind of acousmatic listening to the distilled voices of bereaved daughters, wives, and mothers. To put it somewhat differently, the closest approximation to the voice masquerade that Jameel performs is one of the vocalic body in ventriloquist performance. Steve Connor proposes that the vocalic body "is the idea—which can take the form of dream, fantasy, ideal, theological doctrine, or hallucination—of a surrogate or secondary body, a projection of a new way of having or being a body, formed and sustained out of the autonomous operations of the voice."[25] The concept of the vocalic body is an invitation to interrogate voice-body relations.

In the audiocassette renditions of *Dubaikathu*, this relationship acquires additional dimensions. In the cassette, the voice appears as embodied and disembodied at the same time. Distinctions between the singing body and the sung voice, between the live and reproduced media, all make the vocalic body rather complex. Due to recording technology, the voice appears beyond the body that produces it. The virtuosity of the male voice, enabled by mimetic procedures of the recording, reinstates the ontology of the singing body. The projected voice, the lyrical grammatic voice of the song, enhances the instrumentality of the surrogate female body, intruding its identity at the same time.

In exploring Iranian cinema's complex tropes of acousmatic voices to subvert censorship regimes, Farshid Kazemi argues that the voice acts as a signifier of desire and becomes a love object in place of the forbidden erotic configurations of bodies.[26] Circumventing indexical references to the female body and yet retaining its erotic configurations, the slippery indexicality of vocal registers that Jameel devises is manifested in a phantom-like yet strangely embodied voice. While we hear a male voice, we listen to the deep interiority of a woman's being, her desire and anger making it a voice that is partially resonant and yet asynchronous with the body. Much like Kazemi's Iranian film subjects, the disembodied voices in both *dubaikathu* and *marupadikathu* subvert the logic of veiling female voices and offer grounds for critiquing the male subject as the privileged site of subjectivity. The critique acquires a more powerful presence in the *marupadikathu* response song, which while fully retaining the indexicality toward a male body and voice, accepts the critique in lyrics, grammar, and voice codes.

The new, electronic sonic register, recalibrated through acoustic devices of tape recorders, stereo players, and cassettes, helped Mappila Muslims reimagine community, space, and household in invigorating ways. In the response song, a community of husbands is imagined as bereaved and worn down by pressures of labor and emotional distress that generate a moral and ethical crisis in the community. The woman's statement that "a woman is no angel" is experienced as a pointed challenge to manliness. The response song ends with the protagonist's desire to regain his manliness, reclaim his son, and return to the *maniyara* (their nuptial chamber).

> A husband ignorant of his wife's needs
> Alas an Idiot! He is the cause of her sins
> Opportunity is the mother of all needs
> The one who gives no solace, is the one who leads idiocy
> Are we not listening? Are we not seeing?

Clearly, as recent scholarship suggests, the conjugal space that Jameel constructs is informed by the new sexual doctrines in the theocratic states of the Gulf, which shadowed the migrant's sensibilities around sexual pleasure and desire.[27] As Arafath deftly maps, the wide availability of pornographic material in both print and visual forms and the new print culture of popular sensational magazines in Malayalam also underwrote these sexual mores.[28] This erotic poetic resonates in the subsequent audio letter songs tradition. In "Dubai Kathu," Jameel's protagonist sings:

> *Madhuvidhu nalukal manassil thalirkkunnu*
> *Madanakkinavukal marodanakkunnu*
> *Malarmani rathrikal manjil kulikkunnu*
> *Maniyarakkattilo madivilikkunnu*
> *Engine janurangum*
> *Kidannalum Engine urakkam varum.*
> [Our Honeymoon days still spring in my heart,

leaving sweet dreams close to my heart
Beautiful nights wrapped in mist
Our nuptial bed still invites me back
How will I sleep?
How can I sleep even if I lie down?
Even when I sleep, honeyed dreams wake me up
And I begin to embrace my pillow.]

Songs here show the poetic voice, the articulated language of a speaking subject, situated between an inherited culture in flux and a particular unconscious, expressed in lyrics as an individual finding or questioning their identity. In the canopy of this transitional form and transnational erotic, we can find metaphors of suffering comingling with joy and inseparable from the joy of desiring. At the same time, suffering becomes associated in the erotic imagination with the inaccessible feminine, both as its cause and its expression. In assuming a woman's speaking voice, using direct address, and drawing on autobiographical references, the *kathupattu* tradition exhibits a much greater tendency to address the lover directly, which is to say that it invents an ideal other with whom the poetic voice identifies to the extent that he achieves a lost wholeness. Across the registers of this mediated desire, we find the ruptures wrought by the force field of migration in Muslim households and family structure.

Kathupattu subsequently grew into a major audiocassette genre incorporating themes of migration, exchanges between sons and daughters with an absent father, and between mothers and sons and sisters and brothers. As the genre grew, a diversity of voices, including women singers, emerged. With the expansion of new formats like video and digital, *kathupattu* has enfolded itself into VHS, DVD, MP3, and televisual and networked spaces of cyberculture, such as video-sharing platforms, mobile phone apps, and social media.[29]

In its derivativeness, *kathupattu* records a moment where the orality of an older Mappila genre meets the aurality of technoscapes, mutating into sonic registers and permeating the otherwise impermeable ocean space. The advent of lyric poetry in the vernacular, we could argue, is a moment that makes explicit the relationship between writing and acquiring subjectivity. The audiocassette has invoked a new sonotope for the performative song culture not only linked to its production process but also its aural dispersion. I borrow the term *sonotope* from Jacob Smith's work on space and acousmatic sound: "The category of the sonotope can describe the 'intrinsic connectedness' of sound and space in shaping performance."[30] The technical matrices of circulation, sound amplification, and the performative charge of the song number have conjured up a novel aural sensorium that heightens the affective charge associated with the genre. Owing to this quality of the sensate, *kathupattu* was appropriated across classes, agendas, and spaces. This enmeshed universe of the sensate and technological affordances was generative of several other practices around audiocassettes. In the context of migration, the audiocassette emerged, and its mutability became the generative template for such practices. Let us now turn in more detail to the ways in which a multiplicity of practices emerged in audiocassettes.

SONIC MIGRATION, TAPED LETTERS, AND THE INTIMACY OF VOICE

Cassettes were also available as blank tapes, which allowed for personalized home recordings of music, whether from the owner's records, music sampling from another audiocassette, or radio broadcasts. Other possibilities that emerged in the domestication of the tape recorder included creating voice letters for family members at a distance, rehearsing lectures, or amateur music performances—and making radio plays.[31]

Distinct from gramophone, radio, and television, the tape recorder was anchored around user creativity and enfolded itself into the lives shaped by migration.[32] Its usefulness is reflected in the words of Hisham, whose father worked in Muscat for more than four decades: "As children we would perform and record everything we knew from nursery rhymes, poems, and dialogues for our father and uncle. That was one of the things that my uncle wanted us to do when he brought the tape recorder in his first visit from Abu Dhabi."[33] These properties spawned a specific mixtape culture in the 1980s.

The home recording function of cassette recorders prompted many Malayalee migrants to use them as an audio messaging system to communicate with family and relatives back home. Although the number of telephone subscriptions increased at an annual rate of about 8 percent, since the 1970s, the penetration levels of media goods in India remained low—about 1.4 per 100 persons in 1997. Telephone infrastructure was largely restricted to urban areas, leaving rural residents dependent on other means for overseas communication. Tapes were relatively cheap, rerecordable, and in many instances provided a solution for those who were unable to read or write letters. Cassettes allowed them to record messages in their own language, permitting their voices to be heard directly and literally. In their specific medium of communication, cassettes could be both public and private. Watching and commenting on photos during family meetings and listening to recordings required all people present to be involved in the shared activity at the same time. Everyone in the room had to be quiet, whereas people had become increasingly used to combining listening to music with other activities.[34] Surviving letter cassettes are quite rare, as many of the cassettes that were intended for older members of the community were recorded over and reused later. Multiple recordings on the same cassette, with the subsequent degradation in audio quality, also meant that many became unlistenable and ruined over time.

Messages were recorded on a variety of tape lengths, some of which allowed thirty minutes of audio to be recorded on each side, and the cassettes were exchanged between families, delivered either by hand in the instance when a family member or a trusted friend would be visiting from the GCC or in rare instances via the postal system.[35] Cassettes would be listened to individually or collectively by the intended receivers, with messages being recorded and returned in a similar way. By the late 1980s, however, wider technological advances in both music distribution and telecommunications made the use of tapes obsolete, and the use of cassettes as a system for message exchanges began to wane. Salaam Kodiyathur, the chief filmmaker of the amateur Malabar home-film genre, says that in his depictions of migrants using and recording vocal letters, he noted that they would often record letters for different family members on different cassettes or on different sides of the same cassette.[36] The replies were in turn often taped and taken back to migrants via friends who returned to the GCC.

Such recorded letters were sometimes intended for individual listening and on other occasions for group listening. They contained intimate messages between couples and messages between parents and their sons or daughters. At times they were recorded in secret with the intention of proving culpability, such as infidelity of wives and domestic abuse, or to be use as evidence; at other times, they were mere domestic chatter on the weather and an unfamiliar climate. The cassette letters all contain deeply human stories and can be considered significant artifacts both as objects and as aural moments in a crucial phase of Malayalee migration to the GCC. They were recorded in the moment and of the moment and provide fascinating sonographic snapshots and unembellished insights into private family spheres shaped by migration in the time of analog media.

These accounts resonate with love, at once ephemeral and portable, and invite us to think about audiocassette technologies and their place in sonic migration. In Merleau-Pontian phenomenology, every fusion with technology involves certain modes of being, ways of knowing, and ways of making the world. The spread of audiocassettes and the immersive ecology of music and speech in migrant worlds through audio interfaces became part of the dynamic arrangement of embodied experience. Corollary to this is a perspective that considers each of these interfaces as medium specific; each in their medium specificity effects a different mode of embodiment and a different mode of working, moving, and playing with the body. Practices of recording songs, speech, letters, poems, and various other performances on cassettes can be read as a simulation—an important form of ludic play. Structured around the idea of an audience, simulation also includes solitary pretending and imagining new worlds. This analogic role of simulation is significant in inculcating and reproducing social habitus for both adults and children.

Apart from the novelty of recording one's own voice, listening to the human voice, its uniqueness, and its texture of intimacy provides a context for understanding the place of sound media in the entangled space of Gulf cities. The thinking of Italian philosopher Adriana Cavarero is intriguing in this regard. Cavarero attributes uniqueness to the human voice and locates this in the sonorous materiality of our voices.[37] Cavarero recognizes three aspects of voice: unique vocality, relationality, and politics. Of these three aspects, the relationality of voice-over speech, as she argues, "includes that each voice implies a person who listens, is destined for the ear of another."[38] This irreducible singularity of voice and the "relation among uniqueness" is "already active in the vocal emission" and communicated along with the semantic content of the exchange.[39] Because of the pervasiveness of this relationality of the vocalic (something she temporally traces back to the vocalic exchange between mother and child), she protests against its lack of acknowledgment in Western philosophical traditions and critiques a privileging of the gaze in Western philosophy.[40] Cavarero elaborates further on the sonority of the relation among uniqueness by linking it to resonance. "Resonance" in her reckoning, signifies the "spontaneous rhythm" of reciprocal communication among unique voices.[41] Cavarero emphasizes that this "uniqueness in resonance" is a mutual convocation of the "plurality of singular voices."[42] More specifically, convocation is not the product of autonomous individuals who are looking to bond with each other. If we consider the inherent relationality that Cavarero attributes to the human voice in the context of auditory practices of migration, we arrive at a genealogy of listening practices that have developed as an intrinsic relationship to migration. Teasing out the uniqueness of voice and vocality in the technologically mediated voice in these recording practices, that which had previously been perceptible only in close physical proximity is finally audible: the voice with its accompanying sonic materiality and semantic fraught-ness, breathing, tongue movement, swallowing—a physical intimacy brought to life, stored, and carried across the ocean.

The voice thus recorded in its surrounding atmospheric elements was electrical and mediated in its aurality yet was unamplified, distinguishing it from the miked and processed voices of broadcast media and voices recorded by other means. The vocality of these letters clung stubbornly to a voice from another space-time, making it sound more *real*. It calibrated new meanings for an innocent pastime and created a sociocultural practice of existential significance.

CIRCUITS OF AURALITY: TELEVISUALITY AND "KATHUPATTU"

In stark contrast to unamplified, taped letters are the aural performances *of Kathupattu* songs on television and video music albums that started making their appearance in the 2000s. The musical genre took on new relevance as a channel of discourse in television series, video music albums, and content for portable devices. This shift can be linked back to the geographical media elements with which we opened this conversation, namely the absence of a connecting medium before the arrival of satellite technology. Recent scholarship on Malayalam satellite television channels in the GCC demonstrates that satellite television technology emerged through complex partnerships and collaborations in the Gulf cities.[43] Beginning in the early years of 2000s, radio stations in UAE cities responded to the migrant living conditions and schedule through targeted programming that echoed migrant concerns, providing a template for television stations to launch. With the expansion of broadcasting infrastructure and live transmissions, *kathupattu* found a new audience, one that spread across the GCC and Kerala. *Kathupattu* songs became an important part of music reality television shows derived from the *mappilapattu* tradition, such as *Patturumal* on Kairali TV, *Pathinnalam Raavu* (Fourteenth night) on Media One TV (2013–2017), *Kutty Patturumal* (Small silk scarf) on Kairali TV (2016–2018) all of which ran for several seasons. The televisuality of such aural performances yoked together Mappila live-performance cultures with both television and music. I use the term *aural performance* to invoke both hearing and seeing to highlight the ways in which visual tracks might alter sonic meanings and vice versa. In the televisual texts of *kathupattu*, the sonorous seems to manifest a particular form of spectacle in its acoustics. Far from subsuming music under the visual, these aural performances reversed it by foregrounding how the affective as well as the visual properties of popular music augment or in some cases dictate its television incarnation, aesthetics, conventions, and practices.

ACKNOWLEDGMENTS

I am grateful to my editors Alia Yunis and Dale Hudson for their thoughtful comments and patient shepherding. Through their generous sharing of thoughts and experiences, my respondents provided me with great insights into the sonic world-making process. This chapter wouldn't have been able to travel in the various directions it took without Ira Bhaskar's erudite feedback on poetry and performance in Islamicate contexts, and I am grateful for her generosity. Vebhuti Duggal as always points me toward novel readings in the world of sound studies. I would like to thank members of the MEMIC collective , particularly Terri Ginsburg, Iman Hamam and Wissam Mouwad for their comments. I have also benefited from the comments by the anonymous reviewers, which were helpful in further developing some of the ideas in this chapter.

> BINDU MENON is Associate Professor of Media Studies at Azim Premji University. Her work on early cinema, migrant media cultures, and music culture has been published in peer-reviewed journals such as *Biography, Bioscope,* and *South Asian Popular Culture* among others and she is coeditor of *Film Studies: An Introduction* (Worldview Books, 2022). Besides her academic writing she also contributes to public-facing media in her native language of Malayalam and in English and serves on the editorial board of *Studies in South Asian Film and Media* (Intellect Journals). She is a founding member of MEMIC (Middle Eastern Moving Image Collective). She can be reached at bindu.menon@apu.edu.in.

NOTES

1. See Bindu Menon and T. T. Sreekumar, "'One More Dirham': Migration, Emotional Politics and Religion in the Home Films of Kerala," *Migration, Mobility, & Displacement* 2, no. 2 (2016): 4–23; Mohamed Shafeeq Karinkurayil, "The Days of Plenty: Images of First-generation Malayali Migrants in the Arabian Gulf," *South Asian Diaspora* 13, no.1 (2020): 1–14. An exception to these can be found in P. K. Yasser Arafath, "Cassetted Emotions: Intimate Songs and Marital Conflicts in the Age of Pravasi (1970–1990)," in *Cultural Histories of India: Subaltern Spaces, Peripheral Genres, and Alternate Historiography*, ed. Rita Banerjee (New York: Routledge, 2020), 135–148. Also see Irene Ann Promodh, "FM Radio and the Malayali Diaspora in Qatar: At Home Overseas," *Journal of Ethnic and Migration Studies* 47, no. 9 (2021): 1957–1975.

2. Arabi-Malayalam is a system of writing and a transliteral scriptural literary tradition that can be traced back to the early decades of Islam in the Malabar coast in the ninth century. For an insightful history of the Arabi-Malayalam tradition, see P. K. Yasser Arafath, "Polyglossic Malabar: Arabi-Malayalam and the Muhiyuddinmala in the Age of Transition (1600s–1750s)," *Journal of the Royal Asiatic Society* 30, no. 3 (2020): 517–539.

3. Robin Jeffrey, *India's Newspaper Revolution: Capitalism, Politics, and the Indian-Language Press, 1977–1999* (New York: Palgrave Macmillan, 2003).

4. Andrew B. Alter, "Negotiating Identity in the Garhwali Popular Cassette Indus-

try," *South Asia: Journal of South Asian Studies* 21, no. 1 (1998): 109–122; Paul D. Greene, "Authoring the Folk: The Crafting of a Rural Popular Music in South India," *Journal of Intercultural Studies* 22, no. 2 (2001): 161–172; Stefan Fiol, "From Folk to Popular and Back: Musical Feedback between Studio Recordings and Festival Dance-songs in Uttarakhand, North India," *Asian Music* 42, no. 1 (2011): 24–53.

5. Peter Manuel, *Cassette Culture: Popular Music and Technology in North India* (Chicago: University of Chicago Press, 1993); Mack Hagood, *Hush: Media and Sonic Self-control* (Durham, NC: Duke University Press, 2019).

6. Bruno Latour, *Pandora's Hope: Essays on the Reality of Science Studies* (Cambridge, MA: Harvard University Press, 1999), 304.

7. Tejaswini Niranjana, *Mobilizing India: Women, Music, and Migration between India and Trinidad* (Durham, NC: Duke University Press, 2006).

8. Ben Anderson, *Encountering Affect: Capacities, Apparatuses, Conditions* (New York: Routledge, 2017). Vebhuti Duggal, "Aural Infrastructures in Late Colonial India: Structuring Listening Anew?." paper presented at Digital India and State Making virtual workshop at the Centre for the Advance Study of India, University of Pennsylvania, June 26–29, 2022.

9. For an elaborate discussion on the poetics of signaling and sound media, see Jonathan Sterne and Tara Rodgers, "The Poetics of Signal Processing," *Differences* 22, nos. 2–3 (2011): 31–53.

10. Manuel, *Cassette Culture*; Ravi Sundaram, *Pirate Modernity: Delhi's Media Urbanism* (London: Routledge, 2009).

11. Sundaram, *Pirate Modernity*.

12. Interview with Abdul Manaf, shop manager, NAAZ videos, February 17, 2020, Doha. Most of the music shops in the 1970s, as reports from the GCC suggest, were either started or managed by immigrants of Indian, Iranian, and Pakistani origins. See https://youtu.be/xKbCoXz7wfY?t=3.

13. M. H. Ilias, "Malayalee Migrants and Translocal Kerala Politics in the Gulf: Reconceptualising the 'Political,'" in *Diasporas of the Modern Middle East: Contextualizing the Modern Middle Eastern Diaspora*, ed. Anthony Gorman and Sossie Kasbarian (Edinburgh: Edinburgh University Press, 2015), 303–337.

14. Anna Tsing, "The Global Situation," *Cultural Anthropology* 15, no. 3 (2000): 327–360; Filippo Osella and Caroline Osella, "'I Am Gulf': The Production of Cosmopolitanism in Kozhikode, Kerala, India," in *Struggling with History: Islam and Cosmopolitanism in the Western Indian Ocean*, ed. Edward Simpson and Kai Kresse (London: Hurst, 2007).

15. Anna Lindberg, "Islamisation, Modernisation, or Globalisation? Changed Gender Relations among South Indian Muslims," *South Asia: Journal of South Asian Studies* 32, no. 1 (2009): 86–109.

16. Leela Gulati, "Male Migration to Middle East and the Impact on the Family: Some Evidence from Kerala," *Economic and Political Weekly* 18 (1983): 2217–2226.

17. Kunniparampil Curien Zachariah, Elangikal Thomas Mathew, and S. Irudaya Rajan, "Social, Economic and Demographic Consequences of Migration on Kerala," *International Migration* 39, no. 2 (2001): 4–71.

18. For a recent rendition of the song and its history watch https://youtu.be/-uZmhHsT4EQ-. Burmapattu (Burma Song), was the first postcolonial Muslim letter song written by a Mappila. The protagonist of the song conveys how his fortunes were underwritten

by migration to Singapore and how he was waylaid by a woman who solicited him in the streets of Burma. See Arafath, "Cassetted Emotions," 140.

19. Arafath, "Cassetted Emotions," 142.

20. Vilayil Fazila, who was a prominent singer of Mappila song traditions, started singing kathupattukal later in the 1980s. She was troubled by a group of male audience members for singing one of the kathupattus in Kallachi, a small town with substantial pravasi families in the district of Calicut in the early 1990s. Formerly named Valsala, the singer later converted to Islam and changed her name to Vilayil Fazila. See Arafath, "Cassetted Emotions," 138.

21. Interview with Sajith, a long-term resident of Doha, has worked closely with the Video Centre, an iconic Doha Thalassery.

22. Arafath, "Cassetted Emotions," 139.

23. Arafath, "Cassetted Emotions," 139.

24. Christoper Petievich, "When Men Speak as Women: Vocal Masquerade in Indo-Muslim Poetry by Carla Petievich," *Modern Language Review* 105, no. 2 (2010): 513–514. For a reading of desire and Ira Bhaskar, "Desire, Deviancy, and Defiance in Bombay Cinema (1930s–1950s)," in *"Bad" Women of Bombay Films: Studies in Desire and Anxiety*, ed. Saswati Sengupta, Shampa Roy, and Sharmila Purkayastha (New York: Palgrave Macmillan, 2019), 27–44.

25. Steven Connor, *Dumbstruck: A Cultural History of Ventriloquism* (Oxford: Oxford University Press, 2000), 80.

26. Farshid Kazemi, "The Object-Voice: The Acousmatic Voice in the New Iranian Cinema," *Camera Obscura: Feminism, Culture, and Media Studies* 33, no. 1 (2018): 57–81.

27. S. A. Jameel interview on Jeevan TV, YouTube, https://youtu.be/2pQ8komlXUo.

28. Arafath, "Cassetted Emotions," 144.

29. For a video iteration of "Dubai Kathu," see this video version of Dubai Kathu: https://youtu.be/iMFPWCi_ixU.

30. Jacob Smith, *Vocal Tracks: Performance and Sound Media* (Berkeley: University of California Press, 2008), 245.

31. Karin Bijsterveld, "'What Do I Do with My Tape Recorder . . . ?': Sound Hunting and the Sounds of Everyday Dutch Life in the 1950s and 1960s," *Historical Journal of Film, Radio and Television* 24, no. 4 (2004): 613–634.

32. The practice of recording vocal letters seem to have a history as old as sound recording technology. Anthropologist Panopoulos analyzes nineteen 78 rpm records by a Greek migrant in the United States in the late 1950s. For a detailed discussion, see P. Panopoulos, "Vocal Letters: A Migrant's Family Records from the 1950s and the Phonographic Production and Reproduction of Memory," *Entanglements* 1, no. 2 (2018): 30–51.

33. Interview with Prabhashini, December 17, 2021, Pattambi, Kerala.

34. Interview with Shamsudden Kodungaoor, April 17, 2021, Thrissur, Kerala.

35. The lore is that every returnee from the GCC would start a circuitous journey through the hinterlands of the place distributing gifts, knick-knacks, letters, and cassettes and similarly collecting things before their return.

36. Interview with Salaam Kodiyathoor, December 21, 2021, Malappuram, Kerala. The intermedial reference to audiocassettes, listening to Dubai Kathu and vocal letters form an important trope of migrant narratives in both mainstream and amateur Malayalam films.

37. Adriana Cavarero, *For More than One Voice: Toward a Philosophy of Vocal Expression* (Stanford, CA: Stanford University Press, 2005).
38. Cavarero, *For More than One Voice*, 7.
39. Cavarero, *For More than One Voice*, 5, 16.
40. Cavarero, *For More than One Voice*, 78, 181–182.
41. Cavarero, *For More than One Voice*, 199.
42. Cavarero, *For More than One Voice*, 199, 179.
43. Darshana Sreedhar Mini, "Satellites of Belonging: Televisual Infrastructures and the Gulf-Malayali," *Middle East Journal of Culture and Communication* 14, nos. 1–2 (2021): 81–111.

AUDIOVISUAL REFERENCES

Al Malabari. "Mariyakkutty Pattu," Pattinte Katha, episode 1, YouTube, July 2020. Accessed August 12, 2020. https://youtu.be/-uZmhHsT4EQ-.

Aluva, Nasimudheen. "Dubai Kath Original." YouTube, December 3, 2014. Accessed August 12, 2020. https://youtu.be/iMFPWCi_ixU.

Aluva, Nasimudheen. "Dubai Kath Original Marupadi S. A. Jameel." YouTube, December 5, 2014. Accessed August 12, 2020. https://youtu.be/cGYzoymg_OU.

Malappuram Live. "S A Jameel Story." YouTube, September 9, 2015. Accessed October 27, 2021. https://youtu.be/2pQ8komlXUo.

Musiland Audios Jukebox. "Dubai Kathupattukal: Mappila Pattukal Old Is Gold." YouTube, February 23, 2017. Accessed August 12, 2020. https://youtu.be/oAVGM4JnFdk.

Thasleem, T. P. "Dubai Kathu Pattu by SA Jameel." YouTube, November 9, 2009. Accessed August 12, 2020. https://youtu.be/44UDKYKKUbA.

5

Ultimate Slaves in the Dead Zone
Blackness in Iranian Sacred Defense Cinema

PARISA VAZIRI

The spate of Iranian war-themed films known as "sacred defense" cinema, or *sinamā-yi difā'-yi muqadas*, coincided with the theory of an enigmatic spiritual force binding cinema and war.[1] But charged with politically localized interpretations of the Iran-Iraq War, or the "*first* First Gulf War," and wholly undiscovered by international film circuits, sacred defense is a peculiarly arcane genre; being insular, it polices its own abstractness.[2] If domestic critics and audiences both abhor and admire iterations of this genre for, respectively, its didacticism and cinematographic inventiveness, it is perhaps in part because of this masterful homiletic control over abstraction. Unlike the internationally appreciated Iranian art film, sacred defense films bring a literalness to the Iran-Iraq conflict that aesthetic gestures seem unable to universalize. Thus, a characterological satire of the famous art house filmmaker Abbas Kiarostami in Ebrahim Hatami-Kia's *The Glass Agency* (*Azhans-i Shīshah-yī*, 1989) derides Iranian art cinema for its impotence, its incapacity to defend its own abstract themes from the hieratic propulsion of globalized film-festival circuits.

In a genre that lays such a defensive claim to the future of its own meanings, it may seem futile to seek anything other than ideologically circumscribed, coercive politics of war: certainly, critics have yet to locate much else.[3] Yet, despite the realist focus on war documentation, the topoi of trauma that characterize this Iranian film genre (and its kinship with Iraqi postwar literature) maintain sacred defense films' openness to occulted scenes of meaning.[4] Committed to proving "the presence of the divine in national life" by representing military death as martyrdom, sacred defense films often romanticize the Iran-Iraq War by conflating it with a spiritual quest for self-fulfillment and union with God, or, in its second phase, sacred defense narrates everyday disenchantment following the war's failure to live up to expectations of national salvation and pride.[5] Yet even this simplistic plot taxonomy does not account for the ways in which the formal techniques of sacred defense defy predictable meaning. Pyrotechnic nightmares, warped speed, diffracted sound—their cinematic enigmas lie, like trauma itself, protected from the closure of meaning and beyond the realm of fully comprehensible politics.

In this chapter, I argue that two of the most celebrated sacred defense genre films, Mohsen Makhmalbaf's 1989 *Marriage of the Blessed* (*Arūsī-yi Khūbān*) and Ebrahim Hatami-Kia's 1998 *The Glass Agency* (*Āzhāns-i Shīshah-yī*), draw on figures of blackness to articulate the suffering of the disillusioned Iranian war veteran. In being *about* war, sacred defense films, however obliquely and nonthematically, also evoke and encode the history of military slavery in Southwest Asia. Through close readings of these two films, I suggest that cinematic technology, in concert with sacred defense style, gathers together two unlikely and seemingly unrelated themes: blackness and military history in Southwest Asia. But the sacred defense style, manifested as repetition, acceleration, deceleration, and fragmentation of the image, also suggests the troubled coherence of what it assembles into form. In the second part of the chapter, I provide an overview of why military slavery in Southwest Asia itself contributes to the troubled coherence of Indian Ocean slavery and, in particular, of its impenetrable legacies of racialization. If blackness registers a destabilization of meaning in Makhmalbaf's and Hatami-Kia's films, it is because blackness itself lacks coherence, stable intelligibility, and conquerable meaning in the context of Southwest Asia. And thus, like the wartime traumas it mediates through cinema, blackness recurs, articulating what we could call its own inassimilability through enigmatic modes of repetition.

FAMISHED AFRICA IN *MARRIAGE OF THE BLESSED*

Mohsen Makhmalbaf's *Marriage of the Blessed* opens amid the empty fluorescent hallway of a hospital ward. Squeaking wheels on linoleum confuse settings; the noise of an agentless moving cart and its clinking metal objects sound like a battle scene. Moments later the cart arrives at a luminescent, white-walled room where hysterical war veterans pantomime defense strategies, and the camera portrays their reminiscences with cuts to the front line: a desert explodes into clouds of red smoke; planes glide overhead like life-sized bullets. The protagonist, Hājī Pākdil (Hājī), lies supine and lifeless as the doctor injects his vein. A zoom on his glazed pupils cuts to Hājī fallen on the battlefield. Wounded, he clutches his comrade's arm tenderly to his face. The camera's pan left dismembers the severed arm from a blood-soaked torso.

In *Marriage*, traumatic recollection borders on the visually and sonically absurd and defines the film's recurring trope. Convulsive and obsessive memory proxies damaged postwar subjectivity that (unlike the broad-stroke characterizations Gilles Deleuze observes in neorealism's civilians) remain soldered to the soldier's experience.[6] Importantly, this destroyed psychic integrity that is manifested by film form is also an expression of dishonor and decapitated masculinity. Hājī returns to Tehran from the war to marry his fiancée, Mehri, a wealthy Muslim merchant's daughter. But his physical and psychological deterioration arouses the skepticism and derision of Mehri's family, who tries to annul the arrangement. Hājī's cool welcome mirrors the political and ideological shifts produced by the end of the Iran-Iraq War, Ayatollah Khomeini's death, and Hashemi Rafsanji's election in 1989; the wartime ideals so aggressively promoted by the Islamic Republic over the past decade swiftly dissolved in favor of new prescriptions for the mutilated *jānbāzān*—the hundreds of thousands of war veterans returning home from the front lines.[7] The sacred defense tropes of now outdated revolutionary values (honor, martyrdom, asceticism) dissipated with Khomeini's death, replaced by demands for coerced joy, economic prosperity, and general forgetting of the destruction and wreckage caused by the war.

On his first night home from the hospital ward, Mehri seeds pomegranates in the kitchen, while Hājī wilts in a dark corner of her parents' mansion in a wheelchair. A close-up shows Hājī's numbed gaze framed by sweat beads. Mehri's brother Mamali handles a flapping white dove. Mehri walks toward Hājī with her tray of fruit. Her figure disappears before reaching the foreground, where the lit foyer opens onto the larger darkened room. The camera cuts to a close-up of Hājī's face as he watches her. His half-closed eyes shift as he strains to comprehend her disappearance. The camera cuts back to Mehri at her starting point, again she walks toward Hājī and disappears midstride, and Mamali leans toward the doorway with his flapping bird. This scene, repeated three times, culminates with Mehri's fourth progression, now in slow motion. Mamali releases the panicked dove just as Mehri steps through the doorway and flings her tray into the air, surprised by the flapping bird, as pomegranate kernels fly through the room and drown the floor in red juice. In place of the fruit bursting in the air, we see a fire explosion on the field.

Repeated actions and manipulated speed suggest that cinematically, traumatic recollection iterates an indecision about visual potency and the impotence of the image. For it is through the camera's chimeric visualizations that the viewer participates in casting a postwar world whose dystopic qualities adhere to disappearing, illusory referents. Hoping to revive and stabilize Hājī's memory, Mehri wheels him into a small darkroom, where old photographs adorn the walls. (Before fighting in the war, Hājī worked as a photographer in a low-rent studio.) When she begins reeling camera footage on the projector, images of a younger, ideologically pert Hājī in a classroom suddenly morph into documentary footage of anonymous, starving African children. Mehri turns off the projector and says, "These images aren't good for you anymore." Shaken from his somnambulant state, Hājī turns the projector back on and continues to stare at the footage. A mother in tattered clothes crawls on the ground with her infant lying on her back. A half-dead child with bulging eyes stares listlessly into the camera as an off-screen figure holds a cup of milk to his immobile lips. Two scenes in particular seem to adhere to Hājī's—and the viewer's—memory, reappearing later in the film. One image is of a man marking the foreheads of hungry Ethiopians with a cross; another is of an

African mother seating her paralyzed, skeletal child on the dirt ground. The image of the mother Hājī will reimagine at his wedding, when during the celebration a mother lifts her child up from the ground; the former image he will confuse with a memory of being marked with his comrades during the war.

The timeless racial trope of Africa as "total confusion" and the connected spectacular images of starving, almost inhuman black bodies offer, on one level, Hājī's posttraumatic stress disorder a displaced identification.[8] Black suffering, and its representation, is a way to come to terms with the traumatic reality of the war. "This is from before the revolution," Hājī comments, circumventing Mehri's question about when to set their marriage date. "They're starving. They're starving," Hājī sobs. Dark circles coalesce under his squinting eyes. The projector illumines his bloodless face as he moans and swivels back and forth. The frame zooms gradually in on Hājī, while the camera begins to spin on its axis, mimicking the dizzying optical point of view from Hājī's out-of-control wheelchair. The extradiagetic horror-infused refrain of the popular folk wedding song "Mūbārak Bād" returns. Though unidentified in the film, Hājī's claim that the footage refers to a period before the Iranian Revolution (1979) suggests that the images Hājī witnesses and incorporates belong to the 1973 Ethiopian famine.

In the darkroom, Africa metaphorizes a rupture in memory. This rupture repeats itself throughout the film, a spell enacted by the camera's transgression of the rules of continuity editing. In its repetition, this vertigo suggests the *inassimilable*, for what repeats itself in trauma is not an original event but a failure of experience and an impossibility of pure reference. Blackness evokes a quality of *inassimilability* that destabilizes the event of the Iran-Iraq War, such that the war's meaning is no longer contained by what is known—*or could be known*—about it but rather by what has been foreclosed to any actual experience in the past. In their complaints to Iran's Ministry of Culture about the impossibility of war films, war veterans seemed to affirm this psychoanalytic take on repetition. For those who had come back from the front lines, no visual representation could capture an event which, as a spiritual manifestation, lacks material reference and lives at odds with signification.[9] Ironically,

FIGURE 5.1

Still from *Arūsī-yi Khūbān / Marriage of the Blessed* (Iran, 1989; Mohsen Makhmalbaf).

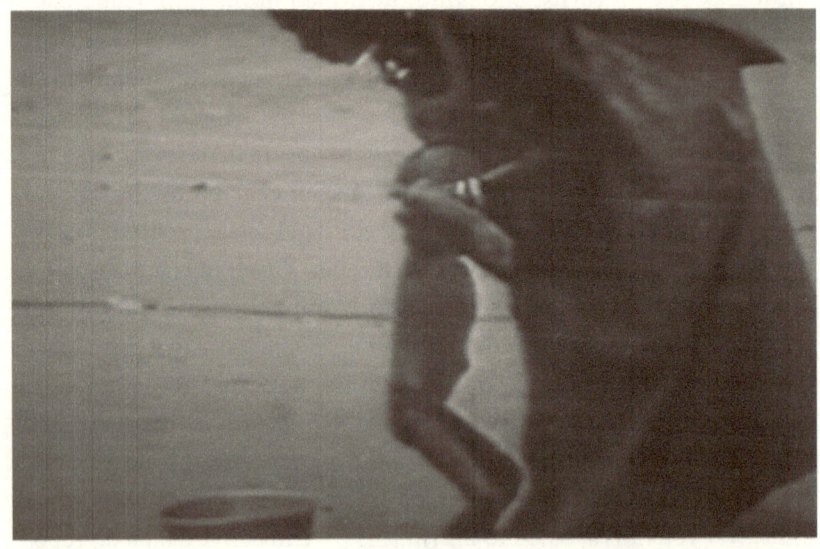

FIGURE 5.2

Still from *Arūsī-yi Khūbān / Marriage of the Blessed* (Iran, 1989; Mohsen Makhmalbaf).

documentary film, the institutionally supported and privileged genre for representing the war in the first years of the Iran-Iraq conflict, was deemed inadequate to the task of authentic documentation. Precisely such concern about the possibilities and limitations of reference propelled the sacred defense genre into its prime.[10]

A stimulant of visceral, paroxysmal attack, the footage of starving African children activates in Hājī a recollection without referent, wherein the dynamic between inside and outside supersedes the content: the simple essence or "is-ness" of the visible image.[11] Memories substituted by the camera's prosthetic, filmic vision both belong and do not belong to Hājī. The film's initial, impersonal shot in the white hospital corridor emphasizes this point as a guiding principle of interpretation, while the scene in the darkroom revisits its thesis. The simultaneous "consciousness of experience" and "experience of consciousness" submitted by the doubled act of perception and expression (recording and projecting) are thematized, put on display in the darkroom scene, and reminding the viewer not only what it means to be watching moving images but, more pressingly, how a film about trauma is always already in its form and content a meditation on history and historical experience.[12]

Makhmalbaf's film refrains from tightly binding images of the war with point-of-view shots that would unambiguously position such images as the optical contents of Hājī's memory. But in the darkroom scene, Makhmalbaf's camera nevertheless appears to anticipate the conflation of the traumatized war veteran with the black body. This is conveyed most clearly by Hājī's visceral reaction to the images and the particular image of marked foreheads that he recalls as his own memory. At the same time, what is collapsed in this very identification recurs throughout the film, is repeated, and leaks from identification's failure.

BLACKFACE AS DISINTEGRATION IN *THE GLASS AGENCY*

Makhmalbaf's film exemplifies the shift from a first phase of ideologically naïve sacred defense films celebrating death as martyrdom to a second, more internally fraught phase of critical reflection on the sobering consequences of the war.¹³ In Hatami-Kia's film, another *basījī* war veteran, Hājī Kāzim, havocs a travel agency in a symbolic political protest against Iranian society's new state-sanctioned embrace of capitalist prosperity and degraded respect for Iran-Iraq veterans. When his former comrade Abbas comes to Tehran on the eve of Nowruz seeking medical help for limb numbness, Kāzim takes Abbas to a doctor who informs them of itinerant shrapnel shifting fatally close to Abbas's jugular vein. Abbas's survival depends on traveling to London for surgery—a trip neither can afford. As Kāzim pleads with a travel agent in the Cactus Travel Agency to keep their tickets on hold as they await veteran government aid to pay for the flight, another Hājī in blackface, Hājī Fīrūz, enters the agency in search of drinking water. Hājī Fīrūz is a black-faced jesterlike figure who prowls the streets during the Persian New Year, warbling traditional jovial tunes and proverbs that gesture toward a slave origin: *Arbāb-i ḳudam salām-ū ʿalaykum, Arbāb-i ḳudam sar-i tū bālā kun!* ("Ma masta, hello! Ma masta, lift ya head up!"). (The grammatical and phonetic distortions that characterize Hājī Fīrūz's language make translating his speech a challenge; these distortions are also, in addition to his blackened face, what mark his blackness as well as his—albeit controversial—status as slave.)¹⁴ Before arriving at the agency, Kāzim briefly notices the Hājī Fīrūz character sitting behind a car in the alleyway but not yet blackened with makeup.

Profound border insecurity, one of Saddam Hussein's primary reasons for attacking Iran in 1980, evokes a mythic anxiety between Iranian and Iraqi rulers, one that long precedes Iraq's transformation from an Ottoman territory into a state in 1921. Iran's perceptual claim to Mesopotamia, or *Iraq-i Arab*, stems from the region's geospiritual significance to Shi'ism, purposefully reanimated in language used on both sides of the war to describe military attack strategies. Reminiscing about the front lines with Abbas Hāj Kāzim refers numerous times to Karbala Five, one of the most important offensives the Iranians launched against Iraq (also known as the Siege of Basra). This citation of the celebrated seventh-century battle between Imam Husayn and the Umayyads, celebrated annually by Shi'is in the processions known as 'Ashura in the month of Muharram, also reactivates one of the primary schisms between Shi'i Iranians and Sunni Arab neighbors, narrating the war in the rhetorical terms of an originary religious tension that has for centuries undergirded Iranian national difference. Karbala in modern-day Iraq is the geographical and "emotional core" of Iranian Shi'ism.[15] Indeed, anxious about the sizable Shi'i population in Iraq, Saddam Hussein, like the leaders of multiple regimes before his, sought to manage this difference by suppressing the potential for Iraqi sympathy for Iranians and expelling Iraqis of Iranian descent.[16]

Reflecting the Islamic Republic's propagandist efforts, *The Glass Agency*'s Karbala citation reanimates the fraught intimacy between Iran and Iraq, positing a charged temporality that is doubly expressed by film form. The editing techniques central to the film's pivotal moments formulate a diachronicity that, like the structure of trauma that it reflects, challenges the simple logic of chronology. Reservoirs of virtual traces, filmic cuts rearrange time in unrecognizable, unforeseeable ways.[17] As other commentators note, the violent, hyperbolically stylized montage sequence following Kāzim's rejection at the travel agency departs from action genre conventions, appearing to articulate a "new film language" resonant with the unique aura of sacred defense motifs. The "breathtaking rhythm" and "choralesque" sound in *The Glass Agency*'s heist montage suggest a "higher or alternate consciousness" expressed in a similar way by *Marriage of the Blessed*'s temporally manipulated shots (sped up, slowed down) and mutated folk-song soundtrack.[18]

If Iran-Iraq War rhetoric overlays multiple, connected, but disjointed histories of territorial and spiritual conflict, so too does the sacred defense montage, by reflecting this symbolic apparatus, suggest unlikely potentialities of experience. In this sense, sacred defense style is an analog for a historical time that cannot be properly represented by the normative, chronological temporality of history. In the heist montage that marks the early climax of Hatami-Kia's film, a glass window shatters, replicating the spiny kaleidoscopic patterns of breaking ice. Each subsequent tracking shot in the montage is slowed, shifting between crisp and blurred movement, as if to question the certainty of the visible, the time of action, the relation between before and after, as well as the distinction between significant and insignificant details. One shot focuses on Hājī Fīrūz lunging forward in slow motion with his tambourine in midair, as if moving toward another dimension, blurring into a nondescript frame of color.

FIGURE 5.3

Still from *Azhans-i Shīshah-yī / The Glass Agency*
(Iran, 1989; dir. Ebrahim Hatami-Kia).

FIGURE 5.4

Still from *Azhans-i Shīshah-yī / The Glass Agency*
(Iran, 1989; dir. Ebrahim Hatami-Kia).

Karbala Five repeats rhetorically the ambiguous conjoining of the time of the present and the time of the past. During the war, early Islamic citations such as these were intended to evoke prefabricated, uncontestable meanings that would in theory be perfectly legible and unambiguous to both Iranians and Iraqis. By contrast, the blurred movement and manipulated speed in *The Glass Agency*'s montage sequence retracts legibility, challenging the retrospective significance of these historical citations as it probes the viewer's assumptions about the relation between the image, memory, and history. Hājī Fīrūz's intrusion into the montage shapes a resistance to the usual and unquestioned significations of historical and religious eventuality. The language of martyrdom and honor imbued in the signifier "Karbala" charges the military operation of the Siege of Basra with spiritual significance. But from the standpoint of the slave that is evoked by Hājī Fīrūz's intrusion, Basra accumulates historical meanings incompatible with a normative, heroic Shi'a narrative. In the sixteenth century the Iranian Safavid and Turkic Ottoman empires fought over Basra, one of the most significant Persian Gulf ports and the Ottomans' only channel to the Indian Ocean. As an important stopover for the hajj sojourn to Mecca, Basra also housed a vibrant slave market, from which slavers trafficked captives through southern Mesopotamia and eastern Syria.[19] Situated opposite Basra at the junction between the Tigris and Euphrates, Khorramshahr (formerly, Muhammara), another important geographical site of the Iran-Iraq War, also played an important role as a slave depot.[20]

The history of Indian Ocean slave trading in Southwest Asia places Hājī Fīrūz—the contemporary sign that mocks the figure of the slave through an aberrant blackness—at odds with the possibility of fidelity or belonging to either side of the war. Bereft of allies and of relation, the black-faced figure empties the territorial conflict and fills it with a different kind of antagonism. He also opens up the possibility of a perspective that is immanent, but not present, to the scene.

Because it is shared among three characters within the comparative frame produced by these two famous sacred defense films, hājī—a common term of respect for Muslims who have fulfilled their religious pilgrimage to Mecca—bears a particular weight. The honorific "hājī" crafts an unthought similitude between Makhmalbaf's Hājī Pākdil, Hatami-Kia's

Hājī Kāzim, and Hājī Fīrūz. In addition to its more famous connotation as a holy shrine for Muslims, Mecca in Saudi Arabia, like Basra in modern-day Iraq and Khorramshahr in modern-day Iran, was historically a major West Asian slave market and one of the locations where slave smuggling persisted longest.[21] Acknowledging fulfillment of an important religious pillar, hājī is a ubiquitous (if mundane and overused) term of respect and honor. The narratives of *Marriage of the Blessed* and *The Glass Agency* lament that Iranian society has lost such respect for the self-sacrificing basīj. The deserved honor persists only in the irony of an exploited title. "You keep calling me hājī, but you know I've never been to Mecca," Kāzim tells Abbas. Abbas responds that every soldier who fought in the battle of Khaybar deserves the respect of a hājī. (Like Karbala Five, Khaybar, another important battle in the Iran-Iraq War refers to the seventh-century battle at Khaybar between Muslims and Jews.) If hājī enshrines the honor of the one who has made the pilgrimage to Mecca for Hājī Kāzim and Hājī Pākdil, for Hājī Fīrūz, the name marks the dishonor of the one whose pilgrimage originates in the coercion and violence of enslavement—dying to become a surrogate for the master (slave) rather than dying to become a surrogate for God (martyr; *shahīd*).[22] Hājī Fīrūz's farcical blackness holds the dishonor of enslavement, doubly reiterated by his name. The dynamic of honor and dishonor that colors the master-slave relation produced by the figure of Hājī Fīrūz repeats to infinity the commutation of death for the slave, a commutation that is remembered and symbolized, however falsely, as black.

The Glass Agency's Hājī Fīrūz is a caricature of a caricature. A quasi-mythological, burlesque figure, historians concoct sinuous genealogies to explain his presence. Nationalists defend Persian blackface practices like Hājī Fīrūz by recourse to apocryphal genealogies, connecting Hājī Fīrūz's blackface to ancient Sumerian rituals.[23] His blackness, as black*face*, is incoherent; this is primarily because it is perverse, derisive, and false. And also because it is justified by recourse to lineages that flout the history of racial blackness in favor of the mythological. Meanwhile, scenes like the one in the travel agency's managerial office, where Hājī Fīrūz seems to impel Hājī Kāzim's dramatic actions, express Hājī Fīrūz's paradoxically finespun yet superficial centrality to *The Glass Agency*'s plot. As if designed to evade discovery, the blackened figure blurs the distinction between signifying and meaningless details in the film while remaining illegible, clothed by winding logics. *The Glass Agency*'s atypical, muscular action-based plot obscures Hājī Fīrūz's accessory presence. Like the life-sized cutouts of airplane stewards populating the travel agency's floor tiles, he is a prop, incidental and ornamental to the film, yet conspicuous and strangely implicated in the major turning points. His repetitive, infantile pleas for freedom distinguish him from the crowd of other hostages that Kāzim detains and who represent an anonymous microcosm of Iranian postwar society in which contrasting dialogues challenge the univocal viewpoint on the Iran-Iraq War that many earlier state-sponsored films of the period upheld. A woman who has been living in Switzerland confesses she does not understand the *basījīs*' complaints and offers them a blank check; a merchant who has been living in Dubai suggests a vacation; a man shouts that ordinary citizens paid for the war. One exasperated woman deprived of her heart medication chastises Kāzim and Abbas for taking more than their share, referring to war veterans' privileged access to government programs and preferential employment and education opportunities. In contrast to the coherent standpoints expressed by both the basījīs and the citizens, Hājī Fīrūz's character delivers no legible opinion, as if positioned outside the community that nevertheless secretes and seems to need his presence. Instead of delivering a coherent perspective, Hājī Fīrūz repeatedly voices a primal desire to be freed. When Hājī Kāzim lends him a phone to call to his family, Hājī Fīrūz's sarcasm affirms an implied but illegible status: *"Khūnah kudūm ghabristoon-i būd, akhah?"* (What graveyard should I call my home?) The response suggests that Hājī Fīrūz's "outside" is in fact a nowhere and a nonplace: a *ghabristūn*, a graveyard.

Defense cinema shows how the Iran-Iraq War tightened fraternal loyalty rituals newly coalescing between millions of mostly working-class Iranian foot soldiers known as the *basījīs*, mass mobilized by Ayatollah Khomeini just after the 1979 revolution. In both *Marriage of the Blessed* and *The Glass Agency*, as in the historical context of the Iranian Revolution, blackness appears unquestionably available for the taking, as it provides a pretext for identification and comradery. For Hājī, starving Ethiopians recall his revolutionary ideals and the failure of the Iran-Iraq War to realize them. For Kāzim, Hājī Fīrūz provides a perverse relief (when Hājī Fīrūz attempts to sneak out with one of the captives, Kāzim aggressively pulls Hājī Fīrūz back; even within the context of the already absurd plotline, such an action lacks a clear point). During Ayatollah Khomeini's mobilization of Iranians for the revolution, black people—localized as the oppressed of the Western world—provided the referent for a kind of universalizable suffering that helped consolidate ill will toward the imperial capitalist West.[24] Revolutionary intellectuals like Ali Shariati read and translated Frantz Fanon; the civil rights movement and Third World liberation movements grounded grievances that revolutionaries could extend to the Pahlavi dynasty, condemning Muhammad Reza Pahlavi Shah's political collusion with the United States. Shortly after 1979, the Iranian government issued a postage stamp of Malcolm X. And yet, unlike these more recognizably modern political gestures toward a self-serving and strategic solidarity with African Americans, the examples of blackness in sacred defense films belie a more challenging kind of relationality, one that would need to account for the buried and blurred history of African enslavement in the Indian Ocean, as well as of the recurring trope of African inhumanness presumed, in its easier-to-avow interactions with colonial modernity, to be detached from this history.

"ULTIMATE SLAVES" IN THE DEAD ZONE

Though the trajectory of themes had shifted, by the turn of the millennium, Iranian filmmakers had produced around two hundred sacred defense films.[25] Early films of the genre champion the necessity of war, upholding the difference between Iranians and Iraqis, Shi'is and Sunnis. The Islamic Republic's aggressive intervention into cultural representations of the war through state sponsorship of films ensured that the war's necessity would appear clearly inflected with the religious overtones promoted by other forms of political propaganda and religious discourse.[26] But later cultural artifacts, like the 2007 Iranian film *Night Bus* (*Utubūs-i Shab*), highlight the artificiality of the difference between Iranian and Iraqi comradery, insisting that the state-wielded distinction blights the historical intimacy between these populations in popular consciousness.²⁷ Academic scholarship mirrors this critique of an overemphasis on distinctions between Iran and Iraq.²⁸ The analogy between the Iranian basījīs and the Ba'ath Party, Popular Army, or Fadayīn-Saddam underscores the commonality of the region's military histories, even if it collapses many specificities of postrevolutionary military reorganization and the "para" nuances of these paramilitary organizations.²⁹ The ideological terminology crafted at the height of the Iran-Iraq War, which defense cinema repurposes, itself recalls a historical legacy in which the heritages of Iran and Iraq intertwine; war-period rhetoric links both Iranian and Iraqi forces to a longer and broader West Asian military history that includes, as one of its central (if underthought) components: the institution of slavery.

Indeed, it is impossible to understand the rapid development of the Trans-Saharan and Indian Ocean slave trades, which supplied Southwest Asian and North African territories with enslaved labor without accounting for the significance of military slavery. In contrast to the largely agricultural purpose of chattel slaves associated with Atlantic world slavery, in the early centuries of Islamic expansion, slavery was primarily a cultural, political, and military phenomenon.³⁰ Though the slave military history of Southwest Asia remains a specialized and somewhat marginal topic usually ignored by both military historians and economic and social historians of slavery,³¹ for some time now scholars have argued for the centrality of military slavery to any understanding of the development of Southwest Asia. David Ayalon argued that Islam's territorial frontiers would not have survived without slavery.³² Other scholars have shown that military slavery's centrality transcends its traditional historical referents (the Abbasid, Mamlūk, and Ottoman empires) proving equally significant to the consolidation of the Safavid dynasty and to the history of the region today recognized as Iran.³³ "The importance, scope, and duration of military slavery in the Islamic world," writes Reuven Amitai, "have no parallel in human history."³⁴

Because he was capable of achieving positions of high power, the military slave is a paradoxical conjunction, and historians have agonized over whether "slave," which in the English context evokes extreme degradation, is the appropriate translation for the mamlūk military slave.³⁵ Though it is not usually recognized by scholars who take up his work, Orlando Patterson's potent concept of social death coalesces mainly out of this question. Patterson's extensive comparative research on slavery in Indian Ocean societies, in fact, draws specifically from scholarship on Islamic military history. Insights into the status of mamlūk slaves and the Ottoman *devshirme* in Islamic military slavery, in particular, help to consolidate social death by offering limit cases to test its conceptual integrity.[36]

In his chapter "The Ultimate Slave," Patterson admits that the institution of military slavery may contradict the entire edifice of his theory of social death, which emphasizes the origin of slavery as a commutation of a literal would-be death, as a condition of general dishonor and exposure to gratuitous violence: with the military slave, "we seem here to be at the very limit of the concept of slavery, if not well beyond it."[37] Rather than exclude the figure of the "elite slave" from his analysis, Patterson concedes that limit cases are precisely where theory tests its sharpness, adding that limits can reveal forms of analytical value not otherwise apparent in "less problematic" cases.[38] What is extreme about Islamic military history is the movement between two polarities of utter powerlessness and political domination, as in the case of the Mamlūk sultanate, which marks an era of political and military rule over Egypt and Syria by foreign, primarily Turkic and Caucasian slaves.[39]

In articulating how military slavery seems to contradict the concept of social death by evincing the slave's power, Patterson frequently makes recourse to comparisons between the "Zandj" (an arguably racialized catchall for black African) and the mamlūk: "What could a favored Mamluk in ninth-century Baghdad either before or after his manumission have in common with a lowly African Zandj toiling in the dead lands of lower Mesopotamia? Or to take the most extreme contrast possible, in what sense is the word 'slave' meaningful when applied to both a grand vizier of the Ottoman Empire and an Ethiopian domestic slave in the household of a modest merchant?"[40]

Though he suggests it is the specter of slave "mobility" and slave power elicited by figures like the mamlūk that constitutes a limit to the category of slavery, it is equally so that it is the tension introduced by the figure of the "Zandj" that produces a conceptual dead zone.[41] The normative referent for the Islamic military slave is the Eurasian mamlūk and not the enslaved African.[42] But the contrast between these figures that threatens to delegitimize slavery as a unified analytic term is also what coheres it. Is the Mamlūk the ultimate slave? Or is it the Zandj? Or, rather, is the limit of social death the dead zone that remains after blackness has been detached from the concept of slavery? Medieval chroniclers praise the mamlūk, but the African military slave is shrouded in a textual oblivion and nonsignificance.[43] Thus observes Bacharach: "Arab chroniclers rarely treated the activities of African military slaves as germane to the major, contemporary power struggles they were recording. It was not unusual to find references to African slaves in Iraq without any warning of when and how they got there or what happened to them after the specific event was recorded."[44]

By performing the memory of enslavement, the mythical, ahistorical figure and cinematic character of Hājī Fīrūz confuses the facts of Indian Ocean slavery; instead, he embodies a legacy that contradicts them. In *The Glass Agency*, Hājī Fīrūz's blackface *remembers* and racializes slavery as black in a retrospective act, despite the lack of any historical authenticity to a claim that would overrepresent African slaves in the history of slavery in Southwest Asia. Notes a historian of Ottoman history, "In most Muslim societies, the Ottoman one included, slavery was associated with African origin."[45]

Why, we must ask, rather than simply observe and pass over this dead zone information as if it ought to be so, was and is it the case that blackness evokes slavery *in spite of* the historical facts and Indian Ocean slavery's exceptionalisms? The available, fallible historical data about slavery tells a different story than the legacy of slavery; and this difference between information and its mode of transmission suggests something enigmatic about the retrospective significance of slavery in Southwest Asia as it interacts with the global legacies of racial blackness. It is also why the *discourse* surrounding Hājī Fīrūz forecloses any facticity to that which his figure remembers and stores. Like the "Zandj" that confounds the ultimate slave, blackness confounds the facticity of Indian Ocean slavery. In rearranging temporal possibilities through assemblage and manipulated speed, sacred defense style articulates a confusion that is always already internal to the possibility of fact.[46]

The cinematic basījīs, Hājī Kāzim in *The Glass Agency* and Hājī Pākdil in *Marriage of the Blessed*, draw oblique identifications with blackness through a common unremarkable title, Hājī, and through the cinematic strategies that mimic optical point of view. Yet there is at least a third sense to their triangulation, one that centers around polarized relations to military institutions. For, as I have indicated, in their distant and not-so-distant pasts, both modern-day Iraq and modern-day Iran drew on military slavery for territorial integrity and sustenance.[47] Volunteers, not slaves, the basījīs (Hājī Pākdil and Hāj Kāzim) of the "people's militia" deserve the gallantry and respect of the military mamlūk but, in a postwar context, identify with the lowly Zanj, the inhuman Ethiopian, the peripheral African infantryman, the self-degrading black-faced jester, collapsing the fragile distinction between honor and dishonor that the military slave embodies and transgresses in his person. (Aptly, basīj refers to the broader organization *Sāzmān-i Basīj-i Mustazafān*, or *Organization for the Mobilization of the Oppressed*.) In the films, blackness symbolizes the disrepute into which the formerly honorable basīj has fallen. But from the *black* perspective thus suggested, if never explicitly articulated—and never fully claimed by the subject of these two sacred defense films—the Iran-Iraq War is nothing more than a zone of dissipation, or a conflict between two masters.[48] The spectacularized conflict of war shrouds a deeper antagonism that is reactivated by figures of blackness (famished Ethiopian, fungible Hājī Fīrūz): "The history of battle is primarily the history of radically changing fields of perception."[49]

CONCLUSION

For modern Iranian society, the plight of the basījī is at best marginal. In a recent chronicle of the development of the basīj paramilitary force, one scholar expresses a common sentiment: ordinary citizens' captivity to the military and paramilitary forces of the Islamic Republic of Iran (current and former basīj) trumps whatever romanticism for the basīj one perceives in the bounded ideology of the sacred defense field. Civic resentment erupts in recurrent contemporary protests that agitate against the extreme violence of the Islamic Republic's state apparatus, such as the July 1999 student protests, the 2009 Green Movement, and more recent protests over gas prices. Somewhat less ideologically weighted than Makhmalbaf's film, Hatami-Kia's *The Glass Agency* supplements sympathetic views of the basījīs with more critical ones—the innocent citizens in the travel agency and victims of the siege balk at the basījīs' newfound privileges. The sympathetic image of the basīj is not a majority view today (if it ever was). Still, if the basīj are portrayed as slavelike and dishonored in sacred defense film, today many Iranian civilians have no problem comparing their own status to slaves or "captives" of the basīj who are paramilitary proxies for state power.[50] And just as the *mustazafin* (oppressed) wielded identifications with descendants of the formerly enslaved in the years leading up to the Islamic Revolution, such identifications with black suffering are in fact widespread, unbounded by the religiously coded and, in truth, unconfinable to the propriety of analogy.

Exploited as a symbol of suffering, blackness is easily repurposed and its plasticity exemplarily expressed by Makhmalbaf's and Hatami-Kia's films. At the same time, as markers of what cannot be experienced, of fragmentation and psychic abyss, in sacred defense films, figures of blackness also appear as resistance to knowledge, even to claims of perceptibility. Hājī Fīrūz's slowly blurred lurching launches him out of the cinematic frame into the discontinuous beyond, as his cloudy genealogy thwarts consensus. Mutations in the image point toward a realm of being beyond the bounds of cognition. African bodies appear in recorded footage but also as hallucinations that recur throughout Hājī Pākdil's life, undermining safe referentiality. Rather than transparent, universal, or pliable signifiers, figures of blackness thus appear instead as the very suspension of signification, suggesting that the history of blackness remains anything but complacently restful within our inherited narratives, selective histories, and their self-sealing claims to positivist truth.

> PARISA VAZIRI is Assistant Professor of Comparative Literature and Near Eastern Studies at Cornell University. She holds a PhD in Comparative Literature from the University of California, Irvine. Her research overlaps interests in critical theory, black studies, Middle

Eastern cultural production, film and media studies, philosophy, and anthropology.

NOTES

1. Paul Virilio's 1989 translation of *Guerre et Cinéma: Logistique de la perception* into English coincides with the burgeoning Iranian film genre of sacred defense. Virilio argued for the original relationship between the technology of war and of cinema.

2. Arta Khakpour, Mohammad Mehdi Khorrami, and Shouleh Vatanabadi, eds., *Moments of Silence: Authenticity in the Cultural Expressions of the Iran-Iraq War, 1980–1988* (New York: New York University Press, 2016), 1.

3. Comparisons between sacred defense cinema and the melodramatic prerevolutionary commercial mode known as filmfārsī suggest a critical disdain of sacred defense cinema, as Pedram Partovi argues in "Martyrdom and the 'Good Life' in the Iranian Cinema of Sacred Defense," *Comparative Studies of South Asia, Africa and the Middle East* 28, no. 3 (2008): 514. On some scholarly literature that, by contrast, takes sacred defense cinema as a serious object of inquiry, see Khakpour et al., eds., *Moments of Silence*; Kamran Rastegar, *Surviving Images: Cinema, War, and Cultural Memory in the Middle East* (Oxford: Oxford University Press, 2015); Pedram Khosronejad, ed., *Iranian Sacred Defence Cinema: Religion, Martyrdom and National Identity* (Canon Pyon: Sean Kingston Publishing, 2012); Roxanne Varzi, *Warring Souls* (Durham, NC: Duke University Press, 2006).

4. As in the Islamic Republic of Iran, the Iraqi state media worked hard to propagate lexicons for the Iran-Iraq War experience (*tajrubat al-harb*) in favor of an Iraqi nationalist subject. See Dina Rizk Khoury, *Iraq in Wartime: Soldiering, Martyrdom, and Remembrance* (Cambridge: Cambridge University Press, 2013), 9. However, the economic blows to Iraqi institutions following the double catastrophes of the Iran-Iraq and the Gulf wars destroyed the state's power to financially support institutions like cinema for the dissemination of officially sanctioned discourses. While Iraqi cinema has never attained the level of institutional robustness of Iranian cinema, postwar novel writing in Iraq experienced a blossoming similar in scope to the Lebanese literary scene after the 1975 civil war. See Haytham Bahoora, "Writing the Dismembered Nation: The Aesthetics of Horror in Iraqi Narratives of War," *Arab Studies Journal* 23, no. 1 (2015): 189.

5. Partovi, "Martyrdom and the 'Good Life,'" 420.

6. Gilles Deleuze, *Cinema II: The Time-Image*, trans. Hugh Tomlinson and Robert Galeta (London: Continuum, 1995).

7. As Behrooz Ghamari-Tabrizi points out, there is no word for "war veteran" in Persian. The term *jānbāzān* (life-surrenderers) offered an approximate neologism. See "Memory, Mourning, Memorializing: On the Victims of Iran-Iraq War, 1980–Present," *Radical History Review* 16 (2009): 109.

8. Achille Mbembe, *On the Postcolony* (Berkeley: University of California Press, 2001), 3. As Susan Sontag points out about representations of African famine in the twentieth century, "The ubiquity of those photographs, and those horrors, cannot help but nourish belief in the inevitability of tragedy in the benighted or backward—that is, poor—parts of the world." *Regarding the Pain of Others* (New York: Picador, 2003), 71.

9. Varzi, *Warring Souls*, 85.

10. Roxanne Varzi, "A Ghost in the Machine: The Cinema of the Iranian Sacred Defense," in *The New Iranian Cinema: Politics, Representation and Identity*, ed. Richard Tapper (London: I. B. Tauris, 2002), 157; Partovi, "Martyrdom and the 'Good Life,'" 416.

11. Common knowledge about trauma includes as one of its primary symptoms what the official DSM description calls "intense or prolonged distress at exposure to internal or external cues that symbolize or resemble an aspect of the traumatic event(s)." American Psychiatric Association, and American Psychiatric Association DSM-5 Task Force. *Diagnostic and Statistical Manual of Mental Disorders: DSM-5*, 5th ed. (Washington, DC: American Psychiatric Association, 2013). The capaciousness and imprecise popular usage of the term "trauma" embodies the enigmatic intimacy between trauma and experience, while the postmodern theory of trauma has made the proximity between trauma and experience, or interpretation of trauma as a proxy for the philosophical interpretation of experience, one of its central themes, most famously in the field-defining work of Cathy Caruth in *Unclaimed Experience* and *Trauma: Explorations in Memory* (Baltimore: Johns Hopkins University Press, 1996).

12. Vivian Sobchack, *The Address of the Eye: A Phenomenology of Film Experience* (Princeton, NJ: Princeton University Press, 1991), 22.

13. Rastegar, *Surviving Images*, 135.

14. Hājī Fīrūz's figure is the object of both defense and protest within the Iranian community in Iran and in the diaspora. The approach I take to this figure in the present chapter elides the fraught discourse over his legacy. For a discussion of the contentious discourse over Hājī Fīrūz's origins, as well as my perspective on what media communicates about his challenging historicity, see Parisa Vaziri, "Antiblack Joy: Transmedial Sīyāh Bāzī and Global Public Spheres," *TDR: The Drama Review* 66, no. 1 (2022): 62–79. See also Vaziri, "Thaumaturgic, Cartoon Blackface," *Lateral: Journal of the Cultural Studies Association* 10, no. 1 (2021), https://csalateral.org/forum/cultural-constructions-race-racism-middle-east-north-africa-southwest-asia-mena-swana/thaumaturgic-cartoon-blackface-vaziri/#fnref-7767-15 as well as Beeta Baghoolizadeh, "The Myths of Hājī Fīrūz: The Racist Contours of the Iranian Minstrel," *Lateral: Journal of the Cultural Studies Association* 10, no. 1 (2021).

15. Khoury, *Iraq in Wartime*, 23. A film made during the war, *Muharram in Muharram*, about a 1982 military operation, drives home the spiritual temporality activated by the war.

16. For a discussion of Saddam Hussein's legitimation of the Ba'thist war on Iran through representations of Iranian racial and religious difference, see Arshin Adib-Moghaddam, "Inventions of the Iran–Iraq War," *Critique: Critical Middle Eastern Studies* 16, no. 1 (2007): 63–83.

17. Domietta Torlasco, *The Heretical Archive: Digital Memory at the End of Film* (Minneapolis: University of Minnesota Press, 2013), 3.

18. Shahab Esfandiary, *Iranian Cinema and Globalization: National, Transnational and Islamic Dimensions* (Bristol: Intellect, 2012), 171. Kamran Rastegar, "The Glass Agency: Iranian War Veterans as Heroes or Traitors?" in *Traitors: Suspicion, Intimacy, and the Ethics of State-Building*, ed. Sharika Thiranagama and Tobias Kelly (Philadelphia: University of Pennsylvania Press, 2010), 192.

19. Rudi Matthee, "Boom and Bust: The Port of Basra in the Sixteenth and Seventeenth Centuries," in *The Persian Gulf in History*, ed. Lawrence G. Potter (New York: Palgrave, 2009), 105–37; Behnaz A. Mirzai, *A History of Slavery and Emancipation in Iran*, 56.

20. Mirzai, *A History of Slavery and Emancipation in Iran*, 56.

21. On Mecca as entrepôt for slave-trading, see Hend Gilli-Elewy, "On the Provenance of Slaves in Mecca During the Time of the Prophet Muhammad," *International Journal of Middle East Studies* 49, no. 1 (2017): 166. See also Henri Lammens, *L'Arabie occidentale Avant l'Hégire* (Beirut: Impr. Catholique, 1928), 12. On Portuguese observations of the Meccan trade in slaves from East Africa, see Randal Pouwels, "Eastern Africa and the Indian Ocean to 1800," *International Journal of African Studies* 35, nos. 2–3 (2002): 418. On the persistence of the slave trade in Mecca into the twentieth century, see Ahmed Chanfi, *AfroMecca in History: African Societies, Anti-Black Racism, and Teaching in al-Haram Mosque in Mecca* (Newcastle upon Tyne: Cambridge Scholars, 2019), 21.

22. For Mohammad Ennaji, slavery's dishonor is tempered by the position of the master: the more noble the master, the more noble the slave. This correlation explains the valorization of the slave figure, 'abd, in religious rhetoric, as well as its ubiquity in Arabic and Persian practices of naming. Mohammad Ennaji, *Slavery, the State, and Islam* (New York: Cambridge University Press, 2013), 57.

23. Hāshim Razī, *Jashnhā-yi Āb Nawruz Savābiq-i Tārīkhī tā Imrūz Jashnhā-yi Tīrgān va Āb-Pāshān* (Tihrān: Intishārāt- i Bihjat, 2004), 201–202. On the Sasanian enslavement of Abyssians in the sixth century, see Gilli-Elewy, "On the Provenance of Slaves in Mecca," 165.

24. The 2015 conference on anti-discrimination, where the IRI invited Black Americans to speak about anti-Black police violence in the United States, provides a contemporary example of this (https://www.telegraph.co.uk/news/worldnews/middleeast/iran/11895197/Iran-invites-families-of-black-men-shot-by-police-to-a-Tehran-anti-discrimination-conference.html). Even more recently, an ayatollah on Iranian state television proclaimed in a speech that Black Americans were protesting in the streets in favor of a government more like Iran's, abusing the lie to retrench justification for animosity toward the United States (https://www.youtube.com/watch?v=OMWBJRXO_CQ).

25. Hamid Naficy, *A Social History of Iranian Cinema: Volume 4, The Globalizing Era: 1984–2010* (Durham, NC: Duke University Press, 2012), 7, 524.

26. Among others, the government-backed organizations that supported the production of sacred defense films included the Ministry of Culture and Islamic Guidance, Anjuman-i sīnamā-yi difā'-yi mūqadas (Council of Sacred Defense Cinema), and the Voice and Vision of the Islamic Republic.

27. Abdollah Givian and Zohreh Tavakoli, "Image of Iraqis in the Cinema of Sacred Defense," *Taḥqīqāt-i Farhangī-i Īrān* 4, no. 2 (2011), 87–107.

28. Houchang Chehabi, for example, criticizes academic rhetoric that repeats the ancient mythic rivalry between the two countries, arguing that "the 'Arabness' of Iraq and the 'Persianness' of Iran are ideological constructs." H. E. Chehabi, "Iran and Iraq: Intersocietal Linkages and Secular Nationalisms," in *Iran Facing Others: Identity Boundaries in a Historical Perspective*, ed. Abbas Amanat and Farzin Vejdani (New York: Palgrave Macmillan, 2012), 192.

29. Saeid Golkar, *Captive Society: The Basij Militia and Social Control in Iran* (Washington, DC: Woodrow Wilson Center Press, 2015), 4. For a discussion of Saddam Hussein's Ba'ath Party, see Joseph Sassoon, *Saddam Hussein's Ba'th Party: Inside an Authoritarian Regime* (New York: Cambridge University Press), 2012.

30. Though, this is not to suggest that slavery in the Atlantic world was not also, in addition to being a primarily economic institution, equally important to the development of Western culture and politics.

31. Barton Hacker, "Firearms, Horses, and Slave Soldiers: The Military History of African Slavery," *Icon* 14 (2008): 63.

32. David Ayalon, *Outsiders in the Lands of Islam: Mamluks, Mongols and Eunuchs* (London: Variorum, 1988), 321–349.

33. Sussan Babaie, Kathryn Babayan, Ina Baghdiantz-McCabe, and Massumeh Farhad, eds., *Slaves of the Shah: New Elites of Safavid Iran* (London: I. B. Tauris), 2018.

34. Reuven Amitai, "The Mamluk Institution, or One Thousand Years of Military Slavery in the Islamic World," in *Arming Slaves: From Classical Times to the Modern Age*, ed. Christopher Leslie Brown and Philip D. Morgan (New Haven, CT: Yale University Press, 2006), 40.

35. Hacker, "Firearms, Horses, and Slave Soldiers," 73; Ehud R. Toledano, *As if Silent and Absent* (New Haven, CT: Yale University Press, 2007), 21.

36. The *devshirme*, instituted in 1395, was the Ottoman practice of recruiting and educating young Christian males from the Balkans to work at the royal court as pages, officers, administrators, and soldiers. See John L. Esposito, ed., *The Oxford Dictionary of Islam*, (Oxford, UK: Oxford University Press, 2003), s.v. "Devshirme."

37. Patterson, *Slavery and Social Death*, 300.

38. Patterson, *Slavery and Social Death*, 300.

39. In English scholarship, the term "Mamlūk" is usually capitalized when in reference to the Mamlūk sultanate, and written with lowercase letters when referring to regular military slaves.

40. Patterson, *Slavery and Social Death*, 299.

41. On the concept of a "dead zone," see Joy James, "The Dead Zone: Stumbling at the Crossroads of Party Politics, Genocide, and Postracial Racism," *South Atlantic Quarterly* 108, no. 3 (2009): 459–81.

42. Slaves from the Black Sea were the single largest group of military slaves in the medieval era.

43. As Ayalon writes, "What is significant and unique about the Turks is that the unparalleled number of highly appreciative statements about their warlike ability and the quite consistent policy of the Muslim rulers in enlisting them militarily are in full agreement. No other ethnic group could pride itself with anything resembling even remotely that combination of those two elements" ("The Mamluks," 311). See also Shaun Marmon, "Black Slaves in Mamlūk Narratives: Representations of Transgression," *Al-Qantara* 28 (2007): 435–64.

44. Jere L. Bacharach, "African Military Slaves in the Medieval Middle East: The Cases of Iraq (869–955) and Egypt (868–1171)," *International Journal of Middle East Studies* 13, no. 4 (1981): 473.

45. Ehud R. Toledano, "Representing the Slave's Body in Ottoman Society," *Slavery & Abolition* 23, no. 2 (2002): 64–65.

46. See Parisa Vaziri, *Racial Blackness and Indian Ocean Slavery: Iran's Media Archive* (University of Minnesota Press, forthcoming).

47. Hacker, "Firearms, Horses, and Slave Soldiers," 63.

48. Foregrounding the foreclosed position of Black spectatorship would entail an entirely new level of analysis, one that might imagine a catachresis of trauma from the context of war tropology to the context of spectatorship and violent self-encounter.

49. Virilio, *War and Cinema*, 7.

50. See Golkar, *Captive Society*.

6

Dreams for Sale or the Challenges of Representing UAE through the Lens of Malayalam Cinema

SEBASTIAN THEJUS CHERIAN

In the Malayalam-language film *Pathemaari / The Dhow* (India, 2015; dir. Salim Ahamed), a migrant worker on a visit to the rocky coast of Khor Fakkan ponders: "Who would have been the first Malayali to arrive on these shores?" His partner responds: "Whoever it was, they definitely weren't tourists on a pleasure trip. They must have been desperate to get their families out of grinding poverty and starvation." Their question and the search for a logical response have intrigued historians, sociologists, economists, and filmmakers alike. This curiosity to historicize, imagine, and re-create the engagement of Malayalis with the Persian Gulf has been a constant among filmmakers of the South Indian state of Kerala where Malayalam is spoken. Salim Ahamed's film ponders this question just as another film, the subject of this chapter, had done forty years ago.

The modern cities of the Gulf have become a prominent feature in many Malayalam films made after 2000. *Arabikatha / Arabian Tale* (India, 2007; dir. Lal Jose), *Khaddama/Housemaid* (India, 2011; dir. Kamal), *Diamond Necklace* (India, 2012; dir. Lal Jose), *Pathemaari, Jacobinte Swargarajyam / Jacob's Kingdom of Heaven* (India, 2016; dir. V. Sreenivasan), *Deira Diaries* (India, 2021; dir. Musthaque Rehman Kariyaden), and *Meow* (India, 2022; dir. Lal Jose) were made after extensive location filming across Dubai and other sites in the United Arab Emirates (UAE). These films do not merely use the landscapes, built infrastructure, and spectacular skyline of the Gulf as backdrop and location for their narratives; they are deeply involved in recounting the long history that Keralites have had with the Gulf, stressing not only on their labor and intellectual contribution to the establishments, infrastructure, media industry, and culture of the states of the Gulf Cooperation Council (GCC) but also on the huge impact that the Gulf has had on Kerala's economy, its social life, and its peoples' aspirations over the past half-century. They examine the spaces of the Gulf as important nodes in the cultural memory of Keralites. So deep runs the Gulf's ubiquity in contemporary Kerala society that its presence in Malayalam films would seem but a natural expression of a sociocultural reality. However, it is interesting to note that the number of Malayalam films that represent or depict Gulf spaces has been highly disproportionate, and it is only in the past decade that this trend has changed as a result of liberalization in policies related to transnational exchange in both India and across the GCC states. By examining a broad spectrum of these films, one can put together a mosaic of experiences that constitute the regional cinematic imaginary of migrant life in the Gulf.

This chapter critically examines the Malayalam film *Vilkanundu Swapnangal / Dreams for Sale* (India, 1980; dir. M. Azad) to identify and analyze the challenges faced by filmmakers in their attempt to create a fictional story of Keralite migrants' life in the Gulf. As the first Indian film to be shot in the Persian Gulf, it becomes a key text in understanding the imagination of Gulf spaces by the film's creators as they attempted to bring to Malayalam screens a vision of the place, via the lived landscapes and architectural sites, where many Keralites worked and many more aspired to go. Apart from becoming an important contribution to the archive of moving images of the UAE and its social history, these filmic scenes of Dubai, Sharjah, and Khor Fakkan of the late 1970s are also a valuable resource for film scholars interested in the depiction of landscapes, built spaces, and the cities imagined by cinema. Such films inspire potential migrants and contribute to the cultural memory of the region. I use theories of space and place to study these cinematic depictions and processes examining the circumstances under which the filmmakers explored, interacted with, and filmed various sites to create a transnational imagination of desire and crisis. Critical transnationalism is used as a conceptual tool to understand this imagined canvas of Malayali lives in the Gulf.

VILKANUNDU SWAPNANGAL AS A TRANSNATIONAL FILM TEXT

Vilkanundu Swapnangal is a critical text to examine, as it was the first feature-length film to capture the subjectivities of Malayali migrants and their everyday challenges in the inhabited spaces of the UAE. The focus on the life of these migrants and the depiction of Gulf cities and infrastructures at a specific moment in history make *Vilkanundu Swapnangal* a defining text that inaugurates a transnational cinematic practice between the Gulf and the Malayalam film industry. Most of the widely available British or US film productions that predate this film were documentary-style explorations of the "transition of traditional Arabia into oil-rich Sheikhdoms" genre. Made from a highly Orientalist perspective, they viewed all of the Arab populace as either Bedouins or Sheikhs, who are either innocent to the "ways of the modern world" or fanatics in defending their traditions and religion.[1] *Vilkanundu Swapnangal* thus presents an alternate perspective that differs from the dominant regimes of representation from both the Western Orientalist point of view and that of the traditional and powerful ruling families of the Gulf states.

With a title that refers to the materialist nature of the interaction with the Gulf, where dreams and desires can be purchased, the film's narrative traces the departure from Kerala of an unemployed youth and his encounter with new environments and other migrants in Dubai. After the harrowing experiences of traveling to Dubai illegally and doing odd jobs on construction sites, a lucky Rajan becomes successful and progresses to a well-paid managerial position in a large Emirati-owned firm that contracts business with establishments across the world. Eventually, Rajan makes his first visit to his village to enjoy the experience of living in a house built with his Gulf earnings and to plan his marriage. The end of the film shows a depressed Rajan returning to the Gulf after putting his dream house on sale.

As a film conceived for Malayalam speakers and assuming their identification with the migrant working class in the film, it can be considered as "a narrative from below" that seeks to reflect on the effects of the circulation of transnational capital, tracing the paths of the numerous workers and enterprises that depend on, thrive, or are ensnared by the global flow of capital. Narratives of border crossing, unemployment, diverse linguistic expression, encounters with law enforcement authorities, and the search for a new identity are often presented along with the longing for one's homeland; these are also the principal themes that proponents[2] of transnational cinema have highlighted. Such narratives become piercing critiques of postcolonial and transnational experiences in former colonies of France and Great Britain as can be seen, for example, in the films of Ousmane Sembène.[3] Within the category of transnational films, Hamid Naficy identifies a corpus of films by exile filmmakers that he categorizes as "accented cinema"[4] or an "engagé cinema," which he further identifies as an offshoot of Third Cinema, a style of militant filmmaking in 1960s' South America that prioritized the voices of the exploited and downtrodden through an amateurish, imperfect, and spontaneous documentary form. In this essay, I seek to include *Vilkanundu Swapnangal* within such a body of film texts that explored themes of transnational migration, "people caught in the cracks of globalization,"[5] and alienation. Although it may not quite adhere to the terms of Fernando Solanas and Octavio Getino's manifesto on Third Cinema,[6] *Vilkanundu Swapnangal* presents an innovative and detailed perspective of migrants working in the Persian Gulf.

A 1980 film review asserts: "The MT [Vasudevan Nair] touch pervades throughout the film. Marunadan movies' 'Vilkanundu swapnangal' was not made with a view to show you the dumb skyscrapers and other construction wonders in the Gulf countries. It has a solid story and though fiction, it is the true, tragic story of every ambitious young man and woman who finds [sic] the El Dorado they struggled to reach a dry, dusty jail without bars, of sand dunes, stony hearts and piercing solitude."[7]

By the end of the 1970s, the Gulf had become an important influence in Kerala's cultural landscape. With many youths employed in both the formal and informal sectors of the developing oil industry, the economic effects of their remittances came to be known as the "Gulf phenomenon." Print media of the late 1970s and early 1980s devoted prominent space to issues related to travel to the Gulf, the economy of the GCC states, and their policies on foreigners' employment and also featured numerous advertisements by travel agents and recruitment agencies with a Gulf focus. This transnational capitalism that linked Kerala with the Gulf states and the wealthy Western customers of Gulf oil generated both keen interest and corresponding anxiety[8] that clearly dominated the discourse of the 1980s.

It is the engagement with this discourse that *Vilkanundu Swapnangal* presents in the form of a popular imagination of the Gulf from a migrant's perspective. The filmmakers' imagination projects the interaction between the Gulf and Keralites, intended to portray to curious spectators back home "the true stories of Keralites' life in the Gulf" as advertised in the prerelease posters. In his work on the immaterial city, James Donald emphasized the role that literature, art, and mass media can play in imagining a region or city: "The way we experience cities is profoundly shaped by the immaterial city of word, image, and myth. It is through them that we learn not only to see cities, but also to live in them."[9] In this sense, through its narrative and exploration of spaces, *Dreams for Sale* reveals and challenges the popular notions and myths relating to the Gulf.

Scripted by the celebrated modern Malayalam novelist M. T. Vasudevan Nair, the film benefited from the work of two Film and Television Institute of India (FTII)–trained professionals, M. Azad as director and Ramachandra Babu as cinematographer. Several of MT Vasudevan Nair's literary works chronicled the challenges faced by the dominant Hindu community in the wake of major land reforms enacted by the state in the 1960s. This screenplay focused on the Gulf's magnetic and transformational aura and "the revelatory truth" that can be gleaned by traveling to the Gulf with a movie camera. The producer, VBK Menon, was a Dubai-based film distributor (Marunadan Movies) in the 1970s and was instrumental in overcoming the challenges of filming in the UAE. Menon's familiarity with the region and with the UAE Minister of Information and Broadcasting was crucial in getting the necessary permits to film in Dubai, Sharjah, and Khor Fakkan.[10]

The film commences with scenes of Rajan and other young men on a dhow that crosses the Arabian Sea and illegally casts them off the coast of Khor Fakkan. They swim the last few kilometers to reach the beach and then undertake a treacherous trek across dry rocky hills to reach a motorable track. Hitching a ride in a pickup truck, Rajan manages to reach Dubai and starts a search for a friend named Mammukka from his native village, who can help him find employment. The search takes him to several of the city's construction sites, marketplaces, and crowded labor camps inhabited by South Asian migrants. The quest seems futile, and Rajan starts work on a construction site to survive, settling into a shack at the on-site labor camp. After his first day of work as a construction laborer, he is shown jotting down his experiences in a diary. Eventually, Mammukka finds Rajan in the labor camp, secures better accommodation facilities for him, and even arranges a meeting with the manager of a construction firm where Rajan is eventually hired. The Emirati sponsor (played by a Keralite in Emirati costume) appreciates Rajan's work, and he eventually rises in the firm through hard work, intelligence, and critical thinking, achieving the dream of becoming the firm's head. From this powerful center, he is seen connecting with companies across the world for business expansion on a global scale. His privileged position provides all the luxuries available to the successful executive. He befriends a Keralite nurse, and they tour the city in their leisure time, frequenting cafés and malls. They also go on a road trip to Khor Fakkan, admiring the natural landscapes of the desert. In the final UAE scene, Rajan is shown at the Sharjah airport terminal dressed in a business suit, bidding goodbye to his friend Mammukka and ascending the escalator to take a flight home—the epitome of the successful migrant who has achieved everything he had aspired to in the Gulf. *Vilkanundu Swapnangal* also develops an empowering portrayal of two female characters, the nurse Malini and Rajan's personal secretary, Alice; they are migrant workers for whom Dubai is the staging ground for upward social mobility. Through these three characters' transformative stories, the filmmakers connect Dubai's prosperous and multicultural ambience with Kerala's social and economic aspirations.

Vilkanundu Swapnangal represents a highly ambitious cultural project to sculpt a place that already exists in the imagination of Keralites. Space is often accorded secondary importance and made subordinate to narrative causality in Malayalam films; however, in *Vilkanundu Swapnangal* the Gulf as a place and the relationship of the protagonists with the spaces around them holds sway over the narrative. The Gulf landscape hence emerges as one of the most important "actors" in these films, serving, in Henri Lefebvre's terms, the third category in his triad of historicity, sociality, and spatiality.[11] Lefebvre considered spatiality as an equally important dimension alongside history and society. Space is not neutral and inert but multilayered and produced through complex processes of the imagined, the political, and out of the public's everyday spatial practices.

The scenes of Rajan's ramblings within the city to unravel and understand Dubai's topography is evocative of the privileged spatial relationship the migrant has with the city. Dubai is witness to a concentration of transnational workers from economically underprivileged regions of the world and concentrated around construction sites and labor camps, commercial centers, and public places, engaged in transforming the anonymous spaces into a modern metropolis. If Rajan represents the "alienated subject of the modern world" in Georg Simmel's terms, the unknown and alien space inhabited by the stranger becomes the abstract space of the migrant in Malayalam cinema where the staging of the migrants' homelessness and the quest for a new identity takes place. The migrant worker's labor transforms unfamiliar spaces into recognizable and meaningful places: functional buildings, public parks, and important city landmarks. The migrant worker then moves on to another construction site, leaving no personal traces in the built structures.[12] Film is hence a snapshot of the space in the process of transformation into place. The visual residue left on film is the imprint of the worker's fleeting activity, his bodily presence, and the outcome of manual labor that caused this spatial transformation. Such films are hence embedded with temporality, nostalgia, and exilic melancholy in their renditions of the migrant's presence in the Gulf. It is this fleeting view of Keralite workers of late 1970s Dubai that gets archived in the film and marks their place in UAE's social history.

VISIONS OF THE GULF LANDSCAPE: FILMING DUBAI ONE DREAM AT A TIME

In the publicity material of *Vilkanundu Swapnangal* (newspaper advertisements published in the *Indian Express*), one witnesses this promise

FIGURE 6.1

Newspaper ad for *Vilkanundu Swapnangal / Dreams for Sale* (India, 1980; dir. M. Azad) in *Indian Express* (Trivandrum), May 7, 1980.

of spectacular views of Dubai promoted in no uncertain terms. The film is projected as a treat to all those who wish to travel through the region and learn about it. It becomes the virtual window that invites the spectators to live the life of the Gulf migrants. One of the newspaper ads declares:

> The first Indian picture shot at Gulf countries! Another wonderful masterpiece of Mr. M.T. Vasudevan Nair!! [sic]

> For the first time a film is being made with the Gulf as the backdrop.[13]

Another advertisement says:

> A Fertile Land For Dreams—Impossible To Be Numbered!

> A Desert Of Dreams, For Most, Dead And Buried!

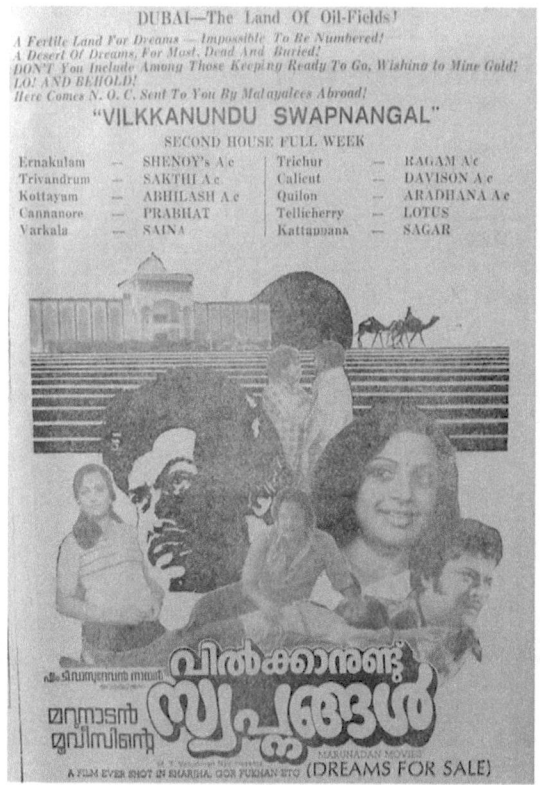

FIGURE 6.2

Newspaper ad for *Vilkanundu Swapnangal / Dreams for Sale* (India, 1980; dir. M. Azad) in *Indian Express* (Trivandrum), May 23, 1980.

DON'T You Include Among Those Keeping Ready To Go, Wishing to Mine Gold?

LO! AND BEHOLD!

Here Comes N.O.C. Sent To You By Malayalis Abroad! [sic][14]

A third publicity poster features the characters' faces among gold coins and doors that open into the sky and clouds, along with the following

FIGURE 6.3

Ad poster for *Vilkanundu Swapnangal / Dreams for Sale* (India, 1980; dir. M. Azad).

captions: "The first Indian picture filmed in Dubai—The Dream land of Malayalis—A screenplay creation of matchless imagination of M. T. Vasudevan Nair, thrilling to the very depth of the human mind, made into a magnificent artistic production now running to packed houses in all screening centres [sic]."

It becomes clear that the spatial imagination is of primary concern to the filmmaker. Dubai's landscape plays the central role in situating the narrative and is eventually the film's subject, drawn from the collective memory of workers and endowed with an agency that can transform people in distant lands.

The presence of such a multidimensional cinematic exploration prompts us to consider Giuliana Bruno's cartographic perspective of film as a means to discover how the camera takes us on a journey to map the route taken by an imaginary traveler:[15] in our case the ubiquitous Keralite migrant in the Gulf. Bruno perceives the activity of cartography as one that produces knowledge. A map can only be drawn after one has traveled or gained sufficient information about the space one is investigating. Her primary approach to studying film is hence more cartographic and historical than narrative driven. For Bruno, the filmic gaze is not just about the visual or the optical perspective gleaned by a voyeur. Rather, she stresses the characteristic of film's mobile spatiality that transforms the spectator from a voyeur into a voyager or traveler. This has been the case since the early days of cinema when the technologies of cinema, locomotion, electric power, and the architectural space of the modern city emerged together. Mobility is crucial to the development of the modern city; cinema embodies this aspect of flânerie and caters to a spatiovisual desire for circulation or travel through new modern spaces. The spaces of the Gulf, especially those of Dubai, emerge as important sites of modernity and spectacular city life on moviegoers' cinema screens.

The exploration of the landscapes of the UAE, or more specifically Dubai, is done in a progressive shift from rural outer fringes to the inner urban center, much like Walter Ruttmann's 1927 film *Berlin: Die Sinfonie der Großstadt / Berlin: Symphony of a Big City*. From the coast of Khor Fakkan, the camera follows Rajan as he traverses perilous desert landscapes to arrive in Sharjah. The spectator is introduced to the twin cities of Sharjah and Dubai through the eyes of an arriving migrant, with Rajan's point of view of the city becoming the default perspective of any immigrant to the Gulf.

The panoramic scenes that track Rajan are but a means of transporting the Keralite spectator-voyager across the various sites of the region, spanning highways, streets, sidewalks, construction sites, labor camps, petty shops, parking grounds, and the harbor. By mapping out the cities of Dubai and Sharjah, the spectators travel in and out of various "e-motional" spaces[16] that represent the various classes of the Gulf-settled Keralite migrant. From the interiors of a crowded wooden shack of the labor camp—where numerous construction workers sleep, wash, and cook—to the relatively better-off air-conditioned room that houses six to eight blue-collar workers or petty traders, the nurses' women-only hostels, and the senior executive's air-conditioned furnished villa: the film's wide canvas explores the whole range of living spaces occupied by the Gulf-*karan*, the Malayalam term for "Gulf resident." This genre of cartographic cinema of the late 1970s corresponds to the need to creatively depict the effects of deterritorialization that Arjun Appadurai considers as one of the phenomena of globalization as it brings laboring populations into the lower-class sectors of wealthier societies.[17]

CHALLENGES FOR THE FIRST GULF-BASED MALAYALAM FILM

Location shooting for *Vilkanundu Swapnangal* prioritized outdoor scenes unique to Dubai, Sharjah, and Khor Fakkan that could not be easily re-created in studios back in India. The rocky coast of Khor Fakkan, Dubai Creek and Abras, the Blue Souq in Sharjah, and the international departure terminal of Sharjah Airport are some important sites that were filmed in 1979. The producer reveals that the team finalized the script after visiting the various possible sites and having extensive discussions with MT Vasudevan Nair. VBK Menon was himself an accountant for a private concern in Dubai, but he also ventured into film distribution in the UAE. His contacts in the Ministry of Culture, Ministry of Information, and censor authorities helped to obtain the permit to film in Sharjah. The cost of the permit was the equivalent of around two hundred thousand rupees, but they were required to wrap up the entire filming schedule in less than two weeks. The skeleton crew of technicians and actors was hence on a tight schedule, as they could only shoot until 10:00 a.m. and after 5:00 p.m. to avoid the heat of the day. Menon adds that he was a "cook, driver, lights technician, interpreter, etc." apart from hosting the visiting crew in his residential apartment. Several Keralites working in and around Dubai

FIGURE 6.4

Photograph of director M. Azad and cinematographer Ramachandra Babu at Dubai port, scouting for suitable locations—from the personal collection of Ramachandra Babu.

and Sharjah were roped in as extras and assistants, with most volunteering to work just for the pleasure of being part of a creative venture that was happening for the first time in their foreign work environment. The actor Bahadur handled the reflector during some shots, and the character Chandran, who dies after arriving on the Khor Fakkan coast, was played by Menon's nephew. Prema A. Kurien mentions the role of such unofficial channels linked to family-based or community-coded networks crucial to sustaining migrants' employment and shelter.[18] This degree of informality and improvisation is prevalent in Third Cinema films that use amateurish methods for filming on low budgets and in unauthorized locations, often to expose the painful labor and living conditions of their subjects.

Permission to shoot at outdoor public locations was obtained only within Sharjah, but the team took a risk by clandestinely filming in Dubai and at a labor camp en route to Khor Fakkan. As in many real-life situations where the migrant worker relies on unofficial networks or personal contacts to achieve the objective of finding accommodation and employment or getting the NOC (No Objection Certificate, similar to a work permit) to carry out business, the film producer and his crew also relied on his friendship with the extended members of Sharjah's ruling family to be able to secure the authorization for filming within Sharjah. Menon further persuaded an official from the Ministry of Information, an Emirati, to accompany the team while they filmed without authorization in Dubai, constantly under the threat of being accosted by local law enforcement authorities. The filming was hence carried out hurriedly, improvising on the way, depending on the relative safety available in public spaces for shooting without attracting the attention of the police.

According to the cinematographer Ramachandra Babu, permission first had to be sought from India's Ministry of Information and Broadcasting.[19] This involved justification for filming abroad and sharing the script and details of the timeline for filming. The Indian government had at the time placed restrictions on foreign currency taken outside the country, and the producer had to sign a declaration to the effect that the film would bring in revenue upward of three times the amount being spent abroad. Hence a skeleton crew was organized, and minimal equipment with basic lighting and reflectors was prepared for the mission.

Many shots were filmed from a moving vehicle, done furtively and without much leeway for retakes. The shaky shots that pan across desert landscapes, Dubai port or creek sides, local marketplaces, or the road trip to Khor Fakkan were filmed without a tripod. In the eye-level shots, one can sense the cameraman's movement as he tracks Rajan's meanderings on foot across the built spaces. Numerous scenes were filmed through the window of a moving car, depicting the fast pace of traffic flows and the dynamism of local markets, but the angled waist-level shots are also evidence of the clandestine strategies that permitted the inclusion of these scenes of everyday life in Dubai.

Unlike the more popular Gulf-based films produced recently, which focus on Dubai's spectacular vistas and gleaming high-rises, *Vilkanundu*

Swapnangal presents a more objective perspective. While documenting the frenetic bustling of the commercial center (the port, modern US-made automobiles, and the illuminated shop fronts displaying the latest consumer goods from around the world—Sony Trinitron TVs and Citroën cars), the camera equally commits to exposing the dark inner structure of the upcoming towers and the harsh conditions under which laborers toil in unprotected and dangerous work environments. The numerous under-construction buildings that dot the city's landscape are an unavoidable reality of the 1970s and 1980s in Dubai and Sharjah.

I suggest that these aspects of the formal aesthetics of *Vilkanundu Swapnangal* can be interpreted as traces or imprints of the conditions of labor that migrant workers endure during their Gulf stint. The film gets materially embedded with the same obstacles that migrant workers face in their daily lives. The camera records and transmits these actions that are inadvertently captured in the cinematographer's field of view. Jacques Rancière stresses the conflict between two important types of views offered to film spectators. One is the cinematographer's perspective, which offers a view of the action that is at the core of the narrative, while the second is the camera lens's view of the background and landscape that is mechanical and unintentional. The combination of these two conflicting views is what defines cinema as a modern art par excellence.[20]

The protagonist Rajan's stint as an accountant in a construction firm provides a window into the imagination of the global traffic of goods and financial flows, and the team felt it necessary to portray the global connectivity that Dubai represented through its high-tech modern infrastructure. Rajan's conversations over multiple office telephone lines to important financial capitals like Sydney and Bombay, snippets of conversation about Japanese companies, and discussions about foreign engineers working on the construction of a harbor: all point to Dubai's links to the world's important trading centers. The film's narrative emphasizes the valuable role played by expatriates, including Indians, in the economic growth of the region.

The Sharjah airport and Blue Souq were completed in 1978 and had just begun operations. At the time of filming, Sharjah Airport was not ready for passenger traffic, and only a few cargo flights were operating on a trial basis. According to the producer and cinematographer, they "needed to create a crowd at the departure terminal as it looked desolate and empty with hardly any staff and no passengers around. Luckily a few Emiratis had accompanied our Ministry of Information official and they agreed to appear in the scenes, lending authenticity to the scene of the departure terminal." The Sharjah Airport departure scene was chosen as the "puja shot," the inaugural shot of the film that is taken with much fanfare and prayers, as is the custom on an Indian film set. The choice of the airport scene as the auspicious opening for this transnational film project attended by all the off-site team members indicates the importance accorded to the techno-modern outlook conceived by the creative team. The scenes of the airport interior are a series of panoramic shots that capture the grandeur (for 1979) of the terminal's luminescence and expanse, encompassing the illuminated central pillar and the escalators through low-angle shots that lend a dreamy impression of a successful Rajan finally achieving his Gulf dream and ascending majestically and magically on a mechanical carpet on his way to the upper floors and onward to the homebound flight.

Cities like New York, London, Paris, and Mumbai have a very strong screen presence, and their cinema history has often been linked to their industrial and creative prowess. *Vilkanundu Swapnangal*, filmed on location in 1979, may be considered one of the defining films of UAE's encounter with Malayalam cinema and an important first step in announcing Dubai's arrival on the transnational cinema scene. Notwithstanding its "poor aesthetics," the imperfection and unsteadiness in camera movements, and the collective and artisanal mode employed in the production process, it shall remain a critical film text in Malayalam cinema's corpus of transnational texts.

If it did turn out to be a profitable venture for VBK Menon's Marunadan Movies, *Vilkanundu Swapnangal* can be said to have drawn its success[21] not just from the novelty of the spectacular Dubai and Sharjah landscapes but possibly also from the "sense of place" that it conveyed to Keralites back home: it provided an important template for generating an imagining of the much-discussed Gulf space.

SEBASTIAN THEJUS CHERIAN is Assistant Professor at the Centre for French and Francophone Studies at Jawaharlal Nehru University (JNU). As part of his doctoral work at JNU's School of Arts and Aesthetics, he examines Malayalam cinema's interaction with the Gulf, studying the depiction of phenomena related to transnational migration in film texts but also the investments made by Gulf-based Keralites in the Malayalam film and television industry and the distribution and circulation of film media across both official and illegal networks.

NOTES

1. See, for example, *Air Outpost* (UK, 1937; dir. Ralph Keene and John Taylor) and *Farewell Arabia* (USA, 1967; dir. David Holden).
2. Elizabeth Ezra and Terry Rowden eds., *Transnational Cinema: The Film Reader* (London: Routledge, 2006), 1–10.
3. In *La Noire de . . . / The Black Girl* (Senegal, 1966 dir. Ousmane Sembene) a female protagonist realizes that by traveling abroad she has been exploited by her "wise, white employers" and can never return to her homeland alive. *Mandabi / The Money Order* (Senegal, 1968 dir. Ousmane Sembene) explores the repercussions of a remittance in foreign currency sent by a migrant worker in Paris to his extended family in Dakar, Senegal.
4. Hamid Naficy, *An Accented Cinema; Exilic and Diasporic Filmmaking* (Princeton, NJ: Princeton University Press, 2001).
5. Ezra and Rowden, *Transnational Cinema*, 7.
6. Fernando Solanas and Octavio Getino, "Toward a Third Cinema," *Cinéaste* 4, no.3 (1970–1971): 1–11.
7. *The Sunday Standard* published by *Indian Express* (Trivandrum), May 18, 1980.
8. Prema A. Kurien, *Kaleidoscopic Ethnicity: International Migration and the Reconstruction of Community Identities in India* (New Brunswick, NJ: Rutgers University Press, 2002), 65.
9. James Donald, "The Immaterial City: Representation, Imagination, and Media Technologies," in *A Companion to the City*, ed. Gary Bridge and S. Watson (Malden: Blackwell, 2003), 45–54.
10. Interview with MBK Menon, September 27, 2017.
11. Henri Lefebvre, *Production of Space* (London: Blackwell, 1991).
12. It is relevant to recall Dubai's "Plywood City," an immense labor camp built with waste packaging material and construction debris, which was dismantled and leveled in 1973 to create Safa Park on the same site. The Dubai Canal construction in 2015 saw the park being uprooted again.
13. *Indian Express* (Trivandrum), May 7, 1980. Author translation from Malayalam.
14. *Indian Express* (Trivandrum), May 23, 1980.
15. Giuliana Bruno, *Atlas of Emotion: Journeys in Art, Architecture, and Film* (London: Verso, 2002).
16. Ibid.

17. Arjun Appadurai, *Modernity at Large: Cultural Dimensions of Globalization* (Minneapolis: University of Minnesota Press, 1995).

18. Prema A. Kurien, *Kaleidoscopic Ethnicity: International Migration and the Reconstruction of Community Identities in India* (New Brunswick, NJ: Rutgers University Press, 2002).

19. Interview with Mr. Ramachandra Babu, Trivandrum, Kerala, October 17, 2015.

20. Jacques Ranciére, *La Fable Cinématographique* (Paris: Editions du Seuil, 2001), 205.

21. According to VBK Menon, the film completed five weeks in theaters in several districts of Kerala between May and June 1980.

7

Transnational Coproductions and Questions of International Festival Films from Saudi Arabia and Oman

KAROLINA GINALSKA

Transnational coproduction in a highly globalized world is ordinarily considered a force that drives development and encourages integration. In the case of cinema, this mode of coproduction may translate into, for instance, enhanced technical quality and narrative style in coproduced films or vastly improved exhibition opportunities. However, transnational coproductions of feature-length narrative films can involve funding and distribution mechanisms that perpetuate existing unwritten rules governing relationships of power, authority, and legitimacy while limiting authenticity or *realness* in developing cinema narratives under the "national" umbrella. In the context of the Gulf, this chapter explores the different consequences and compromises needed for suitable international festival exposure and distribution deals. It does so by examining the purpose and practice of transnational coproduction in the German-Saudi coproduction *Wadjda* (2012; dir. Haifaa Al-Mansour) with the locally financed Omani *Alboom / The Dawn* (2006; dir. Khalid Al-Zadjali), both promoted as the first feature-length narrative film productions from their respective countries. *Wadjda* exemplifies how funding and distribution mechanisms create power imbalances amplified by the fact that narrative films from the Arabian Peninsula rarely appear in international film festivals. When they do, they are categorized as "national cinemas" while simultaneously conforming to Western notions of "festival films." *Alboom* is a film about Omani sea heritage produced without international funding or guidance and thus did not meet international festival criteria. *Wadjda* was made under European guidance and funding and *did* meet those criteria.

Despite certain similarities, *Wadjda* and *Alboom* are very distinct in terms of financing, modes of storytelling, and cinematic styles. *Wadjda* involved seventeen production companies—only two of which were Saudi. The others included seven in Germany, four in the United Arab Emirates (UAE), two in the United States, one in Jordan, and one in the Netherlands. *Alboom* was produced solely by the Oman Film Society, an organization supported by the Ministry of Culture and Heritage and founded in 2002 by Khalid Al-Zadjali, the director of *Alboom*. According to the *Los Angeles Times*, *Wadjda*'s production budget is believed to be "a little less than US$2.5 million," and the film is reported to have grossed almost US$8 million in box office receipts.[1] *Alboom*'s budget is reported to have totaled 1.5 million Omani rials (almost US$4 million), but the box office data is unavailable.[2] Transnational cooperation contributed to *Wadjda*'s international commercial success, but the absence of this cooperation prevented *Alboom* from attaining the same recognition. More significantly, it is worth examining the impact of transnational coproduction on Al-Mansour's decisions with regard to *Wadjda*'s content versus Al-Zadjali's relative freedom in decision-making.

TRANSNATIONAL FUNDING IN THE GULF

Shekhar Deshpande and Meta Mazaj insist that the transnational opportunities that currently exist in the areas of filmmaking, production, and exhibition constitute a promise of world cinema having "the power to create and connect disparate worlds" and help "us to recognize plurality and seek egalitarianism in thought and practice."[3] This understanding of world cinema and its transnational potential evokes the ideals of critical transnationalism, which according to Will Higbee and Song Hwee Lim, seeks to "interpret more productively the interface between global and local, national and transnational."[4] Critical transnationalism additionally implies that world cinema should be refigured as a *world of cinemas*, thus no longer centered on Hollywood and European art cinema.[5] Instead, it should occupy a position on the polycentric map of the cinematic world.[6] In addition to its polycentrism, the transnational potential of world cinemas acknowledges polymorphism as an "interconnected assemblage of various forms: national, transnational, postcolonial, diasporic, small and minor cinemas."[7] It is also their polyvalence that demands an "understanding [of] how each film is viewed and interpreted differently in different parts of the world," or, in David Martin-Jones's words, "how we are to understand the 'transnational gaze' that is required of us as viewers."[8]

Transnational potential of world cinemas lies in polycentrism, polymorphism, and polyvalence; yet these qualities are overshadowed when international cooperation is discussed primarily in the context of funding and distribution. However, as Saër Maty Bâ and Will Higbee have argued, considering transnationalism as a concept that "simply indicate[s] international coproduction and artistic personnel from across the world" obscures "real consideration of what the aesthetic, political or economic implications of such transnational collaboration might mean."[9] Reduced to areas of financial support and staff exchange, transnational coproduction could, as Dolores Tierney points out, "threaten to homogenize the very important diversities between national cinemas, flattening out differences between them, while simultaneously connecting them in a globally networked film economy."[10] This threat, however, may be reduced by looking at transnationalism through the lens of polycentrism, polymorphism, and polyvalence; therefore, it is crucial that the term "critical" be attached to the concept of transnationalism.

Mette Hjort believes that transnational cinema can act as "a resistance to globalization as cultural homogenization; and a commitment to ensuring that certain economic realities associated with filmmaking do not eclipse the pursuit of aesthetic, artistic, social, and political values."[11] Her proposed typology of the different kinds of transnationalism distinguishes between those that "reveal resistance to purely economic thinking" such as the epiphanic, affinitive, milieu-building which appear to be in line with critical transnationalism proposed by Higbee and Lim, and, for instance, opportunistic transnationalism "involv[ing] giving priority to economic issues to the point where monetary factors actually dictate the selection of partners beyond national borders," which can be partly associated with what is referred to here as "transnational" practices.¹² Closely aligned with "polycentric multiculturalism" and "de-Westernizing," critical transnationalism, as opposed to transnationalism alone, yet again offers an opportunity to encourage and promote intercultural exchange and thus enhance intercultural understanding by questioning asymmetrical power relations in transnational coproductions.¹³ But does this close the door to transnational audiences for films like *Alboom*, which did not meet the narrative or aesthetic expectations of outside funders and producing partners (whereas *Wadjda* did)?

If international film cooperation, which in recent years has resulted in "an epidemic" of transnational coproductions, is defined as financial support for production, distribution, or exhibition, then it often creates "the uncomfortable and unequal dependence of filmmakers from the so-called Global South on Western entities."¹⁴ In Latin America, such dependence stems from reduction or withdrawal of public funding for cinema, resulting in a situation where for the last twenty years Latin American independent filmmakers, previously supported by national film institutes, have largely relied on European and North American funding.¹⁵ Viola Shafik and Gönül Dönmez-Colin find a comparable condition in the Middle East and North Africa. Shafik notes that Arab cinema filmmakers "have only two options: to rely either on public subsidies or on foreign producers."¹⁶ As a result of the latter, "Public film organizations as well as private producers increasingly consider coproduction or the advance sale of European rights a good way to lower production costs and save hard currency."¹⁷ Dönmez-Colin confirms: "Faced with production obstacles, lack of funding and distribution, censorship, satellite TV and piracy, [filmmakers] rely on foreign backing [...] the majority of North African films are financed by former colonial powers, in particular France."¹⁸ For example, Wissam Mouawad discovered that of the eighty-five Lebanese films produced between 1990 and 2018, more than 75 percent were supported by international funding bodies, predominantly from France, Lebanon's former colonizer.¹⁹ As a result, seeking financial support from the West or Global North may extend an imbalance of power that directly or indirectly challenges the illusion of national and regional filmmakers' autonomy to tell their stories without outside influence.

While not formally colonized, Saudi Arabia and Oman were under British protectorates, and their film funding stories are similar to those of former colonized nations, despite, according to the International Monetary Fund, Saudi Arabia and Oman belonging to the group of wealthy countries with very different economic situations than those prevalent elsewhere in the Middle East, such as Egypt and Turkey with their long-established film industries and dominance in the region.[20] It could then be inferred that government funding is available to finance cinematic projects without the need to seek foreign financing. However, at the time, film industries in both Saudi Arabia and Oman remain largely undeveloped and struggle with funding and lack of infrastructure.[21] Additionally, it is not uncommon for the Gulf Cooperation Council (GCC) governments to encourage "appropriate" projects, that is projects that promote a specific vision of their nations while seeking transnational support and international cooperation: a symbiosis that benefits both the GCC governments and Western funding bodies, as will be detailed below. *Wadjda* had funding from US and European producers and to a lesser degree a semigovernmental Saudi media company and Gulf festivals. *Alboom*'s funding came only from one Omani fund. Whereas *Wadjda* answered to many funders with Western expectations, *Alboom* had to answer to only one source of funding, a semigovernmental organization promoting Omani heritage locally.

EXPECTATIONS BY INTERNATIONAL FILM FESTIVAL AUDIENCE

Two recurring topics in discussions about relationships between funding bodies and funded projects are *the commercial role of international film festivals* in promoting films branded as world cinema, which continues to be understood as "any film that is not in English [. . .], something reserved for intellectuals and other culture vultures," and the *narrative and aesthetic strategies* in films that are dubbed "festival films," which are often conceived as "only designed and directed to gain recognition on the festival circuit, without any distribution beyond it."[22] According to Jeffrey Middents, transnational coproductions are "specifically designed for international distribution [...], particularly to be screened at international film festivals."[23] Moreover, Marijke de Valck notes Western preference and demand "dictate which projects get funded by festivals."[24] Consequently, festival films are required to be "readily identifiable as from their countries of origin to international audiences that may not be familiar with the subtleties a national audience might" or "universally understood."[25] Furthermore, according to Tierney, "The transnational funding bodies are not insignificant in determining the aesthetic and cultural identities of the film."[26] In other words, for the purpose of simplifying complex cultures to appeal to international audiences, festival films often perpetuate visual and narrative stereotypes that international audiences expect and embrace.[27]

Dönmez-Colin confirms this bias in funding for films in the Middle East and North Africa. She explains: "It would be naïve to think that European dependence would not determine the direction and destination of the end product [since festivals] also play a certain part in the proliferation of films that are supposed to be for a universal audience but are in fact made for festival audiences with little to offer to their home audience."[28] She uses an example of "village films," whose alleged exoticism Western audiences find appealing for "reinforcing Orientalist thinking that assumes the East as the 'other' of the West, an 'othering' that underpins stereotypes and reduces whole cultures to one dimension."[29] *Alboom* is indeed set in a village, but Shafik reminds us of "the exoticizing tendency by which international film festivals tends to only notice Arab, Iranian, and Turkish films that deal with 'hot topics,' such as terrorism, poverty, the oppression of women and religion."[30] *Wadjda* fulfills this need, managing to not show Saudi Arabia's wealth. *Alboom* does not fulfill these criteria: the film does not deal with terrorism, suppression of women, or religion; and although it is set in a poor rural community, the film does not view the situation as a tragedy but rather a source of community solidarity in the face of a Western businessman. In the transnational *Wadjda*, there is a film festival aesthetic in terms of audience expectations of repressed women in the Gulf and a certain exoticizing of the neighborhood the film is shot in, while *Alboom* follows its own locally driven aesthetics, thus precluding it from the festival circuit.

While not tied directly to finances, script development is dictated by funders, who make film financing contingent on the shooting script. Apart from the festival-friendly themes, *Wadjda*'s aesthetics, including its Hollywood three-act structure and a strong central character—a heroine who goes on to become a symbol of resistance—appeal to Western audiences accustomed to the institutional mode of representation associated with Hollywood and Europe. Being more episodic, *Alboom* does not conform to a Hollywood structure, as it did not go through rewrites supervised by a Western funder.

A GIRL'S SUBVERSION GONE GLOBAL: *WADJDA*

The timely topic of the oppression of women in Muslim societies lies at the heart of *Wadjda*. Hailed by Western journalists as groundbreaking, this transnational coproduction was marketed as a tale of firsts. It is considered the first Saudi feature made entirely in Saudi Arabia's capital, Riyadh, by the first Saudi-born female filmmaker. "Widely distributed and universally admired" and "exhibited under the banner of World Cinema [...] as forming part of a global category of art cinema, poised against commercial Hollywood," *Wadjda* took five years to make due to issues with funding and obtaining filming permissions.[31] In the end, Al-Mansour managed to secure funding from seventeen production companies, the most prominent of which is the German company Razor Film, which coproduced the feature with Saudi Rotana Studios and High Look Group, with the support of fourteen other companies. It was Rotana Studios, a television production company owned by Saudi prince Al Waleed bin Talal, that asked Al-Mansour to direct *Wadjda* "after she won several awards in the Middle East and Europe for documentary films about women."[32] *Wadjda* offers a glimpse into a largely inaccessible and conservative part of Saudi society that is still considered one of the most hostile places in the world for women, thus a project worthy of Western investment. For this reason, the fact that it took the director half a decade to secure the funding may appear incomprehensible unless Al-Mansour's original script, which according to her was much bleaker, had to be negotiated to meet the expectations of the European and consequently Saudi producers seeking to work with them.[33]

An inevitable question then is to what extent *Wadjda* is a Saudi film considering the significant transnational input that it received. The story focuses on an enterprising and resourceful ten-year-old girl named Wadjda, who tries to renegotiate social and familial restrictions imposed on her. She performs small acts of defiance that earn her a reputation as a troublemaker, particularly with a strict headmistress, who is forever denying Wadjda the right to follow her dreams. Wadjda's greatest wish is to own a bicycle that would ostensibly allow her to race her friend Abdullah, a boy who, by custom, is allowed to have one. Wadjda decides to buy a green bike from a local shop. Employing her ingenuity and sharp wit, she takes on the challenge of raising the money herself. The most lucrative of all the money-making prospects turns out to be winning the Qur'an recitation competition. Despite lacking interest in religious studies, Wadjda begins the preparations and wins the contest. Her elaborate plan fails when the headmistress decides to give away Wadjda's winnings as charity to "the Palestinians." But the girl's fierce determination continues. She eventually gets her dream bike and, along the way, manages to challenge some of the preconceived ideas about women's position in Saudi society. For instance, she convinces her mother, who struggles to break from established conventions, to secure a bike for her. Wadjda's spirited resistance and determination to realize her dreams can also be seen as a promise of change for a new generation of men, like Abdullah, who supports her in her cycling endeavors.

Wadjda is often considered a pioneering film by Western media, but it can only be a groundbreaking transnational production when polyvalence is applied to the film's narrative.[34] Deshpande and Mazaj explain that polyvalence "is not so much about uncovering suppressed voices, either in the filmmaking or academic sphere, as it is about *reorientation*, seeing the world from a different perspective to bracket commonplace assumptions about meanings and relationships between films."[35] Western readings of *Wadjda* do not, however, adopt the polyvalent approach, but rather they appear in line with the Western perceptions of an ultra-conservative society. Western media praised *Wadjda* as a feature that denounces women's oppression in modern-day Saudi Arabia, with the source of this oppression being presented as strictly religious, thus capturing viewers' attention with at least two of the favored themes listed earlier.³⁶ The *New York Times* mentions "the severe limitations placed on women in the name of custom, Islam and family honor"; the *Guardian* called it "the first film by a woman in Saudi Arabia [which] exposes the country's denial of women's rights"; *Sight & Sound* points out "the limitations and humiliations conferred by [Wadjda's] sex"; and the *Independent* refers to women as "very much the second-class citizen in the Saudi social hierarchy."³⁷ English-language newspapers like *Arab News* conform to a Western reading of the film and focus mostly on *Wadjda*'s commercial success and awards it earned at numerous film festivals.³⁸

Wadjda's central themes figure permanently and prominently within Western anti-Islamic agendas. Among the most sensational narrative elements for an Islamophobic festival film are child brides and suicide bombers, with a mention of the proverbial seventy brides awaiting them in heaven as a reward for their martyrdom. In reality, such subjects are extremely complex issues that require the application of profound insight, professionalism, and sensitivity. Yet both are inserted into the film in an ambiguous manner. For instance, when Abdullah tells Wadjda that a family's son became a suicide bomber, Wadjda asks whether it hurt. Abdullah solemnly announces: "If you die for God, it's like a pin prick. And then you fly up and you have 70 brides!" The issue of a child bride is introduced when Wadjda's classmate Salma shows the rest of the kids photos of her wedding. When questioned by the Qur'an teacher, the girl reveals that her newly married husband is twenty years old. She is reprimanded for bringing the photos to school. With these stories central to an Islamophobic agenda, Western reviewers of the film noted that "the religious and social strictures of a kingdom literally shrouded in sexual anxiety, misogyny and severe repression," and that Saudi Arabia is "fundamentalist Islamic society," or that "Ms Hussa (the headmistress) and her female staff are doing their best to teach young girls how to behave modestly according to their conservative, narrow interpretation of the Koran."³⁹

By contrast, Saudi fiction writer and essayist Tariq Al Haydar criticizes the film: "Al Mansour apparently felt compelled to insert herself into the narrative and indulge in lengthy exposition about what she perceives to be the roots of women's repression in Saudi Arabia: polygyny, child marriage, terrorists who commit violent acts in order to obtain seventy-two virgins (apparently, terrorists lack political motivation)."[40] While he observes that not all critics failed to notice that "discussions of child marriage and suicide bombing feel shoehorned in, as though Al-Mansour realized at the last minute that she'd finished the screenplay without mentioning either," he concludes that "*Wadjda*'s reception reflects that old imperial dream, what Gayatri Spivak described as 'white men saving brown women from brown men.'"[41] As Al Haydar argues, the film itself demonstrates that "Saudi 'society' is patriarchal, repressive, backward and sexist." This narrative feeds into a postcolonial / neocolonial misperception of Islam that persists in Western feminism, in which women's position in a Muslim society is determined by obedience and dictated by the Qur'an, ignoring religious scripture that needs to be contextualized to prevent misinterpretations.[42]

The film perhaps misses an opportunity to debunk the myth that it is the Qur'an that demands absolute obedience from women rather than the government. It instead reinforces these Western beliefs by enveloping Wadjda and other schoolgirls in carefully selected and quoted Qur'anic verses on obedience from the Al Nisa (Women) sura (a chapter of the Qur'an), which perpetuates this one-dimensional view of women in Islam and consequently is likely to endorse anti-Muslim sentiments in Western audiences. The film ignores the presence of strong female characters grounded in the long history of the region, such as Khadija, Prophet Muhammad's first wife, a businesswoman referred to in Hadith as "[one of] the best women of the world and the ruling females in heaven."[43]

Finally, *Wadjda* has a tendency to distort reality in order to suit an accepted narrative. For instance, it is rare for Gulf Arab women to receive degrading treatment from South Asian migrants, as Wadjda's mother receives from her South Asian driver: the driver displays what would be considered arrogance toward Wadjda and her mother within the ethnoracial hierarchies of the Gulf. Comparably, a construction worker makes a sexually inappropriate comment toward Wadjda. South Asian expatriates are rarely in a position to behave in such a way toward Gulf Arabs or even other expatriates. Also, the contrast between the female- and male-dominated areas in Wadjda's family house is too stark, even when taking into account the fact that the family is lower middle class. Wadjda's mother struggles with the kitchen's shabby interior and a broken hair iron. Wadjda's bedroom includes a makeshift antenna and an old cassette player for her "haram" ("forbidden") music, whereas the living room where her father, who works as an oil-rig worker for a company called Oils KSA, spends his leisure time playing on the latest model of a video game console in front of a flat-screen television. These examples demonstrate that the film's interest lies partly in rewarding Western biases rather than demystifying them.

In this regard, *Wadjda* fulfills Western festival preference for individual struggles over social ones. Sean Foley believes this element to be one of the most fundamental reasons why the film "was aggressively marketed in Europe and North America as a potential Oscar contender in 2014 [...] [and] has received extensive favorable coverage in both the Arabic and English-language domestic press" yet is unpopular in Saudi society. He accuses Al-Mansour of "adopt[ing] individualistic approach [and] embodying the core principles of the auteur theory of film," both in choosing Wadjda to be the focus of her film and "seek[ing] to be *the* female director in a society whose most successful producers of culture have consciously shunned individualism in favor of a group model of creativity."[44]

The film also follows other Hollywood conventions. The film's colorful props—Wadjda's Converse sneakers, a symbol of Western fashion, and the longed-for green bicycle—are emphasized by shot composition, depth of field, and focus to support a character-driven narrative. Most scenes with Wadjda apply shallow focus with a small depth of field, emphasizing character and actions while reducing the visual context of other female characters. Early in the film, these props become symbols of Wadjda's rebellious nature. The shoes appear several times within the first three postcredit minutes and are presented in a series of close-ups (some extreme), preceded or followed by medium shots of other girls' purportedly proper and gender-appropriate footwear. Wadjda's startling contrast to her classmates reflects her individuality and rebelliousness. The bicycle first appears in the eleventh minute in an almost oneiric sequence enhanced by the nondiegetic sound of mellow music, becoming Wadjda's obsession and a tool that she believes will help her to free herself from the constraints of her gender.[45]

FIGURE 7.1

Converse shoes signify Wadjda's recalcitrance in *Wadjda* (Germany/Saudi Arabia, 2012; dir. Haifaa Al-Mansour).

Wadjda is also about the narrative built around its director. Al-Mansour is hailed as a trailblazer and a hero who shot her feature film from the back of a van; this was an act of defiance performed in secret (as implied by interviewers) but also a misconception that the director rectifies: "Just to be clear, we weren't filming this secretly, the authorities knew that we were making this film. We got permission from the Ministry of Culture." She also insists that she filmed from a van out of respect for the culture.[46]

Al-Mansour appears to believe that polyvalence is a way forward: "I think cinema is a medium to open society and build cultural bridges between people."[47] In another interview, she explains that it was important for her to be organic and to work with what was given to her. "I wanted to start a dialogue and speak to people. [. . .] I don't want to be accusative but give a slice of life in Saudi," she adds.[48] The real question is whether this position is also evident in *Wadjda* and whether the element of power—and more specifically foreign funding—in the intricate triangle of power, authority, and legitimacy, has hampered Al-Mansour's ability to tell an original story and allowed the film's complexities to be fully acknowledged.

LOCAL WITH A CAUSE: *ALBOOM*

Like *Wadjda, Alboom* was also promoted as the first feature film ever made in its country of origin, Oman. Unlike *Wadjda, Alboom* has neither appeared at major international events nor in film scholarship. Also unlike *Wadjda,* there can be no doubt about *Alboom*'s "nationality" given that it was funded entirely by the Oman Film Society, which received financial support from the Ministry of Heritage and Culture. Despite the lack of international exposure, recognition, and transnational contribution, Omani and Gulf newspapers seem to regularly report on the work of Khalid Abdul Rahim Al-Zadjali, who directed the only three Omani feature films made to date: *Alboom* (2006), *Aseel* (2012), and *Zayana* (2018).[49] *Alboom* was screened in 2006 at the Muscat International Film Festival, which was created by Al-Zadjali, and Nantes Festival of Three Continents. It also took part in Abu Dhabi's Emirates Film Competition before that festival was integrated in 2011 into the Abu Dhabi Film Festival, an international film festival with much higher visibility to Westerners.

The eponymous Alboom is a small and increasingly derelict fishing village on the Omani coast whose residents rely on the sea for their income. Alboom is also the name of a type of boat in the region. The village faces challenging times as the fish seem to have disappeared, and boats are getting set on fire by what is believed to be an evil spirit, Abu Sanasil. At the same time, a rich and influential resident of Alboom, Sheikh Ibrahim, offers to purchase the redundant boats and old homes to realize an investment: a commercial beach resort, encouraged by foreign powers that are never fully revealed to the residents. The sheikh meets opposition from the villagers led by Salem Abu Zahir, an elder and wise captain turned fisherman. The resistance is motivated by the villagers' love for the sea and their traditional sustainable way of life, which is endangered by the spreading tourism industry. Salem Abu Zahir has a particularly strong connection with the sea, which has claimed the life of his son, Zahir, who went on a fishing trip and never returned. In the end, it is this senior member of the community who uncovers the full extent of the planned foreign investment, which is set to transform the village into a tourist resort. He also manages to expose what is behind the actions attributed to Abu Sanasil and save the village. But he also pays the ultimate price: he gets shot by the foreign businessmen and dies from his wound. Rather than pander to the West, the film lays blame on outsiders for changing the village's way of life.

Whereas *Wadjda* is currently available digitally on Amazon, iTunes, and Netflix, as well as on DVD and Blu-ray, *Alboom*'s availability is extremely limited. On the surface, the film would appear to have little international appeal and weak transnational potential for wider recognition due to low production values and a culturally specific story without an individual protagonist and clearly defined conflict.[50] *Alboom* proves Armes's point that "[the work of] many of the Gulf filmmakers [. . .] is largely unavailable in the West, and there seems to be no distribution point in the Gulf itself."[51] In the case of *Alboom*, its lack of distribution is certainly partially due to the film's unmarketability according to international festival criteria. Indeed, a copy of *Alboom* on YouTube reveals that the film is not technically and artistically proficient by Western standards of direction, acting, and cinematography as *Wadjda*. Shortcomings in sound and editing—sound quality, overabundance of nondiegetic sound, or abrupt and imprecise cutting—may create onscreen chaos and confuse viewers. *Alboom* is hardly *festivable* or suitable for distribution for audiences uninterested in Oman.

As a result, the film runs the risk of being deemed technically inept. In an interview, Al-Zadjali recognizes that as a result of budget constraints and lack of facilities and film infrastructure, film quality and distribution suffer in Oman. As he says, "Producing a film in Oman is not easy. Funding is a big issue, and everything else stems from that. We face difficulties at every step, right from finding a sponsor to arranging equipment to getting technical support and so on. The industry is still underdeveloped, and we have a long way to go."[52] Transnational funding, whose potential *Wadjda*'s Al-Mansour recognized and fought for five years to secure, would have perhaps helped *Alboom* to meet international standards in terms of technical support, aesthetics, and exhibition, consequently increasing the film's chances of reaching international audiences. It remains unclear, though, whether Al-Zadjali, who is also the chairman of the Omani Film Society, is actually interested in international publicity for his work. Official channels of communication with the director/producer are either unavailable or inefficient; and despite contact eventually being established through social media, the director's reluctance to engage in discussions about his work has not yielded answers to this author's questions nor has it facilitated access to his films.

Since *Alboom* is not a transnational coproduction, the power and authority over artistic choices belong exclusively to the director and presumably the country's cultural institutions, although it must be stressed that it was not possible to establish whether and/or to what extent the Ministry of Heritage and Culture influenced the director's decision and whether there was an agenda for a portrayal of a community that would support nationalist interests. Although the film carries a theme of neocolonialism (local communities that continue being oppressed by foreign powers), a common one in world cinema, *Alboom* does not engage in any of the issues indicated earlier that typically constitute an integral part of narratives from the Islamic and Arabic-speaking countries screened by international festival audiences, such as poverty, religious violence, or oppression of women. Despite being a film that takes place in a village, *Alboom* does not fit into this narrative of what Dönmez-Colin disapprovingly refers to as a "village film."[53]

The narrative framework within which Al-Zadjali wants to establish his film seems to be that of cultural heritage as a source of pride and strength, which may indicate that *Alboom* is a nationalist project that follows the Omani government's agenda to portray a community in a certain way, as noted by Mirgani, as well as Yunis and Hudson.[54] The actions of Alboom residents are motivated by their desire to preserve their community and lifestyle that, albeit unsophisticated, is also sustainable and evidently what they seek. The film's narrative also does not fit the Hollywood style of storytelling, which features individual rather than social struggles. The community's fierce attempts to preserve its cultural identity and their sustainable and self-sufficient lifestyle may evoke associations with a sense of nostalgia associated with festival films; in this case, however, it is not the lost past that the villagers want to reclaim but the present they do not want to lose.[55]

Another theme favored by Western audiences, migration—or in this case reemigration—does take place, from the capital city Muscat back

FIGURE 7.2

In *Alboom* (Oman, 2006; dir. Khalid Al-Zadjali) the camera favors the community rather than individual characters.

to the village.[56] In fact, a character returns to Alboom to support the opposition against the sheikh's plan. Unlike in *Wadjda*, female characters in *Alboom* are not subject to oppression. Despite a tendency to portray them in a slightly infantile manner, they enjoy respect and are equipped with strong personalities, particularly a girl named Noor. *Alboom*'s more realistic portrayal of Omani life could potentially be less acceptable to certain audiences, those unwilling to "travel"—leave their comfort zone—because it may confound their expectations of Western audiences.

Dönmez-Colin believes that "for a cinema to exist, it is imperative to engage in a productive dialogue with its own social context," which is perhaps the film's main strength.[57] *Alboom* acknowledges an entire community, not only in the script but also through the cinematography. Quite a number of medium shots and extreme long shots, several high-angle shots, and deep focus indicate that the narrative focuses on community and nature rather than the community's individual members.

The camera willingly registers the villagers' get-togethers, which also include local music and dancing, as well as united efforts against a common enemy. Admittedly, like in *Wadjda*, there exists a strong and charismatic leader, Salem Abu Zahir. But unlike Wadjda, he does not attempt to fight the foreign powers single-handedly, although it is his supreme sacrifice that benefits the entire community. In his fight, he is supported by an organized group of equally committed villagers: a collective protagonist with a common goal. Perhaps despite this clearly pronounced goal of saving the community, accepting this collective protagonist may present a challenge to international audiences accustomed to an individualist Hollywood-style protagonist. *Alboom* is a village film, yet it focuses on attempts to preserve cultural heritage without resorting to "fetishizing and commodifying the past or alterity and [...] offering it up to mass-market consumption on a global scale."[58] *Alboom* opposes cultural homogenization, but in order for Western audiences to appreciate the film, they would need to be prepared to adopt a polyvalent approach that involves abandoning preconceived ideas about a place. Unlike Saudi Arabia, Oman is not a country perceived by the West as being oppressive or being rife with human rights violations, particularly with regard to women. Oman does not need to counter Western media biases against it as Saudi Arabia does, which may also contribute to the film's lack of appeal to a wider audience who may not have notions of what needs fixing in Oman.

A PRICE WORTH PAYING?

Transnational cooperation often carries the sort of clout that can be used to unlock the potential of world cinemas into what Giuliana Bruno calls "site-seeing" spaces. "Sightseeing has become site-seeing [...] [it] implies a departure from a defined path," she explains.[59] The power that rests with transnational coproductions should give audiences a chance to be taken on a journey through a world of cinemas to "let us know the territory differently, whatever territory it is that a film comes from or concerns,"[60] particularly if these cinemas are viewed through critical transnationalism. But those concerns may not be the same for festival audiences and citizens of the country in question. Nor can we consider one film to speak for countries as prominent in population, cultures, and landscapes as Oman and Saudi Arabia. One of the primary criticisms that Al Hayer makes of *Wadjda* in the form of a few questions is: "Has *Wadjda* received universal acclaim because it is an exceptional work of art, where the director has successfully grappled with the problems she set up in her 'project'? Or does it have more to do with the fact that this is the first film shot entirely in Saudi Arabia, and, more importantly, that its director happens to be a Saudi woman?"[61] Answers to these questions cannot be unambiguous. *Wadjda*'s commercial success owes much to Al-Mansour's celebrity as a female Saudi director. Despite my criticisms earlier in this chapter, the film also diversifies the representations of the Middle East (and Saudi Arabia in particular) in subtle ways, including avoiding Orientalist Arabian tropes and images of lavish petro-wealth and lifestyles. Perhaps pandering to Western audiences is a strategy to help films get noticed and take advantage of transnational practices in the area of funding, distribution, and exhibition; it is a means to an end that Mette Hjort refers to as opportunistic transnationalism.[62] For instance, at the ninth Dubai International Film Festival (DIFF), where *Wadjda* won two prizes, Hamza Jamjoom, director of the short film *Factory of Lies*, openly admits that although his film is based on a true story, "obviously it has been twisted and turned to be fitting to a Hollywood model. We collected a number of stories that happened in Saudi Arabia and added the Hollywood flavor to it."[63]

Meanwhile, free from economic ties and Western influences, *Alboom* tells a story that, as an all-Omani production, sets a precedent for how Omani cinema might be perceived and acknowledged as having a unique style. The film's autonomy from external agencies and potential pressures that international cooperation might involve means that *Alboom* does not need to satisfy foreign audiences' expectations or conform to stereotypes that are, as Steven Rawle asserts, "something which often creates or relies upon a limited image of the nation in question."[64] *Alboom* is anything but an imagined community of nationhood. Alboom residents *are*, in fact, members of "a coherent, organic community, rooted in a geographical space with well-established indigenous traditions."[65]

One film alone can address the multiple issues that any one nation faces. However, in its transnational production, *Wadjda* is asked to do so by its international producers and festival audiences. Meanwhile, *Alboom* only addresses a community in Oman without being asked to explain all of Oman in two hours for the benefit of a foreign audience. These films suggest two very different approaches for filmmakers from the Arabian Peninsula: *Wadjda* guarantees an international film festival audience but comes with certain expectations that might compromise self-perceptions of Saudi stories that need to be told; the other, *Alboom*, does not register with international audiences but offers a creative freedom that reflects Omani self-perceptions about filmmaking and narratives that need to be told. The film helps us consider whether reaching international festival audiences is a price worth paying.

> KAROLINA GINALSKA is Teaching Fellow at the Centre for Preparatory Studies at Nazarbayev University in Astana, Kazakhstan, teaching English for Academic Purposes while completing her PhD in film studies at the University of Birmingham, UK. Her research interests include world cinemas, transnational cinemas, magical realism, Latin America and the Middle East, Indigenous cinema, and village film.

NOTES

1. Rebecca Keegan, "With *Wadjda* Haifaa Mansour Makes Her Mark in Saudi Cinema," *Los Angeles Times*, September 6, 2013, https://www.latimes.com/entertainment/movies/la-et-c1-saudi-movie-20130906-dto-htmlstory.html; IMDb, "Wadjda," IMDb Pro, n.d., https://pro.imdb.com/title/tt2258858/boxoffice.
2. IMDb, "The Dawn," IMDb Pro, n.d., https://pro.imdb.com/title/tt0843995?rf=cons_tt_atf&ref_=cons_tt_atf.
3. Shekhar Deshpande and Meta Mazaj, *World Cinema: A Critical Introduction* (London: Routledge, 2018), 1.
4. Will Higbee and Song Hwee Lim, "Concepts of Transnational Cinema: Towards a Critical Transnationalism in Film Studies," *Transnational Cinemas* 1, no. 1 (2010): 10.
5. Ella Shohat and Robert Stam, *Unthinking Eurocentrism: Multiculturalism and the Media*, updated version (New York: Routledge, 2014); David Martin-Jones, "Film Philosophy and the Transnational Gaze," in *Teaching Transnational Cinema: Politics and Pedagogy*, ed. Katarzyna Marciniak and Bruce Bennett (New York: Routledge, 2016), 106; Deshpande and Mazaj, *World Cinema*.
6. Lucia Nagib, Chris Perriam, and Rajinder Dudrah, *Theorizing World Cinema* (London: I. B. Tauris, 2012).
7. Deshpande and Mazaj, *World Cinema*, 5.
8. Deshpande and Mazaj, *World Cinema*, 6; Martin-Jones, "Film Philosophy," 108.
9. Higbee and Lim, "Concepts," 10.
10. Dolores Tierney, "Transnational Filmmaking in South America," in *The Routledge Companion to World Cinema*, ed. Rob Stone et al. (New York: Routledge, 2018), 98.
11. Mette Hjort, "On the Plurality of Cinematic Transnationalism," in *World Cinemas, Transnational Perspectives*, ed. Nataša Ďurovičová and Kathleen Newman (New York: Routledge, 2010), 15.

12. Hjort, "On the Plurality of Cinematic Transnationalism," 19.
13. Bâ and Higbee, *De-Westernizing*.
14. Julia Echeverría, "Moving beyond Latin America: Fernando Meirelles's *Blindness* and the Epidemic of Transnational Co-productions," *Transnational Cinemas* 8, no. 2 (2017): 113; Marijke de Valck, "Screening World Cinema at Film Festivals," in *The Routledge Companion to World Cinema*, ed. Rob Stone et al. (New York: Routledge, 2018), 397.
15. Tierney, "Transnational Filmmaking."
16. Viola Shafik, *Arab Cinema: History and Cultural Identity* (Cairo: American University of Cairo Press, 2016), 40.
17. Shafik, *Arab Cinema*, 40.
18. Gönül Dönmez-Colin, *The Cinema of North Africa and the Middle East* (London: Wallflower, 2007), 9.
19. Wissam Mouawad, "Lebanese Cinema and the French Co-production System: The Postcard Strategy," in *Cinema of the Arab World: Contemporary Directions in Theory and Practice*, ed. Terri Ginsberg and Chris Lippard (Cham: Palgrave Macmillan, 2020), 71–86.
20. IMF, "GDP Per Capita, Current Prices," International Monetary Fund, n.d., https://www.imf.org/external/datamapper/NGDPDPC@WEO/SAU/OMN; Roy Armes, *New Voices in Arab Cinema* (Bloomington: Indiana University Press, 2015), 2.
21. Emma Jones, "Saudi Arabian Film-Maker Break Boundaries," BBC, July 8, 2013, http://www.bbc.com/news/entertainment-arts-23195482; Vibhuti Arora, "Dr Khalid Al Zadjali," BroadcastPro Middle East, May 12, 2013, http://www.broadcastprome.com/interviews/dr-khalid-al-zadjali/.
22. Paul Willemen, "The National Revisited," in *Theorizing National Cinema*, ed. Valentina Vitali and Paul Willemen (London: Palgrave Macmillan, 2006), 29; Andrea Cabezas Vargas and Júlia González de Canales Carcereny, "Central American Cinematographic Aesthetics and Their Role in International Film Festivals," *Studies in Spanish & Latin American Cinemas* 15, no. 2 (2018): 180.
23. Jeffrey Middents, "The First Rule of Latin American Cinema Is You Do Not Talk about Latin American Cinema: Notes on Discussing a Sense of Place in Contemporary Cinema," *Transnational Cinemas* 4, no. 2 (2013): 155.
24. De Valck, "Screening World Cinema," 399.
25. Middents, "First Rule," 155, 156.
26. Tierney, "Transnational Filmmaking," 98–99; Middents, "First Rule," 156.
27. Middents, "First Rule."
28. Dönmez-Colin, *Cinema*, 9–10.
29. Dönmez-Colin, *Cinema*, 9–10.
30. Dale Hudson, "Review of Transnational Cinema/Media Studies Conference," *Transnational Cinemas* 6, no. 1 (2015): 89.
31. Armes, *New Voices*, 1; Yael Friedman, "Guises of Transnationalism in Israel/Palestine: A Few Notes on *5 Broken Cameras*," *Transnational Cinemas* 6, no. 1 (2015): 17; Jones, "Saudi Arabian Film-Maker."
32. Sean Foley, *Changing Saudi Arabia: Art, Culture and Society in the Kingdom* (Boulder, CO: Lynne Rienner, 2019), 135.
33. BBC, "Female Saudi Director: 'I Had to Film from a Van.'" BBC, March 11, 2013, http://www.bbc.co.uk/news/av/entertainment-arts-21746195/female-saudi-director-i-had-to-direct-from-a-van.

34. Ibid.; France 24, "Haifa al-Mansour: The Director Breaking Boundaries for Women in Saudi Arabia," France 24, July 10, 2018, https://www.youtube.com/watch?v=fyBtxWhqUEg; Alexandra Alter, "A Pioneering Saudi Director on Her New Film, *Mary Shelley*," *New York Times*, May 23, 2018, https://www.nytimes.com/2018/05/23/movies/mary-shelley-haifaa-al-mansour-saudi-arabia.html.

35. Deshpande and Mazaj, *World Cinema*, 10.

36. BBC, "Female Saudi Director"; Jones, "Saudi Arabian Film-Maker"; France 24, "Haifa al-Mansour."

37. Anthony Oliver Scott, "Silly Girl, You Want to Race a Boy?," *New York Times*, September 12, 2013, https://www.nytimes.com/2013/09/13/movies/haifaa-al-mansours-wadjda-a-saudi-girls-discoveries.html; Rachel Shabi, "*Wadjda* and the Saudi Women Fighting Oppression from Within," *Guardian*, August 7, 2013, https://www.theguardian.com/commentisfree/2013/aug/07/wadjda-saudi-women-fighting-oppression; Hannah McGill, "Film Review: *Wadja*," *Sight & Sound* 28, no. 2 (2013): 90–91; Anthony Quinn, "Film Review: *Wadjda*," *Independent*, July 18, 2013, https://www.independent.co.uk/arts-entertainment/films/reviews/film-review-wadjda-pg-8717978.html.

38. Rima Al Mukhtar, "Dubai Rolls Out the Red Carpet for a Celebration of Film," *Arab News*, December 19, 2012, https://www.arabnews.com/lifestyle/dubai-rolls-out-red-carpet-celebration-film; William Mullaly, "Haifaa Al-Mansour Hopes to Empower Young Women with Her Latest Film *Mary Shelley*," *Arab News*, July 1, 2018, https://www.arabnews.com/node/1330281/lifestyle.

39. Ann Hornaday, "Film Review: *Wadjda*," *Washington Post*, September 19, 2013, https://www.washingtonpost.com/goingoutguide/wadjda-movie-review/2013/09/18/73e63734-1fae-11e3-94a2-6c66b668ea55_story.html?noredirect=on; Frank Swietek, "Film Review: *Wadjda*," *Video Librarian* 29, no. 2 (2014); Tricia Youlden, "Education," New South Wales Teachers Federation, April 7, 2014, http://education.nswtf.org.au/april-7-2014/reviews/film/.

40. Tariq Al Haydar, "Haifaa Al Mansour's *Wadjda*: Revolutionary Art or Pro-state Propaganda?," Jadaliyya, 2014, https://www.jadaliyya.com/Details/30078.

41. Ibid.

42. Ibid.

43. Barbara Freyer Stowasser, "Khadīja," in *Encyclopaedia of the Qurʾān*, ed. Jane Dammen McAuli (2005), http://dx.doi.org.ezproxyd.bham.ac.uk/10.1163/1875-3922_q3_EQSIM_00247.

44. Foley, *Changing Saudi Arabia*, 136, 137.

45. The power of the symbolism associated with Wadjda's bike and sneakers caused several European and Latin American countries to strip the heroine of her centrality and give the film a different title. *Wadjda* became *The Green Bike* in Spain, Italy, Sweden, and Norway (*La bicicleta verde, La bicicletta verde, Den gröna cykeln, Den grønne sykkelen*, respectively), *The Forbidden Bicycle* in Greece (*Το Απαγορευμένο Ποδήλατο*), *Wadjda's Dream* in Latin America and Portugal (*El sueño de Wadjda, O Sonho de Wadjda*), or *A Girl in Gym Shoes* in Poland (*Dziewczynka w trampkach*). A legitimate reason for this change could be a possible misunderstanding of the name "Wadjda" as a girl's name by non-Arabic speakers, but in Germany, for instance, the film's title was changed only slightly to *Das Mädchen Wadjda* ("das Mädchen" means "a girl"), which allowed Wadjda to maintain her titular presence.

46. BBC, "Female Saudi Director."
47. France 24, "Haifa al-Mansour."
48. BBC, "Female Saudi Director."
49. Sunil Vaidya, "First Omani Movie Hits Screen at Film Festival," *Gulf News*, January 25, 2006, https://gulfnews.com/world/gulf/oman/first-omani-movie-hits-screen-at-film-festival-1.222405; Sarnga Dharan Nambiar, "Not Just a Filmy Location," *Oman Observer*, April 28, 2017, https://www.omanobserver.om/not-just-filmy-location/.
50. The director claims not to own a copy, and the author's requests addressed to Muscat and Dubai Film Festival authorities remain unanswered. In this case, a poor-quality version available for free on YouTube (https://www.youtube.com/watch?v=FGJvSBobzxo) must suffice. But finding the film can also be difficult since the name of the video file does not contain the actual film title in English or Arabic.
51. Armes, *New Voices*, 301.
52. Arora, "Dr Khalid Al Zadjali."
53. Dönmez-Colin, *Cinema*.
54. Mirgani, "Making the Final Cut: Filmmaking and Complicating National Identity in Qatar and the GCC States," in *Cinema of the Arab World: Contemporary Directions in Theory and Practice*, ed. Terri Ginsberg and Chris Lippard (Cham: Palgrave Macmillan, 2020), 45; Alia Yunis and Dale Hudson, "Introduction Film and Visual Media in the Gulf," *Middle East Journal of Culture and Communication* 14 (2021): 7.
55. James Chapman, "British Cinemas. Critical and Historical Debates," in *The Routledge Companion to World Cinema*, ed. Rob Stone et al. (New York: Routledge, 2018), 163.
56. Stephanie Dennison, "Debunking Neo-imperialism or Reaffirming Neo-colonialism? The Representation of Latin America in Recent Co-productions," *Transnational Cinemas* 4, no. 2 (2013): 186.
57. Dönmez-Colin, *Cinema*, 10.
58. Daniela Berghahn, "The Past Is a Foreign Country: Exoticism and Nostalgia in Contemporary Transnational Cinema," *Transnational Screens* 10, no. 1 (2019): 37.
59. Giuliana Bruno, *Atlas of Emotion* (London: Verso, 2002), 16.
60. Dudley Andrew, "An Atlas of World Cinema," *Framework* 2, no. 45 (2006): 21.
61. Al Haydar, "Haifaa Al Mansour's *Wadjda*."
62. Hjort, "On the Plurality."
63. Al Mukhtar, "Dubai Rolls."
64. Steven Rawle, *Transnational Cinema: An Introduction* (London: Palgrave Macmillan, 2018), 21.
65. Andrew Higson, "The Limiting Imagination of National Cinema," in *Transnational Cinema: The Film Reader*, ed. Elizabeth Ezra and Terry Rowden (New York: Routledge, 2006), 16.

8

IMPORT-REEXPORT
Reconsidering the Film Festival as a Port Economy[1]

KAY DICKINSON

Port cities feature prominently on the film festival map, from Busan to Rotterdam. Yet scholarly inquiry into this locational particularity remains rare and is typically relegated to discussions about how cultural activity might revitalize—or "Bilbao-ize"—a postindustrial quarter.[2] *Active* ports, however, encourage us to think beyond these immediate geographies and toward how film festivals afford correlations, more so exchanges, between different and distanced territories. Invigorated by the current volume's attention to the Gulf as a meeting place and a conduit, this essay examines how these same qualities characterize both the port and the film festival via an annual event where all three (the region, the port, and the festival) have coincided: the Dubai International Film Festival (henceforth DIFF). During its period of operation (2004–2017), DIFF coordinated not only a rich program of movies from around the world but also production support and training for nonnationals, cross-border coproduction facilitation, schemes for pairing talent with investors, and film markets that brought together creative personnel, buyers, and distributors. Because DIFF was a festival rooted in a port economy, delving into this interrelationship opens up ways through which we might better grasp the fundamental coadjuvancy between cinema, transnational commerce, networks of transportation, and people on the move.

Given Dubai's hulking status as an international entrepôt—at the time when the festival was running the ninth busiest in the world, the largest between Singapore and Rotterdam, and the only one in the top ten outside East Asia—urban waterfront regeneration surveys are clearly not the avenues to pursue.[3] Situated on the sea edge of a meager hinterland with little latitude to develop space-hogging industries—but in a handy location between Africa, Europe, and Asia—Dubai has striven hard to establish itself as one of the twenty-first century's "superterminals," home to companies from over 130 different states.[4] The port is supplemented in this capacity by the airport, which, from 2014 until DIFF's demise, registered the most international traffic of any in the world, with a second, set to be the world's largest and dedicated predominantly to cargo, partially opened in 2010.[5] The limited land mass thus generates revenue by instead temporarily enticing traffic from around the world, in and out, always in motion, and rarely staying put for very long; this is an environment into which a week-long film festival fits snugly.

Certainly the newness of the United Arab Emirates (UAE) as a nation, established only in 1971, means one should not dismiss the festival as an exercise in promoting the country. However, Dubai's much-longer history as a port welcomes thinking beyond the academic tendency toward defaulting to foregrounding place branding or nation building in festival studies.[6] Instead, foregrounding the intimacy between the festival and the port brings us into the throes of how contemporary transnational trade functions (including for cinema), through the mechanics of reexportation, logistics, supply chain building, free zoning, and just-in-time manufacturing. Such operations have become central to global commerce and to the success of global giants like Walmart and Amazon—not to mention Netflix—yet these sadly remain outlying concerns in how we study visual cultures. Examining DIFF less as a forum for exhibition targeted at general audiences (which it also was) and more as a film market shaped by and adopting these practices brings us closer to methods and focal points that benefit critical analysis of sites well beyond this particular one.

To begin, it is essential to take on board how ports actually function. Dubai's largest, Jebel Ali, specializes in reexporting, or transshipment, as it is often called: the cheap, efficient, and reliable redirection of goods received from elsewhere. The Gulf ports have long served as points where cargoes were moved from one ship to another. From the tenth century, smaller vessels traveling down the Euphrates/Tigris were swapped for larger ones fit for the voyage to India or China.[7] Since the 1970s, Dubai has established itself as a strategic stopping-off point to split, manage, and redirect the flows of goods globally, from here progressing onward to over two hundred countries, with a recurrent accent each year on India, Iran, Iraq, Hong Kong, and Saudi Arabia.[8] By the time DIFF was in full swing, reexportation amounted to USD 38 billion worth of trade to Asia alone, and Dubai registered as the world's third-largest reexport center after Hong Kong and Singapore.[9] Dubai sometimes also acts as a crossroads where trade sanctions, such as those upheld between the United States and Iran, can be (covertly) overridden; more pervasively, the port allows clients to take advantage of various free trade and bilateral agreements.[10] These lessen costs, as is possible with movement in and out of the Gulf Cooperation Council (GCC) single market—home to leaders in regional television, like Orbit, Rotana, and MBC—where no further taxes on goods are deducted after entry into Dubai. In short, very few commodities start or stop their lives in Dubai, and the same was explicitly true of the emirate's expansion into cinema via the festival, its film rights sales, and its production financing. In both sectors, the aim is to speed through and generate revenue from the *passage* of commodities by reducing friction on their movement.

The emirate's specialization in reexportation and its interests in cinema also share a history of building infrastructure for movement that preceded and took precedence over local manufacturing. In order to keep its transshipment port competitive, Dubai's broader matrix of facilities boasts reliable onward transportation by road or air; minimal bureaucracy; low or no taxation; and a range of quality services, from ship repairs and on-site light manufacturing to freight-forwarding and business networking facilities. Although I may appear to be describing maritime transport here, I hope to reveal how Dubai increasingly does its utmost to profitably avail the global film industry of analogous amenities too. Just as Dubai amassed key infrastructural elements like ports, airports, and an airline as a priority, so too has its entrance into the film industry progressed, not with a national body of film works but a network for dissemination—an international film festival. UAE-sited production, still largely international, gained momentum after, not before, the establishment of the festival.

Successful transshipment depends on logistics, which is another of Dubai's most buoyant economies. Logistics is the art of keeping things in motion, of saving on time and humanpower so as not to impede the fast, economical distribution of commodities. Logistics, as a management science, has plenty to offer cinema. Given film's typical timeline of years between conception and consumption, movies persistently figure as highly unreliable wares, many productions sinking in their efforts to complete this journey, pulling investments down with them and rendering profits difficult to predict or even generate. Add to this how supply chain management, deeply inspired by port-instantiated logistics, has taken over not just how products reach us but also how their elements are sourced and manufactured by the most powerful multinationals of our age. Logistics can promise to hasten the traffic along cinema's supply chains from preproduction, principal photography, postproduction, distribution, and costly marketing to exhibition or unit sales. This being the case, we should grapple with how a port—and, in Dubai's case, an airport as well—no longer simply register as interchanges where goods or passengers are loaded and unloaded. They are competitive global hubs that distinguish themselves by driving down transport costs and adding value, indelibly altering the character of contemporary capitalism, their tactics now extending, as we shall see, into other realms. By rolling out this model beyond port management, Dubai began to forge new economies and practices for film distribution and manufacturing that challenge the way festivals work.

Following suit, DIFF positioned itself as a facilitator of dependable and fleet transactions rather than as a direct merchant of (film) goods, expedited by its muscle in the spheres of reexporting and logistics. DIFF never sought to become a major player in distribution in the classic sense. In 2009, it dabbled briefly in this area by striking arrangements with Picturehouse to curate a run of highlights from its program and with Front Row to coordinate DVD releases.[11] Yet despite the growing regional market, distribution and exhibition seemed less central to overall objectives. Both are hazardous ventures, given the degree to which multinational chains have dominated these circuits, the expense of the marketing and releasing patterns needed to attract a contemporary audience, and how much viewer taste leans toward the fare of more established industries like Hollywood. Predictably, such enterprises folded over the years with Shivani Pandya, DIFF's former managing director, tellingly declaring to me in a 2009 interview, "We're not calling ourselves distributors.... Our objective is to help, assist and encourage in the process."[12]

What, then, was DIFF up to? To what extent did it recapitulate and diversify Dubai's long-held strengths in port management? And how might following those channels usefully fortify our grasp of the politics and economics of film festivals? In what follows, and drawing on interviews and observations from participation in DIFF's 2009 and 2014 editions, I outline the advantages this brings to assessing how Dubai profits from the temporary congregation of industry personnel and the easing of product movement; the festival's role in guaranteeing and brokering these exchanges; the ways in which Dubai might add value to already-existing (media) entities; how DIFF kept a canny eye on so-called emerging markets and the currency differentials that render them lucrative; and the concomitant measures to bolster other established local economies, particularly tourism, transportation, and real estate. Cinema, I hope to illustrate, adheres more closely to the logistics industry's priorities than we might imagine, and an awareness of how ports function in today's world not only exposes this but emphasizes their centrality to contemporary global capitalism.

The film markets that are increasingly common to film festivals the world over provide straightforward entry points for penetrating these logistical dimensions. Jane Williams, former DIFF industry office director, explains a DIFF core objective: "We've set up a whole series of meetings for filmmakers to meet with potential partners . . . for people who've got money to come and be involved in and work with us in developing Arab talent. And that's really been our motivating force throughout this. It's been about saying to the international community, but also to the region, there is an enormous source of talent in this part of the world."[13]

To streamline the process, DIFF took on the logistical tasks of handpicking invitees, insisting that film directors were already paired up with a producer capable of handling budgets, and keeping a weather eye on growth sectors, be they from television, as was the case originally, or video on demand (VOD) later on. To access those benefits, Williams argued, one had to come "here"—enabled, one way or another, by Dubai's transport infrastructures. Dubai would keep the wheels of production and distribution oiled, with beneficial stopovers in its hinterland but without too much cost to itself in terms of its own manufacturing or merchandising capabilities, steering a wide berth around the financial burdens incumbent on owning film properties or preserving an end stake in their unpredictable retail.

DIFF thus built resourcefully on the UAE's broader fortuity as a junction amid the trade corridors between Europe, Africa, and Asia. Profiting from such convergences began in at least the Middle Ages when a web of regional *funadiq* (inns; more on hotels to come) levied tariffs, stored goods, lodged merchants, and acted as a space for negotiating and fixing prices, as well as buying and selling.[14] Born of this cultural and commercial legacy, DIFF could present the emirate as something of a "contact zone" in Mary Louise Pratt's sense of an actual location for encounters between dispersed people, goods, and ideas; a site where, for long-serving programming consultant, Antonia Carver, "We bring people together from around the region and get them to teach each other.... People ... who can then invest in these films." Carver was convinced that Dubai could do that "better than anywhere else."[15] The emirate's logistics and tourism supremacy would seem to substantiate this, assisted by a centuries-long tradition of both hospitality and a consummate ability to facilitate trade between more prolific manufacturing and consumption centers to its east and west across an often Dubai-administered network of routes. No wonder, then, the slogan on DIFF's logo, "Bridging Cultures, Meeting Minds," embraced a connective infrastructural metaphor. The festival, like Dubai at large, was a means to various geographically distanced ends.

In unfortunate league with these particularities were others stemming from contemporary regional strife. During DIFF's run and into today, the evident dangers of voyaging to other countries in the region (Syria or Palestine, for instance) in search of hot cinematic properties weighed heavily in favor of Dubai's purportedly tranquil ambience and ease of access to citizens from the entire Arab world—and beyond. The cultivated and sustained "neutrality" of Dubai within international opinion has rendered it something of an ideal site over most others in the Middle East to do such business. Dubai, its port, and the festival itself thus become more than just thoroughfares or meeting points.

In addition, they all furnish superlative skills and technologies in situ, ones developed as part of the country's journey to logistical ascendancy. Included within are systems for coordinating across multiple locations and commercial sectors, which are worth pausing to examine before scrutinizing their uptake in the film festival context. Logistics subsumes a raft of services that transport companies now outsource at ports, including storage, fueling, unloading and loading, adding extra components to half-finished goods, repackaging, splitting, and then dispatching goods onward as quickly, cheaply, and as free from time-consuming bureaucracy and inspection as possible.[16] Being able to keep track of goods in transit is an essential requirement of modern commerce, and Dubai's government harmonizes these components in line with a master plan that has top-down streamlined an unbeatable combination of transport infrastructure, minimal bureaucracy, political stability, trustworthiness, low labor costs, and all the latest technologies, while eradicating many customs duties so as to sky rocket not only traffic, but also the services it requires. Sea, land, and air transport services (plus the port) work together to generate revenue for the emirate under the aegis of Dubai World and Dubai World Central Logistics City free zone, which legislatively eases transnational involvement.[17] Capitalizing on the booming markets of India and China and trade between Asia, Africa, and Europe, the UAE generates over USD 9 billion a year in revenue from logistics, whose ventures reached outward to the film industry via DIFF.[18] In the opinions of marine transport specialists John Mangan et al., "It is now generally accepted that supply chains, and not individual firms or products, are the basis of much marketplace competition"; logistics are as fundamental to film markets as to any others, particularly within a digital landscape of torrenting and piracy.[19]

As in the logistics industry, DIFF dedicated great attention to updating technologies to ensure the rapid movement of goods. The sooner a product arrives, the sooner its merchants make money, with the transport

FIGURE 8.1

The Cinetech booths at Dubai International Film Festival.

and logistics industries profiting by facilitating the transfer. During shipping, high-speed cranes have replaced human dockworkers, while computer systems track and thereby minimize the number of empty containers in transit.[20] Developments such as these have now reduced the journey of a ship's cargo from Jebel Ali to an aircraft at Dubai airport to four hours.[21]

DIFF designed an equivalent in the form of Cinetech, proudly launched in 2009, a first-of-its-kind touchscreen interface that linked industry delegates to a bank of over three hundred screeners, as well as *each other*. Ziad Yaghi, then director of the Dubai Film Market, a trained media lawyer and ex-head of acquisitions for regional television giant Orbit, came on as Cinetech's cheerleader: "Lots of people do acquisitions and sales at the festival, but they do it on the side, in the restaurant or the coffee bar. Why don't we create a professional platform to do so?"[22] By reducing human interaction to a more efficient minimum, Cinetech allowed industry representatives to search by categories such as title, genre, country, and actor to home in on what they were looking for. Each movement on the forum was personalized and tracked; then the data was returned to the sales agents and filmmakers with the option always available to leave information for them to arrange a face-to-face sales meeting if that seemed advantageous. Cinetech conforms to what Ned Rossiter labels "logistical media," whose "primary function is to extract value by optimizing the efficiency of living labor and supply chain operations." He goes on to warn us that "logistical media—as technologies, infrastructure, and software—coordinate, capture, and control the movement of people, finance, and things. Infrastructure makes worlds. Logistics governs them."[23] Yaghi corroborates these characteristics of Cinetech, continuing through the prerogatives of logistics: "It is designed to assist buyers, distributors, and broadcasters in the screening process while allowing them to maximize their time."[24] In 2014, DIFF extended this opportunity online to registered delegates, inviting them to continue browsing the catalog and making sales arrangements for several months after the event.

Rossiter's observations about governance and control persist in how DIFF trumpeted Cinetech as a water-tight apparatus. Yaghi elucidates how the unprecedented availability Cinetech could offer was managed in an uncertain environment rife with the illegal movement of film copies as digital files were replacing physical, trackable objects: "[The industry has] trust in the festival, because a lot of people are scared to hand over a DVD because of pirates, but, because of the trust they gave us in the first year, and in the Dubai film festival itself, people have now given us 120 more titles."[25]

Faith of this order has proven essential to Dubai's larger industry of reexportation. Firstly, in a competitive port, goods cannot wander off, get stolen, or become clogged up in processing. Known for many years as the "Pirate's Coast" (well before Cinetech fended off video pirates), the inhabitants of what is now the UAE were once such a threat to international shipping that deals were struck between the most powerful families in the area and overseas (mainly British) interests. The former's political ascendancy, still maintained to this day, was shored up in return for the protection of foreign ships in its waters and within the ports of its coastline—Rossiter's sense of logistics-as-governance writ large and literal.[26] Dubai's ruling elite still doggedly cultivates this image of not only transactional but also economic and political steadiness. Dubai can assert economic dependability (ultimately it is guaranteed by its wealthier UAE neighbor, Abu Dhabi), particularly in contrast to historic but often war-torn regional banking centers like Beirut. However, logistics analysts Chin-Shan Lu et al., after having conducted extensive empirical, survey-based research, conclude that "political stability is the most important incentive."[27] The UAE tirelessly nominates itself as a literal port in the Middle East's political storms, a projection that spilled over, as I will soon delineate, into DIFF's programming objectives. Insuring all these forms of security is exactly what has allowed Dubai's port to prosper as a point of interchange for low-weight, high-value goods such as precious stones and metals. Such reliability remains crucial to traders' use of particular ports—and film festivals too.

Promising security in situ has ever been married to facilitating safe onward movement in Dubai. As noted above, DIFF never fully involved itself in the riskier dimensions of film distribution proper, wherein a merchant takes stock of wares. One might liken DIFF's role here to the warehousing capabilities that flourish across the emirate. Instead of concentrating on acquisition, and as is typical to many film markets (and therefore instructive for comprehending others), DIFF preferred to eschew the liabilities of actual ownership in favor of offering space for negotiation or for the bridging of (sales) cultures. The role that comes to mind, rather, is *brokerage*. And, when directly asked if DIFF considered itself to be acting in this capacity, Pandya responded, "We are."[28] Relatedly, Ziad Yaghi asserted, "We really try to become a platform for them [the films] to go into Cannes and other festivals which is what happened with *Amreeka* [USA/UAE/Canada/Kuwait/Jordan, 2009; dir. Cherien Dabis].... We want to become a hub for helping Arab, Asian, and African filmmakers have their films shown everywhere."[29]

By providing a space for these transactions (physical or screen-based), alongside other corresponding services, DIFF simultaneously operated like another entity that expedites trade: the clearing house. I take this comparison from the actual language of festival personnel. Jane Williams again:

> What became clear last year was that we're becoming like a clearing house at the DFC [Dubai Film Connection—the festival's coproduction platform]. There are two things that we've done that are really important. One is that we go through 120, 150 projects every year and select fifteen to twenty and so we're like a clearing house; we do the selection and we have an international group of people who do that selection operating in the international marketplace, so they have an idea of what to look for and what might find partnerships on the international market and so people started to recognize that this was a really good place if you were looking for good projects, to come to the DFC and meet with those projects and those filmmakers. And when those companies were coming to the DFC they also had the opportunity to see the international interest in those projects, so they could also see if they wanted to take steps towards working in the international market, they had the opportunity to evaluate whether these projects would find partners elsewhere.[30]

A clearing house conventionally performs as an intermediary, guaranteeing, through trust and collateral, a safe transaction between two or more trading partners. While a clearing house typically assesses financial credibility, here DIFF appears to be assuring *cultural* viability, which will then garner its own value in the markets that any film later enters. DIFF thereby shoulders none of the risk or culpability of a real clearing house. These actions, again, can trace a long heritage back to the ports of the Middle Ages, to the *wakil al-tujjar*: an agent acting on the authority of overseas traders, handling legal matters, storing wares, and buying and selling on behalf of absent clients.[31]

This "brokering," I wish to stress, came in culturally translational incarnations, with DIFF creating an environment where, for instance, Palestinian filmmakers could raise foreign consciousness by "exporting" evidence of their colonial condition. The Q&As, the invitations to filmmakers and the sometimes-extensive program notes that DIFF provided over the years, helped set certain values in motion that above all consolidated Dubai's status as not only security conscious but also "safe" in other ways. On many occasions, DIFF seemed almost to be offering a particular cushioning for the outsider delegate against the thornier elements of, say, Middle Eastern politics. A survey of what DIFF has screened over the years unequivocally presents an attention to such matters at the level of political expression. *Chaque jour est une fête / Every Day Is a Holiday* (France/Lebanon/Germany, 2009; dir. Dima El-Horr) stands as exemplary of the kind of film DIFF showcased. Beautifully shot but keeping its narrative more "human" and its politics at arm's length, this Lebanese feature film focuses more on the interrelationship and transformation of a diverse group of women on their way to visit prisoners than on the jail itself or the reason for their relatives' incarceration as political detainees. Such gestures are handy for marketing a film to an imagined general consumer audience.

Similarly, a search for the "personal" sprang up repeatedly in my interviews with DIFF's core selection staff. Jane Williams even edged toward how this emphasis becomes a substitution:

> We've been most successful in finding partners for films with a more personal voice... there is a real interest to encourage film-makers from the region to develop their work from being very issue-based and politics-based to stories that have emotional relations in the foreground rather than politics... to do with their characters rather than their politics.[32]

Michel Khleifi, one of Palestine's most prominent filmmakers, had just completed his DIFF-supported film *Zindeeq* (Palestine/UK/Belgium/UAE, 2009) when he substantiated this perspective in a panel discussion: "My movies put the politics in the background and concentrate on the humanitarian."[33] The languages of the individual and the human(itarian) collude more squarely with Western capitalist and NGO standpoints than those of the Arab region's struggles for independence.

Even though this type of output was not the be-all and end-all of DIFF's program, the festival certainly aimed to hallmark (as most such events do) its chosen films to establish a form of "quality control," part and parcel of the "cultural legitimization" that Marijke de Valck notices emanating from well-regarded festival institutions.[34] Working toward this impression were DIFF's raft of awards, a customary tool of most film festivals. Accolades raise the competitive edge of the winning movies in a flooded market and subsequently advertise the festival when these films move onward. Again, such practices did not arrive unexpectedly in the UAE with the advent of their film festivals. As a stopping-off point along supply chains, Dubai has long ventured into "value added" provision to often near-complete commodities, these services typically dominating, as has been observed, over large-scale from-scratch industrial production.

Dubai's history as a reexporting hub, therefore, allows us to comprehend that DIFF's sidestepping of sinking hefty sums into creating film commodities from scratch was a familiar profit model with fewer financial hazards typical of film production, distribution, and exhibition. Rather, DIFF looked to establish itself as a service provider (facilitator, negotiator, guarantor, translator) in the movement of those goods. With this being the case, it remains crucial to attend to the specific circuits of trade that DIFF nurtured, given that these inevitably built and bolstered the uneven power dynamics that are the lifeblood of commercial transactions.

As we have already seen, Dubai's position as a barrier-free gateway to the Gulf region, but also to other international markets, enabled DIFF to designate itself as a guardian of cinematic reexportation, and these moves represent significant affinity with Dubai's broader placement within patterns of circulation. By 2013, Dubai was steaming ahead toward its fellow members in the GCC common market where trade had swollen by 28 percent over just two years.[35] In efforts to replicate this regional boom, Shivani Pandya recognized that one of the festival's core priorities was to create a culture of spectatorship—a market for cinematic wares: "We'll build and educate the audiences and that will help with future distribution and future acquisition."[36] Toward the end of the millennium's first decade, DIFF spotted that Arab media outlets, particularly the large television corporations like ART and Rotana, were attracted more and more to their market. As Jane Williams describes, "There's an increasing interest in producing Arabic-language material for an Arab market," something also registered by the hike in regional film financing too.[37] The Dubai Film Connection, which assisted with coproduction arrangements until it folded in 2014, certainly did progressively contribute to a rise in regional filmmaking. By more than doubling the projects it supported throughout this millennium's first decade, DIFF directly created products for its own program and saw some of these projects premiere at top-tier festivals like Cannes and Toronto.[38] No wonder, then, that in 2014 DIFF eventually dropped its AsiaAfrica strand to concentrate instead on its Arab categories. It seemed more driven by the exact priorities of global capitalist expansion that logistics have eased into place. As part of Dubai businesses' moves into fresh realms like the media economy, they need a way to identify their most profitable markets, which includes the Gulf itself.

However, throughout its longer history, DIFF's programming priorities mirrored the South-South flavor of Dubai's broader trade relations. Looked at from a wider angle, we can see the reason for this. Dubai availed itself early to containerization, fully equipping its Jebel Ali port for this now-dominant mode of goods transportation, thus making possible its first container routes to India by 1980.[39] At the time of DIFF's heyday, India was first on the emirate's list of top reexporting destinations (worth USD 6.53 billion) followed by Iran and then Iraq.[40]

But how DIFF narrated trade with countries like these within the Global South is striking. The language of emerging markets—both labor markets for film production and consumer markets for watching this output—stood strong within DIFF's self-presentation. Nashen Moodley, the director of the AsiaAfrica strand in the 2009 edition, for example, described his program as "designed to stimulate and expose filmmaking from emerging markets," while one of the festival's strategic aims was that DIFF would "become a center for discovering and showcasing excellence in cinema from emerging markets defined as Asia & Africa."[41] Note also the vocabulary of exploration, as if these territories were terra incognita, with Dubai then playing the host, perhaps even the *patron*, to choice specimens from these locales. The chosen foci blended seamlessly into broader patterns of Gulf ownership and private foreign direct investment (FDI) across exactly those regions, including within their media.[42] Sights fell on definitively cheaper ("competitive") labor markets where paid-for media consumption was simultaneously on the rise. While DIFF was also apt to express such affiliations in the languages of dialogue and diversity, we should nevertheless take seriously how port-derived logistics and a globally dispersed supply chain ethos seek to boost production statistics (including within filmmaking) beyond the richer orbits of the Global North.

Regularly, the talk was about "making South–South relationships," to quote Antonia Carver. Dale Hudson expands on this prerogative as it was experienced within Emirati film culture: "Small nations, then, can help other small nations (especially stateless nations) convey their perspectives in feature films for international audiences."[43] Key DIFF staff framed this through precise geopolitics, with Carver saying that "we can find funding for films in the region, and that means we don't have to go to Europe."[44] Further, as Jane Williams points out, "As soon as a European funder comes on board, the perspective changes . . . most filmmakers would really like to see they could find money here."[45] The resulting autonomy came as a welcome relief to many in the sector against a historical backdrop of transnationalized inequity of access, commercial domination, residues of military occupation, and of course the pressures erupting from regional differences in taste.

Yet such deliberate diversions, localized optimisms about self-sufficiency, or gestures of solidarity must toil against the privatized normalities of film production and the piecemeal, decentralized funding structures they engender. One DIFF-supported film, *Fix Me* (Raed Adoni, 2009), for example, additionally drew on Swiss and French money, including France's arguably neocolonial Fonds Sud. DIFF itself sought financial assistance for training from European Audiovisual Entrepreneurs (EAVE), whose name leaves little space for doubt as to its politics and whose mission was to answer questions about a project's viability or its maker's ability to penetrate international (read: European) markets. More generally speaking, and as scholars like Marijke de Valck highlight, festivals have somewhat cornered less commercially viable markets with the aid of regional subvention, rendering the launch of uncompliant variants of independent filmmaking and dissemination trickier than ever.[46] Festivals and these backers command considerable influence within a highly unbalanced ratio of cinematic production to distribution and exhibition.

Situational compromise, case by case, is one thing and recapitulation of a systemic ethos another. DIFF, along with most other film festivals that sponsor or invigorate production by drawing together multiple backers, coax cinema further away from national(ized) models that have, historically, proffered more stable support (including by employing creative personnel as public-sector workers, as was the case in nearby countries like Syria, Egypt, and Algeria), sheltering them from the maelstrom that multiple interests and the ensuing understanding of value and profit can whip up. A standard feature of festivals, whereby filmmakers compete for one-off awards like those offered by DIFF's Enjaaz scheme, helps cement this change. Likewise, might DIFF's Dubai Film Connection's encouragement of filmmakers to broker coproduction deals outside their country of origin effectively palliate long-term state divestment (even as these haphazard funds are heralded as governmental largesse)? Dubai here also cleaves to the tactical aloofness endemic to port trading and reexportation.

Within this constellation, the festival becomes not simply a place for dialogue, not even just an environment for honing the necessary critical acumen and diversity of experience for an effective knowledge economy, but, beyond this, a motor for the generation, commodification, and retailing of thought and cultural expression. When I talked to Antonia Carver in 2009, she called attention to how "Dubai has always been this trading capital, a place where *ideas* as well as goods get traded."[47] Its free port status, Carver affirmed, has meant that "Dubai has a very different entrepreneurial spirit in business" from that of its neighboring countries, one that has "tipped over into culture."[48]

That all these initiatives should materialize within an (admittedly state-fostered) private sector is a measure of a broader trend spearheaded by the likes of the World Bank and the International Monetary Fund (IMF) to reorganize production (including in cultural form) outside public management and provision.[49] The withdrawal of such backing in poorer countries, often coerced by these transnational bodies, has more than simply enticed their filmmakers to DIFF as a haven offering support of a radically different nature than was provided by national(ized) industries in the twentieth century. It has also impelled large numbers of their populations to migrate to Dubai for work. Practically none are granted lifelong secure residency, a status reflected in festivals' own built-in transience.

Yet it would be misleading to conclude that there are no stable structures benefitting from the exchanges that festivals like DIFF have cultivated. Permanent architectures of profit attach to such events, just as

FIGURE 8.2

DIFF's logo is eased into place at the Madinat Jumeirah; the Burj Al Arab hotel looms in the background.

they do to the workings of a port. Within the latter, these include customs houses, warehouses, and the like. In the past, inns for traveling merchants also counted among the buildings siphoning revenues from passage, and this has carried over to DIFF. When Shivani Pandya stated, "We've become a destination for that [moving films around the world] and that's what we hoped to do,"[50] she divulged the part DIFF would play in Dubai's large-scale conversion from a transit hub to a place where people would actively aspire to vacation and spend money. DIFF ultimately employed more staff in its Guest Relations and Hospitality Department than it did in programming, and no wonder, given the UAE's growing stakes in tourism over the same period. By 2014, Dubai was the Arab world's most-visited city and fifth in the world, racking up 12 million visitors, a ratio of 4.8 to every resident, who collectively spent USD 10.95 billion, thus delivering an important flow of foreign cash into Dubai.[51] Unsurprisingly, over the years, backers for DIFF regularly came forward from the UAE's tourism portfolio: Emirates (its airline), Dubai Airports, the Jumeirah Group (a hotel chain), and Dubai Duty Free. These sponsors promoted their services to delegates and guests and expanded DIFF's capacity to bring its films' directors into town for postscreening Q&As. Shivani Pandya explained that this was part of a "coordinated effort.... Everyone's aware of the goals we're trying to achieve in the next few years, so we're fairly streamlined."[52] It is important to pause and take stock of her recourse to the ergonomics of movement here. With a lick of logistics expertise spurring them along, industry business meetings—long a staple of film markets—could avail themselves of hospitality from local hotels and restaurants, contributing to the surge in event, conference, and business tourism at the beginning of the millennium.[53] A rising niche within the tourism industry at that time, business events (such as DIFF) worked within Dubai's more established infrastructures—its transport sector, for instance—to diversify and cross-promote newer investments. Profit was secured within ancillary sectors—the malls, hotels, and airports—and goodwill accrued to Dubai as a competitive site for the knowledge and creative industries. With Dubai relying on established revenue earners less volatile than film, the riskier financial transactions were left to the festival's buyers and sellers, whether they were involved in film creation or acquisition.

Longer-term rentals than hotels might also prove popular and generate profits in this landscape. Over DIFF's duration, its administration had been housed in the free zones that Dubai dedicates to media production. Free zones have always been attached to ports. They offer exceptional tax-exempt status for manufacturing, eradicate custom duties on imports or reexports, and in the UAE, welcome proportions of foreign ownership that are otherwise curbed by law in the country proper. Now thriving even more than they were at the time of DIFF's operation, these sites have become populous and their properties leased as regional headquarters by large multinationals and the smaller companies that feed from related contract work and a rise in regional media production. In helping build an audience and a market for film and television, DIFF put Dubai on the cultural map. Look closer, and that map increasingly displays everything from office and studio space to housing, all inhabited more continuously and profiting from greater FDI than any hotel could be during a one-week event.

Much to the film community's surprise, DIFF announced a hiatus in April 2018. Initially, a 2019 edition was promised along with a slowing down to biannual appearances; but at the time of this writing, these events have yet to materialize. As mercurial as the logistical strategies it took advantage of, DIFF faded away with little fanfare. My own conjecture follows from the argument I have just presented: that there were tidier and steadier profits to be made from this sector through real estate, itself a bastion of the emirate's post-oil economy. By 2018, DIFF had perhaps served its purpose as a beacon alerting the world to Dubai's potential as a site for creative labor. That these media free zones are likewise governed by the lean production models of logistics, and that they draw a usefully transient (albeit longer-term) international crowd, is another chapter in Dubai's history—one I explore in more detail elsewhere.[54]

> KAY DICKINSON works in the University of Glasgow Film and Television Studies department and is the convenor for MA Creative Arts and Industries. She is author of *Arab Cinema Travels: Transnational Syria, Palestine, Dubai and Beyond* (BFI Publishing, 2016), *Arab Film and Video Manifestos: Forty-Five Years of the Moving Image Amid Revolution* (Palgrave, 2018), and *Supply Chain Cinema: Producing Global Film Workers* (BFI, 2024).

NOTES

1. This essay is an updated and shortened version of the final chapter of its author's monograph, *Arab Cinema Travels: Transnational Syria, Palestine, Dubai and Beyond* (BFI, 2016). The extract is republished with permission of the British Film Institute and Bloomsbury Publishing Plc.

2. See, for instance, Marijke de Valck's treatment of Rotterdam in Marijke de Valck, *Film Festivals from European Geopolitics to Global Cinephilia* (Amsterdam: Amsterdam University Press, 2007), 171–72, and Patricia Avery's more general discussion of regeneration

via the media and cultural industries in Patricia Avery, "Born Again: From Dock Cities to Cities of Culture," in *Tourism, Culture, and Regeneration*, ed. Melanie K. Smith (Cambridge, MA: CABI, 2006), 151–62.

3. World Shipping Council, "About the Industry: World Top 50 Container Ports," http://www.worldshipping.org/about-the-industry/global-trade/top-50-world-container-ports.

4. Melodena Stephens Balakrishnan, "Dubai—A Star in the East," *Journal of Place Management and Development* 1, no. 1 (2008): 168–69.

5. Terry Macalister, "Heathrow Airport Overtaken by Dubai as World's Busiest," *Guardian*, December 31, 2014, http://www.theguardian.com/uk-news/2014/dec/31/heathrow-airport-dubai-world-busiest; Macalister, "Dubai Remains World's Busiest International Airport," Emirates 24/7, January 24, 2017, https://www.emirates247.com/business/dubai-remains-world-s-busiest-international-airport-2017-01-24-1.646965.

6. de Valck's *Film Festivals* is a particularly deft and involved example of the latter type of scholarship.

7. George F. Hourani, *Arab Seafaring in the Indian Ocean in Ancient and Early Medieval Times* (Princeton, NJ: Princeton University Press, 1995), 70.

8. Dubai Exports, *Dubai Trade Profile, 2006–2011* (Dubai: Government of Dubai, 2012), 15–16.

9. B. Ramesh Kumar, "The UAE's Strategy Trade Partnership with Asia: A Focus on Dubai," Middle East Institute, August 19, 2013, http://www.mei.edu/content/uae%E2%80%99s-strategic-trade-partnership-asia-focus-dubai#_ftnref1.

10. Here are some of the trade agreements and organizations to which Dubai belongs: the Gulf Cooperation Council (GCC), the Greater Arab Free Trade Agreement (which incorporates eighteen Arab countries and four associate members from the Organization of Islamic Countries), the GCC and Singapore Free Trade Agreement, Bilateral Trade Agreements with Syria, Jordan, Lebanon, Morocco, and Iraq, the Arab League, the Organization of Islamic Countries, the World Bank, the World Trade Organization, and the United Nations Conference on Trade and Development (Dubai Exports, An Agency of the Department of Economic Development, Government of Dubai, "Re-export from Dubai Mainland.").

11. Dubai International Film Festival, "DIFF to Strengthen Outreach of Regional Cinema through Distribution Support," Press Release, December 15, 2009; Shivani Pandya, interview with author, December 15, 2009.

12. Shivani Pandya, interview with author, December 15, 2009.

13. Jane Williams, interview with author, December 9, 2009.

14. Olivia Remie Constable, *Housing the Stranger in the Mediterranean World* (Cambridge: Cambridge University Press, 2003), 73.

15. Mary Louise Pratt, *Imperial Eyes: Travel Writing and Transculturation* (London: Routledge, 1992), 4. Antonia Carver, interview with author, December 10, 2009.

16. Chin-Shan Lu, Chun-Hsiung Liao, and Ching-Chiao Yang, "Segmenting Manufacturers' Investment Incentive Preferences for International Logistics Zones," *International Journal of Operations and Production Management* 28, no. 2 (2008): 108, 110.

17. John Mangan, Chandra Lalwani, and Brian Fynes, "Port-Centric Logistics," *International Journal of Logistics Management* 19, no. 1 (2008): 35.

18. Department of Economic Development, Government of Dubai, "Exporting and Re-exporting from Dubai," http://www.dubaided.gov.ae/en/startbusiness/Pages/ExportingRe_exportingFromDubai.aspx.

19. Mangan et al., "Port-Centric Logistics," 35.

20. For a readable account of all these technological developments and their social and economic impact, see Marc Levinson, *The Box: How the Shipping Container Made the World Smaller and the World Economy Bigger* (Princeton, NJ: Princeton University Press, 2010).

21. World Port Source, "Port of Jebel Ali: Port Commerce," http://www.worldportsource.com/ports/commerce/ARE_Port_of_Jebel_Ali_1423.php.

22. Ziad Yaghi, interview with author, December 12, 2009.

23. Ned Rossiter, *Software, Infrastructure, Labor: A Media Theory of Logistical Nightmares* (New York and London: Routledge, 2017), 4–5.

24. Ziad Yaghi, interview with author, December 12, 2009.

25. Ziad Yaghi, interview with author, December 12, 2009.

26. Mike Davis, "Sand, Fear, and Money in Dubai," in *Evil Paradises: Dreamworlds of Neoliberalism*, ed. Mike Davis and Daniel Bertrand Monk (New York: New Press, 2007), 56; Ahmed Kanna, *Dubai: The City as Corporation* (Minneapolis: University of Minnesota Press, 2011), 23; James Onley, "Transnational Merchants in the Nineteenth-Century Gulf," in *Transnational Connections and the Arab Gulf*, ed. Madawi Al-Rasheed (London: Routledge, 2005), 72–73.

27. Lu et al., "Segmenting Manufacturers' Investment," 106.

28. Shivani Pandya, interview with author, December 15, 2009.

29. Ziad Yaghi, interview with author, December 12, 2009.

30. Jane Williams, interview with author, December 9, 2009.

31. *Letters of Medieval Jewish Traders*, trans. and ed. S. D. Goitein (Princeton, NJ: Princeton University Press, 1973), 14–15.

32. Jane Williams, interview with author, December 9, 2009.

33. Michel Khleifi, "Palestine on Film," panel discussion, Dubai International Film Festival, December 11, 2009.

34. de Valck, *Film Festivals*, 211.

35. Haseeb Haider, "Dubai Non-Oil Trade Growth to Cool," *Khaleej Times*, May 19, 2014, http://www.khaleejtimes.com/biz/inside.asp?xfile=/data/uaebusiness/2014/May/uaebusiness_May301.xml&section=uaebusiness.

36. Shivani Pandya, interview with author, December 15, 2009.

37. Jane Williams, interview with author, December 9, 2009; Layali Badr of television channel ART claims that 60 percent of the budgets of Arab films come from television now (Layali Badr, "The Arab Film Industry and the Financial Crisis," panel discussion, Dubai International Film Festival, December 12, 2009).

38. Shivani Pandya, speech, delivered December 8, 2009.

39. Stephen J. Ramos, *Dubai Amplified: The Engineering of a Port Geography* (Farnham: Ashgate Publishing Limited, 2010), 111.

40. Dubai Exports, *Dubai Trade Profile*, 15–16.

41. Nashen Moodley, Director of AsiaAfrica Programme, speech, delivered December 8, 2009; Dubai International Film Festival, *5th Dubai International Film Festival Executive Summary* (Dubai: Government of Dubai/Dubai Technology and Media Free Zone Authority, 2008), 4.

42. Adam Hanieh, "Egypt and the Gulf: Rethinking the Nature of Counter-Revolution," (Conference paper, Historical Materialism Conference 2012, SOAS, University of London, London, UK, November 8, 2012).

43. Dale Hudson, "Locating Emirati Filmmaking within Globalizing Media Ecologies," in *Media in the Middle East: Activism, Politics, and Culture*, ed. Nele Lenze, Charlotte Schriwer, and Zubaidah Abdul Jalil (New York: Palgrave Macmillan, 2017), 189.

44. Antonia Carver, interview with author, December 10, 2009.

45. Jane Williams, interview with author, December 9, 2009.

46. de Valck, *Film Festivals*, 105.

47. Antonia Carver, interview with author, December 10, 2009.

48. Antonia Carver, interview with author, December 10, 2009.

49. For a fuller picture of how this has played out in the Arab world, see Chad Haines, "Cracks in the Façade: Landscapes of Hope and Desire in Dubai," in *Worlding Cities: Asian Experiments and the Art of Being Global*, ed. Ananya Roy and Aihwa Ong (Chichester: Wiley-Blackwell, 2011), 162.

50. Shivani Pandya, interview with author, December 15, 2009.

51. Yuwa Hendrick-Wong and Desmond Choong, "MasterCard: 2014 Global Destination Cities Index," MasterCard Worldwide Insights, http://newsroom.mastercard.com/wp-content/uploads/2014/07/Mastercard_GDCI_2014_Letter_Final_70814.pdf, 4–6, 23, 24.

52. Shivani Pandya, interview with author, December 15, 2009.

53. See Johnny Allen et al., *Festival and Special Event Management*, 3rd ed. (Milton: Wiley, 2005), 481; Sandro Formica, "The Development of Festivals and Special Events Studies," *Festival Management and Event Tourism* 5, no. 3 (1998): 135 for empirical data on the rise of these types of tourism. There is even an academic journal entitled *Festival Management and Event Tourism* dedicated to its study.

54. See the longer version of this paper, Kay Dickinson, "'Travel and Profit from It': Dubai's Forays into Film," in *Arab Cinema Travels: Transnational Syria, Palestine, Dubai and Beyond* (London: BFI, 2016): 119–162, as well as Dickinson, "'Make It What You Want It to Be': Logistics, Labor, and Land Financialization via the Globalized Free Zone Studio," in *In the Studio: Visual Creation and its Material Environments*, ed. Brian Jacobson (Berkeley: University of California Press, 2020), 261–80.

9

Peeking behind the Curtain
Gulf Filmmakers Imagine the Lives of Female Migrant Domestic Workers in the Arabian Peninsula

SUZI MIRGANI

Since most of the Arabian Peninsula states do not offer official political participation—neither to their citizens, nor to their foreign migrant populations—other forms of informal political engagement have emerged, especially within the arts.[1] Some filmmakers in the Gulf Cooperation Council (GCC), both citizen and foreign resident, are performing roles more closely associated with civil society, among other interest groups, by highlighting sensitive sociopolitical issues and broaching them in creative ways. Irrespective of the fact that the film industries in the Gulf are state sponsored, filmmaking has emerged as a platform for vibrant social commentary.[2] Even though many of these cultural productions are constrained by the overarching systems in which they are produced and under which they operate, these works nonetheless open up new channels for social critique—most often subtle but sometimes pointedly political as I demonstrate in this study.

While "criticism of society beyond the superficial" is rare in the Gulf states, in this chapter I argue that many Gulf filmmakers have been creatively advocating for a variety of social concerns that have hitherto been more fully and critically explored in academia—from women's rights to migrant worker issues.[3] Through textual and contextual analyses of Gulf-made films, I explore Gulf citizens' artistic engagements with particular social subjects. Specifically, I examine several short fiction films that are overt or covert sociopolitical statements about the Gulf's most silent—and silenced—demographic: female migrant domestic workers. Without losing sight of the obvious skewed power relationship between Gulf filmmakers and their migrant subjects, I argue that some artists have opted to use their public platforms and privileged positions to highlight the uneven and tense relationships between Gulf citizens and the millions of foreign female domestic workers—those publicly visible, and yet invisible, economic migrants to the Gulf states, including maids, nannies, cooks, and cleaners.

I examine five short fiction films whose subject matter concerns the unequal power relationships between Gulf citizens and foreign female domestic workers: *Dunya's Day* (Saudi Arabia, 2018), *Elevate* (Qatar, 2017), *Beshkara* (United Arab Emirates, 2014), *Is Sumiyati Going to Hell?* (Saudi Arabia, 2016), and *Soap* (Kuwait, 2014). These films are all written and directed by Gulf citizens. Even though the films under investigation are all narrative fiction, they can still be considered visual ethnographies that reflect broader social realities. If we acknowledge that film "texts constitute sites around which the pre-eminently social affair of the struggle for the production of meaning is conducted," then there is much to learn from how certain social groups are portrayed and framed by Gulf filmmakers through their creative works.[4] Gulf filmmakers are providing a window into the innermost sanctums of Gulf households, inviting audiences to peek behind the curtain into the imagined intimate relationships between Gulf families and female migrant domestic workers as they unfold in living rooms, kitchens, and bedrooms.

FOREIGN DOMESTIC WORKERS AND SOCIAL FRICTIONS

While the Gulf's economic growth over the past few decades has meant improvements in standards of living—and maids, nannies, cooks, and cleaners relieve Gulf families of the daily burden of housekeeping—migrant domestic workers remain a source of friction within Gulf societies. This is especially the case when Gulf families in general, and children in particular, are necessarily influenced by their proximity to the foreign cultures, languages, and values imparted by migrant domestic workers.[5] These contentious issues are a feature of the alarmist regional media, highlighting public debates about "concerns for the integrity of the local family... as well as the perceived vulnerability to the erosion or loss of a cohesive local cultural tradition."[6] This contemporary condition—being simultaneously grateful to and yet inconvenienced by foreign domestic workers within the private space of the home—is reflected in Gulf-made films: some containing warning messages about the threat these migrants pose, while others advocating on the migrants' behalf. In either case, however, the persistent presence of a foreign figure is "a constant source of domestic disquiet."[7]

In Gulf homes, "household labor is one of the few arenas in which people of differing nationalities regularly interact."[8] Indeed, for many Gulf citizens, "the presence of foreign workers in the house is... their most direct and intimate source of knowledge" regarding migrants in the country.[9] In the academic literature, "the impact of these vast migration flows upon the families indigenous to the Khaleeji states [...] remains one of the most unexplored facets of the migration literature concerning the Gulf States."[10]

The nature of domestic work means that these female migrants are largely confined to the privacy of the home, and their private sponsorship status under *kafala* regulations has meant they occupy a precarious legal space[11] most often highlighted by advocacy groups, academic and policy studies, and the media.[12] In order to add nuance to whatever academic inquiries exist, I examine how female migrant domestic workers are represented and imagined by Gulf filmmakers. If we consider film to be a type of "self-study" through creative text, then Gulf "filmmaking provides an important site for critical inquiry that generate new questions within larger fields, such as film studies or Arab media studies."[13]

Gulf-made films reveal a distinct gendered dimension to how low-income migrants are represented. This is because "while many aspects of local social relations influence household labor relations, such as religion, class and ethnicity, gender is a primary structuring force."[14] Since Gulf households are generally divided according to gender, with male and female areas, many of the tasks a female helper performs are a tolerated necessity (whether as a nanny, cook, or cleaner), but the presence of a male domestic worker (whether a gardener, handyman, or driver) within the privacy of the gender-segregated household is tolerated as an uncomfortable necessity.[15] The films I analyze single out female migrant domestic workers for sympathetic treatment, but these positive representations can be compared with many other more negative portrayals of male domestic workers—a complementary subject of investigation that is beyond the scope of the current study.

The films I analyze in this chapter were produced locally in various GCC states, most funded by GCC government-sponsored film institutions, leading to the conclusion that the Gulf's growing film industries are opening up a space for critical social reflection through the arts. The fact that the films I examine are either directly or indirectly critical of the Gulf's labor systems and of privileged behavior in Gulf societies demonstrates the critical positions Gulf filmmakers occupy: a space that engenders public debate and social critique that is both reflective of and relatable to Gulf audiences. Intended for public viewing, most of these works are either available online or were screened publicly at various Gulf film festivals, most of which have now been discontinued.

THE MISTRESS AND THE MISTREATED

Several Gulf-made films highlight the fraught relationships between a mean mistress and a mistreated maid. These films present a scenario in which a female Gulf-citizen employer must learn from, or at least acknowledge, her petulant behavior—the result of being overly privileged—even if the films do not conclude with the "madame" completely sympathizing with the hardship of her maid. The films I analyze in this study all contain some kind of reflection on the part of the Gulf protagonist but not to the extent of catharsis—defined as "a purification or purgation that brings about spiritual renewal or release from tension."[16] In most cases, even though there is some kind of retribution on the part of the domestic worker, the films conclude with a kind of meditation on the events occurring in the film but without fully reforming the relationship—the films are an invocation to engage in reflection rather than redemption.

Raed Alsemari's short film *Dunya's Day* (Saudi Arabia, 2018) highlights the tensions between a wealthy Saudi citizen and her foreign domestic help. This was the first Saudi film to premiere theatrically in the kingdom after the thirty-five-year-old ban on public cinemas was lifted.[17] It was also the first Saudi film to be included in the Sundance Film Festival and to win the Short Film Jury Award for International Fiction prize.[18] These "firsts" already speak volumes about the role of film in fueling the social reforms currently sweeping through the conservative kingdom and the new role of art in both reflecting and reforming Saudi society.[19]

Dunya's Day follows an exquisitely dressed Dunya—wearing a fur shawl in the desert majlis setting of her graduation party—who screams the names of her domestic workers "Maria," "Rose," and "Abdo," to which she receives no response.[20] The increasingly loud, angry, and desperate screams already tell the audience much about why "hours before her esteemed guests arrive, all the domestic help take off—fed up with 'Madame' Dunya's antics."[21] Even though the domestic workers are physically absent from the screen for most of the film, the specter of their absence is very much present. Through their absence, the runaway domestic workers drive the action, and precipitate all the ensuing events.

Since seventy-three guests have already been invited, Dunya and her two friends must figure out how to go ahead with preparations for the planned party without the "help." The women abandon their lavish gowns and unceremoniously dress down in maids' uniforms—a reversal of fortune in which they are all "ugly stepsisters" forced to go to the kitchen instead of the ball. Despite all three women being in the same disadvantaged position, Dunya remains her haughty self and—just as she would have done with the domestic workers—orders her friends to do the dirty work while she supervises by reading instructions from the internet.

Although the film does not redeem Dunya nor highlight her awakening to the hardships of domestic labor, this "reversal of fortune" genre gives the audience the satisfaction of seeing the spoiled and wealthy Dunya put herself in her maid's shoes—Louboutins notwithstanding. When the evening gets out of hand, Dunya's humiliation is such that she decides to avoid all responsibility for the party by quite literally burying her head in the sand, leaving the guests to look for her and call out her name all evening. In a more politicized reading, the multiple calls to Dunya—meaning "world" in Arabic—become an invocation for the world to watch. The

FIGURE 9.1

Dunya ordering her friends around in *Dunya's Day* (Saudi Arabia, 2018), courtesy of Read Alsemari.

film offers an Arabian schadenfreude in which the audience—the film's spectators as well as Saudi Arabia's international onlookers—delights at Dunya's downfall and that of everything she represents.

Hamida Issa's short film *Elevate* (Qatar, 2017)—which received a Doha Film Institute Qatari Film Fund Grant and premiered at the 2017 Ajyal Film Festival in Qatar—similarly addresses the subject of "Latifa, a rude and vain woman and her long-suffering maid Rosie."[22] When the two become stuck in an elevator—in Latifa's ostentatious house—"Latifa becomes downright nasty in her treatment of Rosie, even going so far as to blame her for the mechanical failure," and berates the maid for regularly using the elevator instead of taking the stairs.[23] The longer the two women remain in the elevator, the more angry and panicked Latifa becomes, until Rosie can no longer take the verbal abuse and responds—seemingly for the first time in their relationship—in an explosion of pent-up anger at her years of mistreatment.

The fact that Rosie's outburst is in her native language, Tagalog, irritates Latifa even more; not only is Latifa trapped, she is also being attacked and alienated in a foreign language. Meanwhile, English-, Arabic-, and Tagalog-speaking viewers become insightful observers who are able to understand Rosie's anguish through her speech and through the film's

FIGURE 9.2

Latifa and Rosie stuck in an elevator in *Elevate* (Qatar, 2017), courtesy of Hamida Issa.

English and Arabic subtitles. Through this shared understanding, everyone involved in the film—the filmmaker, the character of the maid, and the audience—create a common bond at Latifa's expense and that of all those she represents. Finally, Rosie resorts to speaking English, crying: "I left my daughter in the Philippines to work here. I left her there, even if I know that I cannot see her growing up."[24] Latifa is stunned at the ferocity of the accusations leveled against her and takes some time to process Rosie's words. However, before Latifa has a chance to respond to Rosie, the elevator doors mysteriously open.

In the film's ensuing magical realism episode, the elevator doors open toward another dimension—a portal to Qatar's past. Latifa disembarks into the desert landscape and follows the voice of an old woman through the vernacular architecture of a fishing/pearling village. As an ancestral specter, the old woman, in traditional *batula* (face mask), advises Latifa: "Go back to your roots." The ancestor reminds the entitled protagonist of her humble origins and criticizes the Gulf's contemporary consumerism, saying: "People are running after the material. Money does not buy peace of mind."[25] The film's synopsis notes that Latifa "confronts her own egotistical nature and rediscovers the lessons of humility and respect she learned as a child," which is only visible to the viewer through a final sympathetic look shared by Latifa and Rosie.[26] Latifa is left looking over the horizon, meditating on Rosie's harsh words and the old woman's advice. Although the audience is not privy to the future of this relationship, the camera's slow pan over the mangroves and the folk song in the background signal that a lesson has been learned and that something is about to change for the better.

Another Gulf-made film that tackles the relationship between a female domestic worker and her female employer is the United Arab Emirates (UAE) short *Beshkara* (2015), directed by Abdulrahman Al Madani. The film was produced by the New York Film Academy Abu Dhabi and premiered at the 2015 Dubai International Film Festival. The word *beshkara* means "housemaid" in colloquial Emirati Arabic, with origins that reportedly go back to the period of British protectionism. Nadia Buhannad notes that "whenever the Englishmen's cars broke down, and they needed help pushing it to kick start the engine, they would call the workers and ask them to 'Push Car.' It seems that the repetitive usage of the phrase when dealing with workers, who were likely Asian at that time, caused Khalijis to begin referring to Asian workers, especially domestic workers, as '*beshkar*.'"[27] During the preindependence 1960s, when the word *beshkar* gained popularity, there were roughly equal numbers of citizens and migrants in the Emirates, and all were subjected to British rule.[28] The subsequent postindependence decades were fueled by hydrocarbon revenues and infrastructural developments, as well as a dramatic increase in the migrant labor population, creating increasingly unequal power relations between Emirati citizens and millions of low-income migrants.

The film *Beshkara* highlights these new relationships of power and wealth disparities in the contemporary period. A cranky old Emirati woman named Fatima, as an ultimate sign of power over another individual's life and mobility, performs the illegal (yet common) act of confiscating her maid's passport, disbarring Mariam from leaving the country to visit her sick child back home in the Philippines.[29] When Mariam asks Fatima for her passport, the employer responds: "What passport? I told you to never mention this word."[30] Even though the film is fiction, it is a reflection of the very real situations many domestic workers find themselves occupying. The film highlights the kinds of contentious issues that occur regularly behind closed doors and opens these for discussion and public debate wherever the film is screened, including during Q&A sessions at its world premiere at the Dubai International Film Festival in 2015 and subsequent screenings around the Gulf states, which experience similar concerns about the power relations between Gulf employers and migrant domestic workers.[31]

The director gains sympathy for Mariam—especially from Muslim audiences—from the very first scene in which she wakes up to the sound of the *azhan*, the Muslim call to prayer, and walks past a stack of strategically placed books: the Qur'an in English and Arabic, and guidebooks for converts to Islam, *The New Muslim Guide* and *The Choice*. One of the film's many themes highlights how "tens of thousands of domestic workers—migrant women of diverse ethnonational, linguistic, educational and religious backgrounds—have converted to Islam," an act that has been "developed through their gendered experiences of transnational migration and their relations and work centered on household spaces."[32] From the outset, through Mariam's hijab, Islam becomes a visible shield protecting her from the denigration of prejudiced audiences and elevates Mariam to a more honorable position in the viewer's estimation.

Mariam's passivity is represented in stark contrast to the mean-spirited nature of her employer, Fatima, who orders her to get out of the way of the television and to sit down on the floor beside her as she watches a show. Fatima's abuse of Mariam continues when she makes fun of the maid's accent and then prevents her from using the phone, saying, "Don't you have work to do besides use your phone?!" Fatima then confiscates Mariam's device, depriving the maid of any communication with the outside world.[33] Any privacy Mariam tries to find, whether in her bedroom or in the kitchen, to process the bad news that her daughter has fallen ill back in the Philippines, is disrupted by a cheerful electronic call bell alerting her to return to work. When Mariam has had enough of the injustice, and

FIGURE 9.3

Mariam and Madame. Still from *Beshkara* (UAE, 2015), courtesy of Abdulrahman Al Madani.

her frustrations reach the boiling point, she enacts her civil disobedience by dismantling the call bell and ignoring her employer's needs.

Beshkara admonishes modern Gulf societies in which old, helpless, and lonely grandmothers can be left to fend for themselves, with their foreign caretakers as their only company. When Fatima's daughter and eye-rolling, iPad-watching teenage granddaughter come to visit, the audience understands that they do not live together as a family—a growing condition of increasingly fractured Gulf societies.[34] While once extended Gulf families lived together within the same vast household, the contemporary period has been defined by a more nuclear family structure. The film's text of citizen-migrant relationships, and its subtext of transformations in traditional ways of life, are pointed critiques of modern social mores, failing family relationships, and lack of filial piety.

When Mariam finally faces up to her employer, pleading for her release, she asks, "Why can't you just find another maid, Madam?" Fatima breaks down, crying: "No want another, I want no one else but you. No want you go. Please." In the end, the audience sympathizes with Fatima, who is just a cranky, sick old woman, alone in the world, with neither family nor maid for company. The fact that Fatima is played by Moza Al Mazrooei, a famous Emirati actor, and "mother of Emirati theatre" creates a more empathetic context for the old woman, while also soliciting further audience consideration of the film's message.[35] Fatima finally understands that disbarring Mariam from going back home is a situation in which nobody is happy, and everyone feels equally trapped. If Fatima is sick and lonely, then surely Mariam's daughter must be feeling the same way. Finally, Fatima gives back Mariam's passport but expects her to return within a month. This is a temporary truce. As a recurring theme in the films I examine, the Gulf female employer softens toward the plight of her female domestic worker but is not entirely transformed.

Putting oneself in another's shoes is the central theme that runs through many of these Gulf-made films. *Beshkara* highlights many issues pertinent to contemporary Gulf society, including the violation of labor laws. Since domestic workers perform a variety of tasks that go beyond any one job description and cater to multiple household members simultaneously, they are often themselves afforded little in the way of privacy and are effectively "on call" throughout the day. This is a situation that has been recognized as requiring mediation by Gulf governments, many of whom have issued new laws requiring employers to give domestic workers at least one day off—even if this is not always practiced or enforced.[36]

The new laws have caused public debates in Gulf societies, soliciting the infamous response from Sondos Alqattan, a Kuwaiti beauty blogger. She released a video to her millions of followers where she "described the new worker protections, which include the right to keep their passports and mobile phones, a guaranteed rest day each week and set rest hours a day, as 'pathetic.'"[37] Even though Alqattan is a "social influencer," and her opinions are shared by many of her millions of followers, she received public backlash from other Kuwaitis, admonishing her unethical stance—and, importantly, one in which she opposed official government policy—resulting in her deleting the post, being dropped by the makeup labels that sponsored her, and earning her a hashtag #boycottsondosalqattan.[38]

Mehsal Al-Jaser similarly sympathetically highlights the plight of a female migrant domestic worker in *Is Sumiyati Going to Hell?* (Saudi,

2016), which received support from Saudi's General Commission for Audiovisual Media and the King Abdulaziz Center for World Culture. The film screened at international film festivals and is currently available on Netflix Middle East as part of *Six Windows in the Desert*, a collection of short films from Saudi Arabia. *Is Sumiyati Going to Hell?* tells the story of an Indonesian maid/nanny who "has to navigate and survive a horrible job due to her racist employers."[39] The story is seen through the eyes of seven-year-old Layan, who attempts to understand the maid's role in the home environment. After the mother informs Layan that everyone apart from Muslims will go to hell, the girl inquires: "Is Sumiyati going to hell?" She receives no reply.

The film is shot as an experimental fairy tale narrated by the little girl and accompanied by an eerie music-box soundtrack. Layan introduces the audience to Sumiyati by noting how the maid's identity has been effaced, saying: "To begin with, Sumiyati is not her name. Her name is Almira. Sumiyati was the name of the maid before, before, before, before Almira. They called her Sumiyati because grandpa couldn't pronounce her name. He doesn't have time to memorize new names because he's old."[40] The current maid's identity has thus been erased; she is presented as a disposable figure in a series of servants, none of whom can be properly distinguished from the other as individuals.

The only time Sumiyati is afforded any rest is when she is locked up in her room at night; her dreams of prosperity in the Gulf spread out on a Disney-themed blanket on the floor. The film serves to highlight the illegal practice of limiting the mobility of domestic workers through physical imprisonment when Layan asks her grandfather, "Why does mom lock Sumiyati up?" He responds: "We lock Sumiyati up so she won't escape." This is presented as being in the maid's best interest: otherwise, "Sumiyati will go to dangerous places. Then she'll go to jail." One of these dangerous places is presented as the bedroom of the family's male driver—a slow-motion caricature of a sweaty, sleazy, smoking South Asian man who reclines suggestively on his bed, making clear his unscrupulous intentions.

Fears of the foreign are highlighted when the film takes a supernatural turn. Whenever Layan hears Sumiyati crying over the phone to her son in another country, the girl gives toys to the nanny to pass on to him.

When the mother discovers that Sumiyati has been hiding these items in her room, she accuses the maid of theft and of practicing witchcraft on the family. In a voice-over narration, Layan explains to the audience that "Sumiyati is a witch... Mom always says so. I hope she doesn't put a spell on us." Trying to make sense of it all, Layan wonders why Sumiyati continues to "make breakfast, lunch, and dinner every day" if she is a witch with supernatural powers. The specter of Sumiyati makes a flash frame appearance, as she haunts different scenes of the film and represents media-infused fears that some domestic workers practice witchcraft.[41] Nisha Varia, senior researcher for women's rights at Human Rights Watch notes that, in some instances, "There's a real belief, and it's something that can be prosecuted through the Saudi courts, that black magic or witchcraft is real.... Domestic workers are especially vulnerable to these types of accusations because of cultural differences."[42]

Describing his work in general, the film's director Al-Jaser said: "I love to focus on minorities, because more often than not they're the ones who struggle to have their voices heard, and I believe that their stories deserve to be heard."[43] By focusing on the story of a domestic worker, the director notes how he hopes the film will affect Saudi society: "My goal is freedom and ending racism.... We had a maid in my home and I want her to be proud of me. It's her opinion I care about."[44] As I have argued throughout this chapter, Gulf filmmakers are representing domestic migrant workers in creative and empathetic ways that are indicative of the many nuanced perspectives about what happens behind the closed doors of Gulf family homes.

I conclude with an analysis of an art film that departs significantly—both in content and form—from the previous films under investigation but that directly addresses decades of Gulf household stereotypes. Monira Al Qadiri's *Soap* (Kuwait, 2014) is an eight-minute video in which she inserts her own fictional footage of domestic workers into existing scenes from already-televised Kuwaiti *musalsalāt*, or soap operas. In an accompanying text titled "The Workers Will Not Be Televised," Al Qadiri explains that the project "hijacks excerpts from Gulf soap operas to superimpose images of domestic workers onto their unrealistic settings, making the presence of migrant laborers both undeniable and surreal."[45] The Kuwaiti artist argues that "the title of the piece conflates the first word 'soap' from

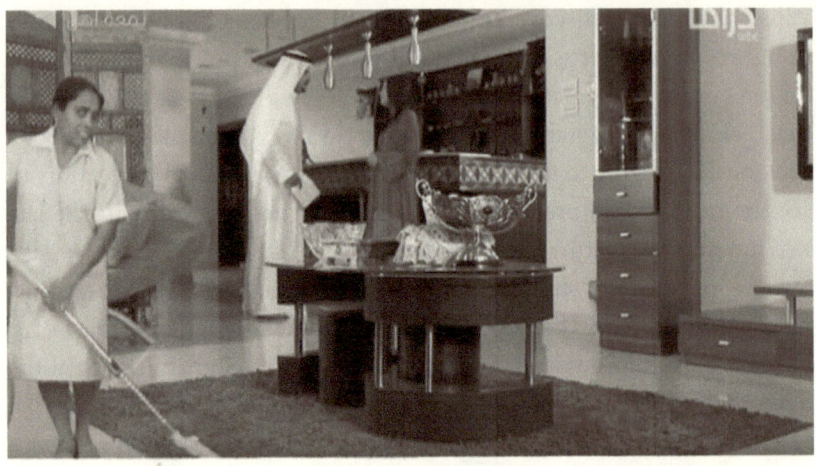

FIGURE 9.4

A domestic worker superimposed into a Kuwaiti soap opera scene in *Soap* (Kuwait, 2014), courtesy of Monira Al Qadiri.

Soap Opera, and a bar of soap—the temporary disappearing object that magically creates sanitary conditions in its wake; a disregarded existence, very much like the precarious case of the migrant worker."[46]

Al Qadiri's video demonstrates how Gulf *musalsalāt* focus on a sanitized version of the Gulf family; they "do not show the domestic laborers, cooks, cleaners and maids who are part of the everyday reality for Gulf Arabs.... Instead Gulf Arabs seem to magically accomplish all household chores by themselves in these soap operas."[47] By playfully superimposing domestic workers into the immaculate, gilded living rooms of Kuwaiti family dramas, Al Qadiri (re)introduces their presence and demonstrates with powerful simplicity how domestic workers "live alongside the family, but not within its fabric."[48] In this film, domestic workers and their employers are shown to occupy oppositional ends of the power spectrum; although they live within the same space, they inhabit parallel existences and have drastically different experiences.

Al Qadiri invites both the audience and the superimposed domestic workers to engage in a mischievous knowing relationship and to have a sly laugh at the expense of the characters in the *musalsal*—as well as at the expense of the shows' creators and original audience. By presenting the *musalsal*'s original actors as the unknowing dupes of a hoax, Al Qadiri invites the audience to poke fun at them. By sharing the "secret" of the domestic worker's presence with the audience, Al Qadiri lets the viewer in on the prank. The artist, the audience, and the domestic workers conspire together in this tongue-in-cheek critique. If soap operas or *musalsalāt* are meant to "offer lessons and examples of how to relate to family, others, and how to or how not to approach ethical and moral choices," then this subversion of the genre offers an added political dimension and complexity to some of the simple stereotypes of Gulf households.[49]

In a playful carnivalesque upsetting of hierarchies and reversal of power, Al Qadiri enacts a shrewd representational revenge that provides the domestic worker with "temporary liberation from the prevailing truth and from the established order."[50] Such films that make visible the domestic worker "have the potential to move the worker from the periphery to the center of the field of vision both within the artwork itself and in society more broadly."[51] In this filmic palimpsest, Al Qadiri overwrites the original story, redirects the original intention, and generally makes a mockery of social dramas that are meant to represent Gulf society. The asymmetrical relationship between employer and domestic worker is highlighted at the same time as it is ridiculed. In Al Qadiri's work, while domestic workers remain in their servitude by performing their labor, they are also simultaneously *performing* their labor by acting for the camera.

CONCLUSION

Even though "the widespread presence of foreigners in the GCC states, and particularly their presence in GCC households, has brought the traditionally insular families of Arabian society into close contact with individuals from a wide variety of cultural backgrounds," there are few studies that highlight the relationships between Gulf families and domestic workers.[52] According to Diop et al., in the growing literature on migrants to the Gulf, "scholars have paid little attention . . . to the views and attitudes held by citizens or nationals towards migrant workers in the Middle East."⁵³ This chapter has tried to add nuance to this scholarly gap by highlighting some of the ways in which the relationships between GCC citizens and migrant domestic workers are creatively represented in Gulf-made films.

In this study, I argue that there is a gendered dimension to how domestic workers are portrayed in these creative texts. Female domestic workers are often represented as victims of harsh treatment at the hands of a female employer and rendered as sympathetic characters on film. It becomes apparent that the key theme running through the films under investigation is simply to put oneself in another's shoes, to either personally experience the hardship of labor performed by a female domestic worker, or to reflect on the conditions of being mistreated, alone, and away from home and family.

Importantly, the films analyzed in this study are works that have been created by GCC citizens, thereby reflecting some of the perspectives held by this creative cohort of Gulf society. These films are reflective of the broader discussions currently occurring in the Gulf about the place of migrants in society in general and the place of domestic workers within the private space of GCC family homes in particular. These creative representations help to reflect various debates currently taking place in Gulf society and in the media—an ambiguous friction between advocating for migrant domestic worker rights and highlighting fears of the foreigner. The films discussed depict these daily conflicts between the Gulf employer and the migrant domestic worker by humanizing and adding nuance to these fraught relationships.

> SUZI MIRGANI is Assistant Director for Publications at the Center for International and Regional Studies at Georgetown University in Qatar. She is author of *Target Markets: International Terrorism Meets Global Capitalism in the Mall*. She is editor of *Informal Politics in the Middle East*; *Art and Cultural Production in the Gulf Cooperation Council*; (with Mohamed Zayani) of *Bullets and Bulletins: Media and Politics in the Wake of the Arab Uprisings*; and (with Zahra Babar) of *Food Security in the Middle East*. She is a writer, poet, and independent filmmaker working on highlighting stories from the Arab world.

NOTES

Special thanks goes to Chaïmaa Benkermi, Shaza Afifi, and Younis Al-Agha, all of whom helped with the research conducted for this study. English translation of Arabic titles and quotes was by Shaza Afifi. I am also grateful to the filmmakers selected for this study, who all provided permission to publish images of their films as part of my research.

1. Amr Hamzawy, "Debates on Political Reform in the Gulf: The Dynamics of Liberalising Public Spaces," in *Popular Culture and Political Identity in the Arab Gulf States*, ed. Alanoud Alsharekh and Robert Springborg (London: Saqi, 2008), 154.

2. Dale Hudson, "Locating Emirati Filmmaking within Globalizing Media Ecologies," in *Media in the Middle East: Activism, Politics, and Culture*, ed. Nele Lenze, Charlotte Schriwer, and Zubaidah Abdul Jalil (London: Palgrave Macmillan, 2017), 165–202.

3. Alia Yunis, "Film as Nation Building: The UAE Goes into the Movie Business," *Cinej Cinema Journal* 3, no. 2 (2014): 58.

4. Tony Bennett and Jane Woollacott, "Texts and their Readings," in *The Film Cultures Reader*, ed. Graeme Turner (New York: Routledge, 2002), 14.

5. Doaa, "Adrar Tarbeyat al-Khadimat li-l-Atfal" [The dangers of domestic workers raising the children], *Almrsal*, May 23, 2018, http://www.almrsal.com/post/652081; *Al Eqtisadiah*, "'Fobya al-Khadimat' Turbik al-Bayt al-Sa'udi . . . wa-l-Aba' Akthar Qalaqan" ['Phobia of maids' overwhelms the Saudi house . . . and parents are anxious], July 20, 2013, http://www.aleqt.com/2013/07/20/article_771848.html.

6. Andrew M. Gardner, "Gulf Migration and the Family," *Journal of Arabian Studies* 1, no. 1 (2011): 19.

7. Wanning Sun, "Making Space for the Maid," *Feminist Media Studies* 9, no. 1 (2009): 60.

8. Sharon Nagy, "'This Time I Think I'll Try a Filipina': Global and Local Influences on Relations between Foreign Household Workers and their Employers in Doha, Qatar," *City and Society* 10, no. 1 (1998): 85.

9. Nagy, "'This Time I Think I'll Try a Filipina,'" 85.

10. Gardner, "Gulf Migration and the Family," 19.

11. Attiya Ahmad, "Beyond Labor: Foreign Residents in the Persian Gulf States," in *Migrant Labor in the Persian Gulf*, ed. Mehran Kamrava and Zahra Babar (London: Hurst, 2012), 22; Simeon Kerr, "Gulf States to Reform Contracts of Domestic Workers," *Financial Times*, November 26, 2014, http://www.ft.com/content/82c820aa-756b-11e4-a1a9-00144feabdc0.

12. There is a growing academic literature on the conditions of migrant domestic workers in the Gulf states. See, for example, Attiya Ahmad, *Everyday Conversions: Islam, Domestic Work, and South Asian Migrant Women in Kuwait* (Durham, NC: Duke University Press, 2017). For discussions about the threat of domestic workers, see Dina Aboughazala, "The War of Words over Who Does Saudi Arabia's Housework," BBC, April 25, 2016, http://www.bbc.com/news/blogs-trending-36112484.

13. Hudson, "Locating Emirati Filmmaking," 166.

14. Nagy, "'This Time I Think I'll Try a Filipina,'" 92.

15. Rana Sobh and Russell W. Belk, "Privacy and Gendered Spaces in Arab Gulf Homes," *Home Cultures* 8, no. 3 (2011): 317–340.

16. Merriam-Webster, "Catharsis," 2020, http://www.merriam-webster.com/dictionary/catharsis.

17. Melanie Goodfellow, "Arab Stars of Tomorrow 2019: Raed Alsemari, Filmmaker (Saudi Arabia)," *Screen Daily*, November 24, 2019, http://www.screendaily.com/features/arab-stars-of-tomorrow-2019-raed-alsemari-filmmaker-saudi-arabia/5145020.article.

18. Pranav Vadehra, "Raed Alsermari's [sic] Dunya's Day wins jury prize at Sundance," Digital Studio Middle East, February 13, 2019, http://www.digitalstudiome.com/production/content-business/31323-raed-alsemaris-dunyas-day-wins-jury-prize-at-sundance.

19. For an in-depth discussion on the role of art in modern Saudi society, see Sean Foley, *Changing Saudi Arabia: Art, Culture, and Society in the Kingdom* (Boulder, CO: Lynne Rienner, 2019).

20. Raed Alsemari, dir., *Dunya's Day* (Saudi Arabia, 2019).

21. Urban World, "Dunya's Day," 2019, http://www.urbanworld.org/2019/dunyas-day.

22. Hamida Issa, dir., *Elevate* (Qatar: Doha Film Institute, 2017), https://dohafilminstitute.com/filmfestival/films/elevate.

23. Hamida Issa, dir., *Elevate*.

24. Hamida Issa, dir., *Elevate*.

25. Hamida Issa, dir., *Elevate*.

26. Hamida Issa, dir., *Elevate*.

27. Nadia Buhannad, "Ma'ani al-kalimat w 'oqul al-'arab al-moghaiyyaba" [The meanings of words and the absent Arab minds], *al-Arab*, November 9, 2014, http://bit.ly/2YESRaY. Quote translated from Arabic to English by Shaza Afifi.

28. Adam Hanieh, "Temporary Migrant Labour and the Spatial Structuring of Class in the Gulf Cooperation Council," *Spectrum: Journal of Global Studies* 2, no. 3 (2010): 77.

29. *Kuwait Times*, "92 Percent of Employers Hold Domestic Workers' Passports: Study," December 9, 2018, https://news.kuwaittimes.net/website/92-percent-of-employers-hold-domestic-workers-passports-study.

30. Abdulrahman Al Madani, "Beshkara (Housemaid)—Short Film," YouTube, February 18, 2017, http://www.youtube.com/watch?v=tommThO420M.

31. Sharjah Art Foundation, "Programme 1," January 18, 2019, http://sharjahart.org/sharjah-art-foundation/events/sharjah-film-platform-programme-1.

32. Ahmad, *Everyday Conversions*, 5, 6.

33. Abdulrahman Al Madani, dir., *Beshkara* (UAE/UK, 2015).

34. For more on changes to Gulf family structures, see multiple articles in Elizabeth Wanucha and Zahra Babar, eds., CIRS Special Issue of *Hawwa* 16, nos. 1–3 (2018).

35. Ola Salem, "Award Just the Beginning for Mother of Emirati Theatre," *The National*, October 15, 2010, http://www.thenational.ae/arts-culture/award-just-the-beginning-for-mother-of-emirati-theatre-1.495282.

36. The law for domestic workers has been recently updated in many Gulf states, outlining basic rights for domestic workers and basic obligations for employers; see, for example, Government of Kuwait, Department of Domestic Labour, "The Domestic Worker," Kuwait Society for Human Rights, 2016, http://www.ilo.org/dyn/natlex/docs/ELECTRONIC/101760/132163/F1794745336/KWT101760%20Eng.pdf; Government of United Arab Emirates, "UAE Policy on Domestic Helpers," 2019, https://government.ae/en/information-and-services/jobs/domestic-workers/uae-policy-on-domestic-helpers; Human Rights

Watch, "Qatar: New Law Gives Domestic Workers Labor Rights," August 24, 2017, www.hrw.org/news/2017/08/24/qatar-new-law-gives-domestic-workers-labor-rights#.

37. *Gulf Business*, "Kuwait Social Media Star Unapologetic after Filipino Maid Comments," July 24, 2018, https://gulfbusiness.com/kuwait-social-media-star-unapologetic-filipino-maid-comments.

38. Twitter, #boycottsondosalqattan, 2018, https://twitter.com/hashtag/boycottsondosalqattan?src=hashtag_click.

39. Meshal Aljaser, dir., *Is Sumiyati Going to Hell?* (IMDb, 2016), http://www.imdb.com/title/tt6811134.

40. Meshal Aljaser, dir., *Is Sumiyati Going to Hell?*, collection 1, episode 2, *Six Windows in the Desert* (Netflix, 2020), http://www.netflix.com/watch/81235972?trackId=200257859.

41. Doaa, "Adrar Tarbeyat al-Khadimat li-l-Atfal"; *Al Eqtisadiah*, "'Fobya al-Khadimat' Turbik al-Bayt al-Sa'udi ... wa-l-Aba' Akthar Qalaqan." ['Phobia of maids' overwhelms the Saudi house ... and parents are anxious].

42. Sophie Brown, "Saudi Arabia Pledges to Protect Foreign Workers, as Indonesian Maids Face Execution," CNN, February 21, 2014, http://www.cnn.com/2014/02/21/world/meast/saudi-arabia-indonesia-domestic-worker-agreement/index.html.

43. Esquire Middle East, "The Esquire 100—Meshal Al Jaser," August 29, 2018, http://www.esquireme.com/lists/the-esquire-100-meshal-al-jaser.

44. Susan Karlin, "Exporting Saudi Arabian Culture through Film," Fast Company, November 9, 2016, http://www.fastcompany.com/3065388/exporting-saudi-arabian-culture-through-film.

45. Mona Al Qadiri, "Ramadan Soaps: The Workers Will Not Be Televised," Creative Time Reports, July 11, 2014, http://creativetimereports.org/2014/07/11/ramadan-soaps-workers-will-not-be-televised-monira-al-qadiri.

46. Mona Al Qadiri, *Soap* (2014), http://www.moniraalqadiri.com/videos.

47. Sindelar, "When Workers Toil Unseen, Artists Intervene," 270–271.

48. Jay Weissberg, "Film Review: 'A Maid for Each,'" *Variety*, January 4, 2017, https://variety.com/2017/film/reviews/a-maid-for-each-film-review-1201952631.

49. Michael Allen Mendoza, "Recurring Themes in Gulf Arabic Dramatic Television" (MA thesis, University of Texas at Austin, 2014), 3.

50. Mikhail Bakhtin, *Rabelais and His World*, trans. Helene Iswolsky (Bloomington: Indiana University Press, 1984), 10.

51. Sindelar, "When Workers Toil Unseen, Artists Intervene," 273.

52. Gardner, "Gulf Migration and the Family," 22. There is a small but growing literature on the relationship between Gulf families and domestic workers; see multiple articles in Elizabeth Wanucha and Zahra Babar, eds., CIRS Special Issue of *Hawwa* 16, nos. 1–3 (2018); Nasra M. Shah et al., "Foreign Domestic Workers in Kuwait: Who Employees How Many?," *Asian and Pacific Migration Journal* 11 (2002): 247–269; Nagy, "'This Time I Think I'll Try a Filipina.'"

53. Abdoulaye Diop et al., "Attitudes towards Migrant Workers in the GCC: Evidence from Qatar," *Journal of Arabian Studies* 2, no. 2 (2012): 173.

10

Reorienting the Gaze
Emirati Women behind the Camera

CHRYSAVGI PAPAGIANNI

In 2006 Nayla Al Khaja was awarded the title of the "First Female Filmmaker" in the United Arab Emirates (UAE) by Minister of Culture, Youth, and Social Development H. H. Sheikh Nahyan bin Mubarak Al Nahyan, for her documentary film *Unveiling Dubai* (UAE, 2006), which screened at the Dubai International Film Festival (DIFF). Two years later, another Emirati woman, Nujoom Alghanem, won Best Documentary in the Gulf at the Abu Dhabi Film Festival (ADFF) for her documentary *Al Mureed*. Following *Al Mureed*'s success, Alghanem has produced and directed more than ten films, mostly feature documentaries that have drawn local as well as international attention. But the story of women in film in the UAE goes beyond state feminism narratives of "firsts." Alongside Al Khaja and Alghanem, a growing number of Emirati women have, in the last decade, joined the field of filmmaking in UAE, including Ahlam Al Banai, Alia Al Qemzi, Amna Al Nowais, Hana Alshateri, Jumana Al Ghanem, Majida Al Safadi, Manal Bin Amro, Mariam Al Nuaimi, Muna Al Ali, Nahla Al Fahad, Rawia Abdulla, Sara Alsehhi, Sarah Zohair, and Slatha Masoud. Each attempts to create a space for herself within an emerging local film industry. Although their films are often experimental shorts and not major productions, their presence defies perceptions of the Orientalist construct of the "Arab woman" in foreign media as faceless and voiceless.[1] Their films open up space for the redefinition of female identity not only in the UAE but also in the Arab world.[2]

This chapter focuses on Emirati women filmmakers within Emirati cinema, which has received little, if any, scholarly attention, particularly in studies on Arab, Middle Eastern, or Middle East and North Africa (MENA) cinema.[3] Overall, Emirati women filmmakers break new ground to rise above Orientalist stereotypes, as well as Indigenous forms of patriarchy and state feminism. I purposefully use the term *Emirati women* in the plural to avoid creating yet another category that might reinforce Oriental fantasies already embedded in the terms "Arab" or "Muslim woman." My approach is premised on an acknowledgment of the differences that mark both their work and their positioning within a country where progressive neoliberalism competes with traditionalism for dominance. Following Ella Shohat's call, I abide by the principle of relationality, approaching these women filmmakers and their work "not as hermetically sealed entities but, rather, as part of a set of permeable, interwoven relationships"[4] that is appropriate for the transnational and multicultural reality in which they live and work.

In this light, one should not expect that Emirati women filmmakers and their work can be categorized under extant frameworks. My focus on Alghanem and Al Khaja reflects their status as the two most prolific and acclaimed Emirati women filmmakers, locally, regionally, and internationally. It is also important to recognize that they both come from financially well off, relatively liberal Dubai families that allowed their daughters to study abroad before that was widely accepted. At the same time, Alghanem and Al Khaja exemplify the diversity of contemporary Emirati women as they belong to different generations. Al Khaja often echoes the concerns and aspirations of the younger, globalized generation through her choice of themes that are strongly rooted in the here and now. Alghanem's work, on the other hand, is characterized by nostalgia for the Emirati past and a focus on women's contributions to the country's history. Despite such particularities, Al Khaja and Alghanem both claim the power of representation to tell women's stories against conservative patriarchal and Western Orientalist pressures that intersect with and depart from experiences of other Arab, Middle Eastern, or MENA women filmmakers that lead to new epistemic configurations when it comes to the study of regions and cultures.

Through their choice of subjects and cinematic styles as well as through their presence in a gendered space, Alghanem and Al Khaja complicate existing gender schemata. Alghanem's films often focus on the social tensions between "tradition" and "modernity" as these affect women and inform UAE national narratives. Al Khaja looks at human relationships in daily life as they are shaped by cultural traditions and globalized modernity, often casting a critical glance at both. Together, their work and the stories they tell through their films can reorient patriarchal and Orientalist gazes, question existing epistemologies, and bring to light the need for new theories beyond area studies that can encompass their experiences and films.

State-sponsored film festivals and competitions over the past twenty years have brought Emirati filmmakers and their films a platform. Image Nation, Abu Dhabi's government-funded media and entertainment production company, established in 2008, further promoted the development of a distinct local film culture, with Nawaf Al-Janahi's *Sea Shadow* (2011) as the first feature by an Emirati director to be produced by the company.[5] In 2014, Al-Janahi and director Khalid Al Mahmood launched the Emirati Cinema Campaign (ECC), bicycling in the streets to raise public awareness of Emirati cinema. Notably, they also helped launch #SupportArabCinema campaign in 2015 at the Dubai International Film Festival (DIFF), aimed at further promoting Arab films. DIFF had previously supported African and Asian filmmaking as well. But the campaign reflects these Emirati filmmakers' hunger to connect to Arabic-language cinema. Since its launch, the campaign has more than eleven thousand followers registered worldwide on social media.[6]

These state-sponsored and grassroots initiatives have gradually created a fledgling film culture but with limited international exposure. Al Khaja became the first Emirati to be represented at the Cannes Film Festival in 2018 with the screenplay of her first feature film *Animal*, which had previously won the Jury's Special Prize for Best Short Fiction at the Italian Movie Award in Pompeii in 2017.

However, theatrical exhibition of Emirati films is extremely limited, even though for foreign productions the UAE has one of the biggest box offices in the Middle East.[7] Joseph Gugler calls competition with foreign productions "formidable" and explains how local markets are dominated, for example, by the West, as well as by India, Hong Kong, and Japan.[8] When women filmmakers in the UAE talk about the difficulties and challenges they face, what emerges as a unifying element is not so much gender bias in the workplace but funding and education opportunities that are common to all filmmakers irrespective of gender.[9] The most common concerns shared by the overwhelming majority of filmmakers are censorship, financial considerations, lack of a local talent pool and scant expertise (especially in the area of acting), limitations in production and marketing, as well as societal and cultural taboos.[10]

In the words of Nayla Al Khaja, "In the nascent Arab film industry, we thankfully have less gender inequality when compared to other markets around the world."[11] For her, women's presence in the industry is a clear indication of "a fresh look at film gender equality." Her perception is worth remarking on, especially when one takes into consideration the long-standing complaints by US women filmmakers about sexual discrimination in Hollywood, which culminated in the 2015 lawsuit by the American Civil Liberties Union against the industry.[12] In contrast to women filmmakers in Hollywood, Emirati women filmmakers experience a male-dominated industry that does not, in their view, limit their creative potential or opportunities. Such views destabilize preconceptions about oppressed Muslim and Arab woman that have given rise to "white savior" campaigns by Western feminists. Such views further show that the categories of "Muslim women" and "Arab women" should not be approached as a monolithic group.[13]

As both Al Khaja and filmmaker Hana Kazim have conveyed in personal interviews, women in the industry enjoy not only respect from their male counterparts but also fair treatment, which is indicative of an open-minded attitude at the government level. As a result, many of these women have earned broad recognition both inside and outside the country. As far as state approaches are concerned, UAE is indeed one of the few Arab countries where female empowerment initiatives are actively promoted at the government level through laws that offer equal employment opportunities and through the formation of state organizations that promote women's rights at the workplace.[14] Jillian Schedneck discusses the

UAE's state-sponsored feminist agenda, which is relevant to many Gulf countries. Such an agenda would entail support for women in top-ranking positions as well promotion of female entrepreneurship and leadership.[15] Thus, the experience of Emirati women follows a different trajectory than other Arab women, who often had to circumvent political restrictions and make do with limited financial means.

Despite government support, Emirati women experience other challenges as according to Serra Kirdar, the UAE's "state-sponsored feminism ... does not present a meaningful change on the societal level."[16] Indeed, societal and family pressures seem to weigh heavily on them. They have to overcome some conservative mentalities surrounding not only cinema per se but also the issue of representation in general. What surfaces over and again in various interviews with women who work in the filmmaking industry are the difficulties, often intense, as they struggle to ensure family approval to pursue film as a career.[17] Al Khaja's story of how her family disapproved of her choice is indicative. As she explains, it was only when she started earning local and regional recognition that her family started acknowledging her choices. Such attitudes are not only a result of concerns associated with cultural propriety but also of the fact that filmmaking is not considered a valid or a financially worthwhile career choice for either men or women.[18]

In this context, Emirati women filmmakers disrupt assumptions about Arab and Muslim women in a way that resists Euro-American approaches to the region as a homogenous entity.[19] As such, they cannot be added to what Shohat ironically calls "a pre-existing nucleus" by the "expert intellectual."[20] While similarities exist and should be acknowledged, the socioeconomic and historical conditions that shape the everyday realities for Emirati women should also be taken into consideration, as Florence Martin argues concerning the particularities of Maghrebi cinema.[21] I thus approach Emirati women filmmakers with a recognition of the important differences while also acknowledging connections between Emirati and other Arab, Middle Eastern, and MENA women filmmakers. Such an approach resists compartmentalization and is more in sync with the dynamics of globalization and neoliberalism evident in many Arab societies today the UAE being an apt example. Such an approach also seeks to foreground the connections between the local and global and thus open up the scope of area studies to encompass new cognitive cartographies without foregoing the importance of indigenous perspectives that spearheaded area studies in the first place.

The most important support to this day has been the film festivals that have offered Emirati women a much-needed exhibition venue. As a case in point, both Alghanem and Al Khaja claim that festivals launched their films and their careers. Following the success of *Unveiling Dubai*, for example, Al Khaja was commissioned to make *Arabana* (*Wheelbarrow*), a short film that won the Best Emirati Filmmaker in 2007 at DIFF. In 2010, she received the Muhr Emirati Award at DIFF for *Malal* (*Bored*) for which she had also received the Best Script Award at the Gulf Film Festival (GFF). Her successful career continued with yet another award: Best Emirati Film in the 2014 ADFF for *The Neighbor* (2013).

Comparably, Nujoom Alghanem has earned local, regional, and international awards that brought attention not only to her films but also to the country and its filmmaking. Following *Al Mureed*'s success in 2008, Alghanem, who started as a poet in the 1990s, earned Special Jury Prize for her documentary *Amal* (2011) from the Beirut International Film Festival. Her *Sounds of the Sea* received a Special Jury Prize at the Alexandria Mediterranean Countries Film Festival in 2014. *Nearby Sky* (2014) won Best Non-Fiction Prize in the Muhr Feature Competition at DIFF, as well as Best Documentary from GCC Film Festival in 2016. Her most recent, *Sharp Tools* (2017), a tribute to Emirati artist Hassan Sharif, won Muhr Award for Best Emirati Feature in DIFF 2017. No other Emirati director has had so much festival exposure.

State support should also be acknowledged with Image Nation offering many women filmmakers, such as Alwiya Thani, Fatima Al Dhaheri, Hana Kazim, and Sara Al Sayegh, an opportunity to work in the field. These women work as producers, directors, editors, cinematographers, and writers, and they are actively involved in the company's filmmaking projects, along with other Arab and Western women and men. But these women share the common goal of attaining a theatrical release for their work.[22]

In the last fifteen years, more than ten Emirati feature films have screened in commercial theaters, an optimistic development given the limitations discussed earlier. Yet all of these films were directed by men. As most of the women-directed films are not narrative feature films, this might partially explain the absence of films by Emirati women in commercial theaters. The reasons why women work mostly on short films or documentaries deserve further investigation. Like elsewhere, unconscious and unacknowledged biases within financing, production, and distribution might partly explain these choices, although there is no research confirming that this is the case in the UAE.[23]

REORIENTING THE GAZE

An important question to ask is what stories Emirati women filmmakers tell and why these stories are significant. In the words of Al Khaja, women's participation in the emerging film industry has an undoubtedly interventionist quality. Their voices are bold, and their stories call into question the stereotypical cinematic images often found in popular narratives with regard not only to Arab, Middle Eastern, and MENA women but the population at large.[24]

Foreign industry initiatives, such as the UAE branch of Women in Film and Television (WIFTI), which was launched in Dubai in 2012 by Michelle Nickelson and Dedra Stevenson, provide further support for women. Such western industry outreach needs to be approached with caution since well-intended, western-trained, film-industry professionals, often white women, harbor agendas and preconceptions that can unwittingly undermine Emirati women. Hudson, for instance, discusses the "white-savior myths that Muslim women, do, in fact, need saving *from* Islam" that are reproduced in narratives which capitalize on the view that "women's lives are determined solely by the presence or absence of 'the veil.'"[25]

Despite attempts at more culturally sensitive representations of Arab people in Hollywood, negative stereotypes continue. Al Khaja expresses shock and annoyance. "They labelled us under 'three Bs': billionaires, belly dancers, and bombers," she explains.[26] Indeed, twenty-first-century Hollywood cinema continues to be linked with cultural imperialism as the "eastward gaze" has not changed a lot since the early days of cinema. Spearheaded by tax incentives offered by a country that is keen on diversifying its oil-based economy, Hollywood's interest in the UAE is evident in the array of recent productions fully or partly set in the UAE, including *Syriana* (2005), *Sex and the City 2* (2010), *Mission Impossible 4: Ghost Protocol* (2011), *Fast and Furious 7* (2015), and *Mission Impossible 6: Fallout* (2018). *Sex and the City 2* is actually an apt example showing clearly how little progress has been made in terms of a non-stereotyped representation of the UAE capital of Abu Dhabi as a western Orientalist fantasy. As a matter of fact, the film seems to unabashedly celebrate and build heavily on a wide array of clichés that vilify and belittle Emirati women, as the film revels in images of mysterious veiled Emirati females and ominous, unpredictable, and narrow-minded Emirati males.

A closer look at the other films will also reveal a reliance on stereotypical images of extravagant wealth but also of anachronistic depictions of unnamable threats that linger in the dusty, disorderly, desert landscape. Such portrayals fail to rise above the usual stereotypes despite the fact that the glamour and posh images in the last few years have come to expand the existing repertoire of images associated with this part of the world. Overall, the UAE is depicted as a place to be tamed and consumed. Whether feared or desired, the end result is still the same: the objectifying gaze of the camera attempts to contain a threatening presence or to covet and consume it as fantasy. The "eastward gaze" in the films still "represents, animates, constitutes, the otherwise silent and dangerous space beyond familiar boundaries."[27]

In this context, the need for more nuanced representations becomes crucial for many Emirati filmmakers. That said, these filmmakers should not be limited by the attempt to merely counter Orientalist stereotypes, as such an attempt can be implicated in the same logic of binary thinking that gave rise to stereotypes in the first place. Comparably, scholars should develop new methodologies and interpretative frameworks. To this end, Nadine Naber argues for a "de-Orientalizing theory" that can reorient the gaze from the restrictive focus on counter-stereotypes and toward the extraordinary existing inside the ordinary and the beauty that lies within everyday, quotidian themes.[28]

With their focus on the everyday, Emirati women's films offer a different interpretative framework that will result in a more nuanced representation and understanding of the country and its people. The films made by Emirati women often focus on a multicultural, multilingual, and globalized UAE society that struggles not only with issues of identity and hybridization but also with heritage preservation and tradition. Their approach ranges from satirical to critical as they attempt to define their place within an Emirati society that, as I have argued, is characterized by "a globalized mindset in all but clothes."[29] Some examples are Ahlam Al Bannai's and Jumana Al Ghanem's *I Am Arab* (2009), which is about the tensions surrounding the Arabic language brought about by multiculturalism, a theme also explored in Mariam Al Nuaimi's *Our Accent* (2011). The issue of national identity for children of "mixed" marriage is the focus of Amal Al Agroobi's *Half Emirati* (2012). Sarah Zohair and Majida Al Safadi revisit and rewrite an Emirati female legend in *Um Duwais* (2012), offering a feminist interpretation of the djinn.

Al Agroobi and Zohair have also worked together to create the first female superhero, Hessa, in the 2014 short film *Super Lochal*, which screened in the Short Narrative Competition at the Emirates Film Competition (EFC) in 2014. It is noteworthy that the film's six directors—Mahya Soltani, Majida Al Safadi, Maram Ashour, Omnia El Afifi, Sarah Alagroobi, and Sarah Zohair—have different nationalities and backgrounds. Al Agroobi is the only Emirati in the group. Together they created a film based on converging experiences and the need to remedy injustices that they face as women by helping other women. Overall, the films by Emirati women offer a glimpse into the concerns of a younger, globalized, and thus hybrid Emirati generation, with approaches ranging from playful to grave on social issues that convey a different reality for women than ones imagined by Hollywood professionals who come to advise or teach in the UAE.[30]

Al Khaja describes that her intention is "to show the reality of [her] culture in a realistic way, not over-polishing it and not griming the scenario."[31] What she rejects here is the sensationalism and excess that often characterizes Hollywood productions. Indeed, her preference for universal themes such as love and secret dating (*Once*, 2009), marriage (*Malal*, 2010), authoritative parenting (*Animal*, 2016), child abuse (*Arabana*, 2016), and motherhood (*The Shadow*, 2019), together with her own unique cinematic style, situate her Emirati characters in ordinary, day-to-day life and highlight their humane aspects as they are shown to share the same problems, dreams, and aspirations as everyone.

Alghanem opts for sweeping desert and sea scenes that present her characters in a harmonious proximity to their surroundings, focusing on characters like the elderly healer in *Hamama* (2010), the camel breeder in *Nearby Sky* (2015), a legendary sea singer in *Sounds of the Sea* (2015), and two beekeepers in *Honey, Rain and Dust* (2016). As I have argued elsewhere, her films create "a repertoire of images, sounds, and colors that can awaken Emiratis to a new sense of selfhood" and can bring forth a longing for the not-so-long-ago past that contradicts the monetized nostalgia of tourism and branding.[32]

The reorientation of the camera's gaze is obvious in scenes where the everyday reality of these people is foregrounded. No sensationalism, exaggeration, spectacularism, or romanticism of the country and its people can be found in Alghanem's films. Her symbolic poetic aesthetics are beautifully combined with the realism of documentary cinematography to produce images that capture essences of the country and its people in a more realistic way. Her films invite the audience to adopt the camera's affective gaze, which lingers lovingly and nostalgically on the characters as well as on their surroundings. Far from objectifying the characters or landscapes, the camera assigns to both a prominent position, as both have important stories to tell. In other words, even though these are apparently ordinary people and places, their stories are far from ordinary as they defy popular representations.

In *Hamama*, she redefines popular conceptions and misconceptions about the Gulf, creating a counter-narrative to Orientalist paradigms of "traditional" versus "modern." The use of English subtitles in the film can be read as an attempt to reach a wider audience while at the same time providing a necessary bridge between the past and the multicultural, global present of the Emirati society. The camera's "insider's gaze" shows an everyday reality that is characterized by a Spartan simplicity reminiscent of bygone days. As the film shows the elderly Hamama performing her daily chores and leading a humble, self-sustained life, the break with the country's current narrative that builds heavily on images of opulence and glamour becomes clear.[33] Hamama's self-sustenance celebrates cultural singularity and thus destabilizes the overarching, homogenizing model of global capitalism that promotes materialism and overconsumption. Although she has the choice to rely on hired help, Hamama still opts to perform daily chores herself and thus emerges as an active, strong, and fully fleshed-out individual who finds happiness and meaning in the simple things that life brings.

In terms of gender redefinition, Hamama's strength and independence represents a deviation from what Jane Bristol-Rhys describes as the fragile stories of the contemporary Emirati women, who are either romanticized or largely perceived as lazy and frivolous shop-goers.[34] Alghanem's film "disrupts the story of the contemporary female subject" with a protagonist who despite her age is by no means fragile or ordinary.[35] Moreover, she is not "dislocated" like the women in Bristol-Rhys's description; instead, she is firmly located in a present that feeds directly into a past when people were self-sustained, thus creating a stable basis from which she apparently draws not only her strength but also a purpose in life. To put it differently, Hamama has an integral relationship with her locale, which is obviously connected with the past despite the encroaching forces of global capitalism around her. Firmly rooted in the material geography of the past, she can lead a meaningful life in the present as the film seems to suggest.

This is the case with more or less all the protagonists that Alghanem chooses. For example, Nazzat Makki in *Red, Blue, Yellow* (2013) and Fatima in *Nearby Sky* (2015) are also spirited and willful. In their quest for meaningful lives, they do not hesitate to go against the odds to challenge patriarchal norms. Nazzat steadfastly claims a space of her own as an Emirati female artist. Fatima becomes the first woman to participate in camel beauty pageants and races. Both face strong social and patriarchal pressures; yet both are admirable and indomitable in the pursuit of their dreams. As Alghanem reveals, she has "found it fulfilling to focus on extraordinary female stories from our society or the Arab world that are worth being highlighted."[36]

Overall, Alghanem tells a different story about Emirati women: one that recovers women within the country's narrative and advocates for gender redefinition. As a matter of fact, women's presence and contribution is acknowledged as Alghanem feminizes the country's narrative and literally "inserts" women into the picture. The scene in *Nearby Sky* (2015) where Fatima is seen watching the camel races, a woman alone surrounded by men, is an eloquent example of this insertion. The same is true of Hamama, who enjoys immense respect from the men in the film, young and old alike. Her healing powers are acknowledged and celebrated in an official ceremony by the community, which can be read as an example of "official" history making space for women.

Her healing powers are further celebrated by the camera in scenes where, through slow motion and extreme close-ups on her hands, a mystical atmosphere is created around Hamama that elevates her to the realm of the myth. Alghanem's cinematic language, rich in symbolism and lyricism, can uncover the extraordinary that lies within the ordinary. Indeed, the lyrical realism that permeates the film allows Alghanem to stay away from a mere ontological portrayal of her subject matter and instead cast an affective glance on what has been misrepresented or even left unrepresented.

Feminist theory has often underlined the need for filling in the gaps of dominant narratives, for telling stories that have been left untold, which is exactly what Alghanem is doing as she creates a mosaic of different Emirati women who can stand alongside men and claim their rightful place in the making of the country's history. Even when the apparent protagonist is male, as for example in *Sounds of the Sea* (2016), Alghanem allocates time and space to the story of the woman that materializes as an apparition throughout the film. The female figure softly complements the marine landscape and the marine stories narrated by the fishermen, creating a parallel story to the film's main narrative as we see her time and again treading softly onto the sand.

Another parallel story worth mentioning is the story of a transcultural past, as we see immigrant labors of South Asian, African, and Arab origin actively shaping the maritime tradition of the country. The fishermen's songs reorient the story of the country and of the Gulf itself back to its origins and away from western narratives of homogeneity. The songs, akin to the sounds of the sea, evoke syncretism while the sea itself, both as an image and as a sound, highlights cultural overlaps. As Hudson and Yunis put it, the Gulf is recognized as a "fluid and transcultural space." Thus, Alghanem recognizes a heterogeneous past that is largely absent from dominant accounts, whether national or otherwise.

In a similar way, Al Khaja's films intervene in the existing sociocultural landscape in a subtle but powerful way. Her vision is synonymous with revision as her critical cinematic gaze unsettles sociocultural constructions that undermine women's existence. Her preference for "difficult" and uncomfortable topics, such as arranged marriages and secret dating, creates powerful subplots that share common ground with local and international audiences alike. Such topics make visible alternative narratives about the country itself but also about the Gulf and the wider area. Often her focus is on the patriarchal structures that restrict women and undercut their pursuit of meaningful relationships and fulfilling lives in general. She further "offers a bold insight into human relationships and the human psyche": so bold that it can actually lead to gender redefinition since the topics she tackles have a direct effect on the life of Emirati women and are often responsible for their frustrations and mishaps.[37] Yet, Al Khaja does not want to be strictly labeled a "woman director." The critical gaze that she casts on society aims at bringing about positive change, not only for women but for men as well, given that the lack of meaningful relationships affects them both. Hers, then, is an agenda that subscribes to a feminist approach encompassing people irrespective of gender. Her vision, similar to Alghanem's, is one of unity and not division.

By bringing to light intimate aspects of Emirati women's lives, Al Khaja's films open up space for a more realistic representation, comparable to what many Arab women filmmakers do but also to many women filmmakers worldwide. Arab women in films directed by Arab women are presented not as "victims" but as "strong yet vulnerable personalities."[38] The strength of self-representation and control of the camera's gaze is evident in both Al Khaja's and Alghanem's films, which both show a preference for female protagonists in a variety of contexts that have a strong local flavor and yet at the same time touch on intercultural concerns that foreground, as Shohat says, "discursive links" between regions. Indeed, despite the differences linked to the diverse sociopolitical configurations in the MENA area, the work of Emirati and MENA women filmmakers also shares important similarities. Thus, films by Emirati women filmmakers represent an important intervention that has the potential to reorient the gaze away from universalizing assumptions and toward a more nuanced understanding of the positioning of these women in a dialogical relationship "within, between, and among cultures, ethnicities and nations."[39]

The need to find a voice and overcome the silence imposed by the austere patriarchal environment surfaces over and again in Al Khaja's and Alghanem's films. Al Khaja's short film *Animal*, for example, focuses on a mentally abusive father who instills fear in his wife and young daughter. The daughter's inability to speak during the dinner scene is indicative of the horror that she experiences due to psychological abuse from her authoritative, sociopathic father. Her scream following her stuttering could be again interpreted as fear. Yet it could also be read as a protest against the power structures that suffocate her. In other words, the scream is an acting out, a rebellious deed of courage and audacity that seeks to overturn the stifling regime of voiceless-ness imposed by the family patriarch.

The scream does not come from the mother, who is a mere passive observer of the absurdity around her, but from the young girl. If seen from a broader perspective, it could be an indication of a larger cultural shift as the younger generation of Emirati women brought up within a neoliberal, globalized setting has a bolder voice and does not hesitate to speak out. Even though the girl utters no real words, the sound of her scream has a more profound effect as it commands the audience's attention. Al Khaja's personal investment in the film has been made clear in various interviews. It is the story of her own upbringing, and yet it is also representative of many women who find themselves entangled within suffocating gender frameworks that have rendered them mute and impotent. As *Animal* seems to suggest, overcoming the silence and making their voice heard is the next step for these women, with Al Khaja exploding the silences while exposing the gap that still exists among state-sponsored feminisms that do not go "deep enough to touch people's lives."[40]

The recognition of the film by the Italian Film Festival is an example of the film's international appeal. Nevertheless, the film does not sell out to foreign notions of feminism because it goes beyond western expectations of the silent, victimized Arab woman as its title also suggests. The universal theme of authoritative parenthood, while connected to the specific sociocultural conditions of Emirati culture, simultaneously works between foreign and familiar gender structures creating a new intercultural space of connection where inequalities can be addressed. The feature-length screenplay of the film made it to the Cannes Film Festival in 2018, when it was accepted by the Producer's Network, making Al Khaja the first Emirati filmmaker to be accepted. Such international recognition once again should not be misinterpreted, as it can bring attention to Indigenous perspectives. Hudson explains that the absence of Emirati perspectives, usually due to the predominance of foreign film productions, "allows foreign assumptions and suspicions to frame perceptions about the UAE, often based on ones about neighboring Saudi Arabia and Iran."[41] Countering these assumptions, Al Khaja's film answers Hudson's call for Indigenous productions that will undercut stereotypes by operating "in more discreet and culturally aware ways to address social inequities and human rights."[42] Apart from the inequities afflicting women, the film allows some space for another narrative that is largely missing from the usual repertoire of images about the area. The presence of the immigrant cook, who is also abused by the father, makes a statement, subtle though it may be, about the intersections of race, class, and gender that cannot go unnoticed. Even though the cook is voiceless, he is more than a mere backdrop to the main story. In Mary Louise Pratt's words, the film creates a contact zone where "disparate cultures meet, clash and grapple with each other" as Hudson and Yunis also note in the introduction.

With regard to stereotypes, it is not only the stories that Emirati women choose to tell through their films that are important; their presence in a traditionally male sphere radically revises the existing gender schemata in a country where progress and conservatism give rise to unique sociocultural configurations and epistemic models that merit attention because of the local entanglement with modernity and the fluxes of globalization. Al Khaja, for instance, goes far beyond the usual Emirati female stereotypes. As an advocate for women's empowerment, she leads by example and does not hesitate to tackle taboo topics such as women's abuse. Her presence in the country's cultural scene is vibrant. Her Scene Club in Dubai, UAE's first official film club (which she launched in 2007), shows uncut films that according to reporter and cultural activist Nina Rothe are impossible to view publicly anywhere else in the UAE.[43] Following up on the success of the Scene Club, Al Khaja launched the Aflam Film Club in Abu Dhabi in 2012. Al Khaja's grassroots initiatives[44] represent a bold intervention in the country's stern sociocultural environment and help promote a more vibrant film culture.

Al Khaja and Alghanem use the medium of film as a means of cultural expression and as a means of claiming a public voice to have their stories told. By laying a bold claim on the power of representation they question—implicitly or explicitly—the overarching cultural conservatism and the deeply rooted patriarchal mentalities that limit women's lives similar to other women filmmakers globally. At the same time, they are juggling different realities given the country's globalized outlook and progressiveness. The case of Emirati women filmmakers can then help refocus the discussions on Arab cinema, which has often been viewed as homogenous. Further consideration of the different social, cultural, and financial configurations in the UAE can lead to an epistemological shift for a place whose global reputation usually rests on oil wealth. Scholarly attention and theorization of the area is long overdue and so is the reorientation of the gaze. The question of whose theory should be implemented for this venture and for what purpose remains open and is still fraught with concerns amid ongoing debates centering on Eurocentric models.

> CHRYSAVGI PAPAGIANNI is Associate Professor in the Department of English and Writing Studies at Zayed University and Adjunct Faculty at the University of Patras, Greece. She holds a PhD in film and literature from the State University of New York at Buffalo. Her studies and research focus primarily on anglophone women's literature and cinema with a specific interest on issues of memory and identity.

NOTES

The author conducted personal interviews (together with Christopher Thornton) with Nayla Al Khaja, Masood Amralla Al Ali, Hana Kazim, Alwiya Thani, Fatima Al Dhaheri, Sara Al Sayegh, Alia Al Qemz, and Sara Alsehhi, between October 2016 and March 2018.

1. See Nahed Eltantawy, "Women and Media in the Middle East: From Veiling to Blogging," *Feminist Media Studies* 13, no. 5 (2016): 1. Ella Shohat criticizes Eurocentric

categories and identity designations that have cast Arab women as passive and inactive ("Area Studies, Transnationalism and Feminist Production of Knowledge," *Signs* 26, no. 4, Globalization and Gender [2001], 1269).

2. Although their films do not enjoy wide release and have not made it to the theaters yet, it is not due to gender-imposed restrictions as would be the case for example with other countries in the area with Iran being a prime example.

3. See for example, Viola Shafik, *Arab Cinema: History and Cultural Identity*, rev. ed. (Cairo: American University of Cairo Press, 2017); Gönül Dönmez-Colin, ed., *The Cinema of North Africa and Middle East* (London: Wallflower, 2007); Josef Gugler, ed., *Film in the Middle East and North Africa: Creative Dissidence* (Austin: University of Texas Press, 2011); Oliver Leaman, ed., *Companion Encyclopedia of Middle Eastern and North African Film* (New York: Routledge, 2001).

4. Shohat, "Area Studies," 1269.

5. Image Nation (originally Imagenation) is also actively involved with financing international films, television series, and documentaries. Its international division works together with such transnational media corporations, such as Warner Bros. and National Geographic Films, and many of its productions stream globally on Netflix. According to the company's website, its "mission is to help build the film and entertainment industry across the GCC and MENA" with the combination of local and international talent as the key of its success, evident through two Academy Awards, a BAFTA and an EMMY. Image Nation, "What We Do," *Imagine Nation* (n.d.), https://imagenationabudhabi.com.

6. Image Nation, "Top Industry Professionals and Filmmakers Attend European Launch of #Supportarabcinema at Berlin International Film Festival" (press release), *Image Nation*, February 15, 2016, https://imagenationabudhabi.com/media-center/top-industry-professionals-and-filmmakers-attend-european-launch-of-supportarabcinema-at-berlin-international-film-festival/.

7. Alia Yunis, "Film as Nation Building: The UAE Goes into the Movie Business," *Cinej Cinema Journal* 3, no. 2 (2014): 2.

8. In his introduction to *Film in the Middle East and North Africa*, Gugler calls competition with foreign productions "formidable" (4).

9. Personal interviews with directors (together with Christopher Thornton), Abu Dhabi, 2018.

10. Ibid.

11. Personal interview (together with Christopher Thornton), Dubai, 2018.

12. In May 2015, the American Civil Liberties Union (ACLU) filed grievances with several federal and California-state agencies, including the Equal Employment Opportunity Commission, requesting investigations on the issue of gender discrimination against women in Hollywood. The EEOC vindicated women's cases a few years later. For further discussion see Ben Child and Nigel M. Smith, "Hollywood Prejudice against Female Directors to Have US Equal Opportunity Inquiry," *Guardian*, October 7, 2015, https://www.theguardian.com/film/2015/oct/07/us-hollywood-discrimination-prejudice-female-directors-equal-opportunities.

13. See also Eltantawy, "Women and Media in the Middle East," 1.

14. In "Women Pioneers of Arab Cinema," *Screen* 48, no. 4 (2007), Roy Armes discusses Tunisia's progressive laws that enabled women filmmakers to play an active role in postindependence cinema (518). By contrast, women in Saudi Arabia and the Gulf states had a

totally different experience, although state policies of "female empowerment" were part of the founding principles of the newly formed UAE back in the 1970s. See also Wanda Krause, "Gender and participation in the Arab Gulf," *Kuwait Programme on Development, Governance and Globalisation in the Gulf States* 4 (2009).

15. Jillian Schedneck, "Young Emirati Women: Stories of Empowerment, Feminism and Equality in the United Arab Emirates," *Outskirts* 30, The Gender Games (May 2014): 2.

16. Serra Kirdar, "United Arab Emirates," in *Women's Rights in the Middle East and North Africa: Progress amid Resistance*, ed. Sanja Kelly and Julia Breslin (Lanham, MD: Rowman & Littlefield, 2010), 13.

17. Personal interviews conducted with women filmmakers in Image Nation, spring 2018, as well as with Nayla Al Khaja.

18. As a matter of fact, men face more pressure in this respect as the traditional "breadwinners" that have to opt for a profitable career.

19. See Chandra Talpade Mohanty, Anne Russo, and Lourdes Torres, *Third World Women and the Politics of Feminism* (Bloomington: Indiana University Press, 1991); Amani Hamdan, *Muslim Women Speak: A Tapestry of Lives and Dreams* (Toronto: Women's Press, 2009).

20. Shohat, "Area Studies," 1270.

21. Florence Martin, *Screen and Veils: Maghrebi Women's Cinema* (Bloomington: Indiana University Press, 2011).

22. Personal Interviews (together with Christopher Thornton), Abu Dhabi, 2018.

23. While access to the means of production might be one of the issues in question in the UAE and elsewhere, yet the documentary genre has also been viewed as a consciousness-raising tool and as a privileged site for the articulation of alternative representations when it comes to gender, race, and identity. Janet Walker and Diane Waldman in *Feminism and Documentary* (Minneapolis: University of Minnesota Press, 1999) explain, for instance, that "activists from the second wave of the women's movement were initially attracted to the documentary form for a multitude of reasons, and early feminist film writing enthusiastically embraced these films as well" (6).

24. Personal interview (together with Christopher Thornton), Dubai, 2018.

25. Hudson, "Locating Emirati Filmmaking," 179.

26. Personal interview (together with Christopher Thornton), Dubai, 2018.

27. Edward Said, *Orientalism*, (London: Penguin Classics, 2003), 57.

28. Nadine Naber, *Arab America. Gender, Cultural Politics, and Activism* (New York: New York University Press, 2012).

29. Chrysavgi Papagianni, "The Salvation of Emirati Memory in Nujoom Alghanem's Hamama," *Quarterly Review of Film and Video* 35, no. 4 (2018): 4.

30. Justin Thomas's words are revealing in terms of the discrepancies evidenced in Emirati society today; "It has been suggested that youngsters in Abu Dhabi and New York have more in common with each other than they do with their grandparents," *Psychological Well-Being in the Gulf States* (London: Palgrave Macmillan, 2013), 8.

31. Personal interview (together with Christopher Thornton), Dubai, 2018.

32. See Papagianni, "Salvation of Emirati Memory."

33. For a more detailed discussion of the images promoted by UAE, see Papagianni "Salvation of Emirati Memory," 6; Jane Bristol-Rhys, *Emirati Women: Generations of Change* (New York: Columbia University Press, 2010); Alia Yunis, *Coming*

Soon: Encounters on the Road to Film and Heritage in the UAE (Amsterdam: University of Amsterdam, 2020).

34. Drawing on interviews and oral narratives, Bristol-Rhys's study reveals a younger generation of Emirati women that seems to enjoy less freedom when compared to the older generations not only because they are trapped in a vicious circle of overabundance but also because the public space has been dramatically redefined and confined after the discovery of oil that brought a surge of expatriates to the country.

35. Chrysavgi Papagianni, "Emirati Women Filmmakers," in *Gender and Media Encyclopedia*, ed. Karen Ross (New York: Wiley-Blackwell, 2020), 7.

36. Melissa Gronlund, "Award-winning Dubai Poet and Filmmaker Will Represent the UAE at the Venice Biennale 2019," *The National*, January 29, 2019, https://www.thenational.ae/arts-culture/art/award-winning-dubai-poet-and-filmmaker-will-represent-the-uae-at-the-venice-biennale-2019-1.819538.

37. Papagianni, "Emirati Women Filmmakers."

38. Rebecca Hillauer, *Encyclopedia of Arab Women Filmmakers*, trans. Allison Brown, Deborah Cohen, and Nancy Joyce (Cairo: American University of Cairo Press, 2005), 10.

39. Shohat, "Area Studies," 1272.

40. Kaltham al-Ghanim, "The Intellectual Frameworks and Theoretical Limits of Arab Feminist Thought," in *Arab Feminisms: Gender and Equality in the Middle East*, ed. Jean Makdisi, Noha Bayoumi, Rafif Rida Sidawi (London: Bloomsbury, 2014), 187.

41. Hudson, "Locating Emirati Filmmaking," 173.

42. Hudson, "Locating Emirati Filmmaking," 175.

43. E. Nina Rothe, "Director & Producer Nayla Al Khaja: The 'Exceptional Arab Women in Film' Series," Huffington Post, April 3, 2017, https://www.huffpost.com/entry/director-producer-nayla-al-khaja-the-exceptional_b_58e1ebbae4b03c2b30f6a817.

44. Apart from Al Khaja's film clubs, other noteworthy grassroots initiatives include Cinema Akil, which together with the Sharjah Art Foundation represents an important venue for the promotion of UAE filmmaking.

11

ARABIA'S AMBIVALENT AUTEUR
Meshal Al-Jaser's Cinematic Vision for the New Saudi Arabia

SEAN FOLEY

Over the two last decades, Shahad Ameen, Meshal Al-Jaser, Ahd Kamel, Ali Kalthami, Haifa Mansour, Malik Nejer, Mahmoud Sabbagh, Mujtaba Saeed, and Ali al-Sumayin have emerged as the first Saudi directors with global reach. Even before cinemas in Saudi Arabia were allowed to reopen in 2018, these film directors established the kingdom as a new center of cinema by creating original content in Arabic as films or as YouTube videos—a medium that has become, in essence, a new form of television. Among this new generation of directors, Al-Jaser, whose films and short videos often go viral within days of their release, has a unique position. In the words of Bahraini film blogger Mohamed Sultan, Al-Jaser's "only competition" in Gulf cinema "is himself."[1] In October 2018, before cinemas opened had opened again, the director's YouTube channels had well over 870 million viewers and 8.6 million subscribers.[2] Shocking, hilarious, and wild, Al-Jaser's videos and films blend oppositional Western and Saudi cultural references in commenting on the most sensitive issues facing his country today.

Although Al-Jaser asserts his individuality as an artist and does not "care about the opinion of others,"[3] the Saudi director does not assign meaning or truth to his work; rather, he leaves that up to the audience—or, more broadly, to society. As he observed in 2018, many Saudis loved his 2015 video *Ṭaz bi al-Kuffār!* (*Screw Infidels!*) because they "understood that it was a 'sarcastic'" attack on religious extremism, while countless others, not realizing the video's multilayered messages, "liked it because it was racist."[4] Despite the popularity of Al-Jaser's videos on subjects as varied as the Syrian civil war, religious extremism, and women's rights, he and his colleagues have been largely overlooked by leading scholars of Saudi society.[5]

Using extensive in-country and online research, this chapter aims to fill the aforementioned gap in scholarship by exploring the appeal of the Saudi director's "cinematic vision"—as revealed in his short videos and his longer films. Throughout, I will build on the work that I did for my monograph *Changing Saudi Arabia: Art, Culture, and Society in the Kingdom* along with the insights on humor and online networking in Henry Jenkins, Sam Ford, and Joshua Green's *Spreadable Media*. In this chapter, I argue that Al-Jaser's blending of global cultural norms with Saudi cultural traditions allows him to reach a wide domestic audience while serving in a role that he and other artists in the kingdom now fill—individuals who through the language of culture articulate the feelings that the masses cannot easily articulate. At once mirrors and lamps, reflections of society and leaders, Al-Jaser and his male and female colleagues stand at the forefront of social change, offering innovative ways to approach an increasingly complex world.[6]

THE RISE OF THE MODERN SAUDI ARTISTIC MOVEMENT

For many Arabs and Western observers, the presence of filmmakers like Al-Jaser or an arts movement in Saudi Arabia is unfathomable. They view Saudis as religious fanatics whose loyalty to the Saudi monarchy is the only thing really separating them from the leaders of the Islamic State (ISIS). Typical of these types of views is *On Saudi Arabia*, a study of Saudi Arabia by Karen Elliott House, a Pulitzer Prize–winning US journalist. In her eyes, the high walls of Saudi cities permit Saudis to live in "cocoons" and raise their children in a culture "largely devoid of art and the enjoyment of beauty."[7] Indeed, Noah Feldman, writing in the *Wall Street Journal* in 2012, noted that the Arabic-speaking states of the Gulf had no "indigenous tradition of visual or plastic arts" and were situated "next-door to Wahhabi, art-despising Saudi Arabia."[8]

Such statements reinforce a vision of Saudi Arabia as devoid of film or any art in general—a view that was voiced by T. E. Lawrence when he observed, "There was so little Arab art that one could say Arab art did not exist."[9] One finds a similar perspective among some Saudis. For example, writing in the Saudi daily newspaper *As-Šarq* in 2013, Dr. Abdulsalam al-Wayel, a sociologist at King Saud University in Riyadh, declared: "If we can say that there is a 'Saudi culture,' and it has value, then we can also say with high confidence that the contempt for the arts lies at the heart of its values."[10] Further implicitly reinforcing this argument was the fact that there were no movie theaters in Saudi Arabia and few signs that there would be a domestic film industry that would allow for Al-Jaser and other filmmakers to emerge.

However, an indigenous artistic movement had already begun to emerge in the twenty-first century and was already laying the groundwork for Al-Jaser and a new creative class to emerge. Remarkably, that movement did not begin in the cities of central Saudi Arabia but in Abha, the capital of Asir, a mountainous southern province on the Saudi-Yemeni border. There in the 1990s and early 2000s, Ahmed Mater, Abdulnasser Gharem, and a group of young professionals, none of whom had any artistic training, began to discuss creating an artistic movement that viewed the creation and experience of art as central elements to positive social change in Saudi Arabia—a vision that would fundamentally shape Al-Jaser's films in the 2010s.[11]

Out of their discussions, there emerged a new worldview and model for creating art, which synthesized art from home and abroad, explored cultural and social issues, drew from the online world, and created a common social space. Rather than utilizing the Western framework, in which an artist works in a studio on his or her own—creating art as God created the world—they looked at the creation of culture, and of visual art in particular, as a process that involves many people. What also set the work of the new generation of Saudi artists apart was the extensive use of collage and its exoteric nature: in other words, they did not assign meaning or truth to their work. Rather, they left that up to the audience—or, more broadly, to all of society. While the artists were still in their twenties and thirties, they accepted the input and guidance of Saudis of all ages, including those with whom they fundamentally disagreed.

As one of the artists, Abdulnasser Gharem, once noted, he and his colleagues were not picking sides; instead, they were "trying to be a mirror" to society.[12] But that did not mean that artists in Abha did not want their mirror to serve a greater good and inspire reaction and change. "Sometimes when you become a mirror as an artist and you show your society who they are," Gharem has tweeted, "they get upset."[13]

By taking that approach, the artists invited further discussion about the real meaning of their work. Those discussions effectively extended the process of creating art and culture beyond their group, so that society could have a say in creating culture and be invested in it. As a leading Saudi art critic once told me, Mater "allows people to read into his work what they want... to have their own take, so to speak."[14] Over time, that process transformed these artists and those who followed them, including Al-Jaser, into organic intellectuals who, through the language of culture, expressed the feelings and experiences of their society in ways that could not be replicated by academia, business, or the media. Ambiguity had an important benefit, for it offered these artists a mechanism to explore sensitive cultural, political, and social topics, while still claiming that they and their work were "apolitical."[15]

THE BRIGHTEST BOY BEHIND THE CAMERA

By the second decade of the twenty-first century, the cultural model that Mater and others had pioneered had been adopted by Al-Jaser and a new generation of Saudi artists exploring the same questions as the artists in Asir had done but through comedy. Taking advantage of the limited Saudi state regulation of YouTube, they founded online television networks that became extremely popular. Their shows earned millions of hits online, making Al-Jaser, Hisham Fageeh, Omar Hussein, Ali Kalthami, Malik Nejer, and others household names in Saudi Arabia.[16]

From the start, the comedians sought to hold a mirror to society, moving their audience to thought and eventually social change. This approach reflected a nuanced understanding of humor and its linkage to shared experiences and common history in society—one voiced in *Spreadable Media*, which observes that successful humor reflects relationships and inspires others in society to react, using comedic content for their own purposes.¹⁷ As Hussein noted, humor "reflects something that is happening in our community in a comical manner." But, he adds, "It's up to you to decide what's right and wrong."¹⁸ Indeed, Kalthami, a cofounder of Telfaz11, a popular Saudi YouTube network/channel, argued that he and his colleagues filled a similarly apolitical and positive social role by encouraging viewers to "critique and question, rather than passively receive."¹⁹ Notably, Kalthami, who grew up in the same southern region as Gharem, has sought out the Saudi artist's advice while running his company; he has also proudly displayed his work in the company's office.²⁰

That advice may in part explain one of the key choices of Kalthami and other pioneers in the comedy industry—namely, they deliberately made their videos look homemade and omitted the names of both the directors and writers. Instead, they listed the directors as "the boys behind the camera," while writers were portrayed as "scratchers" or "scribblers."²¹ By omitting both the names of the directors and writers and characterizing them in a humorous way, Saudi comedians camouflaged the authorship of their cultural products, implicitly borrowing tactics that had been employed by Gharem, Mater, and the other visual artists in Abha.

The resulting product did not fit easily into key schools of Western film criticism, either old or new, such as: (a) auteur theory, which holds that a film's director is its author and the one who defines it; (b) Schreiber theory, which assigns that role to the screenwriter; or (c) collaboration theory, which analyzes the contribution that multiple types of employees make to a film, including those who are "above-the-line" (directors, producers, and leading actors) and "below-the-line" (grips, gaffers, or extras). Instead, Saudis pursue a very different strategy for authorship: the "boys behind the camera" and other creatives created content but delegated responsibility for defining movies and YouTube videos to society at large, making their art as exoteric as the work of Gharem and Mater.²²

One of the brightest "boys behind the camera" was Al-Jaser, who started to make films at the age of seventeen for Telfaz11's *Folaim Ya gholaim* YouTube web series in the early 2010s. Remarkably, Al-Jaser, who had dreamed as a child of drawing cartoons for the Cartoon Network, had limited experience with filmmaking, only gaining access to the internet at home in his teens. But it was clear that he had a natural aptitude. After only a few months of having access to the online world at home, he was making films and posting them to his YouTube channel. There he was discovered by Telfaz11 executives, who quickly added him to the company's series, with Kalthami serving as his personal mentor.[23]

When I visited the company's Riyadh offices in 2013 and in 2014, one of the company's star comedians, Fageeh, lionized Al-Jaser's talent—even after Telfaz11's video *No Woman, No Drive* went viral, cementing Fageeh's reputation as a comedian around the world. Fageeh expressed his appreciation for Al-Jaser's vast cultural knowledge and talent as an artist and a director.[24] In fact, he looked on Al-Jaser as an individual whose work could one day be compared to that of leading non-Saudi directors of the past, many of whom were once hailed as master "auteurs."[25] Notably Fageeh, like Al-Jaser, had been discovered by Telfaz11 executives on YouTube,[26] and they have since collaborated on multiple projects, including on *Suriā yā taḥtājak* (*Syria Needs You*), the second video in *Meshal's Short Film Series*. In July 2018, Fageeh told me that he still vividly remembered watching Al-Jaser make the video, which was released in 2012.[27]

THE RISE OF JOHNNY DEPP AL-ARAB

The two-minute video, which is in English with Arabic subtitles, combines several factors that both echo the work of earlier Saudi artists but eventually became the hallmarks of his own film style: images drawn from both Saudi and global popular culture, ironic humor, symbolism, ambiguity, and a sophisticated message meant to provoke a fierce reaction online across class and age groups in Saudi society. The broad audience is especially important to Al-Jaser, who, like the Abha artists, wants his work to reach everyone, not just his own peers and contemporaries.[28]

At the same time, the video incorporated four elements that now define his unique style as a Saudi filmmaker: (a) popular Western music, (b) blood, (c) shocking action and graphic imagery, and (d) violence. As Al-Jaser told *Vice* magazine in a lengthy interview in 2018, he seeks to "challenge" "all segments of society" but to do so while bearing in mind the "mentality of his viewer," whose opinions he wishes to "respect"—even if it differs with his own.²⁹ Moreover, he stresses that his artwork arises out of a deep sense of patriotism, a desire to "correct" what he sees are the wrongs in his country and to improve his community.³⁰

We can see this consciousness clearly from the start of *Suriā yā taḥtājak*. Shot entirely in black and white, the video addresses the Syrian civil war, an event that was then at the forefront of Saudi society, which had deep ties to the neighboring Arab state. Already, some Saudis and non-Saudis had sought to use YouTube videos to galvanize the country to act through song or poetry. By contrast, *Suriā yā taḥtājak* opens with a tired and seemingly dazed Al-Jaser, who is wearing a T-shirt, jeans, and tennis shoes, walking next to a wall adjoining a residential street in Riyadh. He could be any young man living in the Saudi capital, unaware of the violence in neighboring Syria.³¹

But he is suddenly awoken to that war—both physically and intellectually—by sinister music and a stream of blood. When Al-Jaser stops and looks up at the wall next to the stream of blood, we see a black stencil image of Syrian president Bashar al-Assad complete with fake devil's horns. The stencil is situated above words clearly meant to be both horrific and ironic: "Bashar's Fun Land." Now fully awake, Al-Jaser dons the type of white bandana often worn by the young Syrians who frequently appeared on Arab satellite television in demonstrations opposing Syria's government at the time. As the music picks up again, we see Al-Jaser pass a young male demonstrator lifting his left arm in defiance, only to be shot dead. But Al-Jaser continues to walk, passing a child who is being comforted by a woman sitting next to a dead body covered by a white cloth. Behind the body, "What is my fault?" is written on the wall. Al-Jaser then passes by the words "Help Us" and a Syrian flag with a splattering of blood adjacent to it. Al-Jaser eventually stops beside the words "The World" on the wall. There, he removes the white bandana and moves forward out of view. The video ends with an entirely black screen with an English message in white letters meant to shock Saudis into action but that does not instruct the viewer: "You just going to pretend that you didn't see?"

From the moment the video was posted on YouTube, Al-Jaser aggressively promoted it through a process that *Spreadable Media* calls a "participating mechanism."[32] Within this framework, Al-Jaser and other content creators, who lack promotional budgets, court online "niche or subculture communities" who "have strong affinity with their genre or message" and who "will promote the work to like-minded others."[33] Al-Jaser begin this process by posting six separate tweets about the video (four in English[34] and two in Arabic)[35] while tagging Fageeh and other leading Saudi artists and creatives with substantial followings on social media.[36] He also tweeted at Justine Erzak, a US online personality, asking her to retweet the video to her 1.78 million followers.[37] While Erzak did not retweet the video, Al-Jaser's video went viral, earning eight hundred thousand views on YouTube, a very respectable number for a filmmaker who was largely unknown when the video was released in June 2012. Over time, Al-Jaser developed a wide following on social media in Saudi Arabia and abroad, where his dark humor has earned the moniker *Johnny Depp al-Arab* (or "The Arab Johnny Depp").[38] In 2022, Al-Jaser boasted that he had 118,500 followers on Twitter and over 1.5 million on Instagram. [39]

SCREW INFIDELS!

Following his success with *Suriā yā taḥtājak*, Al-Jaser appeared in and directed several successful videos in the *Folaim Ya Gholaim* and *Khambala* series, the most successful of which was *Ṭaz bi al-Kuffār!* (*Screw Infidels!*) In the 2015 video, filmed after he had moved to California to attend film school, Al-Jaser plays a young Arab Muslim man living in Los Angeles, who forces everyone he encounters to adhere to his strict vision of Islam. While the video is largely in Arabic, there are English subtitles.[40] Repeatedly, Al-Jaser's character asserts that he has a pure heart with a desire to remain strong and not "melty like ice cream." Nevertheless, he physically assaults anyone or anything that contradicts his rigid interpretation of Islamic morality, whether they be a young couple in love, a bare-chested male jogger, a man walking his dog in a park, or a boy giving a female teacher an apple. Remarkably, as Al-Jaser knocks away the apple, he admonishes the child for being generous. Then he slaps an Arab Muslim who challenges him to treat non-Muslims with respect. He also burns the toilet paper in a man's bathroom, telling the poor guy that infidels are gross because they don't use bidets. When Al-Jaser finds a mixed group of young revelers at a rooftop pool party, he declares that they are *Mufskeen*, a colloquial Saudi term for "naked," before urinating in their pool to show his disgust.

Further adding to the absurdity of Al-Jaser's actions are his clothes, which include sneakers, multicolored shorts, impossibly dark sunglasses, black hats akin to Rasta caps, beads, and tie-dyed t-shirts emblazoned with the nonsense word *LoLaby* in Arabic script—a parody of names taken on by Arab rappers. Al-Jaser is usually accompanied in his act by Yasin Ghazzawi, who wears the same types of clothes—until he suddenly becomes a romantic ballad singer in a tuxedo, a character that had previously appeared in earlier Telfaz11 videos. Al-Jaser's actions and mode of dress are clearly parodies of videos that have been produced by ISIS, targeting young Muslims who yearn to live in a community that upholds a strict vision of Islam, while demonstrating their manhood by practicing extreme violence, especially against Westerners and non-Muslims.

Clearly, this is a sensitive area for Saudi comedians to exploit. Only Tunisia sent more fighters than Saudi Arabia to serve in ISIS military forces.[41] While many Saudis were amused by the video, others wondered what message it sent to the rest of the world. Nonetheless, the video went viral, striking a chord with millions of Saudis who felt that it expressed their own experiences and worldview. As Al-Jaser has observed, some viewers enjoyed the video because they saw it as an attack on religious extremism, while others liked what they interpreted as the "racist" message, overlooking the video's clear satire of bigotry.[42] By September 2022, the video had been viewed more than 10.3 million times.[43]

Ultimately, what *Screw Infidels!* exemplifies is the vast freedom of Al-Jaser's artistic imagination, which, by 2015, had become shocking, stunning, hilarious, and unpredictable. Discussing the film with me at the time, a friend in Riyadh observed that one cannot kill an idea—no matter how horrific it is.[44] However, by bringing the extremism of ISIS and other complex matters into the spotlight of comedy and extreme slapstick humor, the Saudi filmmaker had awoken Americans and Saudis with a new way to confront some of their darkest fears.

A MATURE VISION

With his comedic reputation cemented, Al-Jaser continued to make popular short videos for Telfaz11 that explored sensitive issues in Saudi society, often by using the same type of shocking, violent humor to make clear that everyone has a role in both causing and potentially solving the major issues facing their society. In *Can I Go Out* (*Mumkin Aṭla'?*), Al-Jaser explores women's mobility and, implicitly, the idea of women driving, another subject where morality and scandal are intertwined.[45] Starring Darin Al-Bayed, the ten-minute video shows the efforts of a "mature" Saudi young woman to see her friend and to shop in Riyadh's famed Taḥlia shopping district. The video is set in the "era when she cannot drive"—an ambiguous phrase that could signal a period in the woman's life when she could not drive or during the period the law banning women from driving in Saudi Arabia was still in effect. Notably, the video opens with a shot of a goldfish swimming in a beautiful clear fishbowl, a potential metaphor for the limited ability of even middle-class or wealthy Saudi women to leave their homes when they choose.

Initially, Al-Bayed is seemingly successful in her plan to go to Taḥlia. Her father delights her by providing SAR 1500 (USD 399), sparking a short song and dance routine in which she imagines what she could do with the money and the freedom it represents. But the scene ends abruptly when her father orders her to check with her mother before leaving, leading to a scene titled "The Interrogation." In that scene, we see Al-Bayed's mother emerge from prayer, setting up an intense series of exchanges between mother and daughter about whether she can go out and whether her friend is morally upright and from a good family. Even after Al-Bayed secures the support of her mother to leave, Al-Bayed must deal with her sister to use the family driver. In a scene entitled "The Battle," the two women engage in fierce verbal and hand-to-hand combat in the family kitchen for the right to use the driver, yelling at each other and eventually throwing glasses and knives at each other.

When the sister vanquishes her, Al-Bayed must turn to her brother Khalid, played by Al-Jaser, in a scene titled "Loss of Dignity." After Al-Bayed accedes to his demand for a glass of orange and carrot juice before he drives her, he refuses to help her, putting on red lipstick and a ridiculous orange suit with a bow tie—all the while singing that he is the *Rajul al-Bait* (the man of the house). He then gives a litany of complaints about the bad weather, including that he has driven her to the mall recently and that he is tired. Al-Jaser also asserts that he can insult her, even though he cannot change a light bulb. Adding to the absurdity of the situation are the inanimate objects that sing, the flickering lights, and that Al-Jaser levitates in the air—recalling scenes from *The Exorcist*, the classic Hollywood horror film. Stymied by her siblings, Al-Bayed decides to go with "Plan B," taking a taxi. But even that choice is filled with peril. On a dark and stormy night, the driver, who is one of the thousands of expatriate South Asians who drive taxis in the Gulf, turns back to her after she tells him where she wants to go and looks lustily at her, holding a rose in his mouth. Terrified, she takes matters into her own hands, lifting out a small pistol and cocking it in the final scene of the video. The viewer does not see if she uses the gun.

Released in December 2017 weeks after the Saudi government announced that the ban on women drivers would be lifted in 2018, *Can I Go Out?* provides a fresh mirror to society and a vision of why women in Saudi Arabia cannot move freely—much as he had done in *Screw Infidels!* Although *Can I Go Out?* has been criticized for not focusing more on how patriarchy and the Saudi guardian system negatively impact the country's women, the film's approach helps us see that Al-Bayed's problems and those of Saudi women reflect the realities of a social system in which men and women, old and young, bear some responsibility and are negatively impacted.[46] We can see this process clearly in the situations of the sister and brother, both of whose crazed actions reflect a clear social logic: the sister cannot drive, while the brother complains about the burdens of driving Al-Bayed and other female relatives. Indeed, the brother's complaint is one commonly voiced by many young Saudi men.[47]

Al-Jaser takes a similarly broad approach to problem-solving in *Taḥt as-Asmint* (*Under Concrete*), which was released in March 2018.[48] In the video, Al-Jaser returns to Syria, the same theme he explored in *Suriā yā taḥtājak* but through the life of a young girl named Deema. She and her family are living in a house with near constant radio and television reports about the brutality and killing taking place in Syria's civil war. While it is not explicitly stated that the family is in Syria, Al-Jaser clearly linked the video to the country and to the Civil War on Twitter, where he wrote "UNDER CONCRETE #Syria" in a March 14, 2018, tweet in which he first released the YouTube link to the video.[49]

At the opening of *Under Concrete*, Deema's family is seemingly living a normal middle-class life in a comfortable house. But after the family starts to eat its breakfast, their house is hit by a rocket attack. Deema, the lone survivor of the attack, is shown covered by a concrete slab and bleeding. She is in excruciating pain because of her badly injured leg. As the video progresses, Deema drifts off into a surreal and dark dreamscape. We see her remembering a happier time when her mother helped her whenever she was sick or injured. In one horrific sequence, we see her mother, while singing Deema a lullaby to help her sleep, transform from a healthy woman into the bloodied corpse she became after the rocket attack. Another striking memory is an argument in the recent past between her parents after Deema asked her father if a missile could strike their house. While Deema's mother seeks to discourage her from thinking about an attack because of her age, her father proclaims that only God knows if they will be attacked. "Let her know," he says to Deema's mother, "that the Arabs have lost their humanity."[50]

Although there is a hint at the end of the video that Deema has been saved or is really experiencing a horrible nightmare, the overall message, as voiced by her father, is clear: innocent people are dying in Syria and elsewhere because the Arabs have remained silent. Here the blame for the conflict and the horror it has caused is collectively shared; it is not just the Syrians and others who have taken part in the conflict that bears the blame. Such a statement is counterintuitive in that it blames millions for a war they have not taken part in. But it also offers hope for a potential solution to a seemingly impossible situation. If Arabs regain their humanity and take action, then Deema and others can be safe and live in a world defined by justice.

Since its release, *Under Concrete* has been a critical success, opening new doors for Al-Jaser. Not only has it been viewed, as of September 2022, over 1.1 million times on YouTube, but it was also named the worldwide winner of the Qomrah competition—an edutainment film contest that provides directors and production houses a grant to produce a short "educating" film of approximately five minutes. A year later, Al-Jaser took part in a United Nations project aimed at helping refugees from Syria and other countries around the world.⁵¹

"IF YOU DON'T SHOCK PEOPLE, THEY JUST WON'T PAY ATTENTION."

That same year, Al-Jaser returned to gender, a theme that has long defined his work but with an approach that is seemingly more daring than the one he used in *Can I Go Out*? In *Rise*, he partnered with Tamtam, a Saudi female singer based in Los Angeles, on a film that explores "the idea of arranged marriage"⁵²—or what he referred more ambiguously on Twitter as *Zawāj Taqlīdī* (Traditional marriage).⁵³ Throughout the four-minute film, which feels more like a dream than a traditional pop music video, we hear Tamtam sing in English about the many travails she faces as a Saudi woman. At the same time, we see her experience the rituals linked to arranged marriage along with those of Saudi domestic life. As Al-Jaser admitted in 2019, these symbols and the rituals linked to them may look odd or even exotic to a Western audience but are "a good representation" of what his "society wants" along with rules that define the life of Saudis. By contrast, "if this was an English music video," he continued, "you might see fish and chips."⁵⁴

In the opening scene of *Rise*, Tamtam wears a dark floral dress that seamlessly blends into the wallpaper of a room, perhaps symbolically suggesting the place of young women in Saudi Arabia. Significantly, she is shown carrying two glasses of orange juice, one of the traditional symbols that a Saudi woman uses to accept a marriage proposal.⁵⁵ Tamtam is then forcefully ushered into another room by an older woman, presumably the groom's mother, who displays a sinister smile while carrying a smoking *mabkara*, another symbol of Saudi society and social gatherings. In that room, Tamtam sits down next to a mustached mannequin dressed in traditional Saudi clothing, presumably her future husband. Then she presents the orange juice glasses to the mannequin. Now that she has seemingly given her consent to marry a person she has never met before, we see images of the two things that she is entitled to as a Saudi bride: a white envelope marked with dollar signs, presumably her dowry, and a mannequin hand on a rotating pedestal with a ring. Notably, the use of a mannequin in the scene is no accident, reflecting an insight that Al-Jaser once had after viewing mannequins in a store window. "Marrying a person without meeting them," Al-Jaser realized at the time, is just "like marrying a mannequin."[56]

Al-Jaser, however, continues the farce far beyond the scene in which Tamtam agrees to marry a mannequin. Following the engagement, the video cuts to a nighttime outdoor wedding party, where a dazed and clearly uncomfortable Tamtam wears an exquisite white wedding dress while sitting in a thronelike chair. She is oblivious to the young women dancing and celebrating around her. Instead, she focuses with increasingly dread at the arrival of the mannequin, who slowly enters the party and sits in a large chair next to her, signifying that he is her husband. The situation is both hilarious and tragic—just as Al-Jaser's other videos have been—but neither patriarchy nor any other force is blamed for the situation. After all, there is no explicit force keeping Tamtam at the farcical wedding, while it was the older woman who ushered Tamtam into the meeting with the mannequin. Instead, the viewer is left to ponder why the older woman or the others in the wedding party would sanction this situation or see it as acceptable that a woman must start a family and spend the rest of their lives with a man they don't know.

The video, however, does not stop at the wedding or the mannequin. Now wed, Tamtam and her husband together experience married life, symbolized by a series of objects that are found in any Saudi home—namely, coffee cups, tea, zatar, Turkish delights, eggs in a skillet, and a birthday cake—all of which appear on the same rotating platform as the mannequin hand with the ring had. We then see the married couple driving in a 1970s-era car on a desert road, with the mannequin at the car's steering wheel while Tamtam sits stylishly dressed with sunglasses in the passenger seat. The video concludes with a dreamlike sequence in which we see the husband inexplicably burst into flames, the blurred images of Tamtam carrying glasses of orange juice, and finally Tamtam driving away from the smoldering mannequin.

Has Tamtam's character really killed her husband and left him in the desert? Or is the video a metaphor for the end of a marriage or a type of

Saudi women's liberation? Might the whole video have been a fantasy or a nightmare of what could have happened had Tamtam entered into an arranged marriage in Saudi Arabia? That is left for the viewer to decide—just as it is left unsaid at the end of *Under Concrete* whether it was real or if it was only a bad dream. Whether real or imagined, the images are unsettling and prompt the viewer to wonder about the meaning of Tamtam's marriage to a mannequin, the position of Saudi women generally, and how a society (men, women, young, old) could accept how women are treated in Saudi Arabia in general. And that was the intent of Al-Jaser and Tamtam: to get a conversation going rather than blame a specific party. Indeed, using language that strikingly echoes Al-Jaser's words about his own work, Tamtam explained in a 2019 interview about *Rise* that she had not burned anyone but instead aimed to "start a conversation, and sometimes, if you don't shock people, they just won't pay attention."[57]

CONCLUSION

When thinking about the role of Al-Jaser, Tamtam, and other Saudi artists, an American writer cannot help but be reminded of the words of American poet Walt Whitman (1819–1892), whose vision of America remains to be fulfilled. These lines from the poet's "Song of Myself" might be appropriate for Al-Jaser's work, especially his views about how his fellow Saudis see his video *Screw Infidels!*:

> Do I contradict myself?
> Very well then I contradict myself
> (I am large, I contain multitudes.)[58]

Whitman is himself recalling another great American writer, Ralph Waldo Emerson (1803–1882), who in his essay "Self-Reliance," famously observed that "a foolish consistency is the hobgoblin of little minds."[59] To be sure, Whitman went further in asserting the equality of women to men. He writes in "I Sing the Body Electric":

> The female contains all qualities and tempers them,
> She is in her place and moves with perfect balance...
> The male is not less the soul nor more, he too is in his place.[60]

Nonetheless, Whitman's vision remains relevant. For Al-Jaser, as for Whitman, it is not a question of "contradiction" but of the acceptance of diversity and the avoidance of dogmatism and of "a foolish consistency." Al-Jaser does not experience diversity or even tribalism as a threat. Rather his faith in Saudi society and its institutions *enables* pluralism—it has been the strength of his belief that has allowed him to admit so much diversity into his consciousness and his work, thus giving Saudi society innovative ways to look at its most contentious issues. In his eyes, almost anything is possible if you can just start a productive conversation among a diverse group of people.

> SEAN FOLEY is Professor of History at Middle Tennessee State University specializing in the contemporary history and politics of the Middle East and the wider Islamic world. He is author of *Changing Saudi Arabia: Art, Culture, and Society in the Kingdom* and of *The Arab Gulf States: Beyond Oil and Islam*. He has conducted extensive primary research in Saudi Arabia and has held Fulbright fellowships in Syria, Turkey, and Malaysia.

NOTES

1. Mohamed Sultan, "The Eccentric Cinema of Meshal Al Jaser," *Asia Cinema* (blog), January 7, 2018, https://theasiancinemablog.com/essays/the-eccentric-cinema-of-meshal-al-jaser/.

2. The Arab Gulf States Institute Washington, "Meshal al-Jaser Filmmaker," https://agsiw.org/associates/meshal-al-jaser/.

3. Meshal al-Jaser, "*Muqābala maʻa mukrij as-saʻūdī Mašʻal al-Jāsr*," interview by Nada Haju, *Vice*, June 12, 2018, https://bit.ly/2MwfoCt.

4. Meshal al-Jaser, "*Muqābala maʻa mukrij as-saʻūdī Mašʻal al-Jāsr*."

5. For a recent discussion of this issue, see Sean Foley, review of *Salman's Legacy: The Dilemmas of a New Era in Saudi Arabia*, by Madawi al-Rasheed et al., *Middle East Journal* 73, no. 1 (Spring 2019): 165–166.

6. Sean Foley, *Changing Saudi Arabia: Art, Culture, and Society in the Kingdom* (Boulder, CO: Lynne Rienner, 2019), x.

7. Karen Elliot House, *On Saudi Arabia: Its People, Past, Religion, Fault Lines—And Future* (New York: Knopf, 2012), 30.

8. Noah Feldman, "Taking It to the Street," *Wall Street Journal*, October 25, 2012, https://www.wsj.com/articles/SB10001424052970204425904578072630892858670.

9. T. E. Lawrence, *The Seven Pillars of Wisdom* (New York: Anchor Books/Doubleday, 1926), 38.

10. Abdulsalam al-Wayel, "*An iḥtiqārna al-Fann ... fauz Muhammad 'Asaf baina al-Ḥadīf wa al-Ğabaran*," *As-Šarq*, June 29, 2013, http://www.alsharq.net.sa/2013/06/29/880540.

11. For more on this period, see David Calverley-Morris, "People Weren't Ready for Us," *Esquire Magazine*, September 2013, 122–127.

12. Aimee Dawson, "Saudi Artist Abdulnasser Gharem to Have First Solo US Show at Lacma," *Art Newspaper*, March 8, 2017, http://theartnewspaper.com/news/saudi-artist-abdulnasser-gharem-to-have-first-solo-us-show-at-lacma.

13. Abdulnasser Gharem (@abdulnasserghar), "Sometimes When You Become a Mirror as an Artist and You Show Your Society Who They Are, They Get Upset," Twitter, June 29, 2017, 4:10, https://twitter.com/abdulnasserghar/status/880382635570233346.

14. Author in conversation with a leading figure in the Saudi entertainment industry, January 2014.

15. Foley, *Changing*, 14.

16. For more on the early history of these companies, see Gilbert Ramsey and Sumayah Fatani, "The New Saudi Nationalism of the New Social Media," in *Political Islam and Global Media: The Boundaries of Religious Identity*, ed. Noha Mellor and Khalil Rinnawi (New York: Routledge, 2016), 187–202.

17. Henry Jenkins, Sam Ford, and Joshua Green, "Designing for Spreadability" in *Spreadable Media: Creating Value and Meaning in a Networked Culture* (New York: New York University Press, 2013), 206–207.

18. Catriona Davies, Rima Maktabi, and Aroub Abdelhaq, "How to Rebel Saudi Style," CNN, March 23, 2012, http://www.cnn.com/2012/03/23/world/meast/saudi-alternative-culture/index.html.

19. Alissa Simon, "Q&A: C3 Films and Telfaz11 Topper Ali Kalthami Talks Internet and the Saudi Film Scene," *Variety*, May 13, 2016, https://variety.com/2016/biz/spotlight/csfilms-telfaz11-ali-kalthami-internet-saudi-film-scene-1201773008/.

20. Author in conversation with Abdulnasser Gharem, August 2013.

21. "Boys behind the camera" was *"Al-'iyāl 'ilaī warā'a Al-Kāmīrā"* and scribbler was *"karbaša."* Alaa Yousef, "Lecture 4: Alaa Yousef" (paper delivered to the Nuqat Mena Conference, Kuwait City, Kuwait, November 9, 2013).

22. Foley, *Changing*, 119–120; Janet Staiger, "Authorship Approaches," in *Authorship and Film*, ed. David A. Gerstner and Janet Staiger (New York and London: Routledge, 2003), 41–42.

23. al-Jaser, *"Muqābala."*

24. Author in conversation with Hisham Fageeh, September 2013.

25. A leading member of the Saudi artistic community recently noted to me that, among Saudis, the term "auteur" is not viewed as a term limited to white male directors. Author in conversation with a leading member of the Saudi cultural community, July 2022.

26. Author in conversation with Hisham Fageeh, Ali Kalthami, et al., September 2013.

27. Author in conversation with Hisham Fageeh, July 2018.

28. al-Jaser, *"Muqābala."*

29. Ibid.

30. Ibid.

31. Folaim (@Folaim Ya gholaim), "Film Folaim: Sūriyā taḥdtājak," YouTube, June 27, 2012, https://www.youtube.com/watch?v=9FtRZXkKlYQ&feature=plcp.

32. Henry Jenkins, Sam Ford, and Joshua Green, "Courting Supporters for Independent Media" in *Spreadable Media: Creating Value and Meaning in a Networked Culture* (New York: New York University Press, 2013), 230.

33. Ibid.

34. Meshal al-Jaser (@MeshalALjaser), "@SaudiShortFilms Meshal Short Films—Episode 2 'Syria Needs You,' http://www.youtube.com/watch?v=9FtRZXkKlYQ&feature=plcp," Twitter, June 28, 2012, 1:08, https://twitter.com/MeshalALjaser/status/218254647234805760; al-Jaser (@MeshalALjaser), "Meshal's Short Films—Episode 2 'Syria Needs You' http://www.youtube.com/watch?v=9FtRZXkKlYQ&feature=plcp," Twitter, June 28, 2018, 00:52, https://twitter.com/MeshalALjaser/status/218250405614854144; al-Jaser (@MeshalALjaser), "@BidzSaleh @Fahad @FatKhairo @kalthami @shugairi @Masameer_tv @YouTube tweet it [for] Syria, http://www.youtube.com/watch?v=9FtRZXkKlYQ&feature=plcp," Twitter, June 28, 2012, 7:28 a.m., https://twitter.com/MeshalALjaser/status/218350079306772480; al-Jaser (@MeshalALjaser), "@SaudiFilmMakers @FMB4 @AFt7ldn Meshal's Short Films—Episode 2 'Syria Needs You,' *Taḥtājuk Sūriyā* http://www.youtube.com/watch?v=9FtRZXkKlYQ&feature=plcp...... RT," Twitter, June 30, 2012, 11:39, https://twitter.com/MeshalALjaser/status/230009813948588032.

35. Meshal al-Jaser (@MeshalALjaser), "@NewsSyRev http://www.youtube.com/watch?v=9FtRZXkKlYQ&feature=plcp... *Sūriyā taḥdtājak – rītūwīt*," Twitter, July 1, 2012, 8:11, https://twitter.com/MeshalALjaser/status/219448271645581313; al-Jaser (@MeshalALjaser), "@TurkiAldakhil, *'ākar Ā'amālī Sūriyā taḥdtājak ilāk*' http://www.youtube.com/watch?v=9FtRZXkKlYQ&feature=g-all-lik... RT Šukran," Twitter, July 19, 2012, 4:54, https://twitter.com/MeshalALjaser/status/225921623969116161.

36. Meshal al-Jaser (@MeshalALjaser), "@BidzSaleh @Fahad @FatKhairo @kalthami @shugairi @Masameer_tv."

37. Meshal al-Jaser (@MeshalALjaser), "@ijustine http://www.youtube.com/watch?v=9FtRZXkKlYQ&feature=plcp.... Tweet It for Syria," Twitter, June 28, 2012, 10:34, https://twitter.com/MeshalALjaser/status/218396875244568576.

38. Al-Jaser, "*Muqābala*."

39. Meshal al-Jaser (@MeshalALjaser). Meshal al-Jaser (@meshalaljaser).

40. Folaim Ya gholaim (@Folaim Ya gholaim), "Screw Infidels! Ṭaz bi al-Kuffār," YouTube, April 29, 2015, https://www.youtube.com/watch?v=GgbJGn4cH-M.

41. Louisa Loveluck, "Islamic State: Where Do Its Fighters Come From?," *Telegraph*, June 8, 2015, http://www.telegraph.co.uk/news/worldnews/islamic-state/11660487/Islamic-State-one-year-on-Where-do-its-fighters-come-from.html.

42. Al-Jaser, "*Muqābala*."

43. Folaim Ya gholaim (@Folaim Ya gholaim), "Folaim: Ṭaz bi al-Kuffār/Screw Infidels," YouTube, April 29, 2015, https://www.youtube.com/watch?v=GgbJGn4cH-M.

44. Author in conversation with Saudi attorney, May 2015.

45. Folaim Ya gholaim (@Folaim Ya gholaim), "Can I go out? Film—Mumkin Aṭla'?," YouTube, December 26, 2017, https://www.youtube.com/watch?v=dhdnVrsIEBk&t=3s.

46. Waad A. Janbi, "Feminist Analysis: Saudi Arabian Women Seize Their Freedom through Cinema" (master's thesis, Long Island University, 2019), 14–18.

47. As a professor at King Fahd University for Petroleum and Minerals (KFUPM) in the Eastern Province noted to me, many of his male students view life at KFUPM as a

liberating experience because they are no longer responsible for driving their female relatives. Author in conversation with KFUPM professor, May 2013.

48. Folaim Ya gholaim (@Folaim Ya gholaim), "Folaim: Under Concrete/Film—Taḥt as-Asmint," YouTube, March 14, 2018, https://www.youtube.com/watch?v=1kMOabw_w3Y&feature=youtu.be.

49. Meshal al-Jaser (@MeshalALjaser), "UNDER CONCRETE #Syria https://youtu.be/1kMOabw_w3Y," Twitter, March 14, 2018, 9:26, https://twitter.com/MeshalALjaser/status/973958543228338176.

50. Folaim Ya gholaim (@Folaim Ya gholaim), *Under Concrete*.

51. The Arab Gulf States Institute Washington, "Meshal al-Jaser Filmmaker."

52. Meshal al-Jaser (@MeshalALjaser), "My Latest Work with @tamtam_sound A Music Video That Talks about the Idea of an Arranged Marriage https://youtu.be/EiePLoe9p7o," Twitter, September 19, 2018, 9:43, https://twitter.com/MeshalALjaser/status/1042454130600468480.

53. Meshal al-Jaser (@MeshalALjaser), *"Zawāj Taqlīdī,"* Twitter, September 19, 2018, 13:00, https://twitter.com/MeshalALjaser/status/1042503684045697024.

54. Suzie London, "Saudi-Born, L.A. Based Singer-Songwriter Tamtam Releases Her New Single 'Rise,'" GIGsoup Music, June 7, 2019, https://www.gigsoupmusic.com/news/new-music-news/saudi-born-l-a-based-singer-songwriter-tamtam-releases-her-new-single-rise/.

55. This is also referencing a classic scene from Arab cinema, where a woman signals that she has accepted a suitor's proposal by placing a tray down on a table with two glasses of juice, one of which she offers to the man.

56. London, "Saudi-Born."

57. London, "Saudi-Born."

58. Walt Whitman, "Song of Myself," in Walt Whitman, *Leaves of Grass: 150th Anniversary Edition*, ed. David S. Reynolds (New York: Oxford University Press, 2005), 43.

59. Richard Brodie, *Virus of the Mind: The New Science of the Meme* (Carlsbad, CA: Hay House, 1996), 82.

60. Walt Whitman, "I Sing the Body Electric", in Reynolds, *Leaves of Grass: 150th Anniversary Edition*, 68.

12

Covering Critiques
Film and New Media Artwork in the UAE

ELIZABETH DERDERIAN

The video is shot from above, we come to realize, perched over a pot on the stove. Mounds of white sugar slowly caramelize into auburn flecks, a small spot at first that darkens and widens as the video continues. The crystals on the edge of the burned spot suddenly become individually visible, white against the brown background, before they too turn brown. As the pot of sugar remains on the stove, the burned spot widens, and curls of smoke rise up toward the lens.

Moza Almatrooshi's "Irreversible Act I: Sugar Rush" (2017) is a commentary on the speed of urban development in the United Arab Emirates (UAE). For the work, Almatrooshi accelerated the video playback so the sugar burns more quickly on screen than in real life. Almatrooshi wanted to highlight how irreversible these changes are: "I want to expose the impossibility and irrevocability of returning to the original—gesturing at the idea that, once change has been made, we can never recover the original."[1] Dubai's rapid development has brought many advantages to the people of the Emirates, including transportation infrastructure such as freeways, standardized health care, and education systems. Yet this development has also spurred sweeping sociocultural changes as well (not to mention the human cost expended by migrant workers to undertake all this construction). The population of the country has skyrocketed, causing real estate prices to rise, and many Emiratis have moved from the traditional neighborhoods in older parts of cities, called *freej*, to spacious new developments where family life is more diffuse. Almatrooshi, alongside a contingent of other "new generation" (*jil al-jadid*) artists like Khalid Mezaina, Hind Mezaina, Asma Alahmed, and Zeinab Alhashemi have produced work that reflects on different valences of these changes, and in the case of Almatrooshi's "Irreversible Act I," offers a cautionary tale on the downsides and attendant losses of large-scale, rapid urbanization. I came across these artists while conducting ethnographic fieldwork in the UAE between 2015 and 2017, studying the changes to the country's art scene with the planned Louvre and Guggenheim museums in Abu Dhabi; my contextual knowledge of the Emirates derives from that fieldwork, and this chapter is based on extensive 2019 interviews with the artists featured here.

In this chapter, I argue that film and new media are particularly well suited for UAE-based artists for a few reasons. First, work created in these media is (arguably) oriented more toward an aesthetically discerning audience rather than a commercial one. Many collectors prefer paintings or sculptures to beautify their homes and office spaces, and therefore new media works can appear less frequently in high-profile commercial galleries where well-heeled observers and people in positions of power would be exposed to it. It can therefore be less visible to unsympathetic viewers, yet carries significant cachet in the contemporary art scene (i.e., it is a trendy or "sexy" medium). Additionally, in their deterritorialized form, video works and digital performances can strategically transcend or avoid local laws, their lack of material or physical sitedness providing an (ostensibly) supranational, supralegal space. Facilitating artists' critical commentary that touches on taboo, forbidden, or illegal topics, new media works often reside on servers outside the state's jurisdiction. Because new media works also often appear in a material form that belies or masks its content, such as an electronic data file or a thumb drive, it is much easier to conceal than the insistent, continuous physical presence of something like a painting or a sculpture: new media works can be more easily hidden and surface only when desired. Film and new media, in their very medium, thus offer a protective cover, or *sitr* (to borrow from the work of Reem Falaknaz, which I discuss below) for the expression of critical ideas.

Being caught speaking out against the state can have terrible consequences: my Emirati interlocutors used the phrase *war'a al-shams* (behind the sun) to describe what happened to individuals taken by the state who were being held in unknown locations. The phrase invokes a sense of deterritorialization and detachment from the reality of physical territories—an almost mythical space. I borrow this construction to analyze the conscious choices of artists to situate their critiques in a kind of deterritorialized space to protect themselves and also to evoke the kinds of power relations involved in making information, or people, appear or disappear. By selectively drawing on the capacity of new media to cover critiques that may be seen as subversive, and yet often doing so in the contact zone of the internet, UAE-based artists assert control over their own expression.

In what follows, I use the work of three UAE-based (or sporadically so) artists to illuminate additional features of film and new media that allow artists' protective cover to present critiques. First, the form of film and new media works also allows for malleability in their legibility. By this I mean that within one work (such as Almatrooshi's, discussed below), an artist may play with the video focus or distort audio in ways that are less available in more material mediums or those that do not have a temporal or performative aspect. Secondly, new media can mimic or appear in forms easily recognizable in the digital era and therein provide space for their critique, such as Falaknaz's series that interrogates the documentary or evidentiary nature of photography in the social media era. Finally, I show how artists use the internet as a platform to circumscribe audiences and minimize potential retribution for expressing their critiques.

Cover, or *sitr*, is desirable because critique in the UAE, and the Gulf more broadly, is a complicated issue due to local slander laws, the politics of polite speech, and a widely held belief that critique is a necessary fixture of a contemporary art scene.[2] First, critique is frequently conflated with criticism, and criticism is coded as a criminal offense in the UAE, regardless of the truth of the claim. Dubai's highest court, the Court of Cassation, has "held that *mere criticism* may be regarded as defamatory."[3] Regardless of how often they are enforced, these laws often have a chilling effect on negative expression and further reinforce a dominant "language ideology," or social connotative practices, of positive expression (or if not outright positive, at least avoidance of directly articulated negative views).[4] Meanwhile, my interlocutors—artists, curators, gallerists, and art center directors—believed critique to be integral to the "proper" functioning of a contemporary art scene and integral to the making of good art.[5] While artists reproduce the prevailing definition of contemporary art as that which is critical, they also reshape the modes of expressing that critique.

The works of Moza Almatrooshi and Reem Falaknaz, as well as the experimental platform Samt, wrestle with important questions of gender and sexual equality; photography as evidence; commodification and authenticity in the internet age; and the constructed nature of history, the nation-state, and borders. The strategic use of new media and film, with its malleable legibility, structural parallels with social media, and the ability to limit distribution digitally provides these artists cover, or *sitr*, in offering these critiques.

RECUPERATING THE QUEENDOM: NEW MEDIA AND LEGIBILITY

After "Irreversible Act I," Almatrooshi continued to work with film in her piece "To Whom the Sun May Be of Concern" (2018). Almatrooshi produced this seventeen-and-a-half-minute video in response to the news that archaeologists working in the Emirate of Sharjah had unearthed coins indicating that the region had once been ruled by a queen. *The National*, the UAE's state-run media outlet, published an article describing the finds and noting that "some scholars now think the word 'Abi'el' may refer to a series of female rulers, which suggests a dynasty of queens could have ruled" the area.[6] Almatrooshi related that the discovered coin was emblazoned with an inscription in Arabian Aramaic: LONG LIVE THE QUEEN. However, when she traveled to the archaeological center nearby, she learned that the guides had not been trained to share this information. After speaking with the center's supervisor, Almatrooshi learned that the archaeologists were unsure whether this queendom was one single queen or possibly a matrilineal line. However, the team considered this a "theory" and elected not to focus on it. Almatrooshi pointed out that "everything in that center is a theory."[7] In fact, archaeology itself is a discipline where scholars offer theories about what may have happened in the past based on limited evidence.

Her video work is an attempt to recuperate an imaginative history of the region's possible queens. The title, which references the sun, refers to the fact that the sun was worshipped as a goddess in the pre-Islamic or Jahiliyya-era Arabian Peninsula. Yet the sun is often labeled as a god in displays in archaeological centers in the UAE—perhaps because Jahiliyya-era history is already a touchy subject, and adding goddesses to the already-problematic pantheon of paganism might be too much.[8] When people get picked up in the UAE and taken to unknown detention locations, this phenomena is colloquially referred to as being taken "behind the sun (*war'a al shams*) . . . it is this place you dip where no one knows anything about you."[9] It also emerges as a location in the film work and "sums up a lot about where these histories go and how they are not cared for."[10] Thus the reference to the sun in the title of the work captures both the negligence and erasure of the history of goddess worship in the region.

With this work, Almatrooshi hopes to "reintroduce this history that we've completely destroyed and have very little access to, if at all. It was very soul-crushing for me to arrive at this point where, we are not only *not* acknowledging that history, but when we have to, we misgender it."[11] The plot of the video work echoes Almatrooshi's own research. At one point in the video, the subtitles read, "We lost the queens all over again to man" (13:50)—much as Almatrooshi lost the desert queens all over again to the men of the archaeological center.

The narrative in the work takes the form of a children's fable, featuring animals as protagonists rather than humans. The story recounts a queen bee who is expelled from her hive and once out, finds a coin in the desert, just as the archaeologists in Sharjah did. With the help of other animals, she traverses the desert and makes her way to a place behind the sun where she can remain with the desert queen's belongings—and presumably become "disappeared," given the imprisonment and detention valences of the phrase "behind the sun." Almatrooshi shared the following: "I'm interested in self-censorship as a necessary means to being safe and still saying what you want to say. That became such an interesting challenge for me. That's where the text came in. I started to write these childlike stories, with quite dark endings or dark content. It's the idea of something coming across as light when it's actually really heavy."¹² Almatrooshi thus uses the genre of the fable to point out the fallibility of stories: that all stories about the past and about why things are the way they are, are just that—stories. They can be rewritten, hidden, or inaccurate.

Almatrooshi shot footage for the work around London's parks and museums with a low-resolution camera, which she intersperses with cropped YouTube clips of popular but controversial pop singers Ahlam and Fifi Abdouh, "women who are so vilified for performing their gender, sexuality, or age in the most exaggerated and 'inappropriate' way."¹³ We can read the inclusion of these characters as commentary on the socially enforced performance of gender and gender norms and also the ways in which women gain public visibility and/or authority. The video is often fragmented, blurry, or thrown into such high contrast it becomes difficult to make out. Woven together, the video does not present a coherent visual narrative but rather offers fragmented visuals that acquire meaning largely through the voice-over audio and the subtitles.

Almatrooshi's layering and borrowing of images in the video work interrogates processes of meaning-making associated with images and how images gain and lose meaning. Because the audio and video have been copied from a copy and reused, they have become degraded and almost unintelligible at points—and Almatrooshi intentionally plays with this legibility, particularly in the audio. The voice-over in Arabic does not always match the English subtitling; at times the subtitles are missing, set in a glaringly neon font that is difficult to read or replaced altogether by symbols. The ambient audio of the video is also at times present and at others removed. The artist commented, "My film isn't silent but like in everything else, there's a lot of silence or different audio. I narrate in Arabic. Even in the film you can't hear the other characters, you can only read a translation."¹⁴ Almatrooshi also made some of the subtitles symbols to purposefully obfuscate meaning and put other subtitles "in this very exaggerated Arabic font that's quite comical. I was using subtitles as this material, where it had power not just to provide access but also to take away that access and what that feels like."¹⁵ The subtitles also contain scriptlike instructions, for example, "self pity and wind blowing intensifies" (0:33), "Enter Good Samaritan" (7:24), "**Enter relief**"

FIGURE 12.1

Still from "To Whom the Sun May Be of Concern" (2018) by Moza Almatrooshi. Image courtesy of the artist.

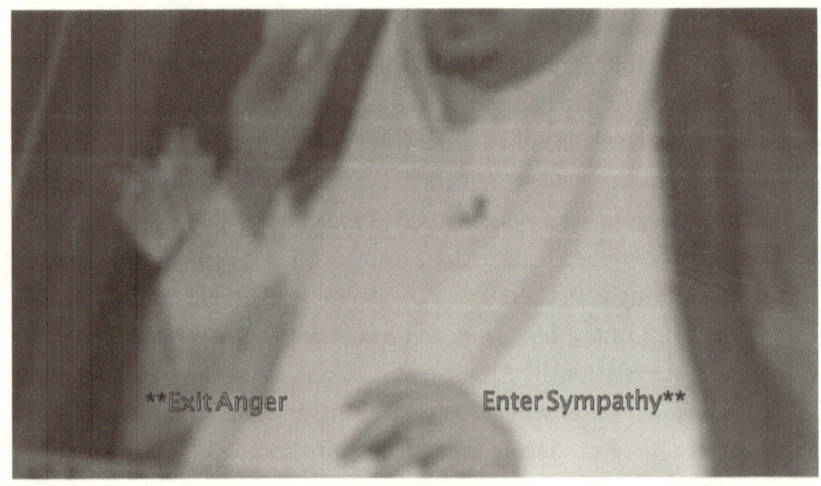

FIGURE 12.2

Still from "To Whom the Sun May Be of Concern" (2018) by Moza Almatrooshi. Image courtesy of the artist.

(16:38), or "**SCREAMS INTERNALLY**" (5:14). The work is layered, such that Arabic speakers and English speakers can access various bits of the story—and bilingual viewers have the most access. The translations Almatrooshi uses are of course themselves political and not neutral, as scholars tell us no translations are.[16] Almatrooshi uses the subtitles—or their absence—as a medium to trouble any easy legibility of the work, a feature available to her because of the forms of new media.

As the fable unfolds, the bee character meets a fox, who reveals the history of the lost queen. The fox shares this story via English subtitles, while ambient audio plays without Arabic narration. The text recounts a king arriving to the queendom and the queen kneeling to the king. Subtitles read: "Her abandonment of the throne to satisfy the desire of man enraged the Sun" [goddess] (12:00) while the video transitions to cropped footage of a woman dancing in a formal ballgown on the beach. Finally, the viewer learns, "The Sun set the city ablaze" (12:07) and the humans lost the language of the animals and migrated away. But the animals tell the bee, "The love our foremothers reserved for the queens stayed with us until today" (12:30). However, the viewer learns that "one day diggers appeared on the land and disturbed the resting place of the Queens" (12:48). The fox continues to narrate that these diggers began taking things—here the video, blurry, appears to be taken from a moving vehicle, paralleling the movement described in the text.

Much as the archaeologists of Sharjah presented the real discoveries as Jahiliyya-era gods, in Almatrooshi's work, the diggers in the fable begin to discuss "uncovering a kingdom of the Sun God" (13:18). Just as the real queens were misgendered into erasure, so are the goddesses of Almatrooshi's fable. Yet Almatrooshi recuperates the location, Behind the Sun, to an extent. The animal characters relate, "We found a place that no human or djinn can trace" (14:36) behind the sun (*war'a al-shams*). Thus, it no longer does it represent only detention and disappearance but also a deterritorialized place and thus offering possible safety and tranquility.

Almatrooshi's film ends with an Arabic phrase in white text on a black screen: *li-an al-shams naseetna li-takhlina 'an amhatuna* (The sun has forgotten us because we have forsaken our mothers). Almatrooshi's work examines the erasures of women in history and draws on two primary methods to do so: first, by playing with the genre of fables and, second, through the legibility of the audio and video in her work. The flexibility and il/legibility of new media allows Almatrooshi to offer a critique of the erasure of Jahiliyya-era queens and religious practices.

PROOF, DOCUMENT, EVIDENCE: NEW MEDIA AS METHOD AND DISPLAY

Meanwhile, Reem Falaknaz uses the very form of new media as a method in her work to produce an exhibition entitled *If a hymen breaks and no one hears it* (2018). Posing as a "fictional character," Falaknaz undertook extensive research on hymen restoration schemes available to women in the Gulf region, including e-*fatwa* (religious rulings available via online services). Falaknaz noted that the online fatwa service, where Muslims may submit questions about appropriate religious practice to determine if something is permitted, universally responded that one did not have to report a missing or damaged hymen to a fiancé: "All the fatwas said, *sitr*. So, a woman for example wears a hijab, a covering, for *sitr*, as a guard, a protector, a piece of clothing that covers. If someone sins in my society they say, *Istiru 'alay*, which means, covering others' misdeeds which deserve prescribed penalties."[17]

According to the Hans Wehr dictionary, sitr can also mean to forgive or to overlook. That is, the religious authorities encouraged young women to protect themselves by not disclosing elements that might lead them to encounter harm.

Artists worked in much the same manner—that is, not actively deceiving but simply not disclosing things that might lead them to harm. UAE-based artists often produce sitr by not revealing the critical elements of their artwork—and in particular, new media lends itself easily to offer sitr, as Falaknaz's work reveals. Because her series uses new media as a method of inquiry and mode of display, it also allows for a thoughtful interrogation of the use of photography as a documentary or evidentiary technique, particularly in a social media era where the internet facilitates immediate global contact and exchange. The series seamlessly blends new and analog media: both in the ways Falaknaz researched the work and in its presentation.

For example, along with e-fatwa, Falaknaz also researched other methods of hymen restoration including herbal remedies, imported temporary hymens available for purchase online, sorcery, and finally, hymen restoration surgery. For the exhibition, she gathered all the research and reproduced it in paper form. She presented a series of WhatsApp messages with an herbalist in a long, red paper printout mimicking the online scroll, or in a series of images of the messages she received on a phone. *If a hymen breaks and no one hears it* thus bridges new and analog media, troubling easy classification: while the series was created using new media, the display itself takes the form of analog photography and printouts.

Falaknaz's work pushes at the construction of photography as reliable or accurate proof—especially in the internet era, where photos are doctored, manipulated, and circulated outside of their original contexts, often without the consent of their original creators.[18] The series raises the question of photography as documentation, evidence, and/or proof on multiple levels: she interrogates the supposed proof offered by these various providers but also in the form of her own work, presenting her findings as if they were to be used in a clinical or criminal trial. The images in the exhibition were often sent to Falaknaz to prove the validity of a particular treatment and to establish credibility, but they have been altered, either by the addition of text or the removal of identifying features for confidentiality. This framing renders the messages almost like evidence in a criminal court or police investigation: the technology on which the words were sent and received becomes part of the work, paradoxically implicating new media while appearing in analog physical form (the paper printout).

Falaknaz also discussed the elements that particular providers "think provide proof of their legitimacy."[19] Many photographs in the series are layered with additional text boxes or obfuscating marks, and therefore even as they were offered to the artist as evidence, they had clearly been altered and their integrity compromised. The artist is the last person to present the image, putting her own spin on it. For example, a blog that offers treatments to regrow one's hymen contained a photograph of a woman's

FIGURE 12.3

Installation view, *If a hymen breaks and no one hears it* (2018) by Reem Falaknaz. Image courtesy of the artist.

hand outstretched, resting on a copy of the Qur'an. The text stamped above the Quran notes that she repents. Falaknaz describes a subsequent image: "You see a woman walking in [to a room] carrying a cake, and the text on her head to cover her anonymity."[20] The woman pictured is holding a white box, and a white box of text appears superimposed over her eyes to conceal her identity. The text reads: "In this office [*sic*] a new life. Amal, on the day of her healing (*shifa-uha*), she carries a gift and a certificate (*shahada*) ... and joy (*farha*)." In another image of Amal, she praises Allah for her transformation, the photo taken midspeech as her hands are outstretched toward the camera; and to her left, a recorder appears, as if to assert Amal's words as official testimony.

Another layered photo depicts a second woman, holding up a note written in French on doctor's stationary with a "medical certificate" (*certificat medical* in original) scribbled at the top, which confirms that the woman, whose name is whited out of the photograph, has been inspected and

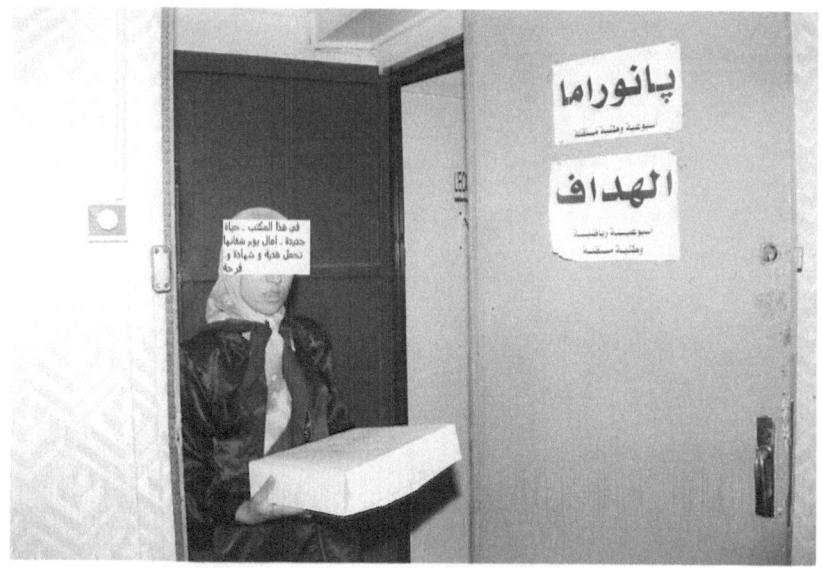

FIGURE 12.4

Image from exhibition, *If a hymen breaks and no one hears it* (2018) by Reem Falaknaz. Image courtesy of the artist.

found to have an intact hymen. The word "virgin" (*vierge*) appears next to a doctor's stamp, over which a signature is scrawled. The woman also holds a handwritten sign that thanks Allah first and the herbalist second for making her a virgin. Two blocks of text are layered onto the photograph, one over the woman's eyes and the second to the right of her face: the first professes gratitude for the herbalist, and the second claims the photo to be owned by the herbalist and is stamped with his contact information. The image also has a timestamp dating from 2014, another modality pointing to the use of photos as ostensibly accurate documentation.

In another part of the exhibition, Falaknaz shows the screenshots of photos another herbalist claimed were sent to him by satisfied customers, including photos of bloody sheets to "prove" the remedies worked and restored their hymens for their wedding night.[21] In addition, Falaknaz was sent images of WhatsApp conversations, which have been superimposed with colorful text extracted from the messages, in particular *"A'shaby"* (my

FIGURE 12.5

Image from exhibition, *If a hymen breaks and no one hears it* (2018) by Reem Falaknaz. Image courtesy of the artist.

herbs), the number of the herbalist, the apparent nationality of the women sending these messages of gratitude, and repeatedly, his contact number.²² Tracing the material life of these messages, these digital chat conversations are copied via screenshots and then dropped into other conversations sent via the internet; then, finally, they are printed on paper and affixed to a wall in the UAE. The viewer in the exhibition sees a copy of a copy of a copy—much like Almatrooshi's copies of images from YouTube and social media.

Photos on social media are easily copied and redistributed, their meanings lost, gained, and adapted based on the context of their usage. These questions—of how meaning accompanies images and texts and how authentic or accurate they can be—are key questions of the contemporary period, particularly with the rise of the "deep fakes" phenomenon. New media work like Almatrooshi's and Falaknaz's ably critiques the modalities of offering and encountering evidence via the internet.

In addition, the internet is also a place of business, a contact zone of commercial exchange, and Falaknaz's series captures the commercial nature of new media as well. "A hymen is a commodity," Falaknaz sighed, with clinics and online services "all catering to girls in the region and making money off them."[23] The series also critiques the commodification of the hymen that has transpired with the emergence of this internet marketplace for hymen restoration and replacement—and the subsequent exploitation of vulnerable younger women in the region. When Falaknaz, as her fictional character, emailed clinics who claimed to offer hymen restoration surgery, she was quoted a price of 36,000 AED/£7500 (approximately 9,500 USD), with a £1000 discount (to approximately 8,100 USD) once the appointment was scheduled and prepaid. Further showing the commodification of the hymen, the artist includes screenshot documentation of a website where "artificial hymens" are advertised for sale for $29.95 apiece, and a five-pack for $114.95 (thus one gets a $7 per hymen discount if one buys in bulk). Like the photos of women's testimonials and the herbalists' screenshots of thank-you messages, the website selling artificial hymens is also stamped with additional text. This additional text in English reads, "1. Marry in confidence—your secret is kept, 2. Spice up your marriage life, 3. No needles, no costly operation." The language of the ads reveals its target audience: engaged or married women.

Arabic text on the screenshot echoes the English at first. Additional text, which does not appear in an English translation, reads, "The method of hymen retrieval is fantastic" (*Tariqat turji' ghasha' albakarha 'ajeeba*) and "very easy" (*jiddan wasahla*). A black box surrounds white Arabic text just above the "Buy now" button, with two notes to the consumer: first, an offer of a complimentary makeup kit with purchase, and finally, "Our company does not encourage illegal practices before marriage" (*sharikatuna*

FIGURE 12.6

Image from exhibition, *If a hymen breaks and no one hears it* (2018) by Reem Falaknaz. Image courtesy of the artist.

leh tushaji' 'ala al-mamarisat al-ghayr shar'ia qabl al-zawaj). In a similar invocation of Islam, the website also reads, *bi-shart al-tawba*, on condition of repentance. These kinds of guarantees, of course, are meant to convey legitimacy to buyers, while also shielding sellers from accusations of promoting indecent behavior. The juxtaposition of marketing language and religious language is jarring but also reveals the savvy of the marketing companies and the intended audience, despite the anonymity of the internet.

But religious language appeared to be another modality of offering evidence or proof, not only for providers as described above but also for

FIGURE 12.7

Image from exhibition, *If a hymen breaks and no one hears it* (2018) by Reem Falaknaz. Image courtesy of the artist.

consumers. Falaknaz was at one point informed she needed to prove she was a female, and to do so, should call the herbalist's office or to "send an audio note praising the Prophet for us to confirm you are female."[24] This modality of proof is predicated on gender performativity but in also, in particular, this requirement assumes that the potential consequence of connecting under false pretenses would dissuade would-be consumers. As with the swearing on the Quran in some of the herbalists' photos or the marketed necessity of repentance as a precondition for buying a hymen online, these religious statements confer an air of legitimacy and are meant to deter potential schemers, drawing on the authority of religion to validate their claim.

Falaknaz's series deftly weaves together multiple themes: a critique of hymen commodification via the internet, an interrogation of the different ways in which photography is offered as proof or evidence despite internet circulation and a reflection on the ways in which religious language—either in person, as online text, or in assumed behaviors—is predicated as a mode of legitimacy. Falaknaz and Samt, the exhibition organizer, released the location of the exhibition by request only. They did not publish the location of it on social media, but they did publish information about the show. This choice allowed the artist and organizer some protective cover, or *sitr*. The exhibition was held in an unoccupied tailor's shop in a residential neighborhood, and they elected to hang curtains over the shop windows for discretion. The internet as an exhibition site was a similar tactic artists used to control access to critical work.

CIRCUMSCRIBING AUDIENCES: THE INTERNET AS PERFORMANCE SITE

Born and raised in the UAE, artist Walid Al Wawi is well versed in its politics of expression. Al Wawi launched Samt.co, an online exhibition space that also draws on Instagram as a primary platform, in October 2017. Because the website has a UK address, it is legally protected and cannot be shut down by potential governments unhappy with the works shown (although the artists themselves do not enjoy such protections, and states can firewall undesirable sites). Samt's mission centers around five pillars (much like Islam has five pillars): the first, "censorship and conversation: Samt's main objective is to assist all users of creative fields, who are living in or have self-limiting relations with, a politically/culturally censored region, to practice their right to free expression through the medium of contemporary art and anonymity."[25] By allowing artists the opportunity to produce work to disseminate via the internet, Samt offers a protective barrier constituted through the anonymity of the virtual and the automatic distance generated through the absence of physical presence. Some participating artists choose to use pseudonyms during the run of their online exhibitions, such as Bu Yousif and Collect.ive. The deterritorialized nature of the internet paired with pseudonyms to protect anonymity can offer artists living under censoring regimes a wide swath of protection and encourage expression. Samt occurs as a virtual platform "for research and exhibition" and "manifests primarily in a digital format to open the receptivity of Art and Discourse from Southwestern Asia and North Africa to an international audience from all regions with no Geopolitical restrictions on humans or art."[26] That is, Samt offers artists a place to share their work that will circumvent the restrictions of individual locales.

"Samt" is Arabic for silence, "making no sound; quiet; still."[27] It is thus a seeming paradox: expression without sound. Silence is safety. The platform also includes "Sawt, Arabic for noise, is the physical parallel to Samt and is a collective of micro-events around the world, that are curated in dialogue with the digital issue and perform as forums for free discussions and verbal feedback."[28] Sawt is also often translated as voice—thus the platform aims to offer artists both voice and silence, depending on their individual needs, preferences, or positions.

CONCLUSION

Film and new media works have the troubling and exciting capacity, in their largely deterritorialized nature, to travel quickly via the internet and achieve viral status in modes that older media do not (that is, a sculpture cannot go viral in the same way that a film clip can). The unique temporal and material qualities of film and new media can also make them excellent vehicles for critique in regions where expression is extensively regulated. However, these advantages are also liabilities: the internet documents for posterity, by virtue of being a contact zone with others in it, and documentation can expose artists to potential retribution. The artists discussed here have drawn strategically on the cover that film and new media offer to produce works that are critical, transgressive, and thoughtful—particularly their flexibility and il/legibility, their parallel uses of photography as a documentary or evidentiary tool, and the deterritorialized nature of the internet as a site of performance or exhibition.

With increased circulation comes attention and potential recognition and fame. But this circulation and portability—while offering artists occasional protection—can also remove the protective *sitr*—or cover. This raises difficult questions for scholars like myself as well: How can we write about and analyze these works without endangering their makers? Do we destroy the *sitr* they have so thoughtfully created, or not give them credit for their ideas and intellectual labor? If we gain the artists' consent, is that enough? Analyzing their work allows us to see the creative ways they have balanced competing concerns and better understand the realities of life on the ground on the Arabian Peninsula. The real question, as Almatrooshi puts it, is: "How can I have an authentic mode of self-expression, and not get into any trouble? Our battles will be different."[29] Perhaps, just perhaps, new media offers one way forward.

> ELIZABETH DERDERIAN is Assistant Professor of Anthropology and Museum Studies at the College of Wooster. She holds a PhD in Anthropology from Northwestern University. She recently served as contributing editor for the Society for Cultural Anthropology's AnthroPod podcast and coeditor of the Middle East section on *Anthropology News*. She is currently co-director of the Pella @ Wooster project.

NOTES

1. Muhannad Ali and Cristiana de Marchi, *Is Old Gold* (Dubai: Ductac, 2017), 54. The work is incorrectly titled in the exhibition catalog and is listed there as "Markings: Act I, Sugar Rush."

2. Elizabeth Derderian, "Authenticating an Emirati Art World: Claims of Tabula Rasa and Cultural Appropriation in the UAE," *Journal of Arabian Studies* 7 (2017): 12–27.

3. Susie Abdel-Nabi and Alexandra Lester, "Defamation and Social Media in the UAE: Clyde & Co," April 3, 2019, https://www.clydeco.com/insight/article/defamation-and-social-media-in-the-uae.

4. Language ideologies are "sets of beliefs about language articulated by users as a rationalization or justification of perceived language structure and use." Michael Silverstein, "Language Structure and Linguistic Ideology," in *The Elements: A Parasession on Linguistic Units and Levels*, ed. Paul Clyne (Chicago: Chicago Linguistic Society, 1979), 193.

5. I conducted primary fieldwork in the UAE between September 2015 and April 2017, thanks to support from a Fulbright IIE grant and a doctoral research grant from the Al Qasimi Foundation. While I was based in Dubai, I conducted interviews and participant observation in Ras al Khaimah, Sharjah, and Abu Dhabi as well.

6. Rym Ghazal, "Sharjah's Mleiha Archaeological Centre—A Step Back in Time," April 6, 2016, https://www.thenational.ae/arts-culture/sharjah-s-mleiha-archaeological-centre-a-step-back-in-time-1.137537.

7. Moza Almatrooshi, interview with author, Skype, London/Chicago, June 30, 2019.

8. Historian Fred Donner is cited as saying that the contemporary Muslim "account of Jahiliyya is a saga of unrelieved paganism, which emphasizes the difference between the darkness of unbelief and the light that Islam brought to Arabia." Elias Muhanna, "A New History of Arabia, Written in Stone," May 23, 2018, https://www.newyorker.com/culture/culture-desk/a-new-history-of-arabia-written-in-stone.

9. Moza Almatrooshi, interview with author, WhatsApp, New Haven/Sharjah, July 24, 2019.

10. Moza Almatrooshi, interview with author.

11. Almatrooshi, interview, June 30, 2019.

12. Almatrooshi, interview, June 30, 2019.

13. Almatrooshi, interview, June 30, 2019.

14. Almatrooshi, interview, June 30, 2019.

15. Almatrooshi, interview, June 30, 2019.

16. Per translation scholars including but not limited to: Kwame Anthony Appiah, "Thick Translation," *Callaloo* 16 (1993): 808–819; Gayatri Spivak, "The Politics of Translation," in *Outside in the Teaching Machine* (New York: Routledge, 1993); Lawrence Venuti, ed., *The Translation Studies Reader* (London: Routledge, 2004).

17. Reem Falaknaz, interview with author, WhatsApp, UAE/Chicago, June 20, 2019.

18. In a seeming paradox, new media can offer greater and uncontrolled visibility (i.e., virality), but new media can also offer circumscribed visibility, as I describe in the next section.

19. Falaknaz, interview, 2019.

20. Falaknaz, interview, 2019.

21. Troublingly enough, this night is colloquially referred to as *laylat-a-dakhla*, or the night of entrance/penetration.

22. The nationality ascribed to these alleged customers is based on the phone numbers by which they contacted the herbalist and therefore are not necessarily Emirati, Qatari, etc., but rather, someone with an Emirati number (who could be of any citizenship status). In the presentation, however, the healer conflates the country's code of contact with their citizenship.

23. Falaknaz, interview, 2019.

24. Falaknaz, interview, 2019.

25. Samt, "About," https://samt.co/School.

26. Falaknaz, interview, 2019.

27. Falaknaz, interview, 2019.

28. Falaknaz, interview, 2019.

29. Almatrooshi, interview, June 30, 2019.

13

The Gulf between Students
The First Decade of the Gulf's Longest-Running Film Festival

ALIA YUNIS and SASCHA RITTER

In 2010, two Zayed University communication majors, Alyazah Al Falasi and Reema Majed, came to my office to share their senior capstone idea: a Middle East–wide student film festival set on our campus in Abu Dhabi. Both had been students in my introductory film production class, and both were very bright and hardworking. Instinctively, I responded that we could not put together a festival with such big ambitions in two months. Prior to moving to Abu Dhabi the previous year, I had worked in Los Angeles with companies responsible for the logistics for festivals like Cannes, Sundance, and Venice, and I had seen how preparations for the next festival began well before the current festival's closing night. But the students' response was: "Why not? We will get sponsorship." At that time, the university capstones were extravaganzas to rival fancy weddings, with students getting major sponsors to host events that included everything from mechanical bull rides to *abaya* fashion shows, and there was a general attitude that more money meant a bigger and better capstone.

Alyazyah and Reema were in fact embracing the United Arab Emirates (UAE) government's massive push into film at that moment, manifested through the establishment of Image Nation (US$1 billion-funded film production company, launched in 2008), twofour54 (a multimedia production hub named for its geographical location, launched in 2008), Dubai Media City (a free zone for international media companies like CNN and

Thomas Reuters, launched in 2000), and Dubai Studio City (home to the biggest soundstages in the Middle East, launched in 2005). Both Dubai and Abu Dhabi had also opened film commissions aimed at attracting international productions.

With the UAE's landscape of construction cranes, there was, to reference a Hollywood film, a general "if we build it, they will come" attitude among the students. Both Alyazyah and Reema had been volunteers at the two-year-old, glamorous, government-funded Middle East International Film Festival (later rebranded as the Abu Dhabi Film Festival), and Reema had gone on a field trip with me to the even more glamorous, government-funded Dubai International Film Festival (DIFF).[1] Both festivals had heavily courted young Emiratis to authenticate the red carpet with local flavor. Student films had no screen time in the festivals, however, even while the abovementioned new organizations were offering filmmaking workshops for young Emiratis, and the federal universities were reorienting communication and media majors from a focus on television news and talk shows to film. In fact, I had been hired to take the film and video program from broadcast ambitions to film education. Similar shifts were happening at the Higher Colleges of Technology, which has campuses in all seven emirates, as well as at the American University of Dubai and American University of Sharjah. Meanwhile, the newly opened New York University Abu Dhabi was launching the UAE's first film and new media major. Thus, I did see the niche for students to have a place to show their films and to get together with other aspiring filmmakers beyond campus walls.[2]

I got swept away by the students' enthusiasm, and as promised, they quickly obtained sponsorship, pitching the festival to businesses with the slogan: "By students, for students." Meanwhile, I began building a film-based network across Middle Eastern universities, reaching out blindly, as there were no regional university film consortiums to tap into.

It is notable that the students aspired to a Middle East–wide festival, not international. And in the years to come, students never expressed the desire for it to be international. In retrospect, this represents two things: (1) a connection that the students continued to feel, at least symbolically, with the greater Arab world, as implied in the very name of the UAE; and

FIGURE 13.1

Q & A Session at ZUMEFF 2018 at Warehouse 421, Abu Dhabi.

(2) a focus on Middle Eastern films was never questioned because the students' attention was mainly on the festival and the red-carpet elements rather than the film criteria. Indeed, Zayed University Middle East Film Festival (ZUMEFF) is not only an exploration of stories of youth through film, it's also a story of finding content and audiences in a place with little history in student and short film culture. At the same time, aspiring filmmakers were growing up in a country that promoted its future as a global cultural leader, as well as afforded an exclusive identity and heritage to its citizens that came with the privileges of a benevolent leadership and the notion of Emirati exceptionalism. These factors would impact both how the festival was organized, how audiences would respond to the festivals, and what films would be featured.

Today ZUMEFF is the longest-running film festival in the Gulf, having outlived Abu Dhabi Film Festival (ADFF), DIFF, and several other festivals that have come and gone, such as the Gulf Film Festival and TropFest Arabia. I worked on ZUMEFF during its first decade. I would not have been able to do this without Sascha Ritter, a colleague who would take over the leadership role of the festival after the first five years. Ritter worked alongside me from the beginning because of his background in producing music and film festivals in Germany, his home country. The heavy workload of faculty at the university, with instructors teaching five classes a semester and higher-ranking faculty teaching four classes a semester, meant other professors understandably declined to participate in the organization of ZUMEFF. What follows is a conversation between Sascha and I in June 2021, reflecting on that first decade ZUMEFF and predicting its future two years after we both left Zayed University and the festival.

Sascha Ritter: I didn't come onboard until the second year of ZUMEFF. But I remember how you were already stressed with fundraising, marketing, media, and curation all being your responsibility.

Alia Yunis: That's why I was so happy when you said you were interested in ZUMEFF. For the capstone students and me, the festival was a one-time graduation project. However, the festival ticked all the university boxes: it received much media attention, getting covered by all the local papers and most of the TV channels, as well as some regional coverage; it allowed the university to add to the nation's ambitious list of firsts (the first regional student film festival); many students attended the opening and closing ceremonies in full make-up and enthusiasm, reflecting school spirit; and the red carpet—yes, a real red carpet—was walked by many media and business VIPs that the sponsors brought with them. The dean of the College of Communications and the university's future provost, Dr. Marilyn Roberts, decided—I must admit to my exhausted dismay—that the festival carry on to the next year and expand its outreach.

SR: Yes, and all without a budget.

AY: Yes, it's a festival that survived despite itself really.

SR: True. Let's start with what was the most interesting aspect of the festival for us: the film curation. I've broken it down by numbers. ZUMEFF has screened films from seventeen Middle Eastern and North African

(MENA) countries, and the number of universities participating has increased, as has the number of submissions.[3] By the second year, to maximize student screening opportunities, the festival, which includes three days of screenings, played approximately fifty short films each year and expanded to include a category for Best Animation. By its tenth year, the festival was receiving nearly two hundred submissions annually, as opposed to twenty-five the first year, from more than thirty MENA institutions. This increase is in part due to the festival being more known, particularly with the increasing use of social media as a way for filmmakers to find out about affordable, easy online submissions as opposed to mail-in submissions. Partly it is because there has been an increase in student production across the Middle East, particularly in the Gulf, especially in Qatar and the UAE.[4]

AY: We definitely saw some patterns emerge. Lebanese films, for example, show more kissing and sexual innuendo, which were against Zayed University rules, so both the students and we knew the university would require them to be censored, as with films dealing with sexual crimes, even though they gave insight into a societal ill.

SR: The students saw the hypocrisy of this, given that they were watching far more explicit shows on television and online. But we opted not to censor films. Instead, we excluded them if the sexual content was not acceptable to the university. I think it was important to teach the students to respect the artists' expression of his or her story, even if it meant not being able to play it. I know this was frustrating for some universities, but they started to send us packages of student films curated to meet our rules. Maybe it's not just GCC [Gulf Cooperation Council] nationals and residents who practice self-censorship to be screened or noticed in the UAE, given it has become the production center of the MENA.

AY: Yes, there are topics we all knew were off-limits. And the framing of topics discussed in Europe or the US under constructs like skin color are so different here. No one talked about why some Gulf citizens are black. Slavery, which was a component of the Arabian trade routes along East

Africa, is not often discussed. We are seeing that change a little, but always with the caveat that, as they married their slaves to get around Islamic prohibition of slavery, it was not slavery in the context of, say, the United States. Funnily enough, mostly Syrian actors play Emirati women in local commercials, as acting [as a profession for a woman] is still largely frowned upon for women, and students have said things like, "They hire these actresses to be Emirati, but they are too pale." And "pale" is said with distinct disdain.

SR: And definitely no speaking of homosexuality. That's the most taboo subject of all. Most students even considered it unspeakable.

AY: In 2011, in one of my classes, a student asked me if she could make a film about a gay friend of hers, although he would not let her show his face. When I played it in class, some students demanded I stop it, and many walked out. Several students complained to the provost. I could actually have lost my job over that one.

SR: In general with the increasing globalization of the UAE and needing as many tourist markets as possible, this is changing. While still not accepted in society, reaction to it is not as virulent as when ZUMEFF started.

AY: The other big topic we could not show was Shiism. I remember the students saying in 2013 when we were looking at the submissions, "Miss, stop the film now. We shouldn't even be looking at this." I can't remember where the film was from, but it was a scene set in a Shiite martyr's funeral. Whereas the students thought the censorship of kisses was silly, Shiism clearly made them uncomfortable. Yet they were always keen to watch any submissions from Iran, as long as they didn't show religious practices. I think they viewed the tensions with Iran (and Yemen) as embedded in religion, while we saw them as political.

SR: In reality, we received very few student films from Iran. The majority of films came from the Levant countries, especially Lebanon, which has the largest number of schools with established film and media programs.[5] Next in number would be Palestinian student films. They have a very solid film school, Dar Al Kalima in Bethlehem. But even Palestinian schools with no equipment have students who find a way to tell their stories. The Gulf was actually the biggest challenge. We were always searching for films from Bahrain, Kuwait, and Oman, for example, but there still isn't much film production happening at higher education institutions there.

AY: In other parts of the MENA, national patterns appear. Students from Lebanon still lean toward stories that negotiate its civil war (1975–1990) and more recently the current Syrian war (2011–present); Palestinian students are entrenched in the ongoing Israeli occupation; and Egyptian students focus on nostalgia for imagined days before mass corruption and poverty, often referencing the peak of Egyptian popular cinema in the 1950s and 1960s in their short films; Moroccan films focus on migration to Europe.

SR: Of course, there are some deviations from these patterns that can be found in student films everywhere. It's that age of angst, with plots involving dying mothers and angry parents, mostly with melodrama. Do you remember how much the students loved *Et Je Vole*, the 2016 Lebanese film by Mannon Namour, in which a young girl is living a charming life, but then her mother dies in the end? These films owe much to television serials, the most abundant form of filmed entertainment on the Arab satellite channels, either dubbed or in Arabic. Students in the early years of ZUMEFF would not have yet been so reliant on Netflix and YouTube programming as they are today.[6]

AY: But the UAE is not as easily categorized as the other countries. Where do stories come from in a country with a Ministry of Happiness? This is not my question—it was a rhetorical question from one of the male ZU students in 2018.[7]

SR: Watching films about the opening of an entertainment center indeed has its limitations. Our students tended to produce films for their classes that play into the consumer culture, mainly filming a new trendy hamburger shop or café. On a positive, there were also a fair amount of films submitted about children with special needs, now called "people of determination" in the UAE. Students have really taken to government efforts to normalize special-needs children. But these are films that, as well-intentioned as they are, tend to be more like public service announcements.

AY: When I first arrived here, so many students wanted to make films about the founder of the UAE, Sheikh Zayed bin Sultan Al Nahyan, or Baba Zayed ("Father Zayed"), as he was often called. He passed away in 2004, but they were keen to interview people who had known him. Students today are too young to remember his passing and don't refer to him as Baba Zayed. But the government is making sure he remains present in people's minds. For example, in 2018, we did include a special competition for films about him to mark his one-hundredth birthday, in keeping with the country's Year of Zayed. We had around five submissions.[8]

SR: The students' love has now been passed down to Sheikh Zayed's son and President of the UAE, Sheikh Mohammed bin Zayed, and the ruler of Dubai, Sheikh Mohammed bin Rashid. Students display a genuine loyalty to the rulers, with images of them on everything from car decals to key chains to phone covers, a mark of appreciation for all the leaders have given them as citizens. And preserved for them.

AY: Today, they don't make films about the leaders but rather about government narratives that tend to be stories about the exceptionalism of the UAE, whether it is the hyperreality of the biggest and firsts or state feminism about women firsts, like the first Emirati woman to climb Mount Kilimanjaro. More than anything, there has been a growing interest in the heritage of the place, as defined by the government, with students often opting to make films in heritage villages about henna, camel competitions, and horsemanship.

SR: I know you have more to say about heritage and film. But I just want to add that we can't really blame the students for not digging into more interesting stories. Faculty across the UAE federal schools will tell you that they are consistently approached by organizations, such as advertising agencies and governmental institutions (not necessarily UAE ones) offering Emirati students a chance to make films promoting some aspect of the UAE.[9] At first, it seems like a great opportunity to give students real-life experience. But as the offers pile up, there are more opportunities than busy university students can handle, and it is questionable what the projects bring in terms of a film education—or the pursuit of societal stories. No one is coming to the students asking them to make films about issues like social disparity.

AY: Definitely. At the same time, I am not so comfortable with the faculty in UAE institutions generally complaining about the films' lack of story, critical thinking, or self-reflection. ZUMEFF's finalists are judged by an international jury that does include at least one Emirati, but one most likely educated abroad as he or she would be knowledgeable about short films. These have included film director Nawaf Al-Janahi, former DIFF artistic director Masoud Al Ali, and founder of Cinema Akil, the only independent cinema in the UAE, Butheina Kazim.[10] But by leaning toward those schooled in what makes a good film by the Western festival and film school standards, are we excluding films that are valid expressions of what the students consider their reality?

SR: That is a tough one to answer. We are all products of societies that have whole bodies of films that uncritically glorify the nation and ignore many alternative narratives. However, as faculty we are also products of Socratic philosophy when it comes to art and education: admit you are ignorant and can learn more—and engage in self-examination. It's interesting because the students who evaluate the films with us tend to dismiss UAE films that are not technically proficient in comparison to the Lebanese films, for example. I think what we, as teachers, are most needed for is to say, "Wait, let's not think about cinematography. Is there an interesting question being asked in the film?"

AY: That's why it's not right to label Socratic thinking as Western philosophy and say that our students are not capable of engaging in it because they are not taught critical thinking. It is human nature to question, if hungry enough. That goes back to what you were saying about Palestinian students always finding a way to tell their stories because they are hungry for solutions and for others to hear them. Here it is different. On the one hand, sure, many Emiratis aren't that hungry, lost in a globalized consumer world in which they have few political and economic worries. On the other hand, some amazing films have been made by the filmmaker simply asking people a question. It might not mean brilliant craft in storytelling, but it reveals a life and history here beyond government heritage tropes and hyperreality.[11] This goes back to the first ZUMEFF. It included student shorts from Egypt, Lebanon, Iraq, and UAE. The winners were flown to receive their prizes, a tradition that has continued every year. The Best Documentary went to *Our Lady of the Rosary* (2009) by Shurouq Abdullah Shaheen from Qatar University, in which two students interview several Qataris about their feelings regarding the opening of the country's first church. The people's responses highlight the conflicted emotions of Qataris and the perceived risks of non-Muslim institutions to their identity. The following year, the Best Documentary went to University of Sharjah student Fatima Ibrahim for *Rabbit Hole* (2011), in which she asks young Emiratis where their identity comes from. The interviews are juxtaposed with images from Western and non-Emirati Arab popstars and products. When the filmmaker asks a young woman what identity means, the young woman repeats back, "Identity?" and looks at the camera, unable to give an answer. This question—Who are we?—haunts many of the Gulf narrative and documentary films screened every year in the festival.

SR: This pattern shows up with expat students as well, who are more often than not born here, with the focus being more on what is a home within UAE identity.[12] In the short documentary *Robbama* (2017) Malak Mansoura, a Palestinian born in the UAE city of Al Ain, asks both Emiratis and expats what the definition of home is. The people she interviews have their passport home, but, in reality, know no other home than the UAE, and they struggle with the answer while showing nostalgia for the life they have had in the UAE and for the home they do not know. Home becomes an imagined place, and the UAE reality.

AY: These expats are not one homogeneous block. They are separated along national, racial, and monetary divides, as well as divides along how many generations they have been in the UAE. Mansoura's film is remarkable in that her focus is not only on Emiratis and Palestinians, but she is a rare filmmaker looking beyond the confines of her own nationality. Another example of that is Indian student Arkus Arkus's film, *Hartom* (2017), about a deaf American reverend in Abu Dhabi who dabbles in magic tricks. He has made a handful of shorts about other interesting, everyday expats he has met, like a Bangladeshi barista.

SR: But these are stories we don't see much. We all respect video artists like Qatari American Sophia Al Maria and her concept of Gulf Futurism, coined with Kuwaiti Senegalese musician Fatima Al Qadir, in which, through video art, she expresses how the future is already here in the Gulf. She chronicles the breakneck speed of technology and construction. But Al Maria is both a product and darling of Western art circles. She speaks their language. She has benefited by Western interest in the Gulf as a concept.

AY: Yes, she is a cosmopolitan creator, as opposed to a grassroots filmmaker. I think of there being two Gulfs: the local Gulf and the global Gulf. The global Gulf is the one that lives inside the malls and towers and tourist sites. But the local lives both inside and outside these borders, not just physical borders but also social borders that are not part of the globalized or cosmopolitan narratives. The local doesn't render the Emiratis a singular stereotype, like we were just saying about the diversity within expats. Thus, film students, with some teacher guidance, are able to dig into questions at the grassroots level, in their own neighborhoods and families, when they explore what has been lost with modernity. They have their own very special window that we can encourage as film teachers and programmers. This grassroots filmmaking triggers questions, and expands the youth's definition of the UAE beyond heritage tropes. In examining contemporary life, they question both the rapidly changing past and future.

SR: I think there is some comfort in this exploration. I remember a film, *A Time to Pray*, from Bahraini student Ahmed Al Kuwait, studying at the American University of Dubai. It's a narrative short in which some men at a mosque take in an Egyptian woman as she goes into labor and help her deliver the baby. The students loved it, even though it was a film with little tension and story, because it confirmed the compassionate identity of Islam and therefore themselves.

AY: Yes, it really showed the passion students have for Islam as part of their identity and their perception of Islam as the unifying element among different groups within the country. It's another rare look at the expats and Emiratis mixing without making it the point of the story.

SR: I think the film *The Gamboo3a Revolution* (2012) by Abdulrahman Al Madani is my favorite of the Emirati films. I really appreciated how the director ask a range of people if they like the gamboo3a or not. The gamboo3a was something that women would put under their shaylas to make them taller. The film asks Emiratis if the gamboo3a is okay in terms of culture and identity and intersperses the interviews with staged acting of a woman walking through the mall with a very big gamboo3a. It's very freestyle, and it shows the intersection of culture and religion as well as modernization in the UAE. It also uses a lot of humor. Humor rarely comes into play in the student films, perhaps because you have to accept the premise of being flawed to engage in humor, and Emirati exceptionalism doesn't allow for too many flaws—or so we are led to think.

AY: Exactly. There is an example of a film that the judges didn't rank highly, but the students went crazy for it. We had to do three additional screenings of the film because of popular demand. We ended up creating a special audience award for it. Students still love it today, even though the gamboo3a was already nearly out of fashion by the time the film was completed.

SR: Yes, it is a film that wasn't made with an audience in mind, certainly not an international audience, which is probably why it resonates locally.

FIGURE 13.2

ZUMEFF student organizers on stage at closing ceremony of ZUMEFF 2011 at Zayed University Abu Dhabi.

I think that's what makes ZUMEFF so valuable. It allows students who are not necessarily from the wealthy, Western-educated families to share stories that are not confined to the slick packaging of the Gulf in tourist films made to meet Western orientalist expectations and hyperreality.

AY: Of course, I do wish we had seen such student interest in other films.

SR: The winners of each ZUMEFF category take part in audience Q&A sessions on stage afterward. In 2017, Ahmed Salah, a Palestinian who had won for Best Animation for his short, *Ayny*, about two refugee kids in an unnamed country losing not only their physical shelter but also their physical parts, came to see his multiaward winning film screen with the other shorts. As he sat in the audience, students were on their phones and chatting and giggling with each other. Saddened, he got up on stage and said to the audience, "Why are you here, if you don't want to watch this film? I don't know if I feel worse for you or me."

AY: Ahmed did not know that he was part of a long line of filmmakers who had watched their films not being watched by students. While ZUMEFF has programmed wonderful, engaging films every year, it has struggled more with being able to say the same about audiences.

SR: Yes, basically, the biggest job of the students working with ZUMEFF was getting an audience. In the end, it was usually me reaching out to faculty across campus, giving them lesson plans to justify them bringing their classes to the auditorium. We had more people willing to come to the festival from other institutions than our own student body. Half the time, it felt like we were holding the ZU students hostage by making them watch films.

AY: When all they really wanted was to have fun outside in the lobby where we had cupcake booths and a popcorn stand. And boys! It was the only event at ZU in which both males and females could attend together.

SR: Even though we had to have separate seating in the auditorium. We actually had student volunteers whose job was to keep them apart.

AY: It was ridiculous on the administration's part because the students mixed together plenty off campus, and we offered options for them to self-segregate by gender if they wanted. In the lobby, the students were negotiating their own social issues, the chance to have a normal university atmosphere, like their counterparts at private universities—and that could never compete with the films on screen. Unless the films were dealing with them—like *The Gambooza Revolution*. Kind of the way people like selfies.

SR: To be fair, they also had never been to a film festival—or watched short films. Come to think of it, the first decade of ZUMEFF was also the decade of social media and internet platforms taking over as the main entertainment, news, and marketing sources, particularly in the Gulf, one of the first and few places in the world to have full smartphone penetration.

AY: Actually, the students really loved making social media promotional films for the festival. Promoting and selling seems to be quite comfortable for the students, perhaps in keeping with the business culture of the country, and they weren't shy to be creative here, with behind-the-scenes videos and red-carpet interviews.

SR: Yeah, if you want to measure by likes and followers, ZUMEFF became more famous on social media than any of the films it played, and that is due to the students working on social media. I think people want to help students, and so top social media influencers would promote the festival with short videos, and they were some of the first on the red carpet. And so many social media videos came out of that the next day.

AY: As ZUMEFF continued to a second year, the dean decided that it would be taught as an upper-division course for tourism and media students. The class quickly filled up, with students remembering the fun of the red carpet on closing night. Within the 2011 class, there was an exceptional group of students who worked hard for us to establish a formal festival and an event manual. But for the six years it was run as a class, it basically ended up being the faculty and a handful of students doing the work, while the others focused on filling up the closing ceremony during a couple of weeks running up to the festival. Of course, the lights and media attention made the administration happy, but how do you grade students who have basically just spent a few days of the semester inviting people on social media to a party they are hosting, and that's about it? We could even get them to promote workshops our sponsors, like Adobe and Nikon, hosted for the festival. They were actually the ones that delivered the only thing the university was interested in—a public relations event.

SR: Yes, the least amount of interest was in the film curation. It would always come down to two or three students interested in screening and evaluating the submissions with us so we could narrow them down to fifteen (five for each category) to send to the judges. Not to mention the students were asked to look for sponsorship, rather than university providing a budget, as if that was a worthy educational skill as opposed to being able to look at film critically.

AY: What is most striking is that when it came to the visiting filmmakers, even the tourism students rarely took an interest in showing them around town. They showed little interest in those visiting from other Arab countries, much like they didn't take much interest in their films.

SR: Luckily, it didn't matter much in terms of hospitality because most of the visiting filmmakers—from Palestine, Iraq, Jordan, Lebanon, even the student from Iran—had family or friends working in the Gulf that they went to see for a tour instead. I think this shows the interconnectedness of the Gulf to the rest of the Middle East. We have even had a couple of Lebanese filmmakers who ended up working in media production in Dubai. But no sense of community was built between the Emiratis and the other Arab filmmakers.

AY: It's interesting, too, because Egyptian, Sudanese, and Levantines formed the bulk of the production staff of television channels from their inception in the Gulf in the 1960s.

SR: I think that goes back to students being fed on Emirati exceptionalism. Remember when twofour54 wanted to offer an internship to the winner, but then when it realized it wouldn't be an Emirati, they asked us to make a special award, Aspiring Filmmaker of the Year, and to make it exclusively for Emiratis! The bar was pretty low for this award. I mean it's just numbers—the UAE population is only ten million people, and 88 percent are not nationals. Then you narrow it down to the numbers who are students completing short films, and that's not a big competition.

AY: I think that's why Arab Film Studio at Image Nation was introduced in 2011 as a one-year training program for aspiring resident filmmakers, Emirati and expat, rather than just Emiratis. Maybe allowing for being more inclusive is why Arab Film Studio has been sustainable, unlike so many of the other workshops and training programs that have come and gone.

SR: Arab Film Studio always submits to ZUMEFF. I have mixed feelings about it. Arab Film Studio's goal is to get films into international festivals and because of Image Nation's investment in Hollywood, it has the connections to be able to do so. While it plays on the word "Arab," it is run by Europeans and North Americans and the films play like they are made for foreigners, not local consumption.

AY: With some exceptions. The 2016 ZUMEFF Best of Best winner was an Arab Film Studio film by Syrian resident Walid Al Madani, entitled *The Sheikh of Mussafah*. It's about a thirty-five-year-old Palestinian carrying on his late father's car mechanic shop in Mussafah (Abu Dhabi's industrial zone), despite the abuse his father put him through.

SR: It's a beautifully shot film, but it did not play as much in international film festivals because it spent no time explaining the UAE to the audience—it assumes viewers know Mussafah. It takes being an expat for granted and gets to a personal story.

AY: I don't remember our students being particularly interested in it, either.

SR: It didn't create a buzz, but I'd like to think there will be a growing number of films set among expats that opens up the definition of Emirati film, sidestepping the "us vs. them" attitude between expats and Emiratis. Emirati students know Arab and South Asian expats of the same socioeconomic class as them and probably have a pretty good idea of their countries' histories.[13] But they are not connecting with them very much, especially if they do not go to school with them. Many expats have told me their few childhood friendships with Emiratis did not carry on to adulthood.

AY: I just realized that we rarely received submissions from non-Arab expats, even from institutions that had large South Asian student bodies.

Maybe the word "Middle East" did feel exclusive. Or maybe they thought that the film had to be about something to do with the Middle East, however you want to identify that. I don't even really know what the point of the word "Arab" is in Arab Film Studio. When I taught a workshop there, I remember that about a third of the students weren't of Arabic-speaking heritage.

SR: Well, maybe film is going to make the unspoken visible. Do you remember the ten-minute Emirati narrative film *Arasian* (2018) by Ahmad Al Tunaiji, a New York University Abu Dhabi student? The film is about a middle school boy who gets picked on because his mother is a Filipina. To prove himself a true Emirati to the other boys in school, he bullies the kind Filipina cleaner, asking her to dig out of the toilet the cakes she had given him that morning and eat them. The film did not do well with the judges, to reinforce our earlier point, but what a Q&A we had!

AY: Right away, a male Emirati stood up, speaking in Arabic, to say he found the film offensive, and the filmmaker should be ashamed of producing a film that makes Emiratis look so bad to an audience that includes non-Emiratis. Another Emirati stood up and said that the film didn't even show how bad it really is. She said her mother is Filipina and that she and her brother were ridiculed at school for being half-half. The male student apologized to her for having had that experience, as if on behalf of all Emiratis, and pointed out that he would never do such a thing but that as a nation, Emiratis shouldn't let the foreigners in the audience, including visiting filmmakers from other Arab countries, see them like this.

SR: I thought, now we have a film festival!

AY: It definitely broke away from Emirati exceptionalism by asking if it is okay to show painful imperfections in the culture to others, which has been a big issue in creating compelling narrative films.

SR: I think that was the year we figured out the key to making it work was to take it off campus so that it was no longer subject to campus rules—therefore the mixing of genders didn't become the big issue, and students really watched the films, at least the ones set in the Gulf. For students by students finally made sense. And the students weren't doing the fundraising—we got a sponsor and host at Warehouse 421.[14]

AY: That was our last year running the festival. It was a good way to end.

SR: Yes, I think ZUMEFF gave space for stories to be shared that were not focused on guessing what outside audiences were looking for from the Gulf. While certainly race and gender are issues here, they are not the only frameworks to look at the Gulf, as these student films show. What other moment stands out for you?

AY: I'll never forget when twenty-year-old Palestinian student, Montamy Arabi, in 2012, who won for Best Documentary, came to the podium and thanked ZUMEFF for bringing him to Abu Dhabi. It was the first time he had ever left the West Bank, and it was a struggle for us to get him a visa. Then he said, "It was the first time I have ever seen the sea. My country is on the sea, but I have never seen it."

SR: My favorite moment also involves a Palestinian student. Mohamad Alfateh Abu-Snenih won the Best Documentary Award in 2014 with his film *Burhan Kashour*, about a young rapper from Jerusalem struggling to quit his career due to depression from the social, economic, and political situation. Unfortunately—due to changing university rules—we were not allowed to bring the winners to the festival that year. In 2015, he submitted his new documentary *Praise of Wounds*, about a mother in Jerusalem and her child who are trying to reach their home near the Al-Aqsa Mosque. He won Honorable Mention, and we invited him to join the festival. He was sitting on the steps at the edge of the cinema while watching his film, and his eyes teared up. He hugged me and told me that he had never been to a cinema and that he had never seen his film on a big screen. This was so touching. Some male ZUMEFF volunteers were close by and overheard our conversation; they went to him and invited him to a movie night in Dubai. So they took him out on a trip and sent me various photos of Mohamad enjoying his time in the big city. Yeah, that makes it all worthwhile.

AY: They couldn't connect to his films, but they could sympathize with never having been to a cinema. I was really proud of those students that day. Not only was it a rare moment where they engaged with the visiting filmmakers, but they also were true hosts. They lived up to a quality they repeatedly say is part of their heritage: hospitality. And they are hospitable. I'm just not sure they know how to connect to people who, aside from speaking the same language, live in a totally different world. I have to say overall the male students were much better hosts than the female students, and I suspect it goes back to them mixing more with others in general, although that might be changing.

SR: But it wasn't moments like that that allowed the festival to survive. Or the films. Ironically, it was the students' passion for hosting events. And that they always filled the red carpet, which made the administration happy.

AY: Maybe our memories of ZUMEFF and the films ZUMEFF screened will be a time capsule for a place that is changing so fast.

SR: I'd like to think so.

AY: Do you think ZUMEFF is going to survive?

SR: It would be the only film festival that has. But who knows? Maybe next ZUMEFF will have Israeli films but not Iranian films, so then how does a film festival define Middle East?

AY: I'm not sure, either. We had a vision that was beyond creating a media-worthy event. When we left Zayed University, no one cared until the new vice president said she wanted ZUMEFF to continue as the university's most high-profile event. Now they want to make it international. Then the soul is gone, and it is mainly about publicity, not film. That is the challenge of sustaining festivals. In the Gulf, how do you keep the programming more valuable than the show?

> ALIA YUNIS is a film and heritage scholar, filmmaker and writer. She is the co-founder of the Zayed University Middle East Film Festival. Her fiction and non-fiction work have been translated into eight languages.
>
> SASCHA RITTER has taught at Zayed University and was director of the Zayed University Middle East Film Festival. He has also worked as a freelance journalist for various music magazines.

NOTES

1. The Abu Dhabi Film Festival was introduced in 2007 as the Middle East International Film Festival. Its name was changed in 2009 when its management was taken over from a local Egyptian television personality by a team of film festival veterans, including a large contingent from the Toronto International Film Festival.

2. Defining "Middle East" would shift throughout the festival's history, depending in part on the practicalities of the film submissions and the political winds. It has always included North Africa. Qatar stopped being included in 2017 due to the UAE's severance of political ties with it. In general, the Middle East has been defined by the festival as Arabic-speaking countries. Turkish and Iranian students have accepted, although due to the limitations of faculty time, no effort has been made to reach out to universities in those countries. Turkish and Iranian students have submitted on their own after hearing about the festival on social media or through friends..

3. The first event, the capstone, was called Zayed University Film Festival (ZUFF); but as a faculty, we changed the name to ZUMEFF from the second year on. This was to better express its purpose and focus less on the university name.

4. Qatar's Doha Film Institute (DFI) also launched in 2008, with several workshops and classes for young filmmakers. In 2009, Qatar hosted the Doha Tribeca International Film Festival, which was canceled in 2013 and replaced with the smaller Ajyal Film Festival, which is specifically geared toward young filmmakers. DFI continues to offer grants to independent filmmakers, as well as workshops for aspiring directors in the country.

5. Most films submitted from Lebanon are from Lebanese American University, Notre Dame University–Louaize, and St. Joseph University. The production values are the highest from these schools within all the film festival submissions.

6. The Arabic satellite channels offer television serials from the Middle East, Latin America, India, and South Korea. Youth consume these shows online rather than on traditional television stations. Based on my surveys with students in ten years of teaching Emiratis, Korean dramas are the most popular, having replaced the Turkish series in 2011, and the Arab-language series were the least popular—deemed "boring" and "slow."

7. The reason I said "male" is that the male and female students have separate campuses within the same building. The male population is one-quarter the size of the female student body, as the university began in 1998 under Sheikh Zayed as an institution to educate the top Emirati females. A full male student program began in 2013.

8. The UAE government often has themed years, including Year of Tolerance (2019) and Year of Reading (2016).

9. NGOs, like UNHCR, which receive significant funding from the UAE, approached us to make films about the UAE's generosity. In fact, my students and I produced a film on the UAE's camp for refugees in Jordan in 2015.

10. Cinema Akil is not a government-funded cinema and has essentially became one of only two places in the UAE to screen films from the international film festival circuit since the demise of ADFF and DIFF. The other outlet was Cinema Space at Manarat Al Saadiyat in Abu Dhabi, a biweekly film series voluntarily programmed and promoted by Mohamed Khawaja, an Indian national born in UAE and a former employee at ADFF (and currently employed at twofour54). However, he stopped programming in 2022. Emirati Hind Mezaina has also developed programming of independent films for Louvre Abu Dhabi and theaters and Mall of the Emirates in Dubai. New York University Abu Dhabi hosts public screenings of Emirati films, as well as film series followed by discussions with scholars.

11. Common heritage tropes include camels, palm trees, and sand dunes. Common hyperreality tropes include the Mall of the Emirates indoor ski slope, the seven-star Burj Al Arab, and multiple theme parks, including Ferrari World, with the world's fastest roller coaster.

12. I use the word "expat" here for lack of a better word, knowing that it has connotations related to upper-middle-class and wealthy Westerners working abroad. Here, it is used to reference students, usually from the Middle East or South Asia, who are the first or second generation of their family born in the UAE.

13. I mention these two groups here because there are several families that have been here for generations, although this can also be the case with other expatriates.

14. Warehouse 421 is a gallery and public venue run by the Sheikha Salama bint Hamdan Foundation to promote art and culture in Abu Dhabi.

INDEX

Aadujeevitham (2023), 27
Abbas, Ali, 18
Abu Dhabi (1969), 18
Abu Dhabi Film Festival (ADFF), 21, 24, 110, 197, 248, 253, 307, 308, 326n1, 327n10. *See also* Middle East International Film Festival
Abu-Snenih, Mohamad Alfateh, 324–25
Abu Sunayd, Abd al-Aziz, 82, 98–99n63
Adoni, Raed, 221
Aflam Film Club, 263
African Studies, 16, 63
Ahamed, Salim, 167
Ahmed, Attiya, 3
Ajyal Film Festival, 21, 234, 326n4
Akinmolayan, Niyi, 28
Al Agroobi, Amal, 256
Al Attar, Ammar. *See* Cinemas in the UAE
Al Bannai, Ahlam, 256
Alboom / The Dawn (2006), 42, 54n130, 185–91, 197–203
Al Falasi, Alyazyah, 306–7
Alghanem, Abdulrahman, 20
Al Ghanem, Jumana, 256

Alghanem, Nujoom, 248–50, 253, 257–61, 263
Al Haydar, Tariq, 32, 193–94
Al-Janahi, Nawaf, 314
Al-Jaser, Meshal, 40, 43, 239–41, 267–82; *Can I Go Out?*, 276–79; *Under Concrete*, 277–79, 281; *Rise*, 279–81; *Screw Infidels!*, 267–68, 274–75, 277, 281; *Syria Needs You*, 272–74
Al Jazeera, 24
Al Kameen / The Ambush (2021), 22
Al Khaja, Nayla, 248–54, 256, 260–63
Al Kuwait, Ahmed, 317
Allouache, Merzak, 36
Al Madani, Abdulrahman, 236–39
Al Madani, Walid, 322
Al Maria, Sophia, 316
Almatrooshi, Moza, 286–94, 298–99, 304
Al Mureed (2008), 248, 253
Al-Nakib, Farah, 91
Al Nuaimi, Mariam, 256
Alobthani, Mohammed, 24–25
Al Qadir, Fatima, 316
Al Qadiri, Monira, 241–43
Al Safadi, Majida, 256

329

Al-Saqr / The Falcon (1965), 18
Alsemari, Raed, 232–34
Al Thawadi, Bassam, 29
Al Tunaiji, Ahmad, 323
Al Waleed bin Talal, 191
Al Wawi, Walid, 43, 302–3
Al-Zadjali, Khalid AbdulRahim, 42, 185–86, 197–99, 200
amateur filmmaking, 6, 41, 42, 76–78, 96n34, 135
Ameen, Shahad, 267
Amin, Samir, 10
Amitai, Reuven, 157
Amreeka (2009), 216
Ana mafi khof min Kafeel / I'm Not Scared of Kafeel (2015), 41
Animal (2016), 261–62
Annaud, Jean-Jacques, 22
Appadurai, Arjun, 9–10, 57, 178
Arabian American Oil Company (Aramco), 79–83
Arabian Sea, 2, 3, 4, 5, 8, 121, 171
Arabikatha / Arabian Tale (2007), 167
Arabs Got Talent (television program), 39
Arafath, P. K. Yasser, 128, 129, 132
area studies, 55–58; expansive geographical approach to, 62–65; Gulf Studies, 58–65; Middle East Studies, 9, 14, 57; South Asian Studies, 14–15, 57, 61; transnational approaches to, 62–65
arenas, 8, 9, 28; maritime arena, 36
Arkus, Akus, 316
Armes, Roy, 198, 264–65n14
Arūsī-yi Khūbān / Marriage of the Blessed (1989), 42, 144, 145–49, 151, 154–55, 160
Attenborough, Richard, 15

audio cassettes: culture of, 122–24; *Dubaikathu* (Dubai letters) and, 121, 128, 130–32; home recordings, 134–37; *kathupattu* (letter songs) and, 42, 122, 127–34, 137–38, 141n20; Mappila Muslim community and, 122, 127–29, 132–33, 138; *marupadikathu* (song in response), 130, 132; as sensory technological objects, 124–26
aural performance, 137–38
Ayalon, David, 157, 165n43
Azad, M., 25–26, 168–82
Azhans-i Shīshah-yī / The Glass Agency (1998), 42, 143, 144, 149–55, 159–61

Bâ, Saër Maty, 10, 187
Bab el-Hadid / Cairo Station (1958), 12, 38
Babu, Ramachandra, 171, *179*, 181
Bacharach, Jere L., 159
Bachchan, Amitabh, 36–37
Badshah, S. M. G., 87, 89
Bahrain Cinema, 74, 83–93
"Bahrain Cinemas" files, 69–70
Bahrain Petroleum Company (Bapco), 18, 78–80, 83–84, 89, 91
Barger, Tom, 79
Barot, Chandra, 37
Bashu, Gharibeye Koochak / Bashu, the Little Stranger (1989), 29
Bas ya Bahar / Cruel Sea (1972), 1, 29–31, 44, 54n130, 111
Beblawi, Hazem, 62
Bedouins, 1, 5, 169
Beizai, Bahram, 29
Belgrave, Charles Dalrymple, 68–70, 74, 76, 78–79, 83–85, 87, 89–91

#BeMyGuest, 23
Berlin: Die Sinfonie der Großstadt / Berlin: Symphony of a Big City (1927), 177
Bhansali, Sanjay Leela, 15
Bhattacharya, Spandan, 16
Bird, Brad, 24
Bishara, Fahad, 9
blackface, 40, 149–56, 159
Black Gold / Day of the Falcon (2011), 22
Bollywood, 10, 15–16, 23, 25, 39, 44, 104
Born a King (2019), 22
Born into Brothels (2004), 15
Boyle, Danny, 15
Brand India campaigns, 23
Branding Global Image (2021), 24–25
Briski, Zana, 15
Bristol-Rhys, Jane, 258
Bruno, Giulana, 177, 201

Cannes Film Festival, 11, 15, 216, 219, 250, 262, 306
Carthage Film Festival. *See* Journées Cinématographiques de Carthage
Carver, Antonia, 212, 221, 222
Cavarero, Adriana, 136–37
Centre for Arab Gulf Studies (University of Exeter), 61–62
Chahine, Youssef, 12, 37–38
Chaplin, Charlie, 19, 82
Chaque jour est une fête / Every Day Is a Holiday (2009), 218
Chaudhry, Haider, 25–26
Chen, Kuan-Hsing, 10
Cherian, Sebastian Thejus, 42
Chidebe, Mac-Collins, 27–28
Ciecko, Anne, 18
Cinema Akil, 24, 207, 266n44, 314, 327n10

cinema closings and demolitions, 102, 104
Cinema El-Housh, 24
cinema posters, 108–9, *109*, 114–15, 116
Cinemas in the UAE (art installation), 102–10; Al Attar on, 111–20; censorship documents, 115; context and contents, 102–10; film distribution, 113–15; origins of, 111–12; promotional posters, 116; Sharjah Art Foundation and, 119–20
Cinema Space, 24, 327n10
City of Life / Dar al-Haya (2008), 20, 28, 50–51n76
Cohn, Bernard, 57
commodification, 201, 222, 289, 299, 302
Connor, Steven, 131
contact zones, 8, 29, 33, 212, 262, 288, 299, 303
Cooley, Claire, 36
Culcasi, Karen, 5
culturalist language, 3

Dabis, Cherien, 216
Dalyell, Eleanor Isabel Wilkie, 76–77
Damascus International Film Festival, 21
Damluji, Mona, 18
Dante's Inferno (1924), 69
Dark Continent myth, 12
Deira Diaries (2021), 167
De Klerk, Nico, 77
Deleuze, Gilles, 8–9, 145
dependency theory, 57
Derderian, Beth, 43
Deshpande, Shekhar, 186, 192
deterritorialization, 56, 178, 287–88, 293, 303

de Valck, Marijke, 190, 221
Devdas (2002), 15
Diamond Necklace (2012), 167
Dickinson, Kay, 42–43
Diop, Abdoulaye, 243–44
Dirks, Nicholas, 15, 93
Disney, Roy Edward, 1, 2
Doha Film Institute (DFI), 21, 234, 326n4
Doha Tribeca Film Festival (DTFF), 21, 326n4
Dokhtar-e Lor, ya Iran-e Diruz va Iran-e Emruz / The Lor Girl, or Yesterday's Iran and Today's Iran (13), 13–14
Dokotum, Okaka Opio, 12
Don (1978), 37
Donald, James, 171
Dönmez-Colin, Gönül, 188, 190, 199–200
Dubai (2001), 26
Dubai (2005), 27, 28
Dubai Chalo / Let's Go to Dubai (1979), 25–26
Dubai International Film Festival (DIFF), 21, 43, 202, 248, 250, 253, 307, 308, 314; Cinetech, 214, 214–15; Dubai Film Connection, 217, 219, 222; port economy and, 207–25
Dubaikathu (Dubai letters), 121, 128, 130–32
"Dubai Kathu" (Jameel), 42, 122, 127–34, 137–38, 141n20
Dubai Presents: A Five-Star Mission (2021), 24
Dubai Runs 1 (2007), 27–28
Dubai Runs 2 (2007), 27–28
Dubai Seenu (2007), 26
Duggal, Vebhuti, 16

Edhay in Abu Dhabi / Dhhayy fi Abu Dhabi (2016), 20
El-Horr, Dima, 218
Elsheshtawy, Yasser, 6
Emerson, Ralph Waldo, 281
Emirates Film Competition (EFC), 24, 52n92, 197, 256
Emirati exceptionalism, 308, 313, 317, 321, 323
encounters, 8, 9, 28, 29, 36; cultural encounters, 34; ethnographic encounters, 77; Indian Ocean encounters, 34; self-encounter, 166n48; transnational encounters, 169–70, 182
errancy, 9, 47n21
essentialism, 3, 11, 65; strategic essentialism, 6
Et Je Vole (2016), 312
Eurocentrism, 10, 14, 17, 55, 263–64n1

Falaknaz, Reem, 287, 289, 294–302
Fanon, Frantz, 80, 156
Faqir, Mohammed, 83–84
Feldman, Noah, 268
femininity, 78, 130, 133
feminism, 261; Emirati cinema and, 248, 249, 251–52, 256, 259, 260, 261–62; state feminism, 6, 13, 248, 249, 251–52, 261–62, 313; Western feminism, 14, 32, 194, 251
Ferguson, James, 57
Festival panafricain du cinéma et de la télévision de Ouagadougou (Fespaco), 21
film festivals: audience expectations, 189–91; port economy and, 207–25; transnational coproductions and, 189–91. *See also individual festivals*
Fix Me (2009), 221

Foley, Sean, 43
Ford, Sam, 268
Fowle, Trenchard Craven William, 86
free zones, 21, 24, 43, 213, 224, 225, 306–7
From A to B / Min Alif ila Ba' (2014), 20
Fuccaro, Nelida, 42
fundamentalism, 3, 38, 40, 193

Gabriel, Teshome, 17
Gallant Lady (1933), 19
Gamboo3a Revolution, The (2012), 317
Gandhi (1982), 15
Getino, Octavio, 170
Ghatak, Ritwik, 15
Ghosh, Amitav, 4
Gillespie, Craig, 24
Ginalska, Karolina, 42
Glissant, Édouard, 8–9
Golden Cinema (aka Plaza Cinema), 103, 107–8, 111–12, 114
Great Depression, 72
Green, Joshua, 268
Green, Nile, 9
Green Movement, 161
Grieveson, Lee, 92
Guattari, Félix, 8–9
Guha, Dulal, 109
Guha, Ramachandra, 12
Gulf Committee, 59–60
Gulf Cooperation Council (GCC): Bedouin Arab identity preference, 3, 5–6; Customs Union, 20; economy and market, 170, 209, 219; GCC Film Festival, 253; government-sponsored film institutions, 232; Image Nation and, 264n5; Iran-Iraq War and, 60; Kerala, India, and, 121–22, 129, 135–36, 138, 168; member states, 46n3, 94n8; migrant domestic works and GCC citizens, 232, 243–44; transnational support and, 189
Gulf exceptionalism, 6, 42, 62, 65
Gulf Film Festival, 24, 253, 308
Gulf Futurism, 316
Gupta, Akhil, 57

Haddad, Saleh, 41
Half Emirati (2012), 256
Halliday, Fred, 59–60
Hamad and the Pirates: The Phantom Dhow (1971), 1, 2
Hamama (2010), 257–58
Happy New Year (2014), 25
Harootunian, H. D., 55
Hartom (2017), 316
Hatami-Kia, Ebrahim, 42, 143, 144, 149–55, 159–61
Hekaya Bahrainiya / A Bahraini Tale (2006), 29
Her Scene Club in Dubai, 262–63
Hickinbotham, Tom, 85–86
Higbee, Will, 10, 186, 187
Higson, Andrew, 11
home moviemaking, 6, 76–78
Homo Arabicus, 60–61
Homo Islamicus, 61, 66n18
Honey, Rain and Dust (2016), 257
House, Karen Elliott, 268
Hudson, Dale, 42, 199, 221, 254, 259–60, 262
Hungama in Dubai (2007), 26
Hussein, Omar, 270–71
Hussein, Saddam, 150–51
Hyder, Pulikkottil, 128

I Am Arab (2009), 256
Ibrahim, Fatima, 315

identity politics, 17, 61
Image Nation Abu Dhabi, 20, 24, 39, 250, 264n5, 306, 321–22
India: Emergency, 36, 123
Indian Cinematograph Committee (ICC), 71–72, 86
International Documentary Festival Amsterdam (IDFA), 11
International Monetary Fund (IMF), 189, 222
Iranian sacred defense cinema. *See* sacred defense cinema
Iran-Iraq War, 5, 29, 35, 46n3, 60; sacred defense cinema and, 143–45, 147, 151–57, 160
Iskanderija, Kaman oue Kaman / Alexandria Again and Forever (1989), 37–38
Islamophobia, 16, 40, 193
Issa, Hamida, 234–36

Jameel, S. A., 127–32
Jamjoom, Hamza, 202
Jenkins, Henry, 268
Jim Crow laws, 19, 82
Jose, Lal, 167
Journées Cinématographiques de Carthage, Les (JCC) aka Carthage Film Festival, 21

kafala (labor sponsorship laws), 2–3, 231
Kalthami, Ali, 267
Kamel, Ahd, 267
Kanna, Ahmed, 5
Kariyaden, Musthaque Rehman, 167
kathupattu (letter songs), 42, 122, 127–34, 137–38, 141n20; *Dubaikathu* (Dubai letters), 121, 128, 130–32;

marupadikathu (song in response), 130, 132
Kauffman, Ross, 15
Kazemi, Farshid, 131–32
Keene, Ralph, 18
Khaddama / Housemaid (2011), 167
Khaleeji, 3, 20, 231
Khalifa, Ali bin Abdullah, 85, 87
Khalifa, Ali bin Mohamed, 85, 87
Khalifah, Isa bin Sulieman, 1, 7
Khalij al-'Arabi, al- (the Arab gulf), 61
Khan, Farah, 25
Khleifi, Michel, 218
Khomeini, Ayatollah, 145, 155–56
Khorfakkan (2020), 22
Khouri, Samir A., 38
Koch, Nathalie, 6
Kodiyathur, Salaam, 26, 135
Korda, Alexander, 69
Kramp, Fritz, 87
Kulthum, Umm, 74, 87

La Cava, Gregory, 19
Lamangan, Joel, 27
La Noire de . . . / Black Girl (1965), 16, 183n3
Larkin, Brian, 70–71, 90
Latour, Bruno, 123
Lawrence, T. E., 269
Lean, David, 15
Lefebvre, Henri, 173
letter songs. *See kathupattu*
Lim, Song Hwee, 186, 187
Limelight (1952), 19, 82
Loch, Percy Gordon, 68–71, 76, 78–79, 84–85, 94n2
Lockman, Zachary, 61
Lu, Chin-Shan, 216
lyric poetry, 128, 133

Majed, Reema, 306–7
Makhmalbaf, Mohsen, 42, 144, 145–49, 151, 154–55, 160
Malayalam cinema, 167–68; imagined landscape and, 174–78; transnationalism, 169–73; *Vilkanundu Swapnangal / Dreams for Sale* (1980), 25–26, 168–82, 174, 175, 176
Mangan, John, 213
Mansour, Haifaa, 29–33, 34, 185–86, 191, 193–96, 198, 202, 267
Mansoura, Malak, 315–16
Manuel, Peter, 123
Mapp, H. V., 89
Mappila Muslim community, 26–27, 122, 127–29, 132–33, 138
Marah fi Robo'a Lebnan / Fun throughout Lebanon (1971), 18
Martin, Florence, 252
Martin-Jones, David, 187
"Marupadi Kathu" (Kameel), 128–29
masculinity, 36, 78, 125, 145
Mater, Ahmed, 269
Mazar, Meta, 186, 192
media free zones, 21, 24, 43, 213, 224, 225, 306–7
Menon, Bindu, 16, 42
Menon, VBK, 171, 178–80, 182
Meow (2022), 167
Merleau-Pontian phenomenology, 136
Meshkini, Marzieh, 29, 37
Middle East Broadcasting Center (MBC), 24, 39, 209
Middle East International Film Festival, 21, 307, 326n1. *See also* Abu Dhabi Film Festival (ADFF)
Middle East Research and Information Project (MERIP), 60

Middle East Studies, 9, 14, 57
migrant domestic workers, 229–30; in *Beshkara* (2014), 230, 236–39; in *Dunya's Day* (2018) and, 230, 232–34; in *Elevate* (2017) and, 230, 234–36; in *Is Sumiyati Going to Hell?* (2016), 230, 239–41; power relations, 232–43; in *Soap* (2014), 230, 241–43; social frictions and, 230–32
Mini, Darshana, 27, 39
Mirgani, Suzi, 43, 199
Mission: Impossible—Ghost Protocol (2011), 24
Mitchell, Timothy, 14, 56, 59, 73
Miyoshi, Masao, 55
modernization theory, 57
Modi, Narendra, 23
Mohammed bin Salman, 38
Mole, Ben, 22
Moodley, Nashen, 220
Morana, Reed, 23
Morel, Pierre, 22
Mostafa, Ali F., 20, 28
Motrescu-Mayes, Annamaria, 76
Mouawad, Wissam, 188
Muscat International Film Festival, 197

Naber, Nadine, 255
Nafas / Breath (2019), 22, 23
Naficy, Hamid, 35, 170
Nagib, Lúcia, 12
Nair, Mira, 22, 23
Namour, Mannon, 312
Nantes Festival of Three Continents, 197
Nasser, Gamal Abdel, 29. *See also* Nasser, Jamal Abdul
Nasser, Jamal Abdul, 16, 60. *See also* Nasser, Gamal Abdul

nationalism: Arab nationalism, 30, 321; Bahrain and, 91; identity and, 3; India and, 123; Iran and, 154; Iraq and, 162n4; language and, 3; Oman and, 91, 199; pan-Arab nationalism, 98n62; in pre-oil cinema, 1; Saudi Arabia and, 14, 22
nation building, 3, 208
Nearby Sky (2014), 253, 257–59
Nejer, Malik, 267
neoliberalism, 3, 23, 25, 50–51n76, 249, 252, 261
Netflix, 24, 39, 118, 198, 208, 240, 264n5, 312
new media, 286–304
Niblock, Tim, 61–62
Nickelson, Michelle, 254
Niranjana, Tejaswini, 123
Nollywood, 26–28
nomadism, 1, 8–9

oil company films, 1, 18–20, 42, 58, 59, 78–83
"oil sheik" stereotype, 6, 31
Oman Film Society, 186, 197. See also *Alboom / The Dawn* (2006)
Omar Gatlato / Umar Qatlatu Al-Rudjla (1976), 36
oral poetry, 17, 39
Orbit (satellite television company), 209, 214
Organization of Petroleum Exporting Countries (OPEC), 82
Orientalism, 3, 9, 12, 15, 22–23, 57, 59, 169, 190, 248–50, 255, 257
Orientalism (Said), 57
Orientalist Studies, 9, 61
Oruc, Firat, 42
Osella, Caroline, 127

Osella, Filippo, 127
Otto, Henry, 69
Our Accent (2011), 256
Our Lady of the Rosary (2009), 315

Pahlavi dynasty, 14, 156
Pan-African Film and Television Festival of Ouagadougou. See Festival panafricain du cinéma et de la télévision de Ouagadougou (Fespaco).
pan-Arabism, 5, 16, 24, 29, 36
Pandya, Shivani, 211, 216, 219, 223, 224
Papagianni, Chrysavgi, 43
Passage to India, A (1984), 15
Pathemaari / The Dhow (2015), 167
Pathemaari, Jacobinte Swargarajyam / Jacob's Kingdom of Heaven (2016), 167
Pather Panchali (1955), 15
Patterson, Orlando, 158
Persian Story (1952), 18
Petiwala, Ada, 23, 25
petrocoloniality, 72–74
"petrodollars," 3, 6, 37–38
policing cinema, 92–93
polycentrism, 186–87
polyvalence, 187, 192, 196
port economy, 207–25
postindependence cinema, 2, 16–17, 236, 264–65n14
postindependence state building, 60
Pratt, Mary Louise, 8, 212, 262
presences, 8; physical presence, 287, 302
private cinema, 74–78
Private Life of Helen of Troy, The (1927), 69

Qalb al-Adala / *Justice* (television program), 39
Quintos, Rory B., 27, 28
Qur'an, 33, 192, 193, 194, 237, 296

Rabbit Hole (2011), 315
Radhakrishnan, Ratheesh, 26
Rafsanjani, Hashemi, 145
Rawle, Steven, 202
Ray, Satyajit, 15
Red, Blue, Yellow (2013), 258
Red Sea, 2
Red Sea International Film Festival, 22
Reisz, Todd, 18
relations, 8–9, 28, 35–37; affective relations, 122–24, 126, 218; artistic relations, 302; asymmetrical relations, 8, 33, 57, 188, 236–37, 243; exchange relations, 13–14; gendered relations, 231, 237; labor relations, 231, 237, 243; military relations, 160; poetics of relations, 9; power relations, 35–37, 56, 72, 188, 230, 232–43, 288; sonic relations, 122–24, 126, 131, 133, 137; trade relations, 220; voice-body relations, 131
rentier state theory, 3, 62
Ritter, Sasha, 43
Robinson, Pearl, 16
Rochiran, Daulatram, 83–84
Roozi khe zan shodam / *The Day I Became a Woman* (2000), 29, 37
Rossiter, Ned, 215–16
Rotana Studios, 191, 209, 219
Ruttmann, Walter, 177

Sabbagh, Mahmoud, 267
Sabry, Tarik, 9, 34
sacred defense cinema, 42, 143–44, 160–61; *Arūsī-yi Khūbān* / *Marriage of the Blessed* (1989), 42, 144, 145–49, 151, 154–55, 160; *Azhans-i Shīshah-yī* / *The Glass Agency* (1998), 42, 143, 144, 149–55, 159–61; blackness and, 144, 147, 149–56, 161; Iran-Iraq War and, 143–45, 147, 151–57, 160; military history and, 143–45, 147, 150–61; themes and tropes, 144, 145, 149–50, 151, 153
Saeed, Mujtaba, 267
Said, Edward, 59–60
Salah, Ahmed, 318–19
Sam, M. A., 84–85
Samt, 289, 302–3
Sarah Balabagan Story, The (1997), 27
scapes, 8, 9–10, 29; ethnoscapes, 9; financescapes, 10; globalizing scapes, 33, 36; ideoscapes, 10; landscapes, 77, 167–68, 172, 177, 180, 182, 201, 257; mediascapes, 9; technoscapes, 10, 133
Sembène, Ousmane, 16, 170
Sen, Mrinal, 15
Sennett, Richard, 64
Shafik, Viola, 38
Shaheen, Bahraini Khalifa, 18
Shaheen, Jack, 12
Shaheen, Shurouq Abdullah, 315
Shahid.net, 24
Shams, Majid, 18
Sharjah Art Foundation (SAF), 119–20
Sharjah Film Platform, 24
Sharp Tools (2017), 253
Shohat, Ella, 10, 14, 17, 44, 249, 252, 260–61, 263–64n1
Siddiq, Khaled, 1, 18, 29–32, 44, 54, 111
sightseeing, 201. *See also* tourism
Simmel, Georg, 173
Simpson, Mark, 73
Sinha, Babli, 86, 90

sitr (cover), 287–89, 294, 304
Slumdog Millionaire (2008), 15
Smith, C. G., 5
Smith, Jacob, 134
social media, 38–43; YouTube, 26, 39–40, 58, 198, 267, 270–74, 278, 291, 298, 312
Solanas, Fernando, 170
sonotope, 133–34
Sounds of the Sea (2015), 253, 257, 259–60
South Asian film studies, 14–15
South Asian Studies, 14–15, 57, 61
Spiro, Julian, 18
Spivak, Gayatri, 6, 89, 194
Sreenivasan, V., 167
Stam, Robert, 10, 17, 44
Standard Oil, 78
Stevenson, Dedra, 254
Stoler, Ann Laura, 93
Story Takes Flight, A (2019), 23
storytelling, 17, 186, 199, 315
strategic essentialism, 6. *See also* essentialism
Sultan, Mohamed, 267
Sumayin, Ali, 267
Sundance Film Festival, 15, 233, 306
Super Lochal (2014), 256
Sweeney, Maurice, 22
Sykes-Picot Agreement, 6

tape recording, 125–26, 128, 132, 134–37
Tariki, Abdullah, 82
These Are the Trucial States (1958), 18
Third Cinema, 170, 179
Thomas, Rosie, 15
Tierney, Dolores, 187, 190

Tiger Zinda Hai (2017), 25
Toronto International Film Festival, 219, 326n1
tourism, 211–12, 223–24, 257, 311, 316, 318, 320–21
transnational coproductions, 185–86, 201–3; *Alboom / The Dawn* (2006) compared with, 185–91, 197–203; film festival audience expectations, 189–91; funding, 186–89; *Wadjda* (2012), 185–86, 189–98, 200–202
transnational gaze, 187

Um Duwais (2012), 256
Unveiling Dubai (2006), 248, 253
Utubūs-i Shab / Night Bus (2007), 156

Vaitla, Sreenu, 26
Van Peursem, Gerrit, 75
Vasudevan Nair, M. T., 170, 171, 174, 176, 178
Vaziri, Parisa, 42
veiling, 3, 132, 254, 255
ventriloquist, 131
Vilkanundu Swapnangal / Dreams for Sale (1980), 25–26, 168–82, 174, 175, 176; filming challenges, 178–82; imagined landscape in, 173–78; as transnational film text, 169–73
village film, 199
Villaronga, Agustí, 22
Vitalis, Robert, 19, 82
vocalic body, 131
voice masquerade, 131
Vora, Neha, 6

Wadjda (2012), 29–33, 34, 42, 185–86, 189–98, 200–202

Wahhabism, 38, 75–76, 268
Wayel, Abdulsalam, 269
Wedad (1936), 74, 87
Wedding Party 2: Destination Dubai (2017), 28
white savior mythology, 12, 251, 254
Whitman, Walt, 281–82
Wilkie-Dalyell, Eleanor Isabel, 76–77
Williams, Jane, 211–12, 217, 218, 219, 221
World Bank, 222
world cinema, 10–12, 186–87, 189, 191, 199, 201
world of cinemas, 186–87, 201

Yaghi, Ziad, 214–15, 216
Yateem, Hussein, 68, 85
Yunis, Alia, 43, 199, 259–60, 262

Zafar, Ali Abbas, 25
Zayed University Middle East Film Festival (ZUMEFF), 309–11, 320–21; Arab Film Studio and, 322–23; audience Q&A sessions, 318–19; expat filmmakers, 315–17; festival promotion, 319–20; film curation, 309–11, 320–21; future of, 325–26; heritage and film, 313–16, 323; history of, 306–9; jury process, 314–17; statistics, 309–10; student films, 310, 311, 315, 321; trends in film topics, 311–13; visiting filmmakers, 321
Zi'ab la Ta'kol al-Lahm / Wolves that Don't Eat Meat / Kuwait Connection (1973), 38
Zimmermann, Patricia R., 78
Zindeeq (2009), 218
Zohair, Sarah, 256

For Indiana University Press

Tony Brewer, *Artist and Book Designer*

Brian Carroll, *Rights Manager*

Allison Chaplin, *Acquisitions Editor and Director*

Sophia Hebert, *Assistant Acquisitions Editor*

Samantha Heffner, *Marketing and Publicity Manager*

Brenna Hosman, *Production Coordinator*

Katie Huggins, *Production Manager*

Nancy Lightfoot, *Project Editor and Manager*

Dan Pyle, *Online Publishing Manager*

Leyla Salamova, *Senior Artist and Book Designer*

www.ingramcontent.com/pod-product-compliance
Lightning Source LLC
Chambersburg PA
CBHW021341300426

44114CB00012B/1036